THE SERIOUS
SHOPPER'S
GUIDE TO
LONDON

Other titles available in **THE SERIOUS SHOPPER'S** series:

THE SERIOUS SHOPPER'S GUIDE TO ITALY
THE SERIOUS SHOPPER'S GUIDE TO LOS ANGELES
THE SERIOUS SHOPPER'S GUIDE TO PARIS

All published by Prentice Hall Press, New York

THE SERIOUS SHOPPER'S

GUIDE TO

LONDON

BETH REIBER

Photographs by Keri Pickett

Prentice Hall Press • New York

Published by Prentice Hall Press
A Division of Simon & Schuster, Inc.
Gulf + Western Building
One Gulf + Western Plaza
New York, NY 10023

Library of Congress Cataloging-in-Publication Data

Reiber, Beth.
  The serious shopper's guide to London.

  Includes index.
  1. Shopping—England—London—Guide-books.
2. Stores, Retail—England—London—Guide-books.
I. Title.
TX335.R39   1988   381.1'09411   87-1326
ISBN 0-13-806852-6

Manufactured in the United States of America

CONTENTS

PART TWO
THE ULTIMATE LONDON SHOPPING SPREE
121

Index
351

MAPS

To Chris Lyons, whose love for London
and life itself is both inspiring and infectious

ACKNOWLEDGMENT

I would like to thank several people and organizations for their gracious help in the preparation of this book: the wonderful staff of the British Tourist Authority; Lufthansa; David Couper; Sean Williams; and Marilyn Wood at Prentice Hall Press.

INFLATION ALERT: While the rate of inflation has declined over the past two years, we don't have to tell you that prices remain volatile. In researching this book we have made every effort to obtain up-to-the-minute prices, but even the most conscientious researcher cannot keep up with the ever-changing shop scene. However, as we go to press, we believe we have obtained the most reliable data possible.

A DISCLAIMER: All information in this book has been obtained from personal visits to each establishment. Because policies and managements change, we cannot be responsible for representations made or implied in this book. We suggest, therefore, that you check the policy of each establishment prior to any purchase.

PART ONE

A LONDON OVERVIEW

A CURRENCY NOTE

The basic unit of British currency is the pound (£), divided into 100 pence (p). As we go to press, the current exchange rate for the pound is approximately $1.50. A few basic conversions, based on the current rate, are listed below. Before you go, check at your local bank for the latest currency exchange rate.

Pence	U.S. $	Pounds	U.S. $
1	.015	1	1.50
5	.075	2	3.00
25	.375	5	7.50
50	.75	10	15.00

CHAPTER 1

AN INTRODUCTION TO LONDON

Shopping is nothing new, especially in London. From the time the Romans first set up camp here in a curve of the River Thames almost 2,000 years ago, people have gathered here to barter, bargain, and trade. Little wonder that one of the world's first shopping streets—Bond Street—was built in London 300 years ago. The wealthy, the fashionable, and the hopefuls were flocking to shops along Bond Street for a look at the latest in clothing and household goods long before people in many other European capitals even imagined such a venture.

However, even though shopping is nothing new, there's no denying the fact that it has become epidemic, elevated from a necessity to an art and a pastime. People travel the world looking for good bargains, visiting certain destinations solely for the items they offer.

With its long history of shops and shopkeepers, London is well prepared to meet the demands of today's shoppers, and in fact has quietly been doing so for a long time. Having leared how to cater to everyone from the English country gentleman to the cockney, London is superb for the variety of what

Only in London

it has to offer. There are street markets selling bric-a-brac, there are jewelers to the Crown, and there is everything in between. What's more, London is a city for walking, allowing for an intimacy you don't find in many large cities.

Where else can you find centuries-old hatters with stacks of bowlers and felt hats; chemist shops with old, family recipes and potions; bootmakers creating leather shoes by hand? There are cigar shops, wine merchants, cheesemongers, and more, and nothing can compare with the delight of exploring these Old World shops. There are also many fine antique shops unrivaled in the quality of their English furniture, along with established art galleries that have been selling paintings of the Old Masters for centuries.

On the other side of the coin are the highly fashionable clothing boutiques that can hold their own against shops anywhere in the world. There are also shops selling the avant-garde and sometimes outrageous fashions of Britain's young designers, beauty salons, glorious china shops, bookshops, and London's famous department stores. There are tobacconists, perfumers, stationers, and tailors, and don't forget about the city's marvelous flea markets.

A list of London's shops goes on and on, with possibilities for shopping that you've probably never even considered. That's why I've written this book. I'm not out to sell you a particular item, nor am I trying to sell a particular store. I simply want you to enjoy yourself, and if you have as much fun going to these shops as I did in researching them, then I will have done my job. With the fluctuation of the dollar, you may not be able to realize huge savings by shopping in London, but in my opinion that's not the point. The joy comes from being in a different country, from buying something you could never find back home, and from exploring London's wondrous stores that bring with them centuries of experience and decades of expertise. You can learn a lot about London, its history, and its people by exploring its shops and meeting the shopkeepers who run them. In short, you are about to embark on an adventure.

BASIC ORIENTATION

With a very cosmopolitan population of approximately 6½ million inhabitants, Greater London sprawls along the River Thames in southeast England. In fact, it was the Thames that drew settlers in the first place, serving as the lifeblood for goods and people coming in and out of the city.

Founded almost 2,000 years ago by the Romans, London has always had a rather cosmopolitan atmosphere, as through the centuries waves of immigrants added to the population. Long ago, however, foreigners were barred from actually entering the city, so they put down roots east of the city in an area that became known as the East End. The East End still has its own distinct personality, characterized by the working-class cockney. Although Jews were originally associated with the East End, they've slowly been replaced by new groups of immigrants, particularly from Pakistan.

As for the old core of London which was originally surrounded by a wall to keep out intruders, it's known today simply as The City. Only one square mile, it is the financial and business district of the capital city. There are few shops in The City, but there are many historic old pubs which still serve pints to London's lawyers, journalists, and businessmen of Fleet Street. As for Britain's politicians, they're a mile upriver in Westminster, where you'll find Buckingham Palace, Westminster Abbey, and the Houses of Parliament.

Just to the west of The City is London's most important shopping district, known as the West End because of its geographical position west of the original walled city. It's here that you'll find London's most famous shopping streets— Oxford Street, Old and New Bond Streets, Regent Street, and Piccadilly. To the east of Regent Street is Soho, famous for its sex shops and nightlife, but also for its trendy cafés and restaurants. South of Soho is London's theater land, bordered by Covent Garden. Once London's main fruit, vegetable, and flower market, Covent Garden is now one of the city's most vibrant shopping areas, filled with boutiques and avant-garde clothing shops. In sharp contrast are the embassies, plush hotels, and expensive restaurants of Mayfair and the charming Old World shops of St. James's and Jermyn Street.

The Arcade: Old Bond Street entrance

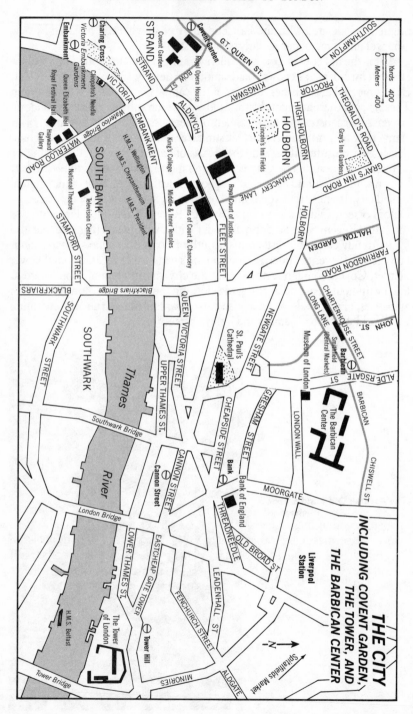

THE CITY
INCLUDING COVENT GARDEN,
THE TOWER, AND
THE BARBICAN CENTER

London was molded from the fusion of many small villages, among these Chelsea and Kensington, which lie southwest of the West End. With its elegant town houses and quaint side streets, Chelsea has been home to both the rich and the bohemian, exploding in the 1970s as the birthplace of punk along crowded and chaotic King's Road. Sloane Rangers, England's chic and manicured version of the American yuppie, have since taken over, populating the expensive clothing boutiques and cafés of Sloane Street and Beauchamp Place. Harrods, one of the world's most famous department stores, occupies a full block on nearby Brompton Road. And within walking distance is South Kensington, home of several of London's finest museums and some of the city's wealthiest people.

To make the job of the postman easier, London is subdivided into dozens of postal codes consisting of letters and numbers. W1 is the most prestigious address one can have, signifying occupancy in the West End or Mayfair. WC2 covers Covent Garden and Holborn, SW3 is Chelsea, and W8 covers most of Kensington.

GETTING FROM THE AIRPORT

Two airports serve international traffic to and from London, Heathrow and Gatwick. Heathrow is the largest and the closest to central London, but both airports are conveniently connected to the city by public transportation.

HEATHROW

London's underground (subway) is the cheapest and often the fastest mode of transportation from the airport. There are two stations right at Heathrow, one serving the newer Terminal 4 and the other one serving Terminals 1, 2, and 3. Both stations are on the Piccadilly Line, which runs from Heathrow Airport through the central part of London where many of the city's hotels are located. Stops include South Kensington, Knightsbridge, Hyde Park Corner, Green Park, Piccadilly Circus, Leicester Square, Covent Garden, and Holborn. In any case, you can make easy connections to any of London's 268 stations, including the British Rail stations for onward travel in Britain. Subway trains depart from Heathrow every four to ten minutes and they run 18 hours a day. The fare to central London is only £1.50 and it takes approximately 40 minutes to reach the town's center.

If you have a lot of baggage or want to see some of the city during the trip to your hotel, take the red **Airbus**. These double-deckers leave from all four terminals at Heathrow approximately every ten minutes. There are two routes: A1 runs to Victoria Station and stops at Cromwell Road and Hyde Park Corner along the way; A2 runs to Euston Station and makes stops at Holland Park Avenue, Notting Hill Gate, Bayswater Road, Lancaster Gate Station, Marble

Arch, Bloomsbury, and Russell Square. It takes approximately 60 to 80 minutes to reach central London and the fare is £3 (children pay half fare). You pay as you board, and U.S., Canadian, French, and German currencies are also accepted.

Another bus service operating between Heathrow and central London is **Green Line's Flightline 767**. It charges £2.50 per person (children pay half fare) and passes Kensington High Street, Knightsbridge, and Buckingham Palace Road before terminating at Victoria Coach Station.

Taxis, of course, are also readily available. The fare runs about £15 to £22 to most points in central London.

Before leaving Heathrow, you may want to stop by the **Heathrow Information Centre**, located at Heathrow Central Station and open from 9 a.m. to 6 p.m. daily. Pick up a map of the city and sightseeing brochures.

GATWICK

Gatwick is farther out from the city's core, making **taxis** impractical and expensive as a means to reach your hotel. If you do opt for a taxi, be sure to ask beforehand what the fare will be.

Most travelers take the train. **British Rail's Gatwick Express** whisks customers to Victoria Station in 30 minutes. Trains depart every 15 minutes during the day and hourly at night, and the fare is £4.60 for second class and £6.90 for first. Another train known as the **City Link** connects Gatwick with London Bridge Station. Travel time is also about 30 minutes and the fare is the same as with the Gatwick Express.

If you want to take the bus, **Green Line's Flightline 777** connects Gatwick with Victoria Coach Station in approximately 70 minutes. Buses run from 6 a.m. to 11 p.m., departing every half hour throughout the day and every hour from 8 to 11 p.m. The adult fare is £3 and children pay half fare.

GETTING AROUND

London is one of the easiest cities in the world in which to find your way around. Although even the natives may occasionally get lost, novices discover that it takes no time at all to familiarize themselves with the layout of the city and the various modes of transportation.

Both London's famous red buses and the underground are managed by the **London Regional Transport**, the symbol for which is a red circle with a horizontal bar bisecting it and which you'll find at the entrance of all underground stations. If you have any questions, the London Regional Transport maintains a 24-hour telephone service at 01/222-1234. It also operates helpful **Travel Information Centres** at the underground stations of Victoria, King's Cross, Oxford Circus, Piccadilly Circus, and St. James's Park, and at Heathrow Airport. Be sure to pick up a free leaflet called "Central London" which contains a map of the city as well as maps of the bus and underground systems. At these centers you can also purchase a variety of travel passes such as the London Explorer Pass or tickets for the Official London Sightseeing Tour, both described in more detail later in this chapter.

SAVING MONEY

If you plan on traveling a lot through the city, you can save a substantial amount of money by purchasing a pass. The **London Explorer Pass**, which you can buy at underground stations or one of the Travel Information Centres described above, is valid for unlimited travel on both buses and the underground and is useful for longer excursions into London's hinterland. You can also use it to and from Heathrow on the tube or the Airbus and on all night buses. Several London Explorer Passes are available: one-day passes cost £3.80, three-day passes are £9.90, four-day passes are £12.65, and seven-day passes are £17.60.

If you want to save even more money, travel like the natives do by purchasing a **Travelcard**. You'll need a passport-size photo. You can purchase a one-day card after 10 a.m. on weekdays and anytime on weekends for £2.20 or £1.85, depending on how far within London you want to travel. Seven-day Travelcards range in price from £5.20 for Central London to £9.20 for transportation throughout most of London. Cards are valid for both the red buses and the underground, as well as the night buses.

THE UNDERGROUND

Traveling by underground in London is easy, fast, and convenient, with ten lines crisscrossing the city and serving both the center of London and the suburbs. Londoners call it the "tube," and each line is color-coded. Trains run every few minutes from approximately 5:30 or 6 a.m. until 11:30 p.m. or midnight, with slightly shorter operating hours on Sunday. Tickets are purchased before boarding from either the ticket window or from automatic machines. Fares vary according to the distances traveled, but destinations and prices are clearly marked. In any case, make sure you hang onto your ticket, which you will surrender to the ticket collector upon completion of your journey.

BY BUS

Although slower than the tube, buses offer the best vantage point from which to see the city, especially if you're upstairs in a double-decker. They are also the best way to travel within the West End along Oxford Street, Regent Street, and Piccadilly. Buses run at frequent intervals from about 6 a.m. to around midnight, followed by what are called the "night buses," which serve a limited number of routes throughout the night. Night buses serve Piccadilly Circus,

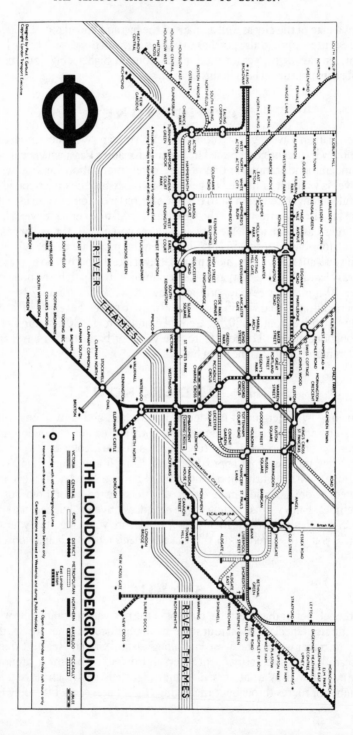

Leicester Square, Victoria, Trafalgar Square, Marble Arch, and other central destinations, and connect them to London's outer regions. Pick up the "Night Owls Guide" with its timetables at a Travel Information Centre.

There are two types of bus stops: those with the red symbol of a circle and horizontal bar, which means that buses will stop automatically; and request stops, which are marked "Request" and which mean that buses will stop only if you raise your hand. Route numbers are listed at the stops, along with timetables.

Although newer buses require that you have exact fare and that you pay the bus driver as you board at the front of the bus, the older ones have a conductor who walks up and down the aisle collecting the fares and making change. The older buses have open entryways at the back, and it never ceases to amaze me to see natives leaping on and off even while the bus is in motion. The less agile among us can indicate a desire to get off the bus by pushing a button or pulling a cord.

TAXIS

There's something grand about riding in a London taxi. Big and black with lots of leg room, taxis here are like relics from another era. Their drivers are among the best in the world and have to pass tough examinations before they can get their license.

Taxis can be hailed from the side of the street. When a taxi's yellow "for hire" sign is lit, it means it's free to take passengers. Once a driver has stopped for you, he's obligated to take you anywhere you want to go within a six-mile radius. The fare is shown on the meter and starts at a basic charge of about 90 pence for the first 90 yards. After that it increases in 20-pence stages per 495 yards or 105 seconds until a £5 fare is reached. After that the rate increases at 20-pence stages per 330 yards or 70 seconds. It's customary to tip drivers at least 10% to 15%.

In addition to the fleet of black taxis, you'll also see private taxis known as minicabs. They can't be hailed from the street but rather operate from telephone calls. Their offices are sometimes located next to underground stations, and I've used them often late at night to get from a station to my destination. Be sure to negotiate the fare beforehand. They're usually cheaper than black taxis for longer distances, and tipping is up to you.

ON FOOT

Armed with a good map, you should have no difficulty finding your way around on foot. In fact, London is a perfect city for walking. In the West End you can easily cover the area bounded by Oxford Street, Bond Street, Regent Street, and Piccadilly. If you get lost, Londoners are very helpful about pointing you in the right direction, as are the legendary bobbies.

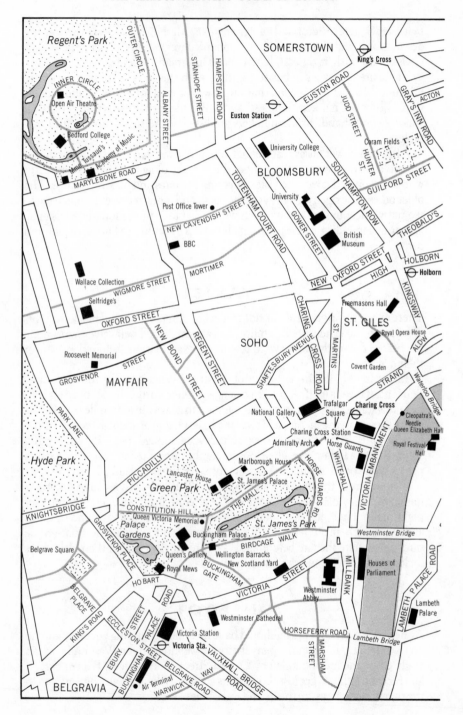

AN INTRODUCTION TO LONDON

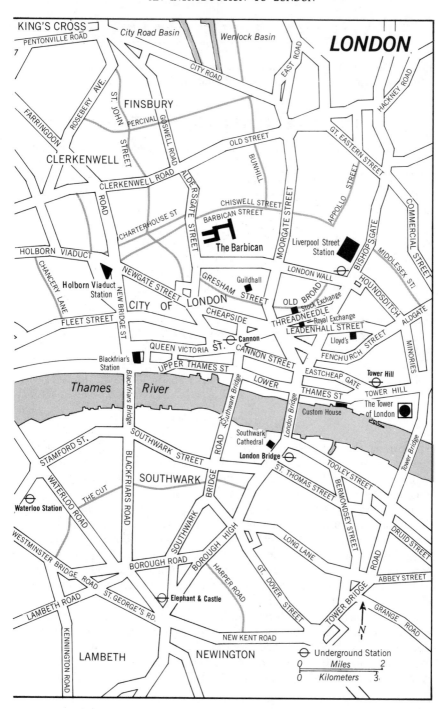

LONDON

KING'S CROSS
PENTONVILLE ROAD
City Road Basin
Wenlock Basin
CITY ROAD
EAST ROAD
HACKNEY ROAD
FARRINGDON
ROSEBERY AVE.
ST. JOHN STREET
PERCIVAL
GOSWELL ROAD
FINSBURY
OLD STREET
BUNHILL
GT. EASTERN STREET
APPOLLO STREET
COMMERCIAL STREET
CLERKENWELL
CLERKENWELL ROAD
ALDERSGATE STREET
CHISWELL STREET
BARBICAN STREET
MOORGATE STREET
BISHOPSGATE
MIDDLESEX ST.
ROAD
CHARTERHOUSE ST.
The Barbican
Liverpool Street Station
LONDON WALL
HOUNDSDITCH
HOLBORN VIADUCT
CHANCERY LANE
Holborn Viaduct Station
NEWGATE STREET
NEW BRIDGE ST.
GRESHAM STREET
Guildhall
OLD BROAD
Stock Exchange
THREADNEEDLE
ALDGATE
CITY OF LONDON
CHEAPSIDE
Royal Exchange
LEADENHALL STREET
MINORIES
FLEET STREET
Cannon
Lloyd's
FENCHURCH STREET
Blackfriar's Station
QUEEN VICTORIA ST.
CANNON STREET
LOWER
EASTCHEAP
GATE
Tower Hill
UPPER THAMES ST
Blackfriars Bridge
Southwark Bridge
THAMES ST
TOWER HILL
Thames *River*
London Bridge
Custom House
The Tower of London
Tower Bridge
STAMFORD ST.
SOUTHWARK STREET
BRIDGE ROAD
Southwark Cathedral
London Bridge
TOOLEY STREET
WATERLOO ROAD
THE CUT
BLACKFRIARS ROAD
SOUTHWARK
ST. THOMAS STREET
BERMONDSEY STREET
Waterloo Station
SOUTHWARK
LONG LANE
DRUID STREET
WESTMINSTER BRIDGE ROAD
BOROUGH ROAD
BOROUGH HIGH
HARPER ROAD
GT. DOVER STREET
ROAD
ABBEY STREET
LAMBETH ROAD
ST. GEORGE'S RD.
Elephant & Castle
TOWER BRIDGE
GRANGE ROAD
KENNINGTON ROAD
NEW KENT ROAD
N
LAMBETH
NEWINGTON
⊖ Underground Station
0   Miles   2
0   Kilometers   3

TOURIST INFORMATION

England is well prepared for the overseas visitor and has a number of free booklets, brochures, maps, and other information on Great Britain.

IN THE UNITED STATES

The smart traveler begins preparing for a trip before leaving home, collecting information on hotels and sightseeing and free pamphlets and maps. There are four **British Tourist Authority** offices in the United States which will be happy to provide you with the information you need. Simply write or call the one nearest you.

British Tourist Authority
40 W. 57th St.
New York, NY 10019
(tel. 212/581-4700)

British Tourist Authority
John Hancock Center, Suite 3320
875 N. Michigan Ave.
Chicago, IL 60611
(tel. 312/787-0490)

British Tourist Authority
Plaza of the Americas
North Tower, Suite 750
Dallas, TX 75201
(tel. 214/720-4040)

British Tourist Authority
612 S. Flower St.
Los Angeles, CA 90017
(tel. 213/623-8196)

IN LONDON

The **British Travel Centre**, 4 Lower Regent St., SW1 (tel. 01/730-3400), opened its doors in 1986 and is one of the best and most efficient tourist information centers I've seen. It's operated by the British Tourist Authority, American Express, and British Rail, making it an excellent one-stop travel center for virtually all your needs. You can change money, buy theater or train tickets, make bookings for coach tours, rent a car, or reserve a hotel room. There are lots of free leaflets and pamphlets on sightseeing in London and the rest of Great Britain, and a travel agency can arrange onward travel. There's also a bookshop with maps, publications, and gifts. Hours are Monday through Saturday from 9 a.m. to 6:30 p.m. and on Sunday from 10 a.m. to 4 p.m., and it's located just south of Piccadilly Circus.

Another large **Tourist Information Centre** is located at Victoria Station with information on London and England, hotels, sights, theaters, and tours. There's also a bookshop with guides and maps for sale. It's open from 9 a.m. to 8:30 p.m. daily. Other tourist information centers are located at Heathrow Airport, open from 9 a.m. to 6 p.m. daily, and at the Tower of London's west gate, open from 10 a.m. to 6 p.m. April to October only. There are also tourist and theater information counters in Harrods and Selfridges department stores.

If you have any questions during your stay in London, you can obtain information by calling 01/730-3488 from 9 a.m. to 5:30 p.m. Monday to Friday.

MAPS AND PUBLICATIONS

London Transport puts out a free map called "**Central London**," which contains maps of the city and of bus and underground routes. I suggest, however, that you invest 45 pence in another map issued by the British Tourist Authority called simply "**London Map**." It's much more detailed and includes a street index as well as an underground map. Armed with this map, you should be able to find almost all the shops listed in this book. If you will be spending a lot of time in London and want to know of every street in the city, "**London A–Z**" is a street atlas and is available in several variations in bookstores, gift shops, and magazine stands.

Available free at tourist information centers are two useful publications. "**London Visitor**" is a small magazine published by the British Tourist Authority with information on sightseeing and eating, a map of London, and articles of interest to visitors. "**Events in London**" comes out monthly and lists special events, fairs such as the Chelsea Antiques Fair, festivals, celebrations, exhibits at museums and galleries, sporting events, daily schedules of walking tours, and other happenings.

There are also two publications available at major newsstands and bookstores that tell what's going on in London. "**Time Out**" and "**What's on & Where to Go**" both come out weekly and give information on the theaters, cinemas, concerts, dance events, fairs, galleries, and other events.

For prerecorded information on what's going on for the day, call **Leisureline** at 01/246-8041.

THE WEATHER

London's rainy weather is no myth, so unless your shopping spree includes the purchase of a raincoat and umbrella you should be sure to bring them with you. The weather can be quite chilly even in midsummer, so be prepared with a jacket or sweater. In the winter you'll need a coat. It doesn't snow very often in London, but the weather can be totally unpredictable. The winter of 1986–1987, for example, was reportedly the coldest of the century, with temperatures plunging below freezing.

Once in London, you can find out what the day's weather will be like by calling a prerecorded information service at 01/246-8091. For individual queries, call the London Weather Centre at 01/836-4311.

SIGHTSEEING TOURS

London has some excellent sightseeing tours that cover parts of the city by bus or on foot. Bus tours tend to offer overviews of the city in general, while walking tours usually concentrate on a certain aspect, such as visits to various pubs.

BUS TOURS

Organized bus tours of London are operated by a number of companies. One of the best-known is the London Sightseeing Tour organized by the **London Regional Transport** (tel. 01/222-1234). It offers a good overview of the city's sights and is especially good if this is your first visit to London. Transportation is aboard a traditional double-decker red bus, which has an open deck during the warmer summer months. Tours depart every half hour (every hour in winter) between 10 a.m. and 5 p.m. daily except Christmas from Piccadilly Circus, Victoria Street, Marble Arch (in Park Lane near Speakers' Corner), and Baker Street Station. Tours last approximately 1½ hours and cover 18 miles, passing such sights as St. Paul's, the Tower of London, Westminster Abbey, Tower Bridge, and Big Ben. Cost of the tour is £5.50 (£3.30 for children under 16) and tickets can be purchased on board the bus, at any London Transport Travel Information Centre, or tourist information centers.

Harrods department store also offers several bus tours, which start and end in front of the store on Brompton Road. The two-hour panorama tour for £13.20 gives an overview of the city, while the all-day tour for £47.30 covers London in much more detail and includes lunch. For more information on these and Harrods' other tours, call 01/581-3603 or visit the booking office on Harrods' fourth floor.

Other companies offering half- or full-day tours of London and the surrounding countryside include **Green Line** (tel. 01-668-7261); **Thomas Cook** (book through any Thomas Cook shop); and **Frames Rickard** (tel. 01/837-3111).

An independent way of seeing the city is aboard the yellow **Culture Bus**, which makes continual runs throughout the city, with 37 stops. Your ticket, which costs £4.40 for one day or £8.80 for three days, allows you to board and depart the bus at your whim as many times as you wish. Buses run every 30 minutes during the week and every 20 minutes on weekends. This permits you to disembark, say, at the Tower of London for a bit of sightseeing and then to reboard for continued travel. You can purchase tickets at the British Travel Centre in Lower Regent Street, at major hotels, from the bus driver, or at the Culture Bus office at 60 St. James's St., SW1 (tel. 01/629-4999).

WALKING TOURS

The best way to see London on a more intimate level is on foot. There are many organized walking tours available, which offer the additional benefit of having an experienced guide right there to answer your questions. Many tours are offered at night, leaving you with your days free to pursue shopping and sightseeing on your own.

Most walking tours center on a particular theme. There's no need to book—simply show up at the appointed time and place, which is usually at the entrance of an underground station. Walks generally last 1½ to 2 hours and cost less than £3. Information on daily schedules is published in "Events in London," "Time Out," and "What's On & Where to Go," or can be obtained from tourist information centers. One company offering walking tours is **Streets of London**, 32 Grovelands Rd., N13 (tel. 01/882-3414), which offers 12 guided tours ranging from "Shakespeare's London—A Lunchtime Pub Walk" to "The London of Jack the Ripper." Other companies include **Cockney Walks** (tel. 01/504-9159), with tours of the Jewish East End and Cockney London, and **The Londoner** (tel. 01/883-2656), with night tours of historic pubs.

BOAT TRIPS

Boat trips on the River Thames offer a pleasant way to see London. Boats depart from Westminster Pier opposite Big Ben and travel either downstream past the Tower Bridge to Greenwich and the Thames Barrier or upstream (summer only) to Kew, Richmond, and Hampton Court. There are also boat trips on the Regent's Canal that run between Little Venice and Camden Lock. Contact the tourist information centers for current schedules of these and other boat trips.

CHAPTER II

SHOPPING STRATEGIES

This chapter is designed to help you plan for your trip and to answer questions pertaining to shopping in London. Read it before leaving home and you should arrive in England prepared and confident, ready to make your shopping spree a pleasurable experience.

WHAT TO DO BEFORE YOU GO

If you have only a few days or less to devote to shopping in London, I can guarantee that you'll go crazy if you arrive unprepared. There are so many stores to choose from, and it's frustrating to learn—perhaps too late—that you've been racing through store after store searching for an item that was available in a tiny shop tucked around the corner from your hotel. Shopping is so much easier when you know what you're looking for and have an idea where you can find it. What part of London, for example, is best for antiques or for avant-garde clothing by Britain's young designers? Will department stores carry most of the goods you want, or is it worth it to seek out the small, specialized shops, some of which have been around for centuries? Of course, the wise shopper will also leave time for exploration. That scruffy-looking shop down the street may well turn out to be a treasure trove in disguise.

COMPARISON SHOPPING

The first thing you must do, of course, is compile a list of items you want to buy in London. Once you have your list, you should research what similar items cost in the United States. Nothing is more aggravating than purchasing goods in a foreign country only to find out that they cost the same amount back home. Visit department stores and boutiques and make notes of prices, model numbers, and other pertinent information. Once you reach England you may find that an item you're interested in costs only $5 less than in the United States, at which point you have to decide whether you really want to lug it home in your suitcase. Be sure also to check annual sales in the United States, such as those held after Christmas, when prices are drastically reduced and may be much lower than what you could ever expect to find on a normal shopping excursion in London.

Another good strategy is to buy American editions of foreign magazines and look at both the articles and advertising to get an idea of what things cost and what's available. Fashion magazines, for example, may display the fashions of leading European designers, along with advertisements for certain boutiques and department stores. It's even better if you can get your hands on British magazines, available perhaps at your local library or at large, international bookstores. British fashion magazines are especially good, among them *Tatler*, *Harpers & Queen*, *Elle*, *Woman's Journal*, and British editions of *Good House-keeping*, *Cosmopolitan*, and *Vogue*. They carry pages and pages of fashion, along with prices and where you can purchase them in London. If you're really serious about fashion, you can even subscribe to these magazines, with addresses obtainable from your local library.

WHAT TO BUY

Whenever people ask me what the good buys are in London, Hong Kong, or other shopping meccas, my first reaction is to answer simply, "Whatever makes you happy." After all, everyone's taste are different and what may be a bargain to one person may be a white elephant to someone else. If you live in a desert or simply don't like Burberrys trenchcoats, they won't be a bargain at any price. If, on the other hand, you've been dreaming of Burberrys forever, you may not mind spending several hundred dollars on one and may even consider it a true steal.

Technically speaking, therefore, all the shop categories listed in this book, from antiques to wines, can be considered as good buys in London. Judging by what visitors lug away in their suitcases and have shipped abroad, however, there are certain items that stand out as popular favorites.

Clothing and fashion accessories are excellent buys in London, with both a wide selection and a seemingly endless parade of stores and boutiques. I personally find sweaters and woolens hard to resist, and at sales it's not unusual to find pure-wool sweaters for less than $20. Handmade sweaters from Scotland and cashmere and lambswool sweaters are of especially good value. Other good clothing items include raincoats, men's and women's hats, bespoke (custom-made) shirts and suits. You can, in fact, have an entire outfit custom-made in London, including your hat, suit, shirt, and shoes. Prices are dear and you may have to wait several months for delivery, but quality is superb. To complete the look, buy an English umbrella or a walking stick.

Another good buy in London is antiques. Although you can spend a small fortune purchasing furniture dating from the Queen Anne period in the early 1700s, there are plenty of collectibles in all price ranges, from snuff boxes and bottles to antique lace, jewelry, and Victorian silver. Antique flea markets are good for picking up inexpensive items, while prestigious antique shops on Bond Street cater to the rich of the world.

To decorate your home there are wonderful buys in china, crystal, and silver. British artisans have been producing masterpieces in all three categories for centuries. Wedgwood, Royal Doulton, Spode, Royal Worcester, Coalport, and Stuart are just a few names readily associated with Britain. There are also great buys in modern art, with contemporary British artists producing glass, pottery, jewelry, and other crafts. Galleries abound in London, from those selling paintings of the Old Masters to those selling the works of living artists.

Add to these the unique finds in antiquarian bookstores, the tobacconist shops, London's famous auction houses, department stores, and—well, you can see that a list of good shopping buys in London is both hard to define and to curtail.

THE DESIGN CENTRE

If you're interested in the very latest of modern British products, you might want to pay a visit to the Design Centre, 28 Haymarket, SW1 (tel. 01/839-8000). As the headquarters of the government-sponsored Design Council, it serves as a showcase for British products that have earned recognition for superior design. A shop sells some of these products, which range from jewelry to glassware to kitchenware.

There's also a photographic index listing approximately 8,000 products that are British-made and designed and that have been approved by the Design Council. These products range from bathroom accessories to sports equipment and fabrics. If you're looking for ceramic tile, for example, it might be useful to look through the photographic index and make note of the style you like and its approximate retail price. The manufacturer's telephone number is listed next to the product, and you can call to find out which shop carries the style you like. If you're in no hurry, you can also fill out a postcard with a description of the product you're interested in and your address and then leave it at The Design Centre. In approximately ten days you'll receive by mail a list of shops nearest you in England that carry the product.

The Design Centre is open Monday and Tuesday from 10 a.m. to 6 p.m., Wednesday through Saturday to 8 p.m., and on Sunday from 1 to 6 p.m.

GREAT GIFT AND SOUVENIR IDEAS

In visiting several hundred shops while researching this book, I came across many delightful items you don't readily find elsewhere. Some of them are strictly British; others are familiar objects made unique by virtue of their form, function, or packaging. Walking sticks, for example, may be much more than just that—they may unfold to form convenient outdoor seats, or they may even conceal a whisky flask.

At any rate, below are some notes I jotted down on items that make great gift and souvenir ideas and yet are not too expensive. The list is by no means complete, nor is it strictly objective. Rather, the recommendations should simply whet your appetite and give you some ideas of your own as you explore London's shops. A much more exhaustive list of gift ideas can be obtained by reading through the list of store categories in Part Two of this book. The categories will also tell you where to find the items listed below.

a tea or coffee "cosy"—this is a tea or coffee pot complete with its own insulation that fits snugly around the pot to keep it warm. Old ones are commonly found at flea markets, particularly Camden Passage, Camden Lock, and Portobello. They usually cost between £15 and £35, depending on the design and the condition.

tea gift packs with several types of teas, available at food halls such as Fortnum & Mason

marmalades, chutney, or mustard

handmade chocolates from Bendicks, Charbonnel et Walker, or Prestat, all of which are famous chocolate shops

a bottle of single-malt whisky, with good selections available at Soho Wine Market, Fortnum & Mason, Selfridges, or Harrods

English toast racks, usually made of sterling silver or silver plate; useful as letter holders and readily available in department stores, silver shops, and flea markets

beautifully packaged **soaps and toiletries**, with good selections at Crabtree & Evelyn

perfumes or toilet waters from one of London's famous perfumers such as Floris or Penhaligon's

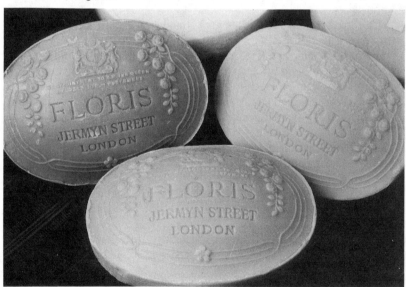

Floris originals

a man's shaving set, consisting of a stand, brush, bowl, and mirror; Geo F. Trumper has one of the largest selections, with prices starting at around £44.

a man's wooden shaving bowl, sold at Yardley for about £8.50

a briar smoking pipe from Astleys, starting at £22

sheepskin boots or slippers from Richard Draper

a Parker writing pen, available at most department stores and at pen shops

a British-made umbrella from James Smith & Sons or Swaine, Adeney, Brigg & Sons; umbrellas that unfold into seats start at around £60.

a walking stick that unfolds into a seat (called a "shooting stick") or conceals a hidden flask for whisky or maybe even a fishing rod

bed warming pans made of copper, available at the Coppershop; also copper coal helmets or coal buckets

a duvet, a thick comforter surrounded by a sheet and used by the British like blankets; sold at linen shops

reproduction coach lamps, originally used with candles on forms of wheeled transport before the discovery of electricity; sold at Christopher Wray's Lighting Emporium

hard cork placemats with a tough, lacquer finish; a set of six begins at around £12, and they're sold at department stores like Selfridges and D.H. Evans

Coalport bone-china flowers, available in various sizes beginning at around £14 and sold in china shops such as Wedgwood

bone-china figurines from Royal Doulton or Coalport, available at china shops

Wedgwood's pendant jewelry made of jasper, or Wedgwood's annual special-edition plates

a Caithness paperweight, made in Scotland with exquisite designs and sold in most department stores, with prices starting at about £10

miniature ceramic cottages, with famous lines produced by Lilliput Lane, John Putnam and David Winter; carried by department stores and gift shops and popular mostly with Americans (a saleswoman at Selfridges told me they'd never sell them if it weren't for Americans!)

brass rubbings—you can make them yourself at the London Brass Rubbing Centre, with about 70 rubbings from which to choose

enamel boxes, sold at Halcyon Days; you can commission one with your own special message or picture.

museum prints and posters

calendars, available at gift shops, museums, and bookstores

old prints, which are usually botanical or depict scenes of London; prices start below £10

Vanity Fair prints of caricatures, including artists, lawyers, literary and theater personalities, jockeys, and hunters; sold for less than £10 at print galleries

costume and paste jewelry or imitation art-deco jewelry, sold in jewelry shops and flea markets

avant-garde and highly original clothing, hats, and jewelry, sold by young designers at stalls set up at Hyper Hyper, Kensington Market, and Camden Town

a scarf from Liberty department store

the British version of Monopoly, sold at the Games Centre and Hamleys

THE ABC'S OF SHOPPING IN LONDON

The following information is provided to make your life easier as you shop your way through London. If by chance you can't find the answer to a nagging problem in these pages, the concierge at your hotel may be able to help you. You can also try calling the tourist information's hotline at 01/730-3488 between 9 a.m. to 5:30 p.m. Monday through Friday. Even if the staff cannot answer your questions, they may be able to refer you to someone who can.

AMERICAN EXPRESS

If you're carrying American Express traveler's checks, the best place to cash them is at American Express offices because you won't be charged commission as you are at other exchange bureaus and banks. If you're cashing something other than American Express traveler's checks, American Express offices will charge a £1.50 commission fee, but it still gives one of the best rates of exchange.

American Express has several locations in London. One of its most convenient branches is at the British Travel Centre, 4 Lower Regent St., SW1 (tel. 01/730-3400), where you can pick up tourist brochures and maps in addition to cashing traveler's checks. Other American Express London offices are located at 6 Haymarket, SW1 (tel. 930-4411); 78 Brompton Rd., SW3 (tel. 584-6182);

Halcyon Days brings back the art of enameling

89 Mount St., W1 (tel. 499-4436); 147 Victoria St., SW1 (tel. 828-7411); and in Selfridges department store on Oxford Street (tel. 629-1234). The Brompton Road office hours are Monday through Friday from 9 a.m. to 5 p.m. (from 9:30 a.m. on Tuesday), on Saturday to 6:30 p.m., and on Sunday from 10:30 a.m. to 4:30 p.m.

AUCTIONS

No matter what you're shopping for in London, chances are you can find it in an auction. Auctions are held several times daily during London's auction season (generally October through July), and some auction houses hold sales the entire year. The list of items sold is vast, including fine antiques, paintings, collectibles, wine, furs, jewelry, carpets, silver, crystal, china, dolls, clocks, stamps, and much, much more. Although prices are sometimes up in the millions, most items are more down-to-earth and may sell for less than $100.

At any rate, just because you've never been to an auction is no excuse to feel intimidated. All auction houses have information desks with a staff willing to answer questions and used to dealing with the curious and uninitiated. Most also sell catalogs listing the items of the next few sales and the expected selling prices. Items are on display in viewing rooms for one day or more prior to the actual auctions, and the public is welcome to come take a look at what's being offered. Even if you don't attend the auction itself, you may find it interesting to drop in to see what kinds of things are sold.

More information on auctions and auction houses in given under "Auctions" in Part Two of this book.

BANKING HOURS

Generally speaking, most banks are open weekdays from 9:30 a.m. to 3:30 p.m. A few banks are open also on Saturday mornings from 9:30 a.m. to 12:30 p.m. Banks are closed on certain public holidays (see "Holidays," below). Refer to "Money Matters" if you need British currency when the banks are closed.

CHAIN STORES

Chain stores have been taking over London, replacing the smaller neighborhood shops that used to predominate in earlier decades. Generally speaking, a chain store is any shop that has two or more outlets. This applies to many shops in London, simply because if a shop proves successful in one part of town, owners are tempted to open a branch somewhere else. Many shops in the West End, for example, have sister shops in Covent Garden or Knightsbridge.

Some chain stores, such as Next and the Terence Conran group of stores, have elbowed their way into public consciousness with brilliant marketing strategies and good products. Others, such as Marks & Spencer, have been

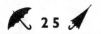
around for a long time and have roots firmly entrenched in the shopping market. At any rate, chain stores have become a fact of life and I've covered them extensively in this book. These include many clothing stores such as Laura Ashley, Monsoon, Take Six, Woodhouse, Warehouse, Next, Miss Selfridge, Mothercare, and Wallis, as well as such specialist shops as Boots pharmacies. Prices are often cheaper in chain stores, because products can be manufactured and ordered in bulk.

CONSUMER COMPLAINTS

The best way to ensure satisfaction is to double-check the goods before purchase to eliminate the headache of returning to a shop or having to send an item back. However, if you purchased an item that is faulty or doesn't do what the store clerk claimed it would do, return to the store and discuss the problem directly with personnel there. Make sure you have your receipt verifying that you did indeed purchase the item in that store. If that doesn't bring satisfactory results, check to see whether there's a **head office** for the shop. Chain stores, for example, have head offices, and management there may be able to help you.

If the store or management refuses to deal with your complaint contact the director of information at the **British Tourist Authority**, Thames Tower, Black's Road, Hammersmith, W8 (tel. 01/846-9000). The director of information is interested in knowing which shops are uncooperative and may be able to help smooth out difficulties.

You can also contact the **Office of Fair Trading**, Field House, Breams Buildings, EC4 (tel. 01/242-2858). They are used to dealing with consumer complaints and can also give you information about shops, including information on head offices.

London also has about 100 branches of **Citizens' Advice Bureaus**, with staff that can advise you on matters relating to infringements of criminal and civil law. They can also find out whether the shop has a head office or whether it belongs to a trade association. You can obtain the address of the nearest advice bureau from the local town hall or from the London telephone directory.

As a last resort, you can also take your case to court. Claims less than £500 go to the **small claims court**, while those more than £500 are settled in county courts under different procedures. Claims more than £5,000 are settled in the High Court, for which you'll probably need a lawyer.

CREDIT CARDS

Credit cards can be used in most of the larger stores, department stores, hotels, and restaurants. The two most commonly accepted cards are MasterCard and VISA. MasterCard is essentially the same as England's Access, while VISA is accepted anywhere that Barclaycard is accepted. Less common is American Express, as is Diners Club. For each shop listed in Part Two, I've given the credit cards accepted using the following abbreviations: AE (American Express), DC (Diners Club), MC (MasterCard), and V (VISA).

If a shop displays on its front window or elsewhere that it accepts a credit card, then it must allow you to pay with that credit card. Just because you don't see a credit card displayed, however, doesn't mean it isn't accepted. I found that a number of shops accept Diners even though it isn't advertised.

Many of London's smaller shops, antique shops, art galleries, and auction houses do not accept credit cards, either because they aren't equipped to handle them or because the sums of money are considered too large. Smaller, specialist shops may accept only cash, though some of them will also take traveler's checks and even U.S. dollars (though the rate of exchange won't be as favorable as at banks). Antique shops and auction houses will accept personal checks, which first must be cleared by a bank.

For **lost credit cards**, call the following appropriate numbers: American Express (tel. 01/930-4411 or 01/222-9633), Diners Club (tel. 0252-516261), MasterCard (tel. 0101-314-275-6690), and VISA (tel. 0604-21288).

CUSTOMS AND DUTY

If your trip takes you only to England and back, you can expect to go through Customs at least twice—in Great Britain and when you return to the United States. Most likely you won't encounter any difficulties, but if you're unclear about what you can and can't take with you, the information below might help. More detailed information regarding U.S. Customs regulations and limitations is available in a free booklet titled "Know Before You Go—Customs Hints for Returning Residents," which you can obtain by writing the Department of the Treasury, U.S. Customs Service, Washington, DC 20229.

United Kingdom Customs

As a visitor to the United Kingdom, you may bring in all the personal effects in your luggage free of duty and tax. All your personal effects must be taken with you when you leave the United Kingdom.

There are, however, restrictions on the amounts of certain items you can bring into the United Kingdom duty free just as in the United Sates. You are allowed to bring in 400 cigarettes or 100 cigars; two liters of table wine plus one liter of a spirit or strong liquor, or two liters of spirits or liquor, or a total of four liters of wine; two ounces of perfume; and nine ounces of toilet water. Any amounts above these allowances are subject to tax.

U.S. Customs

When returning to the United States, you will be given a Customs Declaration form on the plane. Families returning together may prepare a joint declaration, with children claiming the same exemptions as adults (except for liquor).

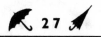

You may declare orally every item purchased or acquired abroad and brought back to the United States if the total value of these items does not exceed $1,400. If your acquisitions exceed a total value of $1,400 or if you have exceeded the liquor or tobacco exemptions, you must declare your items in writing.

Returning to the United States, you are allowed to bring back free of duty $400 worth of personal and household goods obtained abroad, provided you have been out of the United States for at least 48 hours and you have not claimed the $400 exemption within the past 30 days. Included in this duty-free exemption are limitations of 200 cigarettes and 100 cigars, regardless of age. Cuban cigars can be included *only if you bought them in Cuba*. If you are 21 years old or older, you may also include one liter (33.8 fluid ounces) of alcohol if it is allowed by the state in which you arrive.

Anything above this $400 personal exemption is charged a flat 10% on the next $1,000. That means the most you will have to pay on purchases valued at $1,400 (your $400 exemption plus the next $1,000) is $100. Payment can be made either in U.S. currency or a U.S. personal check.

The Customs officer will determine the rates of duty for purchases exceeding $1,400. It's hard to generalize, but it has been found that the average tourist purchase is generally dutiable at about 12%. To give you an idea, non-bone-china tableware valued not over $56 per set is dutiable at 26% of its value, while bone china other than tableware is 6.6%. Other duty charges include crystal at 6%, linen handkerchiefs at 5.5%, jewelry from 6.5% to 27.5% depending on the metals, perfume at 4.9%, leather shoes from 2.5% to 20%, and watches from 3.9% for digitals to 14% for those with gold bracelets. Clothing is even more complicated, with duty rates depending on whether the material is embroidered, cotton, man-made, silk, or wool. If you want more information on duty percentages, send for the free booklet described above.

Although you are required to pay duty on all items acquired abroad—including those shoes you may have worn all over England—there are some items that are allowed free of duty. These include antiques more than 100 years old (you must show proof of antiquity, so be sure to obtain papers from the antique dealer), books, binoculars and opera glasses, exposed film, paintings and drawings done by hand, natural pearls that are loose or temporarily strung without clasp, postage stamps, and diamonds that are cut but not set.

Packages Sent from Abroad

If you find yourself with too much to carry, it's a good idea to send packages through the mail. Packages coming to the United States from abroad are automatically sent to Customs. If the total value of the contents acquired from abroad is determined to be less than $50, the package is sent on to the post office and is delivered to you by your mail carrier. If the value is more than $50, the amount you owe will be collected by the mail carrier upon delivery of your package. Note that it is illegal to mail liquor into the United States.

DISCOUNT SHOPPING

Many of the vendors you see at flea markets sell seconds, that is, merchandise that has some fault or imperfection. For example, clothes may have seams that don't match or colors that are off. A friend of mine bought from a street vendor a pair of jeans with one leg substantially longer than the other. At any rate, you can save money by buying seconds, but be sure to inspect the goods thoroughly.

In London there are also discount fashion houses. Some of these sell leftover items or end of lines from famous designers at greatly discounted prices. I've mentioned a few of these in the "Clothing" section in Part Two. In addition, designers will often rent space and set up a temporary shop for sale items. Since these come and go with great frequency, it's impossible to include them in a book. Sales are advertised, however, in such publications as "Time Out." If you keep your eyes peeled, you'll learn to recognize them.

DUTY-FREE SHOPS

Restricted by British law, duty-free shops are allowed only at airports. Gatwick's duty-free shop is open 24 hours a day, while the duty-free shop at Heathrow is open during all hours that flights are departing from the airport.

Available at duty-free shops are books, magazines, souvenirs, and T-shirts; gift items such as soaps, teas, chocolates, perfume, cashmere sweaters, and other clothing; watches; and of course, cigarettes, cigars, liquor, and wine. Prices are not lower than what I saw elsewhere, but you do save money immediately by not having to pay the VAT (value added tax). The best values are in perfumes and liquor. Otherwise, I suggest you purchase your gift and souvenir items in London's shops where you'll have a greater selection.

EMBASSY AND HIGH COMMISSION

The **U.S. Embassy** is at 24 Grosvenor Square, W.1 (tel. 499-9000), and the **Canadian High Commission** is at Canada House, Trafalgar Square, London, SW1 (tel. 629-9492).

EMERGENCY NUMBERS

To summon the police, ambulance, or fire trucks, the emergency number throughout the country is **999**. The call is free.

HOLIDAYS

All bank and public offices, as well as some shops, are closed on major public holidays. If a holiday falls on a weekend, the following Monday is a holiday.

SHOPPING STRATEGIES

Virtually all businesses close down on Christmas and Boxing Day. Major public holidays are New Year's Day (January 1), Good Friday, Easter Monday (the Monday after Easter), May Day (the first Monday in May), Spring Bank Holiday (last Monday in May), Summer Bank Holiday (last Monday in August), Christmas Day (December 25), and Boxing Day (December 26).

INSURANCE

Most shops that will undertake the shipment of your purchase will also insure it against breakage and loss, but be sure to ask. This may or may not be included in the cost of shipping. All the shipping agencies I've listed under "Shipping" (below) will insure the goods they ship, though the cost is likely to be extra. If you mail packages to the United States through the postal system, you can insure them for amounts up to £1,400.

LOST AND FOUND

If you leave something on a bus or the underground, visit the **Lost Property Office**, 200 Baker St., SW1, located at the side of Baker Street Station. Only personal callers and postal inquiries are accepted. Hours are Monday through Friday from 9:30 a.m. to 2 p.m. A 24-hour prerecorded message can be heard by calling 01/486-2496.

If you've lost something on the street or in a taxi, report the loss to any police station. For taxis, you can also write to **Metropolitan Police Lost Property Office**, 15 Penton St., N1 (tel. 278-1744).

MAIL ORDER

The majority of stores I visited in researching this book indicated that they would accept orders by mail or telephone, and several store clerks told me that mail orders from the United States accounted for a vast amount of their business. England has a long tradition of mail order, and many stores produce catalogs. If you visit a store you like, therefore, ask whether there's a catalog available. Sometimes they're free; sometimes they cost up to £5 or more. Ask to be put on a mailing list for future catalogs and other information that stores send regularly to their customers.

Catalogs usually contain all the information you'll need to order by mail, including whether/what credit cards are accepted, the amount of postage charged, and the delivery time. The VAT is usually automatically deducted when you order goods by mail. Remember, however, that you'll have to pay U.S. duty on goods valued more than $50. If goods you order never arrive, you should first contact the shop. Otherwise you should follow the same procedures outlined above under "Consumer Complaints."

MARKETS

I can't imagine going to London and not visiting one of the city's markets. They're so much a part of what London is—and they're entertaining and fun, and offer great bargains. Markets generally fall into two categories: permanent indoor markets and outdoor flea markets usually held one or two days a week.

Permanent markets, divided into individual stalls, consist primarily of antique markets (Antiquarius, Bond Street Antique Centre, Chenil Galleries, the Chelsea Antique Market, Grays Antique Markets) and avant-garde clothing markets (Hyper Hyper and Kensington Market). Flea markets specialize in everything from antiques (Portobello, Camden Passage, New Caledonian) to avant-garde clothing (Camden Town) and bric-a-brac (Petticoat Lane).

Generally speaking, you should bargain with stallholders. With that in mind, you shouldn't wear your best jewelry. Stallholders will assess what they think you can pay and will ask whatever they think they can get away with. After all, they're here to make money and in most cases must pay a fee for being able to set out their wares on a table.

Although it may sound simplistic to say this, don't let yourself be talked into buying something you don't really want. It happens when you're looking at something and the dealer asks whether you're interested. "How much do you want to pay?" he may ask, and if you answer, you're already negotiating. If he agrees to your price, it's not good form to shrug it off and simply walk away. To avoid such a situation, say "No thanks" when he asks whether you're interested.

For the most part, however, I find stallholders to be reasonably honest, fair, and knowledgeable. I especially like the ones dealing in antiques at Portobello, Camden Passage, Camden Town, and New Caledonian. I've had many conversations with dealers at these markets. Usually they're avid collectors and enjoy talking about the items they've found.

MONEY MATTERS

There are no restrictions on the amount of bank notes or traveler's checks that you can bring in and out of Great Britain.

The Currency

The currency used in Great Britain is the **pound sterling**, which is based on the decimal system. The pound is divided into 100 units, known as pence. Paper notes are issued to the value of £5, £10, £20, and £50, while coins are issued to the value of £1 and 50, 20, 10, 5, 2, and 1 pence.

Changing Money

Banks generally offer the best rate of exchange, but if you need British currency when the banks are closed, you can obtain money at branches of larger travel agents such as Thomas Cook, at many large department stores, at large hotels,

You'll encounter strange juxtapositions at Antiquarius antique market

at Heathrow and Gatwick Airports, and at one of the many bureaux de change in London.

Be sure to check in advance the rate of exchange and the commission charged, since this can vary greatly. Because of the commission fee, it's usually better to exchange money only once or twice rather than on several occasions in small amounts.

Bureaux de Change that are members of the London Tourist Board and with long open hours include **American Express** (refer to the section "American Express," above, for addresses and hours), **Thomas Cook** (a branch at Victoria Station is open from 7:45 a.m. to 10 p.m. daily), **Lenlyn** (a branch adjacent to platform 7 at Victoria Station is open 24 hours every day), and **Erskine** (15 Shaftesbury Ave., open 24 hours every day).

POST OFFICE HOURS AND REGULATIONS

Most post offices are open Monday through Friday from 9 a.m. to 5:30 p.m. and on Saturday to 12:30 p.m. If you need postal service outside these hours, the Trafalgar Square Post Office, Trafalgar Square, 24 William IV St., WC2 (tel. 01/930-9580), is open Monday through Saturday from 8 a.m. to 8 p.m. and on Sunday and holidays from 10 a.m. to 5 p.m.

Regulations for Mailing Packages

If you find you've bought more than you can carry, I suggest that you send packages back home. Packages mailed to the United States can weigh up to 22.5 kilograms (49½ pounds), but only major post offices are equipped to deal with packages weighing more than 10 kilograms (22 pounds). It's prudent to check first, therefore, to see whether the post office nearest you can take heavier packages. The maximum size for packages is 3 feet 5 inches in length and 6 feet 7 inches in length and girth combined. The highest amount you can insure packages heading to the United States is £1,400. And remember, the total value of a package mailed to the United States that is allowed duty free is $50. Amounts above $50 will be charged duty, which will be collected by your mail carrier in the United States.

PUBS

Pubs don't have much to do with shopping except that they are good places to stop off for fortification, as many pubs offer hearty pub lunches consisting of meat pies, casseroles, salads, and daily specials. Pub hours in London are 11 a.m. to 3 p.m. and 5:30 to 11 p.m. Monday through Saturday and noon to 2:30 p.m. and 7 to 10:30 p.m. on Sunday. As we go to press, we note that there is a bill pending that would keep pub doors open from 11 a.m. to 11 p.m.

RETURNS AND REPAIRS

Be sure to ask for and keep all receipts for all your purchases. You'll need them in case the items turn out to be faulty. If the receipt doesn't list all the goods, make sure you do so yourself at the time of purchase, listing the prices for each. Be sure also to keep all receipts on goods that are shipped, either the bill of lading or confirmation of shipment from the post office.

If an item turns out to be faulty or doesn't do what was claimed, you can take it back to the store along with your receipt. All reputable shops will replace the item or will offer a cash refund. You might also be offered a credit slip good toward a purchase of the same value. You can ask for cash instead of the credit slip.

If you purchase an item and then decide you don't want it, the store is not obligated to give a refund (except Marks & Spencer, where there are no fitting rooms and customers take clothes home to try them on). I've found that some stores will nonetheless take items back. Army & Navy cheerfully refunded my money on a purchase I decided I didn't want; Harrods, on the other hand, has a reputation for taking goods back only very, very grudgingly.

ROYAL WARRANTS

If you like dropping names and want to tell the folks back home that you bought your china, chocolates, or jewelry in the same shops that supply the royal family, you have a lot of shops to choose from. Below is a partial list of shops in London that supply Buckingham Palace and members of the royal family with clothing, goods, food, and other items. Stores that have such royal warrants proudly display the Royal Arms, usually on their front façade or window.

Amies, Hardy—dressmakers
Aquascutum—makers of weatherproof garments
Army & Navy Stores—suppliers of household and fancy goods
Asprey—goldsmiths, silversmiths, and jewelers
Berry Bros. & Rudd—wine and spirit merchants
Burberrys—weatherproofers
Cartier—jewelers and goldsmiths
Charbonnel et Walker—chocolate manufacturers
Collingwood of Bond Street—jewelers and silversmiths
Dedge, J., & Sons—tailors
Dunhill—"suppliers of smokers' requisites"
Floris—perfumers and manufacturers of toilet preparations
Fortnum & Mason—grocers and provision merchants
Garrard & Co.—goldsmiths and Crown jewelers
The General Trading Company—suppliers of fancy goods
Gibbons, Stanley—philatelists
Gidden, W. & H.—saddlers
Gieves & Hawkes—tailors and outfitters
Goode, Thomas, & Co.—suppliers of china and glass
Grima, Andrew—jewelers
Halcyon Days—suppliers of objets d'art
Hamleys—toy and sports merchants
Harris, D.R., & Co.—chemists
Harrods—suppliers of provisions and household goods; suppliers of china, glass, and fancy goods; outfitters; saddlers
Hartnell, Norman—dressmakers
Hatchards—booksellers
Hawes & Curtis—tailors

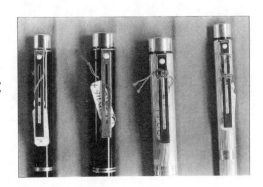

They're not just pens, they're from Asprey

Collingwood: Three royal warrants says it all

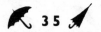
Higgins, H.R.—coffee merchants
Holland & Holland—rifle makers
John, C.—suppliers of carpets
Johnson, Herbert—hatters
Lillywhites—outfitters
Lobb, John—bootmakers
Lock, James, & Co.—hatters
Maggs Bros.—purveyors of rare books and manuscripts
Maxwell, Henry—bootmakers
Paxton & Whitfield—cheesemongers
Penhaligon's—manufacturers of toilet requisites
Phillips, S.J.—antique dealers
Poole, Henry, & Co.—livery outfitters
Prestat—purveyors of chocolates
Prowse, Keith, & Co.—theater ticket agents
Purdey, James, & Sons—gun and cartridge makers
Rayne—shoemakers and handbag manufacturers
Rigby and Peller—corsetières
Simpson—outfitters
Smythson, Frank—stationers
Sparks, John Ltd.—antiquaries of Chinese art
Spink & Son—medallists
Swaine, Adeney, Brigg & Sons—whip and glover makers; umbrella makers
Trumper, Geo. F.—hairdressers
Turnbull & Asser—shirtmakers
Wartski—jewelers
Weatherill, Bernard—riding clothes, outfitters, and livery tailors
Yardley & Co.—perfumers and manufacturers of soap

SALES

Most Londoners wouldn't dream of buying designer clothes, fashion accessories, or fancy household goods except during the annual sales. Department stores are especially legendary for their sales, when items are offered for as much as 50% off. More than 300,000 customers are estimated to pass through Harrods during the first two days of its annual sales, making it necessary to employ an extra staff of 2,000 persons. Harrods can become quite a madhouse, especially in the china and glass departments. As a man was overheard saying in the men's department of Harrods, "You could get trodden to death in there—and by some very respectable people too."

Sales are held by most department and clothing stores twice a year: after Christmas and in the middle of the summer, usually July. Since the crowds can be huge and the best bargains disappear quickly, you have to be prepared, know what you want, and make quick decisions. If you plan to do lots of shopping, it pays to plan your trip for London's annual sales.

SHIPPING

Most antique dealers and fine-art galleries will send your purchases to the United States via ship or plane, either through their own shipping department or through a shipping company. Smaller stores will often send packages through the postal system. The advantage of having your goods shipped is that the VAT is refunded immediately, and I've found that the VAT refund is usually enough to cover the costs of shipping.

If you are purchasing large quantities of furniture, antiques, artwork, or other goods, you may find it easier to make your own arrangement with a shipper to have these goods collected and sent to the United States at the same time. It's best to contact a shipper beforehand, since most shipping companies will arrange to pick up your purchases from the various shops. Below is a list of shipping companies and their specialties.

Alltransport International Group, Unitair Centre, Great South West Road, Feltham, Middlesex TW14 8NT (tel. 01/890-1444). Located next to Heathrow Airport, these shippers will ship anything anywhere, from items as small as an envelope and upward. They will collect your purchases from stores and are especially qualified to handle fine arts and antiques. They offer freight forwarding as well.

C.R. Fenton & Co., Beachy Road, Old Ford, E3 2NX (tel. 01/533-2711). Specialists in fine arts and antiques, they'll even send one cup and saucer if necessary. The company undertakes pickups from stores, packing and shipping to home destinations, as well as freight forwarding.

Featherstone, 24 Hampton House, 15-17 Ingate Pl., London, SW8 3NS (tel. 01/720-0422). Specializes in fine art and antiques but will handle anything. The company can pick up your purchases at stores and takes care of packing and shipment to your home address.

Gander and White, 21 Lillie Rd., London SW6 (tel. 01/381-0571). Specializing in fine arts and antiques, Gander and White can pick up your purchase, pack it, and air-freight it. It can deliver door-to-door and has a New York office as well, at 159 E. 63rd St., New York, NY 10021 (tel. 212/888-1839).

Trans Euro Worldwide Movers, Drury Way, Brent Park, NW10 OJN (tel. 01/459-8080). This company will pack your purchases in a container, and you pay only for your part. It will also air-freight. It will handle single items or more, will pick up your purchases from shops, and can send them to a U.S. port or your home address.

Pitt & Scott Ltd., 20-24 Eden Grove, London, N7 8ED (tel. 01/607-7321). This company specializes in shipping household goods for people who are moving overseas, but it will also ship your purchases and pick them up from the individual stores. It also has an air-freight department and packers knowledgeable in handing fine art.

Vic Pearson & Co. Ltd., 7 Munton Rd., London SE17 1PR (tel. 01/730-8351). This company specializes in fine art but will undertake anything, picking up purchases from shops around London and sending them to your home address.

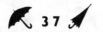

SHOPPING STRATEGIES

W. Wingate & Johnston, 78 Broadway, Stratford, London E15 1NG (tel. 01/519/3211). These enthusiastic shippers will undertake anything, delivering goods door-to-door, to the nearest port or airport. Although they specialize in fine art and antiques, they'll handle any goods.

SHOP HOURS

Most shops in London are open Monday through Saturday from about 9 or 9:30 a.m. until 5 or 6 p.m.; closed Sunday. Generally speaking, the more exclusive the shop, the shorter its business hours. Many antique shops and art galleries along Bond Street, for example, are open only from 9 or 10 a.m. to 5 p.m. and are closed either all of Saturday or Saturday afternoon.

Many shops stay open late one night a week. In the West End, shops stay open until about 7:30 or so on Thursday nights, while in Knightsbridge and along King's Road shops stay open until 7 p.m. or later on Wednesday. During the Christmas season and during August, some shops have longer hours.

SIZES AND METRIC CONVERSIONS

The following chart should help you find clothing and shoe sizes that fit in the United Kingdom. However, sizes can vary, so the best guide is simply to try things on.

Women's Dresses, Coats, and Skirts

American	3	5	7	9	11	12	13	14	15	16	18
British	8	10	11	12	13	14	15	16	17	18	20
Continental	36	38	38	40	40	42	42	44	44	46	48

Women's Blouses and Sweaters

American	10	12	14	16	18	20
British	32	34	36	38	40	42
Continental	38	40	42	44	46	48

Women's Shoes

American	5	6	7	8	9	10
British	3½	4½	5½	6½	7½	8½
Continental	36	37	38	39	40	41

Children's Clothing

American	3	4	5	6	6X
British	18	20	22	24	26

Men's Suits

American	34	36	38	40	42	44	46	48
British	34	36	38	40	42	44	46	48
Continental	44	46	48	50	52	54	56	58

Men's Shoes

American	7	8	9	10	11	12	13
British	6	7	8	9	10	11	12
Continental	39½	41	42	43	44½	46	47

Metric Conversions

Measures: At present, Britain uses miles and inches to measure distances. Weights and measures are, for the most part, already metric.

1 ounce = 28.35 grams (g)	1 gram = 0.035 ounces
1 pound = 0.45 kilograms (kg)	1 kilogram = 2.2 pounds
1 imperial pint = 1.2 U.S. liquid pints	= 0.56 liters
1 imperial quart = 1.2 U.S. liquid quarts	= 0.946 liters
1 imperial gallon = 1.2 U.S. liquid gallons	= 4.5 liters
1 British ton = 1 U.S. long ton	= 2,240 pounds (In the U.S. the more commonly used short ton = 2,000 lb.)
1 metric ton = 1,000 kilograms	= 1.102 U.S. short tons.

TAXES

A **Value Added Tax (VAT)** is levied on most goods sold by shops in the United Kingdom. VAT is usually already included in the retail price and amounts to 15%. Note, however, that there is no VAT imposed on food, most books and newspapers, children's clothes, and most antiques.

SHOPPING STRATEGIES

As a nonresident, you can in many cases obtain a refund of the VAT. It is, however, up to the shop as to whether it will offer this refund. In addition, shops will usually require that you make a minimum amount of purchase in their shop before they give the refund. Most stores require a minimum purchase of £50 to £100, but in my research I've come across everything from shops that require no minimum purchase to those that require a purchase of £200 or more. Some stores charge a service fee. Harrods, for example, requires a minimum purchase of £100, charges a service fee of £2.50, and will give a refund in U.S. dollars for an additional £2.50 charge.

At any rate, be sure to ask whether the shop offers a VAT refund. If it does, the normal procedure is to show the shopkeeper your passport to prove that you qualify for the refund. He will give you a form to fill out, which you then take with you through British Customs at the airport.

At the Customs desk, officers will ask to see both the form and the item purchased. Since the Customs desk is located in the departure hall past check-in and Immigration, you'll need to pack your purchase in your hand-carried baggage. At any rate, the form will be stamped by Customs, after which you drop it into a mailbox next to the Customs desk. Some stores will provide you with a stamped and addressed envelope. If not, however, be sure to bring your own stamp and envelope. Otherwise you'll have to wait until you arrive in the United States before mailing off the form. In any case, once the store has received the form along with the stamp of approval from Customs, the store will mail you a check for the amount of the VAT refund.

Incidentally, if the queue is long at the airport or you've mistakenly packed your purchase in your check-in luggage, you can still get the VAT form certified by your local police or have it notarized in the United States and then mail it to the appropriate shop.

In addition to the method described above, some shops offer other ways of obtaining the VAT refunds. As I've mentioned elsewhere in this book, if you have your purchases shipped directly to the U.S. by the shop, in most cases the VAT will be refunded immediately. Although you may pay nearly as much for shipping as you received for the VAT refund, you will at least avoid the hassles of dealing with the VAT forms, hand-carrying your purchase back to the United States, and cashing a check issued in pounds sterling at your home bank (most banks will charge a fee for cashing foreign checks).

A handful of stores give an immediate VAT refund. The procedure is the same: that is, you receive a form which must be completed at Customs and then mailed back to the store. But you are saved from having to wait for the refund. Since the store is subsequently reimbursed by the government, it's important that you do the necessary work or else the shop will be out the money.

If a store accepts credit cards, the easiest method is to pay for your purchase with a credit card. Methods vary, but some stores will credit your account with the refund when they get back the completed Customs form. Other stores will make up a separate receipt for the VAT amount, which they'll simply tear up and discard once they get the completed Customs form back.

At any rate, it may take up to three months to get a refund. If you never receive your VAT refund, your only recourse is through the shop itself, since it is under no obligation to provide this service. Most shops follow through, however, since it would be bad policy not to satisfy customers.

TELEPHONES

The **area code** for London is 01, which you should omit if you're dialing in London itself. If you don't know a number for London, **information** can be obtained by dialing 142.

Public telephones are generally of two types: older, red telephones that accept 10-pence coins; and newer, green telephones that accept coins (10 and 50 pence) and/or Phonecards. If you're calling from an older-type phone, keep your 10-p coin handy and dial the number; deposit the coin after the party answers. For newer-type phones, you simply put in the coin before you dial, as you do in the US at a payphone. A **Phonecard** is a prepaid card that you can purchase at local kiosks and it can be used for all local, national, and international calls. Cards are sold in units of 10, 20, 40, 100, or 200, with each unit representing 10 pence worth of telephone time. The phone's digital display tells you how many units you have left. Although the cards eliminate the bother of feeding a machine 10-pence coins, I've found that some telephones have an appetite for eating up cards and have charged me extra units—extremely irritating, especially when the one phone booth in the area accepts only Phonecards. I hope the problem of card-mangling telephones will be eradicated in the near future.

TRAVELER'S CHECKS

Traveler's checks are the best way to insure against theft or loss, since they can be replaced. Be sure to keep check numbers listed in two separate places, and mark off each check as it is cashed.

If possible, you might want to get traveler's checks issued in pounds sterling. You can usually use these just like cash, though some of the smaller stores might charge a handling fee. Ask for smaller denominations since small businesses may not be able to make change for large amounts.

Some stores will also accept traveler's checks in U.S. dollars, but the rate of exchange is usually not as favorable as at a bank. Banks will give a better rate of exchange for traveler's checks than they do for cash.

Most banks charge a commission for changing money, but if you go directly to the company that issues the check you will be spared paying such a commission. American Express, for example, does not charge a commission for exchanging American Express traveler's checks.

CHAPTER III

TEN GREAT SHOPPING STROLLS

If someone were to take you by the hand and lead you through Covent Garden, Oxford Street, and King's Road, your first impression of London might well be that it's a city only of shops. While London does have an extraordinary number of stores, the fact remains that most of these shops are concentrated along certain streets and in certain areas of town, making this capital city one of the easiest places in the world for an unbridled shopping spree. Indeed, Oxford, Regent, and Bond Streets are so packed with shops and boutiques that you could blow your whole inheritance in a single afternoon without too much effort—and without walking more than a mile.

The second thing that would probably strike you is how different Covent Garden, Oxford Street, and King's Road are from each other. Each shopping area is like a village in itself, with its own character, atmosphere, and types of shops. Choosing which part of London to shop in, therefore, is the first important decision a shopper must make. Are you interested in books? Then head for Charing Cross Road and charming Cecil Court with its musty antiquarian bookshops. Bond Street is known throughout the world for its fashion boutiques, expensive antique shops, and art galleries, while Kensington has a healthy and eclectic mix of avant-garde clothing stores and family-owned antique shops. London's Old World ambience can be found in tiny specialty shops in the Piccadilly area, but if you're looking for the latest in fashion boutiques, head for Covent Garden or King's Road.

Where you decide to shop might also be governed by what day of the week it is. Many shops stay open late one night a week, and the night is different for different parts of town. Shops in the West End generally remain open until around 7 p.m. on Thursday, while shops in Knightsbridge have late nights on Wednesday. Many shops in Covent Garden remain open until 7 p.m. or later throughout the week.

To help you decide which areas of London would best suit your shopping needs, I've selected ten of the city's major shopping regions and have outlined walking tours through each, highlighting shops you'll pass along the way. More information on each of these shops is given in the shop index in Part Two in the appropriate category. Some of these strolls can be combined, especially those along bisecting streets such as Oxford and Regent. Obviously, the amount of time you spend on each stroll depends entirely on you—it's easy to forget anything as mundane as time when you're captivated by a shop that has changed little in the past 200 years.

At the end of each stroll are suggestions for cultural sights you might want to see while you're in the area. I've also recommended restaurants and coffeeshops where you can stop off for lunch or a light snack. I've chosen establishments that fit into a shopping schedule—that is, easy to find, close to shops, and more often than not, with fast and efficient service. I've also included some restaurants that may lie slightly outside our walking route but offer other redeeming qualities such as great food and good atmosphere.

Remember, too, that pubs usually offer hot pub lunches, which are usually very good for the money and have the additional advantage of being immediately available. Steak-and-kidney pie; a "ploughman's lunch," which consists of cheeses and bread; casseroles; and sandwiches are the usual pub grub. Unfortunately, a very uncivil law in this otherwise very civilized country dictates that you can't buy a pint in the middle of the afternoon. Most pubs, therefore, are open from 11 a.m. to 3 p.m. and don't open again until 5:30, staying open till 11 p.m. On Sunday they're open from noon to 2:30 p.m. and 7 to 10:30 p.m.

To rest your weary shopping bones, you might also want to join in the English tradition of taking an afternoon tea, which might be like a complete meal. In the finer establishments, for example, tea often includes finger sandwiches, scones with clotted cream and preserves, cakes, and a choice of

What say ye to a pint outdoors?

teas. In case you haven't indulged yet, a scone is a small, biscuit-like pastry, over which you heap clotted cream (very rich butterfat) and preserves. It's so sinfully fattening that it's guaranteed to replace any previous guilt you may have had making all those shopping purchases. Tea time is usually from 3 to 5:30 p.m.

THE WEST END

The West End is the heart of London shopping and is the most important shopping area of the entire city. If you have only one day to shop, you should spend it here—after which you'll realize that it's impossible to cover all of the West End in a single day. Oxford Street, New and Old Bond Streets, Regent Street, South Molton, Burlington Arcade, Savile Row, Piccadilly Circus, and Jermyn Street comprise what is one of the swankiest shopping regions in the entire world. Exclusive designer boutiques, jewelry shops, huge department stores, fabric shops, art galleries, cigar shops, antique showrooms, auction houses, tailor shops, and hat shops are just a few of the different kinds of stores you'll find in London's famous West End.

OXFORD STREET AND SOUTH MOLTON

Oxford Street is the most democratic of streets in the West End, with a wide variety of shops and stores that cater to both the rich and the budget-conscious. Stretching more than a mile from Marble Arch to Tottenham Court Road, Oxford Street is home to four major department stores, chain stores, countless clothing stores, shoe shops, banks, and bureaux de change. There are four underground stations along its length—Marble Arch, Bond Street, Oxford Circus, and Tottenham Court Road—and buses make regular runs both east and west. Oxford Street is off-limits to all vehicles except buses and taxis, but the sidewalks are so packed with human beings that you'll probably never notice the lack of cars. The most crowded times are during lunch and just after the shops close, when entire sidewalks become a sea of heads. If Oxford Street becomes too much for you, escape to nearby South Molton Street or St. Christopher's Place, two pedestrian oases with boutiques, restaurants, and outdoor cafés.

An Area Stroll

Let's begin our walk at the **Cumberland Hotel,** which is located right above the Marble Arch underground station. If it's in the afternoon, you might want to pause at the hotel for England's famous traditional refreshment—scones, clotted cream, preserves, and tea. Other suggestions where you can take afternoon tea are given at the end of this stroll.

At any rate, not far from the hotel stretches Hyde Park, and in the middle of

GREAT SHOPPING STROLLS: THE WEST END

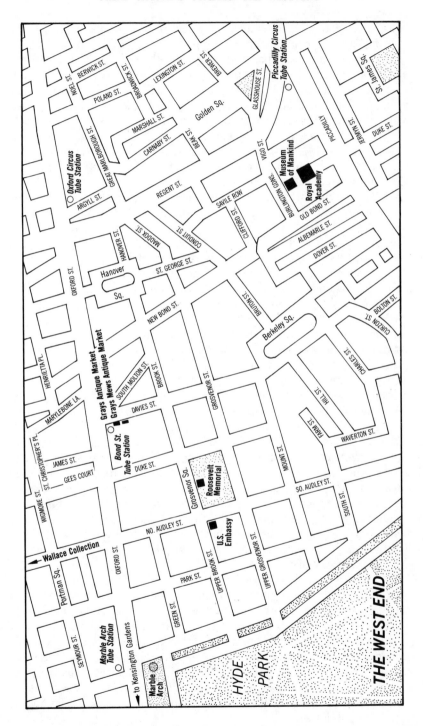

swirling traffic stands Marble Arch, completed in 1827 as a monumental gate to Buckingham Palace and moved to its present site in 1847. The arch stands where Tyburn Tree used to be, a gallows that for 400 years saw the death of some 50,000 "criminals." Executions in the olden days used to draw up to 20,000 spectators, especially if the condemned was a well-known highwayman or a young woman, and death was sometimes by disembowelment or dismember-ment. A rather unpleasant thought, but one that might make the crowds of Oxford Street much more tolerable. After all, it's much less intimidating rubbing elbows with fellow shoppers than with the pickpockets, painted ladies of the night, and troublemakers who used to gather for the express purpose of watching some poor bloke lose his life.

Leaving Marble Arch and history behind you, begin your stroll by heading east on Oxford Street. The first major store you come to is **C&A,** located on the right side of the street and easily recognizable by its rainbow-colored logo. Specializing in affordable clothing for the entire family, this C&A is one of two such stores on Oxford Street and is part of a Dutch-owned group of chain stores. Next door at 499 Oxford St. is **Chinacraft,** a chain store with a dozen locations in London. It stocks all English makes of fine bone china and porcelain, as well as crystal, silver, and gift items. Across the street you'll see **Littlewoods,** a chain of small department stores dealing in moderately priced clothing and goods. **Mothercare,** located on the right side of the street at 461 Oxford St., is a chain store that caters to all the needs of infants, children, mothers, and mothers-to-be. It carries a wide and inexpensive range of mater-nity and children's clothes, toys, and baby furniture.

Almost directly across the street from Mothercare is that monolith of department stores, **Marks & Spencer.** This is where everyone comes to buy the fashions they've seen elsewhere, since prices here are often lower than in other stores. Known to the British as Marks & Sparks, it boasts tremendous values in clothing, particularly underwear. Even Margaret Thatcher admits to buying her underclothes here. The only drawback is that you can't try clothes on before buying them because there are no fitting rooms. Although clothes are easily returnable if they don't fit, having to come back to the store may not be worth the money you save, especially if your time in London is short. In addition, Marks & Spencer can get unbelievably crowded. Still, if you know what you want and you have the time to look for it, shopping at Marks & Sparks may be the best move you make.

Right next to Marks & Spencer is one of my favorite department stores, **Selfridges.** This store is beautiful inside and out—note its stately façade with its columns, plants, and one of the most ornate clocks in all of London, the Lady of Time. Inside you'll find fashion, cosmetics and perfume, housewares and kitchenware, a beauty salon, and a fine gift section with crafts native to Great Britain. On the third floor is the Selfridge Restaurant, where you can pause for a snack or afternoon tea. At the back of the store is the entrance to Miss Selfridge, which has its own address at 40 Duke St. This shop caters to young working women, with fashionable clothes at reasonable prices. It also stocks a good range of casual clothes.

Next on the shopping agenda is **Next for Men,** at 427 Oxford St., a very chic and fashionable clothing boutique for men who are interested in the latest look. This shop is one of many Next stores, a rather new group of chain stores which has taken London by storm. If you can't find what you're looking for here, head farther down the street to **Take Six,** 326 Oxford St. Another chain store of men's clothes, it caters to 20-year-olds and up who are interested in purchasing suits, casualwear, and leather jackets at moderate prices.

Meanwhile, if you want to escape the crowds of Oxford Street, watch for a tiny side street called Gees Court which will lead off to your left after you've passed Duke Street but before you reach Bond Street station. Gees Court leads to St. Christopher's Place, an interesting pedestrian lane with boutiques, pubs, restaurants, and outdoor cafés. Among the shops you'll find here are **Under Two Flags,** which sells model lead soldiers, and **Paddy Campbell,** which specializes in the classic English look with well-tailored clothes for women. **Whistles** and **[ixi:z]** are two shops that sell unique and modern fashions at reasonable prices.

Back on Oxford Street, walk past the Bond Street tube station until you get to Davies Street, where you'll find the **Grays Antique Markets.** Located in an old brick building, this market offers antiques from England, the continent, and the Orient, with goods ranging from books and jewelry to canes, clocks, and porcelain. Just around the corner and a mere 30-second walk away is **Grays Mews Antique Market,** where there are additional stalls selling more of the same.

Just a block west of Davies Street is South Molton Street, a pedestrian lane with fashionable boutiques. **Browns,** which stretches along several storefronts at 23–27 South Molton, is undoubtedly one of London's foremost designer shops. Behind its doors you'll find clothes by Jasper Conran, Bill Blass, Comme des Garcons, Jean-Paul Gaultier, Jean Muir, Sonia Rykiel, and Perry Ellis, to name only a few. Fashion designer **Katharine Hamnet** has her own shop at 50 South Molton, while Joseph Ettedgui has two boutiques on South Molton, **Joseph Tricot** and **Pour la Ville. Zero Four** is a children's clothing store with fashions imported from Italy and France, while 012 is the children's version of the popular Benetton boutique with colorful clothing from Italy. If you're interested in unique hand-knitted sweaters, be sure to drop by **Crochetta,** where feathers, leather, sequins, and beads are ingeniously incorporated into sweater designs.

South Molton is also home to some exciting jewelry stores. **Ken Lane** is the ultimate in fake jewelry and the place to come if you want imitation pearl necklaces or fake diamond rings. **Butler & Wilson** has a dazzling display of costume and paste jewelry, where you can pick up imitation art deco pieces or flamboyant jewelry of the '80s. If you want original jewelry, the **Electrum** is a gallery of handmade contemporary jewelry crafted by artists from around the world.

Vidal Sassoon and **Molton Brown** are two hair salons on South Molton Street, and both shops sell their own beauty products. Sweet tooths can be satisfied by stopping off at **Prestat,** which specializes in delicious handmade chocolates and truffles. In business for 60 years, Prestat even supplies Buckingham Palace with its chocolates. If you're more partial to caffeine than to chocolates, **H. R. Higgins** sells coffee beans from around the world and will grind them to your specifications.

Presuming that the shops on South Molton haven't done you in and you're eager to move on, I suggest you return to Oxford Street for the rest of our stroll. The first large store you'll come to is **Debenhams,** a department store with a large selection of clothing and home furnishings. After Debenhams, you'll reach **Benetton,** 328 Oxford St. This Italian clothing boutique with its bright, colorful casualwear is tremendously popular in London—it has nine shops on Oxford Street alone. Meanwhile, on the opposite side of the street on the corner of Oxford and New Bond Streets is **Next Too,** a woman's clothing store belonging to the Next chain of stores. Next Too caters to the woman in her mid-20s, with clothes for both work and play.

D. H. Evans is the next department store we come to, with its gleaming art deco façade and eight floors devoted to everything from fashion and cosmetics to sports and gifts. Immediately following is another department store, **John Lewis,** famous for its motto "Never Knowingly Undersold." If you buy something here and then find it cheaper elsewhere in London, John Lewis will refund the difference. This department store is where Londoners come to buy their household goods and equipment.

In the following block on the left side is **Wallis,** 215-217 Oxford St., a women's clothing store that sells good imitations of designer clothes at reasonable prices. It has a fine selection of both working clothes with a flair and evening cocktail dresses. Part of a chain, this is one of four Wallis stores in central London. Also in the same block is **British Home Stores,** a chain of small department stores specializing in functional clothing and items for everyday use in the home.

Hennes & Mauritz, 261-271 Oxford St., is a Swedish-owned clothing boutique popular with both men and women in their teens and early 20s. Its clothes are bright, bold, and innovative, with designs that would stand out even in a crowded room full of people. Another clothing store that appeals to young people is **Top Man** and **Top Shop,** located at Oxford Circus. As its name implies, Top Man is for men and carries a large selection of fun, zany, and functional clothing. It has a large selection of men's suit jackets at very reasonable prices. In the basement is Top Shop, for women, with a large selection of work, party, and lounge clothing at great prices. I can spend hours browsing here.

Also on Oxford Circus is **Wedgwood,** home of the famous Wedgwood china. This shop also carries other brands of china such as Royal Worcester, Royal Doulton, Coalport, Spode, and Minton, along with such products as porcelain figurines, Caithness paperweights, and Wedgwood jewelry.

Passing another **Wallis** and **Littlewoods,** you'll come to the newest **HMV** shop at 150 Oxford St., a chain group of record stores. It carries everything from classical and jazz to the latest in pop, and also imports music from around the world. In addition to records, it has cassettes, compact discs, and books on famous musicians.

Italian-designed clothes for men are sold at **Woodhouse,** 99 Oxford St., one of six such shops in London. If you like games of all kinds, be sure to visit **Games Centre,** 100 Oxford St., which sells British versions of Trivial Pursuit and Monopoly as well as children's games, puzzles, strategy, and war games. And last but not least is **Virgin Megastore,** 14–16 Oxford St., another record-and-tape store located not far from Tottenham Court Road tube station. Of modern, contemporary design, this with-it record store could qualify as a tourist attraction in itself and boasts life-size wax models of such famous musicians as Elvis Presley, Madonna, and Boy George.

Sightseeing Suggestions

If, after shopping, you need to recover your sensibilities, the best plan for escape would be to flee to **Hyde Park.** Stretching southwest of **Marble Arch,** this wide expanse of green once served as a hunting forest for Henry VIII and together with adjoining **Kensington Gardens** makes up the largest open space in London. Walking through wooded areas and grassy fields, you can almost imagine you've somehow landed in the English countryside. In the northeast corner of Hyde Park, not far from Marble Arch, is **Speaker's Corner,** where anyone can and does come to speak his or her mind, especially on a Sunday.

Located on charming Manchester Square not far from the Bond Street tube station, the **Wallace Collection** (tel. 935-0687) is one of London's most remarkable museums. The collection itself includes paintings, furniture, porcelain, and armor, primarily French and mostly from the 19th century. Collected by the third and fourth Marquesses of Hertford and donated by Lady Wallace to the nation in 1897, this personal art collection is probably one of the finest selections of French art outside France itself. Even the house is remarkable, built in the 1770s and once serving as the French Embassy. It's as though both the house and its collection were frozen in time, offering interesting insight into what was considered collectible in the 19th century. The Wallace Collection is open from 10 a.m. to 5 p.m. Monday through Saturday and from 2 to 5 p.m. on Sunday.

Luncheon Spots and Drinking Establishments

Justin de Blank, 54 Duke St. (tel. 629-3174), is a cafeteria-style restaurant serving healthy and creative dishes. Using the freshest of ingredients, it serves both vegetarian and meat selections, salads, puddings, and desserts. The menus change daily but might include such creations as pasta-and-avocado salad, broccoli and green leeks in white sauce, white-cabbage soup, or lemon-and-lime cheesecake. With most main dishes averaging about £4, prices are a bit high for a cafeteria, but if you love veggies you won't regret eating here. It's open from 8:30 a.m. to 3:30 p.m. and again from 4:30 to 9 p.m. Monday through

Friday. On Saturday, however, its hours are from 9 a.m. to 3:30 p.m. only. The **Original Crêperie** is located at 56a South Molton St. (tel. 629-4794) and serves various kinds of crêpes filled with everything from chicken to vegetables to chocolate and fruit. Prices start at around £2 for fruit crêpes and average about £3.50 for those with meat. With seating outside in warm weather, it's open from 9:30 a.m. to 8 p.m. Monday through Wednesday, closing at 10 p.m. Thursday through Saturday. It's closed all day on Sunday.

At 46 South Molton St. is **Widow Applebaum's Deli & Bagel Academy** (tel. 499-6710). It also has outdoor seating and is open from 10 a.m. to 9 p.m., except on Thursday when it stays open until 11 p.m. Closed on Sunday, this informal restaurant features such sandwiches as kosher salami on rye bread, lox on a bagel served with cream cheese, reubens, and hamburgers. Most items on the menu cost between £2.70 and £4.40; wine starts at £1 a glass.

Coconut Grove, 3-5 Barrett St. (tel. 486-5269), is located just off St. Christopher's Place and consists of a restaurant and a cocktail bar side by side. With large windows and potted plants, this establishment is very airy and light and is a good place to stop off for a meal or a drink. It's open seven days a week from noon to midnight (until 1 a.m. Thursday through Saturday), but remember that liquor laws restrict the sale of alcoholic beverages to the hours of noon to 3 p.m. and 5:30 to 11:30 p.m. The menu is extensive, listing nine different kinds of salads and entrees ranging from steaks and barbecued chicken to seafood and calves' liver. Most dishes range from £5 to £7, and if you want a cocktail you have more than 40 different concoctions to choose from.

If you're too laden down with packages to travel far, the **River Restaurant** is located on the top floor of the D. H. Evans department store. A cafeteria, it has different counters for various salads, soups, sandwiches, and desserts. Simply pick up a tray, select dishes from the various counters, pay the cashier, and then find a table. The eating area is divided into smoking and nonsmoking sections. Probably the best deal is the set meal of the day, which usually runs about £4.40. From 2:30 to 5:30 p.m. is tea time, during which you can have two scones, jam, butter, cream, and a pot of tea for £1.50.

On the first floor of **Top Man,** Oxford Circus (tel. 629-7179), is an informal snackbar where you can order pastries, salads, quiche, and other dishes, and eat them while observing the shoppers in the store. Snacks are served from 10 a.m. to 6 p.m., with additional hot dishes served from noon to 2:45 p.m.

Fino's Wine Cellar, 37 Duke St. (tel. 935-9459), is a wine bar located in a basement. Usually fairly quiet and relaxed, it metamorphoses into a packed and noisy disco on Friday nights. Wine by the glass starts at £1, but most selections of wine are available by the bottle only. A bottle of Fino's house red wine costs £5, while a bottle of Alsace Gewurztraminer is £9.40. Meals are served from noon to 2:30 p.m. and 6 to 10:30 p.m. Probably your best bet is to order the daily special, which averages £8 for lunch and £11.50 for dinner. The regular menu includes such entrees as calves' liver with bacon, lamb cutlets, fried scampi, and pastas. Closed on Sunday, this establishment is open the rest of the week from 11 a.m. to 3 p.m. and 5:15 to 11 p.m.

Pubs and Pub Lunches

The **Argyll Arms,** 18 Argyll St. (tel. 734-6117), is a restored Victorian pub near Oxford Circus. Featuring original engraved glass and mahogany paneling, this friendly pub serves a good selection of hot food for both lunch and dinner. The changing menu may include steak-and-kidney pie, chicken curry with rice, lasagne, stuffed pepper with tomato sauce, or hot salt beef with carrots. Dishes cost £2.70, and ales start at about £1 a pint.

Henry Holland, 39 Duke St. (tel. 629-4426), is a Georgian pub named after architect Henry Holland, who designed the building. Popular with both shoppers and local business people, it serves a small selection of snacks and sandwiches starting at £1.10.

Lamb & Flag, James Street off St. Christopher's Place (tel. 408-0132), is a typical English pub and has outdoor seating along the sidewalk in fine weather. Closed on Sunday but otherwise open during the usual pub hours, it serves snacks during lunchtime only.

Marlborough Head, 24 N. Audley St. (tel. 629-5981), is located just off Oxford Street in a brick-and-stone building about 150 years old. Open during regular pub hours every day except Sunday, when it remains closed, it serves sandwiches, salads, and other dishes for lunch only. Usually on the menu are steak-and-kidney pie, roast chicken and bacon, and rainbow trout with prawns. A meal here averages about £4.50.

The Tottenham, 6 Oxford St. (tel. 636-7201), proclaims itself "the only pub on Oxford" and is located near Tottenham Court Road next to McDonald's. Receiving a badly needed facelift in 1986, it's a cozy pub with a pleasant Victorian interior. It has its original 1892 fittings, along with old wall murals and mirrors with gold leaf. Pub lunches here are likely to include steak-and-kidney pie, casseroles, and homemade vegetarian quiche, all priced under £3.

Afternoon Tea

The **Selfridge Restaurant,** located on the third floor of Selfridges department store (tel. 629-1234), has a very dignified and subdued atmosphere in which you can take your afternoon tea. Decorated in cool peach and green, with flowers on every table, it serves 14 varieties of tea and a wide selection of sandwiches, cakes, and pastries. For £6.50 you get your choice of tea, scones, and finger sandwiches. Tea time here is from 3 to 5:30 p.m., except on Thursday when it stays open until 7 p.m.

Orchard Terrace is a pleasant restaurant in the Selfridge Hotel, which is located behind Selfridges department store on Orchard Street (tel. 408-2080). It serves tea daily from 3 to 6 p.m. Various tea-and-pastry combinations are offered, starting at £2.10 for tea and toasted teacakes for two persons. If you feel like splurging, go for the £5 version which features two scones with clotted cream and strawberry jam, cake, and a pot of Indian or Chinese tea.

Close by also is the **London Marriott Hotel,** 10 Grosvenor Square (tel. 493-1232), serving an afternoon tea from 3 to 5:30 p.m. daily in the Regent

Lounge. A pleasant and elegant setting with chintz floral curtains and flowers on every table, it offers a cream tea for £7 which includes finger sandwiches, scones, pastries and cakes, and a choice of eight teas.

One of the best deals in town is offered by the **Cumberland Hotel,** located at Marble Arch (tel. 262-1234). Serving a tea buffet daily from 3 to 5:30 p.m. which includes hot scones, cakes, and a pot of tea, you can eat as much as you want for only £3.10. With a deal like this, who needs dinner?

BOND STREET AND BURLINGTON ARCADE

Whereas Oxford Street has stores that appeal to a wide spectrum of the social strata, Bond Street caters unabashedly to the wealthy of the world. In fact, Bond Street has what are quite arguably the ritziest shops in London, including approximately 50 fashion stores, 30 jewelers, some 20 shoe stores, about two dozen fine-arts galleries, and approximately 12 major antique dealers. With names like Sotheby's, S. J. Phillips, Ackermann & Sons, Mallett & Son, Partridge, and Asprey, it's easy to see why the rich come here to dress themselves, furnish their homes, and shop as a form of entertainment. Fortunately, not all prices are sky high, and because this is first and foremost a shopping

Part of the $8 million cache at Partridge

street, most establishments don't mind if you drop in only for a browse.

Recently celebrating its 300th birthday, Bond Street's beginnings were much more humble. In fact, if you had come here for a stroll more than three centuries ago, you most likely would have found yourself flailing in mud up to your arms, since much of the area was nothing more than a marsh. If mud pits didn't get you, robbers probably would have, they being the only sort who might have relished lurking about in muddy shadows.

At any rate, in 1686 this marshy area was elevated to new heights with the construction of a street, named after Sir Thomas Bond, who made his fortune lending money to the king. By the middle of the 18th century Bond Street had become a fashionable address, and famous personalities who have lived here read like a short Who's Who of British history, among them biographer James Boswell, poets Lord Byron and Percy Bysshe Shelley, Sir Horatio Nelson, and historian Edward Gibbon. Even the present queen was born close by, at 17 Bruton St.

Bond Street's beginnings as a center for shopping also date to the 18th century, when women of means flocked here to purchase clothes and to flaunt the ones they had on. Tailors, bootmakers, hatters, and haberdashers all set up shop here, along with a rich variety of shops ranging from cabinetmakers and gunsmiths to fishmongers and cheese merchants.

Today, of course, Bond Street has lost much of its old character and none of the original businesses remain. However, there's a trace of old London in storefronts like Tessiers, Crombie, and Asprey. Whenever I walk down Bond Street, I am humbled by the thought that I am merely following in the footsteps of those 18th-century shoppers who had the foresight to shop just for the fun of it, long before much of the world even imagined it.

An Area Stroll

To begin our stroll of Bond Street, start at its north end where it joins Oxford Street, the closest station for which is also called Bond Street. Bond Street, which is often described as the heart of Mayfair, is divided into two parts, New and Old Bond Streets. New Bond was built around 1721 and stretches south from Oxford Street to Burlington Gardens, where it then becomes Old Bond Street and continues south until it terminates at Piccadilly. It might help to know that the numbering systems for both Bond Streets are completely independent of one another. Standing at the top of New Bond Street and facing south, shops on the left side are numbered from 86 to 1, while those on the right side start at 87 and end at 180. Likewise, the left (east) side of Old Bond runs from 24 to 1, while the right side goes from 25 to 50.

Beginning at the junction of Oxford and New Bond Streets, the first shop you'll notice is **Next Too,** a relatively new and popular clothing store for young women. Walking south on the right side of New Bond Street, you'll see **Kurt Geiger** at no. 95, the first of many shoe shops on this street. Concentrating primarily on Italian makes of shoes, most of its footwear is priced over £100.

Other shoe shops you'll pass on Bond Street include **Bally** (with shoes from Switzerland), **Church's** (English shoes for men), **Rayne, Ferragamo,** and **Russell & Bromley.**

As you continue walking down the right side of the street, you'll pass **Frette,** 98 New Bond, with linen imported from Italy, and **Kansai,** 101 New Bond, the showplace for unique clothing by this Japanese designer. **Cacharel,** 103 New Bond, sells French fashion for men, women, and children. If you're looking for a classy and elaborate evening dress, be sure to drop in to **Lucy's,** 107 New Bond, which sells French and Italian creations that cost up to £5,500. Next door is **Lanvin,** a very stylish men's clothing shop that can provide everything from suits down to the cuff links. Across the street is **Bentley & Co.,** 65 New Bond, which specializes in antique and contemporary jewelry. The helpful staff here will be glad to show you everything from their art deco pieces to their Fabergé and pocket watches.

The next intersection brings you to Brook Street, which has several interesting shops. **Penhaligon's,** 20A Brook St., sells perfume, toilet water, and soaps using the same recipe that was developed by William Penhaligon back in the mid-1800s. **Halcyon Days,** 14 Brook St., is the best place in town to shop for lovely enamel boxes. Along with modern reproductions, this charming shop also sells 18th-century English enamels and will take commissions on boxes with your own special design. You could, for example, have an enamel box with a picture of your home painted on the lid. **Colefax and Fowler,** 39 Brook St., is famous for its floral chintzes, based on traditional designs of the late 18th and early 19th centuries. Fashion designers who have showrooms on Brook Street include **Kenzo** at no. 27-29 and **Roland Klein** at no. 26.

Fenwick is located on the corner of Brook and New Bond Streets. Although small, it ranks as the only department store on Bond Street and sells primarily fashions, cosmetics, and accessories for women. A friendly and helpful staff makes shopping here a pleasure.

After Fenwick come four interesting and diverse shops one after the other. **Smythson** is the most dignified and elegant stationery shop you could ever hope to find and serves as the royal stationers to the queen. Stop here for fine writing papers, writing pens, and leatherbound address books. **Jason's** is a fabric shop specializing in silks and English woolens, while **The White House,** next door, displays the ultimate in expensive lingerie, linens, and a select line of clothing for men, women, and children. You can pick up a silk negligee here for a cool £1,240. **Chappell,** a music store with a strong emphasis on pianos and sheet music, has been selling instruments from the same site ever since it was first established in 1811.

Meanwhile, across the street are the **Bond Street Silver Galleries,** at 111-112 New Bond St., where about a dozen dealers display antique and contemporary silver on the first and second floors (remember, British first and second floors would be the second and third floors in the American system). Next door is **Saint Laurent,** at 113 New Bond, one of several big-name fashion boutiques on Bond Street. This one carries clothes for women, while the Saint

Penhaligon's: Royal perfumeurs

Laurent at 135 New Bond carries designer wear for men. The **Bond Street Antique Centre,** 124 New Bond, is an antique market whose various stall-holders sell such wares as jewelry, porcelain, silver, watches, portrait minia-tures, Oriental antiques, and paintings.

In the next block, on the left side of the street you'll find **Regine,** 43-44 New Bond St., a clothing boutique for men and women with designer wear by Claude Montana, Missoni, Erreuno, and others. **Mallet & Son,** 40 New Bond, is without a doubt one of the most distinguished antique houses in all of London, selling only the finest 18th-century English furniture. Furniture is displayed as though it were in an 18th-century upper-class home, with the top pieces worth half a million pounds. Following Mallett is **Sotheby's,** at 34-35 New Bond, founded in 1774 and one of the most famous auction houses in the world. One or two sales are held weekly (except August and part of September), and objects for sale are displayed two to three days in advance of the auction. Showrooms are open Monday through Friday from 9 a.m. to 4:30 p.m. and I suggest you take a look around even if you have no intention of attending the auction.

Tessiers, 26 New Bond St., is one of my favorite shops in all of Bond Street. From its gleaming, black façade to its old mahogany display cases, Tessiers is a survivor from old London's past. Built in 1720, it sells antique silver, as well as jewelry that dates from the beginning of the 19th century to the present. Note the pictures hanging on the wall—they're designs made with human hair.

Chinacraft, 130 New Bond, brings us back to the present with its large selection of English porcelain and gift items. At 139 New Bond is **S. J. Phillips,** a very expensive shop selling antique jewelry and silver. Founded in 1869, it has a royal warrant.

Housed in what used to be an old Georgian pharmacy at 143 New Bond St. is **Polo Ralph Lauren,** which opened in 1981 as Lauren's first branch overseas. This shop sells both men's and women's smartly tailored fashions. **Partridge,** 144-146 New Bond St., rivals Mallett as one of the most distinguished antique dealers on Bond. Occupying the building originally built as a gallery for the Colnaghi fine-arts dealer at the end of the 19th century, Partridge is a family-owned concern specializing in 18th-century French and English furniture.

Wildenstein, 147 New Bond St., is the first of several top-quality fine-art galleries on Bond Street and specializes in impressionist and Old Master paintings and drawings. Among other famous art galleries you'll pass on Bond are the **Fine Art Society** at 148 New Bond, which concentrates on British and European art from 1800 to 1940, and **Thomas Agnew & Sons,** 43 Old Bond, which first opened its doors on Bond Street in 1876 and which has been selling the Old Masters ever since. **P. & D. Colnaghi,** 14 Old Bond, was established in 1760 and sells Old Master prints, paintings, and watercolors, while **Leger Galleries,** 13 Old Bond, places its emphasis on English oils and watercolors from the 18th and 19th centuries. **Ackermann & Son,** 3 Old Bond, specializes in English sporting, marine, and botanical paintings and prints from 1750 to 1860.

The **Antique Porcelain Co.,** 149 New Bond St., is up on the first floor with porcelain dating back to the time when it was first made in Europe in the 18th century. On the ground floor is **Louis Vuitton** with its famous handbags, luggage, and accessories.

In the following block on the left side of the street is **Moira** at 22–23 New Bond, which specializes in Victorian, art deco, and art nouveau jewelry, and **Fior,** which revels in costume and paste jewelry.

While the main traffic will veer off to the left on Clifford Street, you should continue walking south on Bond Street where you'll see **Watches of Switzerland** with—what else?—timepieces of precise, Swiss design. **Georg Jensen,** 15 New Bond, specializes in Danish products from three manufacturers—namely, Georg Jensen silver, watches, and cutlery; glassware by Holme Gaard; and china by Royal Copenhagen. Opposite Georg Jensen is a side street called Grafton Street, where you'll find the fashion boutique of English designer **Zandra Rhodes** with her fantasy-provoking creations, and **Wartski,** which has an amazing collection of Russian antique jewelry and Fabergé objects.

On the corner of Bond and Grafton Streets is **Asprey,** the ultimate in gift shops. This is where the wealthy come to buy gifts for people who have everything. Where else could you find a paperclip in the shape of a mousetrap, made of 18-karat gold with diamonds and costing almost £3,000? How about a solid-gold toothbrush for about £700? Not everything, of course, is so expensive, and it's worth taking a spin through Asprey for the sheer fun of it. The staff is courteous and gracious, and will help point the way to the various departments, which range from china and silver to books, luggage, antiques, and clocks. Truly, visiting Bond Street without seeing Asprey would be a real shame, for there's no store in the world quite like it.

Established in 1817, **Collingwood,** 177 New Bond St., sells watches and antique and contemporary jewelry, and carries three royal warrants. On the same side of the street are **Karl Lagerfeld,** with fashion for women, and **Cartier,** famous throughout the world for its watches and jewelry.

You've now reached the end of New Bond Street, but before continuing on Old Bond, I suggest you take a left onto Burlington Gardens where you'll then see the entrance to **Burlington Arcade.** Built in 1819, this delightful shopping arcade is a relic of the Regency period and is still patroled by top-hatted beadles, whose job it is to make sure patrons do not "whistle, sing, or hurry."

Take your time, therefore, to explore the various specialty shops. If you're looking for cashmere sweaters, you have a lot to choose from in such shops as **N. Peal, S. Fisher,** or **Berk.** The **Irish Linen Company** sells everything for the table or bed, while **Sullivan Powell** is the arcade's tobacconist. **Simeon** is an antique shop with such collectibles as portrait miniatures and Chinese snuff bottles. If you're interested in miniature soldiers or collector's dolls, be sure to call in at **Hummel,** which also sells toys and novelties.

Retracing your steps back to Old Bond Street, the first shop you'll notice on the right side of the street is **Loewe,** 25 Old Bond. This Spanish leather shop sells luggage, handbags, briefcases, fashion, perfumes, and gift accessories. Next door is **Chanel,** famous throughout the world for both its perfumes and women's fashions. The neighboring **Gucci** shop also needs no introduction, selling its high-quality handbags, luggage, shoes, and scarves, many with the familiar Gucci logo.

No. 28 Old Bond is the address for the **Royal Arcade,** a group of shops that includes **Charbonnel et Walker,** with its handmade chocolates, and **W. Bill,** a family-owned boutique that specializes in cashmere sweaters, kilts, and tweeds. At the end of the Royal Arcade is Brown's Hotel, a pleasant place to stop for afternoon tea.

Charbonnel et Walker: Chocolate suppliers to the royal family

Yardley, 33 Old Bond St., is a traditional perfumery established in London back in 1770. In addition to selling its soaps, after-shave lotions, and perfumes, Yardley also has a beauty salon where you can have facials or your legs waxed. If it's time to visit a barbershop, you could do no better than **Truefitt & Hill,** 23 Old Bond, established in 1805 and serving as the royal hairdressers to the Duke of Edinburgh. Fitted with art nouveau lamps and ceiling fans, this establishment has a very entertaining staff, making it a good place to hear the local news. In addition to haircuts, they also provide face massages and manicures, and offer a complimentary shoe shine.

After you've had your hair cut, your face massaged, and your nails manicured, you may want to stop off at **Sulka,** 19 Old Bond St., for some more pampering. This men's shop is most known for its ties but also has bespoke (custom-made) shirts and other men's accessories.

Sightseeing Suggestions

The **Museum of Mankind,** 6 Burlington Gardens (tel. 437-2224), is located right next to Burlington Arcade. Open from 10 a.m. to 5 p.m. Monday through

Saturday and from 2:30 to 6 p.m. on Sunday, this museum serves as the ethnology department of the British Museum with changing exhibitions designed to illustrate non-Western societies and cultures. Sure to appeal to both children and the kids in us all, its collections come from the indigenous peoples of Africa, Australia, the Pacific islands, North and South America, and from certain parts of Asia and Europe. Admission is free and there's a museum shop where you can pick up handcrafted items from around the world.

Luncheon Spots and Drinking Establishments

In addition to the restaurants recommended here, there are also restaurants listed under the Piccadilly stroll that are easily accessible, especially if you finish this Bond Street walk at Piccadilly. The closest restaurants include Overton's, the restaurants in Fortnum & Mason and the Terrace Garden Restaurant in Le Meridien Hotel.

The **Chicago Pizza Pie Factory,** 17 Hanover Square (tel. 629-2669), is one of the best places in town if you're hungry for pizza. It's owned by American Bob Payton, who pioneered deep-dish pizzas in London, and decorated with Chicago memorabilia and with videos showing Chicago baseball. Pizza starts at about £5 for two. The only drawback is that orders may take long, particularly for deep-dish pizza, but if you call in advance you'll have your pizza waiting for you when you arrive. Open from 11:45 a.m. to 11:30 p.m. Monday through Saturday and noon to 10:30 p.m. on Sunday, this pizzeria is located between New Bond and Regent Streets just south of Oxford Street.

The **Granary,** 39 Albemarle St. (tel. 493-2978), is a cafeteria serving

Gentlemen don't use electric razors at royal barbers Truefitt & Hill

healthy and hearty portions of vegetable and meat dishes. Very popular with local business people, it has a changing menu which may include such dishes as moussaka, curry chicken, lasagne, goulash, beef Stroganoff, seafood pasta, or poached cod in lemon sauce. Main dishes average £4.50, while salads start at around £2.20. There are usually about two dozen dessert selections, with such delectable choices as lemon soufflé, angel cake, Austrian coffee cake, or hazelnut meringue cake. It serves hot food throughout the day from 11 a.m. to 8 p.m. Monday through Friday and 9:30 a.m. to 2:30 p.m. on Saturday.

Milton's, 70 New Bond (tel. 629-2272), is a coffeeshop right on Bond Street which serves breakfast, cold plates, sandwiches, pastries, wine, and daily specials. Sandwiches average about £1.90, and at tea time you can get finger sandwiches, two scones, and a pot of tea for £3.50. With a couple of tables placed outside in warm weather, this place is open from 9 a.m. to 7 p.m. Monday through Friday, to 6 p.m. on Saturday.

Pubs and Pub Lunches

The **Coach & Horses,** 5 Bruton St. (tel. 629-4123), is an interesting, triangular pub only 60 years old which serves a good pub lunch from noon to 2:30 p.m. A staff member told me it was the only building left standing on Bruton Street after World War II. Sandwiches and cold fare are served on the ground floor, but if you want hot food, go up to the first floor. Dishes average £3.50 and the menu usually includes some type of stew, a pie, and a casserole.

The Guinea, 30 Bruton Pl. (tel. 499-1210), is located around the corner from the Coach & Horses. Popular with well-heeled business people who like to drop in for a pint after work, it has both a pub and a restaurant area. If you want a quick lunch, drop in to the pub for a steak pie, chili, or a selection of sandwiches. More formal dining is available in the restaurant section, with such dishes as steaks, lobsters, and seafood, averaging £10 to £15. The pub observes the usual pub hours, but the restaurant is open from 12:30 to 2:30 p.m. Monday through Friday and from 6:30 to 11 p.m. Monday through Saturday. The establishment is closed on Sunday.

Afternoon Tea

The best place to take your afternoon tea is at **Brown's Hotel,** Albemarle Street (tel. 493-6020), which first opened its doors 150 years ago. Tea is served in the lounge area, a relaxing setting with chintz-covered sofas and armchairs and low coffee tables. Wedgwood china and individual little cake stands made especially for Brown's are used to present a tantalizing array of sandwiches, cakes, pastries, scones, and bread. Tea time is from 3 to 6 p.m. and the set price is £8.25 per person. Note that men are required to wear a jacket, collar, and tie.

REGENT STREET AND SAVILE ROW

Because they share space with the many travel agencies, airlines, banks, and other businesses that line this important thoroughfare, shops on Regent Street are not as concentrated as they are along Oxford and Bond Streets. However, there are enough unique and famous stores on Regent Street to rate it as one of London's most celebrated shopping strolls, making it a definite must on any serious shopper's itinerary. With big names like Aquascutum, Laura Ashley, Hamley's, Liberty, and Garrard offering a diverse range of goods, Regent Street presents some delightful surprises to those who like variety in their shopping diet.

As for the history of Regent Street, it was laid out more than 150 years to serve as a grand avenue connecting the Prince Regent's mansion in St. James's to the newly created Regent's Park in the north. However, before the street could be completed the Regent moved from his mansion into Buckingham Palace. Although today none of the original old houses remain, there's still a hint of grandeur in Regent Street's wide lanes and in its gentle curve just before it opens up into Piccadilly Circus. At Christmas, the street is lit up in a festive glow of Christmas lights.

An Area Stroll

Regent Street runs south from Oxford Circus to Piccadilly Circus, with tube stations located at both these ends. Let's begin this stroll at the northern end of Regent Street, where at Oxford Circus we have **Wedgwood,** a famous china shop already introduced in the Oxford Street walking tour. Walking south on Regent Street, the first major shop we come to is **Laura Ashley,** 256–258 Regent St. This is the largest Laura Ashley shop in the world and serves as the designer's flagship store. In addition to Laura Ashley's pretty dresses and pinafores, this shop carries all her home furnishings and fabrics. Although there are more than a dozen other Laura Ashley shops in London, this is the store you'll want to hit if you're a big Laura Ashley fan.

The next store on our agenda is **Dickens & Jones,** the first of two department stores on Regent Street. This five-story establishment has recently changed its image to that of a fashion house, with the goal of providing the largest selection of women's clothes in London. At any rate, there's no denying that it has a great fashion collection with an aim to suit all tastes. It has everything from casual to sports and evening wear, with clothing from Gloria Vanderbilt, Paul Costelloe, Escada, Louis Féraud, Jaeger, Viyella, Windsmoor, Burberrys, and Aquascutum. Its Rose Room on the fourth floor is a good place to stop if you're ready for your afternoon tea.

The next department store is **Liberty,** in my opinion the most beautifully designed department store in London. From its mock-Tudor, half-timbered rear building to its wonderful fabrics and jewelry displays, Liberty is a pure joy in which to shop. In fact, everything in the store is so exquisite and in good taste that I recommend it all! Barring that, if your time is short you may want to take a spin through Liberty's most famous departments, which include its fabrics, jewelry, and Oriental selections. It also has a large Oriental carpet department, designer clothes, antique and modern furniture, and scarves.

After the beauty of Liberty, the gaudiness of Carnaby Street comes as a rude shock. To reach this pedestrian lane, look for the marked side street just past Liberty. The center for all that was new and exciting in the fashion world of the 1960s, Carnaby Street today is crowded with small shops, inexpensive boutiques, and punk clothing stores. You might spot a bargain or two, but this street is recommended mainly as a quick stroll down memory lane.

Back on Regent Street, look for **Jaeger** on the left side at no. 204–206, which usually has very interesting window displays. This British company sells well-tailored clothing for both men and women, at prices here of about half what you'd pay in the United States, according to a public relations spokesman for the store. There are several Jaeger shops throughout London, but this is one of the largest.

Hamleys, 188 Regent, claims to be the largest toy store in the world, boasting six floors of everything from board and electronic games to dolls, toy soldiers, train sets, building blocks, and nursery toys. Many a child has been dragged, screaming and kicking, out of this toy dreamland.

Boots, 182 Regent, is part of a chain of pharmacy shops, with 35 Boots located in the West End alone. This store is one of the largest, selling everything from prescription drugs to cosmetics, perfumes, stationery, housewares, and gardening tools. A great gift here is Boots' own columbine and almond oil face mask, which costs only £2.

At **Berk,** 176 Regent St., you'll find a wide range of cashmere sweaters, while at **Mappin & Webb,** 170 Regent, you can buy everything from a wedding ring beginning at £75 to antique silver serving dishes for several thousand pounds. This plush jewelry and silver store also sells a wide range of watches, and the courteous staff makes shopping here a pleasure.

Next Collection, 160 Regent, is a very trendy store and is one of the most successful of the Next group of chain stores. With a cool, white interior, it caters to the types of shoppers who are lured to Regent Street because of Laura Ashley and Liberty, carrying a more classical range than its other branches. It offers both men's and women's clothes, fabrics, and an espresso bar. **Gered,** 158 Regent, carries mainly Wedgwood china and is a sister establishment to the Wedgwood shop mentioned earlier at Oxford Circus.

Meanwhile, on the opposite side of the street there's **Scottish Woolens** at 193 Regent St., a chain store selling designer knitwear, cashmere, kilts, and suits, with most items made by Scottish designers. Next door is the **Scotch House,** one of a group of stores which sells a more conservative and classical line of woolens, sweaters, tartans, and kilts.

Burberrys, 165 Regent St., is famous the world over for its raincoats. Although its shop at 18–22 Haymarket is larger, this store also carries the full range of Burberrys rainwear for both men and women, as well as knitwear and fashion.

Lawleys, across the street at 154 Regent St., has been at this location for more than 60 years, selling nearly all the popular makes of English china. It now, however, has stiff competition from the nearby **Reject China Shop,** at 134 Regent St., which sells china and crystal at greatly reduced prices. With goods from manufacturers all over the world, its only drawback is that the stock varies according to what's currently available. If you can find your line of china or crystal here, however, the staff tells me you'll recognize savings up to 10% off what you'd pay in other London stores. At 122 Regent St. you'll find **The Little Gallery,** a small gift shop selling souvenirs and British goods, including Caithness paperweights, cork table mats, brass and copper items, model soldiers, and hand-painted pottery cottages by David Winter.

Garrard, 112 Regent St., has the distinction of being the crown jewelers, which means that they are responsible for tending the Crown Jewels. Don't let that scare you off, however. Despite its plush and grand appearance, Garrard is very approachable and its staff is most accommodating. Beautifully designed with a Sicilian marble staircase as the focal point of the store, this shop sells jewelry as well as antique and modern clocks and watches, glass, silver, and porcelain. Up on the first floor is a gift shop, where you can wander among china and dinnerware, desk sets and accessories, and many other items. Prices are high, but so is the quality.

Aquascutum, 100 Regent St., is another big name in rainwear. It presents a classical and fashionable selection of men's and women's raincoats, men's knitwear and jackets, and ladies' separates. On the opposite side of the street you'll find **Airey & Wheeler** at 129 Piccadilly, which specializes in tropical clothing, safari suits, and lightweight casual clothes for men. **Pencraft,** 119 Regent St., is where you can stop to pick up a fountain pen from £6.50 or a brand-name ballpoint pen.

If you want to visit the tailors on Savile Row, turn right on Vigo Street and walk one block. The first tailor's shop you'll see is **Gieves & Hawkes,** at 1 Savile Row. This prestigious-looking shop with its chandeliers, atrium, and ceiling fans carries a large, off-the-peg selection of men's suits in addition to its made-to-measure ones.

Both **Kilgour, French & Stansbury** and **Bernard Weatherill** are located at 8 Savile Row. Catering to men and women, they work together to provide made-to-measure suits, sports jackets, and hunting and riding wear. Other men's tailor shops include **Helman** at no. 10, **Huntsman** at no. 11, **Henry Poole** at no. 15, **Tommy Nutter** at no. 19, and **Anderson & Sheppard** at no. 30. More information on each of these shops is given in the tailor section in Part Two.

Before leaving Savile Row, you may want to visit two other shops. **Hardy Amies,** 14 Savile Row, is unique in that it's a women's couturier in this bastion of men's tailor shops. Established in the 1940s, it has a royal warrant as dressmakers to the Queen. In addition to the wedding dresses, suits, and dresses it will make especially for you, Hardy Amies also has a selection of off-the-peg dresses to choose from.

At 11 Savile Row is **Henry Maxwell & Co.,** which makes handmade-to-measure shoes and boots for both men and women. Established in 1750 as a spur maker for riding boots, this shop claims it can make about anything and also sells some ready-to-wear shoes, leather bags, and attaché cases.

Returning to Regent Street, don't miss **Austin Reed** at 103 Regent St. A famous men's clothing store with well-tailored suits and casual wear, this store also sells women's clothes. And finally, at 56–58 Regent St. is **Dunn & Co.,** a men's store which specializes in traditional suits, Harris Tweed jackets, and hats ranging from tweed caps to bowler hats.

Sightseeing Suggestions

The **Museum of Mankind,** described in the Bond Street stroll, is easily reached from Regent Street via Vigo Street. In addition, the **Trocadero Centre,** listed under sightseeing suggestions for the Piccadilly walking tour, has both **The London Experience,** a slide-show presentation on London and its history, and the **Guinness World of Records,** a museum with visual displays of world records.

If you like open-air markets, the **Berwick Street Market** is held Monday through Saturday from approximately 9:30 or 10 a.m. to 6 p.m. Strung along Berwick and Rupert Streets south of Broadwick Street, this city market has fruit and vegetable stalls as well as vendors selling clothing, jewelry, handbags, and everyday items.

Luncheon Spots and Drinking Establishments

The **Chicago Pizza Pie Factory,** 17 Hanover Square (tel. 629-2669), is an American-style pizza parlor, specializing in deep-dish pizzas. Refer to the restaurant suggestions under the Bond Street stroll for more information on this establishment located halfway between Regent and New Bond Streets.

The most famous place on Regent Street to stop for a coffee, a drink, or a meal is **Café Royal,** 68 Regent St. (tel. 437-9090). Located at the southern end of Regent Street not far from Piccadilly Circus, Café Royal first opened in 1865 and for a long time served as the literary haunt of such distinguished writers as D. H. Lawrence, Oscar Wilde, Virginia Woolf, and Bernard Shaw. The Grill Room, open from noon to 3 p.m. and from 6 to 11 p.m., is one of the most ornate dining rooms in all of London, decorated with gilt mirrors, carved caryatids, murals, and stucco ceilings. À la carte offerings include seafood, veal, duck, chicken, and rack of lamb, with most entrees starting at about £10. The plat du jour is usually around £20. The Brasserie serves lighter meals, while Daniel's Wine Bar offers snacks like quiche and steak-and kidney pie.

Not far away from Café Royal is **The Veeraswamy,** 99–101 Regent St. (tel. 734-1401), which opened in 1927 and rates as London's oldest Indian restaurant. Open for lunch from noon to 2:30 p.m. and for dinner from 6 to 11:30 p.m., it offers a lunch buffet for £10.50 which features meat, fish, chicken, and vegetable dishes, a selection of Indian breads, salad, a choice of desserts, and coffee. The à la carte menu is extensive and includes such specialities as Goan chicken, spicy lentil soup, tandoori dishes, and mutton biryani.

For more dining on Regent Street, try the **Rose Room,** located on the fourth floor of Dickens & Jones, a cafeteria with a changing lunch menu served from 11:30 a.m. to 2:15 p.m. and teas from 3 to 5 p.m. For £2 you can have tea and scones. **Liberty Restaurant,** located on the fourth floor of Liberty department store, is the place to come if you want breakfast, which is served from 9:30 a.m. to noon and costs £5 for eggs, bacon, sausage, toast, juice, and coffee. Lunch, served from noon to 2:30 p.m., offers entrees from £5 for such items as vegetarian hotpot, trout, or roast beef. And if you come for tea, offered from 2:30 to 5:30 p.m., you have choices ranging from £2.90 for tea and two scones to £5.40 for grilled plaice, side salad, sautéed potatoes, bread, and tea.

Cranks Health Food Restaurant, 8 Marshall St. (tel. 437-9431), is London's pioneer vegetarian restaurant, first opening on Carnaby Street in 1961 and moving to Marshall Street in 1967. It has proved so successful that it has opened branches in Covent Garden and other locations. Very popular and crowded at lunchtime, this cafeteria-style restaurant serves salads, sandwiches, pasta, and vegetable dishes. A meal here can cost anywhere from £1 to £5, depending on how many dishes tempt you. Hours are 10 a.m. to 7 p.m. Monday through Saturday.

Oldfields, 70 Brewer St. (tel. 439-6666), offers what it calls "bespoke sandwiches." Located two blocks west of the Garrard jewelry store, this small shop offers more than 20 varieties of sandwiches, with fillings ranging from bacon and avocado to chopped liver, roast beef, or tuna. Prices range from 80 pence to £2.30 and hours are 7 a.m. to 4 p.m. Monday through Friday and 9 a.m. to 3 p.m. on Saturday. The only drawback here is that there isn't much seating, so you may want to avoid this place at peak hours if you prefer to sit down.

Pubs and Pub Lunches

The **Argyll Arms,** located at 18 Argyll St. (tel. 734-6117), is located just southeast of Oxford Circus and was described earlier in the Oxford stroll. This Victorian pub serves a good selection of hot and cold dishes for both lunch and dinner.

The **Leicester Arms,** 44 Glasshouse St. (tel. 734-7641), is located just off Regent Street behind the Garrard jewelry store. It offers hot food throughout the day from 11 a.m. to 11 p.m. every day of the week. The menu changes daily but may include such savories as chili con carne, shepherd's pie, and steak-and-kidney pie, all of which cost about £3.20 and come with two vegetables.

PICCADILLY AND JERMYN STREET

If I were forced to choose what I consider to be London's most interesting shopping area, Piccadilly would be a top contender. Along with neighboring Jermyn and St. James's Streets, Piccadilly has some of the oldest specialty shops in all of London, some of which have changed little in the past 200 years. With its quaint cigar shops, wine merchants, hatters, shoemakers, shirtmakers, cheesemongers, and outfitters of umbrellas and walking sticks, this is the area

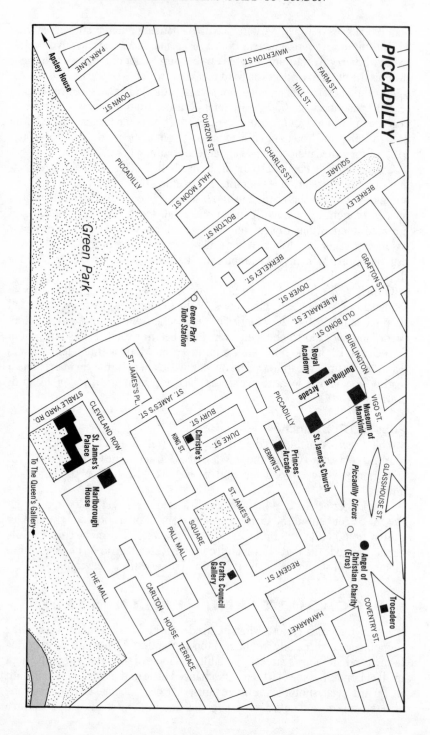

that best fits fantasies of Olde London. It's here that you can stop by an old chemist shop for a glass of the Original Pick-Me-Up, made from a 130-year-old formula. You can have your feet measured for your own wooden last, or purchase a bit of English cheese, a briar pipe, perfume, or a hamper of gourmet food. There are so many specialty shops crowded into this small area that you could easily spend a whole day here.

An Area Stroll

The first destination of this stroll is **Piccadilly Circus,** which has its own tube station of the same name. As the nucleus for the converging streets of Piccadilly, Regent Street, Shaftesbury Avenue, Haymarket, and Lower Regent Street, Piccadilly Circus literally glows at night with flashing billboards and neon signs. With the nearby theaters, the restaurants of Soho, and other entertainment establishments, Piccadilly Circus is crowded with people and traffic both day and night. And in the middle watching over it all is the Angel of Christian Charity, which with its bow and arrow is often mistaken for Eros.

On Piccadilly Circus are two large stores, Lillywhites and Tower Records. Opened in 1863 by a former cricket player, **Lillywhites** has one of the largest selections of sporting goods and sportswear in town and is especially strong in its ski and tennis departments. **Tower Records** is a newcomer to Oxford Circus, opening in 1986 and offering four floors of records, cassettes, compact discs, videos, and related music magazines.

Walking west on Piccadilly on the left side of the road, the first big store we come to is **Simpson,** a men's and women's fashion house with a large selection of Daks clothing. Farther down is St. James's Church, built in 1680 by Christopher Wren. On Friday and Saturday from 10 a.m. to 6 p.m. the **Piccadilly Market** is held in the church's forecourt with stalls set up selling arts and crafts, antiques, and bric-a-brac. In the basement of one of the church buildings is the **London Brass Rubbing Centre,** where you can make rubbings of your own for under £1.

The **Princes Arcade,** 192 Piccadilly, runs from Piccadilly to Jermyn Street and contains more than 15 shops, including those selling bespoke (custom-made) shirts, antiques, rare books, and chocolates. Particularly beautiful is Coleridge, which sells contemporary glass creations such as bowls, vases, paperweights, and scent bottles.

Charming bow windows display the latest arrivals at **Hatchards,** 187 Piccadilly, one of London's best-known bookshops. First opened around 1800 and serving as the royal booksellers to the Queen, Hatchards specializes in the newest bestsellers, paperbacks, children's books, and books covering art, gardening, cooking, wine, ornithology, and travel. **Swaine, Adeney, Brigg & Sons** is another venerable name on Piccadilly, established in 1750 and carrying a delightful selection of Brigg umbrellas, antique walking sticks, and riding gear. Catering to the country gentleman, this is a good place to shop for gifts for the man or men in your life. **Fortnum & Mason,** 181 Piccadilly, has what I consider to be one of the most beautiful food halls in the world. What a pity not all

Princes Arcade

grocery stores look like this. First opening its doors in 1707, Fortnum & Mason offers exquisite food hampers, cheeses, chocolates, teas, biscuits, preserves, wines, and ingredients for gourmet meals. Other departments include fashion, accessories, antique furniture, china, and clocks and watches.

Incidentally, on the right side of the street is an entrance to the **Burlington Arcade** with its shops selling cashmere sweaters, men's and women's fashions, antiques, tobacco, pens, and toys. If you didn't visit this arcade already in the Bond Street stroll, you might want to do so now. Not far away is the Royal Academy of Arts with its changing art exhibitions.

If you continue walking west on Piccadilly, you'll come to St. James's Street, where you should turn left. Once the hub of gentlemen's clubs and shops serving wealthy aristocrats, St. James's today has fallen victim to the 20th century— with the exception of five, delightful stores, four of which are more than 200 years old.

The first of these is **D. R. Harris & Co.**, 29 St. James's St., a family-owned chemist shop and probably the oldest chemist shop in London. With its antique colored bottles in cabinets built in 1845, it looks much the way it always has, with products to match. Selling primarily its own creations, it offers toilet waters, soaps, and body lotions, all made with natural ingredients long before other companies thought of it. For the more adventuresome there are also some fun and unique products, including crystal eye drops, developed 50 years ago and guaranteed to make your eyes sparkle, and the Original Pick-Me-Up, made from a 130-year-old formula and good for everything from hangovers to lack of energy. You can have a glass of this whipped up and administered on the spot for £1.

Robert Lewis, 19 St. James's St., is where Winston Churchill used to buy his cigars. Founded in 1787, Robert Lewis specializes in Havana cigars, which unfortunately you cannot bring back into the United States. Other products include pipe tobacco, Turkish cigarettes, humidors, and snuff.

Lobb, 9 St. James's St., serves as the royal bootmakers to the Queen, her husband, and the Prince of Wales. With an open workshop where you can watch craftsmen making lasts, boots, and shoes, this shop smells wonderfully of leather and sells women's and men's shoes beginning at £686 a pair.

Credited with introducing the bowler hat, **Lock & Co.,** 6 St. James's St., was founded more than 300 years ago. As you look at the window display of old top hats, a police helmet, a bishop's mitre, and a Duke of Wellington hat, think of all the people who must have looked longingly through these very same windows the past three centuries. Suppliers of hunt caps, homburgs, a variety of felt hats, panama hats, and many more, Lock will also make you a cap or tweed hat to match your suit if you bring in the material.

Berry Bros. & Rudd Ltd., 3 St. James's St., has one of the most charming storefronts in all of London, built in 1734. Notice the sign of the coffee mill outside, the origins of which can be traced to the store's beginnings when it first opened as a grocery in 1699. A family business from the start, Berry Bros. & Rudd became strictly wine merchants in 1890. However, you won't find any wine bottles on display. These are kept in the cool wine cellars that extend under St. James's Street. Berry Bros. & Rudd is also famous for its own scotch whisky, Cutty Sark.

Retrace your steps now to Jermyn Street, which parallels Piccadilly and has a number of good stores, including the majority of London's bespoke (custom-made) shirt shops. On the right (south) side of this street, shops are numbered from 65 to 130, while on the left side they go from 64 to 1.

If you're looking for a ready-made or bespoke shirt, you have a number of shops to choose from. **Turnbull & Asser,** 71–72 Jermyn St., is among the best-known shirt suppliers in London, first opening its doors more than 100 years ago. In addition to its bespoke and ready-made shirts, it also sells ties, silk robes, and cashmere sweaters for men. Next door is **Hilditch & Key,** 73 Jermyn St., which also has two other locations on the same street at nos. 37 and 87. Its prices are slightly lower than at Turnbull & Asser, and at no. 37 it sells ready-to-wear shirts for women as well. Other shirtmakers on Jermyn are **Hawes & Curtis** at no. 23, which belongs to Turnbull & Asser; **Harvie & Hudson,** at 77 and 96–97 Jermyn St.; and **New & Lingwood,** 53 Jermyn St., which also makes made-to-measure shoes.

As for the others shops on Jermyn Street, starting at the west end of Jermyn Street where it connects with St. James's Street and heading east toward Haymarket, the first shop you'll come to is **Trickers,** 67 Jermyn St. This store has been handmaking shoes and riding boots since 1829 and has a small selection of ready-made shoes as well. **Taylor of Old Bond St.,** 74 Jermyn St., is a men's and women's hairdressing salon that was founded by the present owner's great-grandfather. The shop also sells a number of hair and skin products and shaving equipment.

If you like antique medical, scientific, and marine instruments, you'll love **Trevor Philip,** 75A Jermyn St. With such unique objects as 18th-century German microscopes, early sundials, compasses, protractors, sextants, and much more, this shop is perfect if you're looking for a gift for the person who has everything, since it's doubtful he or she will already possess the items displayed here. **Dunhill,** located on the corner of Jermyn and Duke Streets, is another good shop for gifts for men, selling everything from its famous tobacco, pipes, and cigars to luggage, wallets, fragrances, and men's wear.

Grima, 80 Jermyn St., is a contemporary jewelry store with a setting to match. The majority of pieces here are one of a kind, based on the philosophy that the shape of the stone should dictate each piece. Antique tapestries and carpets are displayed in the showrooms of **S. Franses,** 82 Jermyn St., and **Mayorcas,** 38 Jermyn St., while **Foster & Son,** 83 Jermyn St., has both made-to-measure and ready-to-wear shoes.

Herbs and spices, soaps and bath oils, tea, coffee, and dried flowers are just some of the items you can pick up at **James Bodenham & Co.,** 88 Jermyn St. Next door is **Floris,** a perfumer's shop since 1730. In addition to its scents, Floris sells a lovely assortment of scent and perfume bottles, porcelain pill boxes, manicure sets, and other gift items.

From its sawdust-covered floor to the huge hams hanging in its front window, **Paxton & Whitfield,** 93 Jermyn St., is a cheesemonger's shop that still conveys the same Old World ambience that it must have had when it first opened in 1797. It sells approximately 300 different kinds of cheese. **Robin Symes,** 94 Jermyn St., deals in antiquities, including Greek, Roman, and Egyptian artifacts.

Briar pipes are the specialty of **Astleys,** at 109A Jermyn St., while hats and nothing but hats are to found at **Bates,** 21A Jermyn St. Be sure to take a look at Binks, a stuffed cat nestled in among piles of hats—it "strolled in as a kitten June 1921 and passed out Nov. 1st, 1926." **Geo F. Trumper,** 20 Jermyn St., is a men's perfumer and serves as the gift shop of the famous Trumper hairdresser's shop on Curzon Street. This location has one of the largest selections of shaving sets and shaving brushes in town.

Sightseeing Suggestions

St. James's Church, located right on Piccadilly, was built by Christopher Wren in 1680 following the Great Fire which destroyed much of London. Both William Pitt and William Blake were baptized here. A small market is held here every Friday and Saturday, while the London Brass Rubbing Centre is located in the basement. Across the street is the **Royal Academy of Arts** (tel. 734-9052), with changing exhibitions of avant-garde art from around the world. Previous showings have included British art in the 20th century and the sketchbooks of Picasso. Hours are 10 a.m. to 6 p.m. daily.

Stretching south from the Green Park tube station is **Green Park,** with its wide expanses of grass and chairs you can rent. If you're feeling energetic, you can walk through Green Park to get a glimpse of **Buckingham Palace** and the changing of the guard, which takes place at 11:30 a.m. daily from May through July and on alternating days in the winter. The **Queen's Gallery** on Buckingham Palace Road displays famous artists' work and is open Tuesday to Saturday from 11 a.m. to 5 p.m. and on Sunday from 2 to 5 p.m.

Also a bit far to walk to, but worth the effort if you're interested in houses and furniture of the Regency period, is the **Apsley House,** 149 Piccadilly (tel. 499-5676). Built in the 1770s and acquired by the Duke of Wellington in 1817, it contains relics, fine paintings, silver, porcelain, and the personal effects of the duke. The closest tube station is Hyde Park Corner, and hours here are 10 a.m. to 5:30 p.m. except on Sunday when it's open from 2:30 to 6 p.m. Note that the Apsley House is closed on Monday and Friday.

The **Trocadero** is a large indoor shopping center located just to the east of Piccadilly Circus. Up on the first floor is *The London Experience* (tel. 439-4938), a slide-show presentation of London and its history, including the Great Fire, plagues, and Victorian England. The show lasts 35 minutes and presentations are given approximately every 40 minutes between 10:20 a.m. and 10:20 p.m. The cost is £2.50 for adults and £1.90 for children.

Also on the first floor of the Trocadero is the **Guinness World of Records** (tel. 439-7331), where you can learn about world records in everything from the tallest to the heaviest humans. It's open from 10 a.m. to 10 p.m. daily and charges an admission of £3 for adults and £1.80 for children.

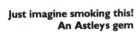

Just imagine smoking this! An Astleys gem

Luncheon Spots and Drinking Establishments

In addition to the restaurants listed here, both **The Granary,** 39 Albemarle St., in the Bond Street stroll, and **Café Royal** in the Regent Street walking tour are conveniently located near Piccadilly.

Bentley's, 11–15 Swallow St. (tel. 734-4756), has one of the oldest oyster bars in London. With its marble-topped bar, wooden booths, and soft lighting, this is a fun place to experience London's famous oysters as well as other seafood dishes. Oyster dishes start at £9.80, with other entrees ranging from scampi and lobster to scallops and plaice. There's a wine bar in the basement and a more formal dining room on the first floor. Hours of the oyster bar are noon to 3:30 p.m. and 6 to 10:30 p.m.

Overton's, 5 St. James's St. (tel. 839-3774), is a small and cozy seafood restaurant that serves oysters and various fish dishes in addition to steaks. Most entrees range from £11 to £20, and hours here are noon to 2:30 p.m. and 6 to 11 p.m. every day except Sunday.

Located on the second floor of Le Meridien Hotel is the **Terrace Garden Restaurant,** Piccadilly (tel. 734-8000). Very bright and cheerful with greenhouse-like windows, lots of plants, and an obliging staff, it's open daily from 7 a.m. to midnight. A changing meal of the day is offered for £13.75, while meals ordered à la carte average £9 per person. Entrees here include sandwiches, salads, seafood, steaks, chicken, veal, and duck. From 3 to 5:30 p.m. you can have afternoon tea for £7.40 which includes a quartet of finger sandwiches, French pastries, scones, and your choice of tea.

Although it's a ten-minute walk farther west from the Green Park tube station, the **Hard Rock Café,** 150 Old Park Lane (tel. 629-0382), is worth the extra effort if you're a diehard rock fan. Located on the corner of Piccadilly and Old Park Lane, this café was established in 1971 and was the first of the Hard Rock Cafés that subsequently opened around the world in cities like New York, Stockholm and Tokyo. The place is so popular that unless you come in midafternoon, you're likely to find yourself waiting in line to get in. More than 150 items from rock 'n' roll history adorn the walls, and there are even brochures on the tables to help you identify all the memorabilia. The café still has some of the best hamburgers around, with prices starting at £3.80. To commemorate your visit, you can buy a Hard Rock Café T-shirt from a booth just outside the front door for £5.80. Hours are noon to midnight daily, but remember that alcohol can't be served between 3 and 5:30 p.m.

Fortnum & Mason, 181 Piccadilly (tel. 734-8040), has several restaurants to choose from. The **Fountain Restaurant** has its own entrance on Jermyn Street and is open in the evening as well, with hours from 9:30 a.m. to midnight Monday through Saturday. Although service is slow, the waitresses are amiable. Besides, this is the restaurant where probably every London native has eaten at least once. The menu includes soups, sandwiches, Welsh rarebit, steak-and-kidney pie, smoked trout, omelets, and desserts, with most items less than £4.

Serving the same menu as the Fountain is the **Patio Bar,** this one located on the mezzanine above the food hall. Both restaurants serve tea from 2:30 to 5 p.m., when you can have two scones and a pot of tea for £3.25. On the fourth floor is the **St. James's Restaurant,** a formal affair that resembles an English drawing room. Dishes here range between £5.50 and £8 for such things as sole, chicken, steak-and-kidney pie, roast duck, or roast beef. Tea is taken here to the relaxing music of a piano, with finger sandwiches, scones, cake, and tea served for £5.40 from 3 to 5 p.m.

In the basement of Simpson, 203 Piccadilly (tel. 734-2002), is **Simpson Restaurant,** which serves everything from sandwiches and salad to steaks, fish, chicken, and roast beef. You can also take tea here: a pot of tea costs £1.20 and scones are £2 extra.

Pubs and Pub Lunches

The Red Lion, 2 Duke of York St. (tel. 930-2030), is located just off Jermyn Street. This Victorian-style pub with its engraved glass, decorative mirrors, and polished mahogany serves mainly sandwiches, with fish and chips offered on Friday only.

Cockney Pride, 6 Jermyn St. (tel. 930-5339), is an upstart compared to the older pubs in London. With bands that often perform in the evenings, it has a large selection of hot dishes ranging from quiche and salad to fish and chips, pork pie, and lasagne. Most items are priced at £3.

Afternoon Tea

In addition to the **Terrace Garden Restaurant,** the restaurants in **Fortnum & Mason** and in **Simpson,** you can also take tea in one of the ritziest places around, the **Palm Court** in the Ritz hotel, Piccadilly (tel. 493-8181). Served in an elaborate dining area representing the zenith of Edwardian style, it offers a selection of finger sandwiches, scones, pastries, and tea for £9.30. On Sunday you can even indulge in another English tradition, the afternoon tea dance, which costs slightly more at £15.90. Tea time at the Ritz is from 3:30 to 5:30 p.m. daily.

TOTTENHAM COURT ROAD, CHARING CROSS, AND SOHO

The only thing Tottenham Court Road, Charing Cross Road, and Soho have in common is their proximity to one another. Located just east of the swanky West End, each of these three areas has its own types of shops and its own character.

AN AREA STROLL

Tottenham Court Road is known for its furniture and electronic stores, while Charing Cross Road, with its secondhand, antiquarian, and contemporary bookstores, serves as a mecca for London's bookworms. Soho, on the other hand, is in a class all its own, with a jumble of sex shops, cafés and pâtisseries, restaurants, and nightclubs living riotously side by side. It's only for the purpose of convenience, therefore, that I've lumped three such diverse areas into one walking tour. Obviously, you may want to tailor the stroll to your own individual tastes, omitting, for example, Tottenham Court Road if you're uninterested in furniture or electronic shops.

The Tottenham Court Road Area

In existence since the 12th century, Tottenham Court Road is known today for its high-class furniture stores and for stores selling radios, videos, and electrical equipment. Along its length are three underground stations—the Tottenham Court Road, Goodge Street, and Warren Street stations. To the east of Tottenham Court Road is the British Museum, with a number of interesting shops in the area.

If you're interested in furniture, begin this stroll at Warren Street tube station, where you'll see **Maples,** 145 Tottenham Court Rd., located just across the street. A large store with everything you need to furnish your home, it has modern furniture imported primarily from Italy and Spain with an emphasis on design that would appeal to the average English home.

Walking a few blocks farther south to the vicinity of Goodge Street station, you come upon two furniture stores located side by side and owned by the same company. **Habitat,** 196 Tottenham Court Rd., is the brainstorm of Terence Conran, who revolutionized the British concept of furniture with the introduction of utilitarian, modern-design furniture. Offering a range of furnishings, kitchenware, and housewares that reflect the 1980s, this store appeals greatly to the British yuppie seeking to upgrade his living environment without going broke. Designs are fun, sleek, and always in good taste.

Next door is **Heal's,** recently acquired by the Conran group of stores. Its furniture is slightly more expensive than Habitat's, and there are also various departments selling linen, bathroom accessories, toys, carpets, lamps, china, silverware, and cooking supplies. Both Habitat and Heal's have their own café serving drinks, snacks, and meals.

While you're in the vicinity, it's well worth taking a right turn down Goodge Street and looking for **Pollock's Toy Museum,** on the corner of Whitfield and Scala. This wonderful museum is actually two little houses joined together, with rooms that are small and connected by narrow winding staircases. On display are dolls, toys, and the museum's specialty—cardboard cutout theaters. On the ground floor of the museum is a toy shop, with old-fashioned toys you don't see much anymore, including cut-out theaters, inexpensive pocket toys, cut-out dolls, limited-edition teddy bears, tin toys for collectors, and antique toys.

Between the Goodge Street and Tottenham Court Road stations are a number of electronic and video stores. One of the largest is **Laskys,** 42 Tottenham Court Rd., with a selection of stereos, compact disc players, televisions, computers, and other equipment. Remember that videos sold in the U.K. don't work on American VCRs without an expensive adapter.

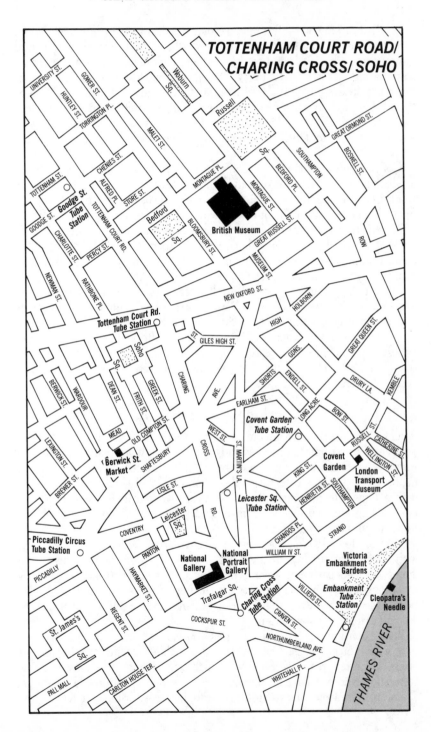

At the bottom end of Tottenham Court Road, turn left onto New Oxford Street. **Cuba,** 56 New Oxford St., is a secondhand clothing store with period fashions from the 1950s and before. If you're looking for men's white cotton shirts dating back to the '20s, ties with designs of stags leaping over meadows, or '50s party dresses, this is the store for you. Across the street is **James Smith & Sons,** 53 New Oxford St., which has been selling umbrellas and walking sticks for more than 150 years. This is a good place to pick up walking sticks or umbrellas that unfold into a seat or one of the handmade umbrellas which start at about £45.

Continue walking down New Oxford Street until you get to Museum Street, at which point you should take a left. There are several interesting shops on this short street, among them **S. J. Shrubsole,** which deals in antique silver and old Sheffield plate, and **The Print Room,** with antique prints dating from 1590 to 1870 depicting old scenes of London, natural history, and caricatures. **Craddock & Barnard** is another gallery, this one specializing in 15th- to 20th-century original etchings and engravings. On occasion they've had works of two of my favorite artists, Albrecht Dürer and Käthe Kollwitz.

Museum Street ends at Great Russell Street, home of not only the British Museum but also two **Westaway & Westaway** shops, both offering great savings in Scottish sweaters and woolens. At 65 Great Russell Street directly across from the museum is where you'll find more traditional cuts of cashmere, lambswool, and Shetland sweaters, some of them starting as low as £15. Down the street at 92-93 Great Russell St., Westaway & Westaway branches out into designer-style sweaters of bright, unique designs.

Charing Cross and Soho

After visiting the British Museum, backtrack to the intersection of New Oxford Street and Tottenham Court Road and then head south on Charing Cross Road where you'll find the largest concentration of bookstores in London. The first major store is **Collet's International Bookshop,** 129–131 Charing Cross Rd., with a large selection of books on Russia or written in Russian, books on left-wing politics and sociology, travel guides, feminist literature, art publications, and international fiction.

Foyles, 113–119 Charing Cross Rd., is the largest bookstore on the street, with strong departments in the fields of technology, medicine, music, and drama. Other departments cover everything in the alphabet from anthropology to zoology, and there's also a catalog with listings of antiquarian and rare books. Be forewarned, however, that Foyles is so large and rambling that it may be difficult to locate what you want.

Before continuing on down Charing Cross Road, you might want to take a right when you get to Old Compton Road, which leads right into the heart of Soho. Just a few years ago Soho was much seamier than it is now, but new coffeeshops and bars have been nudging out the more questionable sex shops. There are quite a few places to stop off here for lunch or a drink, which I've listed at the end of this walking tour. There are also a couple of shopping possibilities here. At 3 Greek St. is the **Soho Wine Market,** well known for its 150 types of malt whiskies, including rare ones 25 years old. A block farther west at 10 Frith St. is the **Fabric Studio,** with an excellent stock of discounted fabrics that come straight from the ends of designer collections. The husband-and-wife team that owns this shop tells me their fabrics run about one-third of the original price, but because the stock changes constantly it's best to drop in "with an open mind." In other words, if you're looking specifically for pink polka dots, you probably won't find it, but you're sure to run across a lot of other fabrics that will catch your fancy.

If you're in the mood for a market, the **Berwick Street Market** is located at the end of Old Compton Street and is open from about 9:30 a.m. to 6 p.m. Monday through Saturday. Stop here for fruit and vegetables, handbags, clothing, and everyday items.

Returning to Charing Cross Road and crossing Shaftesbury Avenue, the first shop to look for is **Zwemmer,** 80 Charing Cross Rd., with books on film and photography, graphic design, fashion, and illustration. Not far away is the **Zwemmer Art Bookshop,** 24 Litchfield St., with books on fine art, sculpture, and arts and crafts.

Snuff is the specialty of **G. Smith & Sons,** 74 Charing Cross Rd., which makes its own and offers 50 different kinds. If you're looking for secondhand books, you might find what you want at **Any Amount of Books,** 62 Charing Cross Rd., **Henry Pordes Books,** at 58–60 Charing Cross Rd., or **Reads,** at 48A Charing Cross Rd.

Cecil Court

After walking a few more short blocks on Charing Cross Road, you'll find Cecil Court leading off to the left. A narrow and short pedestrian lane, it's unique in London in that it has a dozen or so small shops clustered together dealing in rare books and prints. Most of the shops are tiny, personable affairs, making a browse here a delightful experience.

H. M. Fletcher specializes in books written in Latin and Greek, most of them printed before 1500. First editions of late-19th- and 20th-century literature is what you'll find at **Bell, Book & Radmall,** while **Reg and Philip Remington** has a good selection of antiquarian and secondhand books of travel and voyages. Children's and illustrated books dating from the 18th century have literally taken over the tiny shop of Peter Stockham at **Images.** If there's a book you remember from childhood that you wish you still had, you may be able to find it here.

David Drummond's **Pleasures of Past Times** specializes in original posters, playbills, and books dealing with the performing arts, including the circus, musicals, and the theater. This store also had a great selection of Victorian valentines when I was last there, which would make a great surprise for your special someone. They start at £22 apiece.

The **Witch Ball** sells antique engravings of theatrical interest, covering the areas of music, opera, dance, and the theater. **Clive A. Burden** has a wide range of antique maps and prints, including prints of natural history, caricatures from *Vanity Fair,* and architectural prints. You can pick up a small botanical print here for as little as £4.

SIGHTSEEING SUGGESTIONS

The **British Museum,** Great Russell Street (tel. 636-1555), ranks as one of the great museums of the world. Showing the works of man from all over the world from prehistoric times to the present, it has so many departments that it's necessary to choose in advance those you're most interested in. Included in the museum are Egyptian mummies, the Elgin Marbles from the Parthenon, the Rosetta Stone, displays from Roman Britain, medieval artifacts, ancient Greek and Roman art, and the Magna Carta. Admission is free, and hours are Monday to Saturday from 10 a.m. to 5 p.m. and on Sunday from 2:30 to 6 p.m.

Pollock's Toy Museum, 1 Scala St. (tel. 636-3452), is a delightful museum with dolls, cut-out theaters, and toys from yesteryear. The toy shop here is also excellent, with toys for kids and for collectors, including teddy bears, dolls and puppets, cardboard cut-out theaters, and tin toys. It's open from 10 a.m. to 5 p.m. Monday through Saturday.

The **National Gallery** (tel. 839-3321) is located south of Charing Cross Road on Trafalgar Square. Open from 10 a.m. to 6 p.m. Monday through Saturday and from 2 to 6 p.m. on Sunday, it has approximately 2,000 paintings by European artists dating from the 13th to the early 20th centuries. With works from all the major schools of European painting, the museum houses works by Botticelli, Hieronymous Bosch, Bruegel, Dürer, Leonardo da Vinci, Michelangelo, Rembrandt, Rubens, El Greco, Goya, Hogarth, Turner, Monet, Degas, Cézanne, and Renoir, to name only a few. Admission is free.

The **National Portrait Gallery,** 2 St. Martin's Pl. (tel. 930-1552), is a fun museum where you can see what all those famous British people looked like that you learned about in history class. Founded in 1856 with the aim of collecting the likenesses of famous British men and women, the museum pictures such personages as the Brontë sisters, Samuel Johnson, T. S. Eliot, James Boswell, Oliver Cromwell, John Stuart Mill, Charles Dickens, Lawrence of Arabia, Princess Di, and Prince Charles. Exhibitions of varying themes are held regularly at the museum. Hours are 10 a.m. to 5 p.m. Monday to Friday, to 6 p.m. on Saturday, and 2 to 6 p.m. on Sunday.

LUNCHEON SPOTS AND DRINKING ESTABLISHMENTS

To help in your selection of a place to eat or drink, I've divided the following establishments according to area. Most locales are in Soho, which also has the greatest number of nightspots.

Around the Tottenham Court Road Area

The **Valiant Trooper** (tel. 636-0721) is located on the corner of Goodge and Whitfield Streets, just around the corner from Pollock's Toy Museum. Observing the usual pub hours (11 a.m. to 3 p.m. and 5:30 to 11 p.m. Monday to Saturday and noon to 2 p.m. and 7 to 10:30 p.m. on Sunday), this pub is a popular lunchtime retreat for people working in the area. It serves a selection of pies, snacks, salads, and sandwiches.

Oodles, 42 New Oxford St. (tel. 637-4052), is convenient if you're on your way to the British Museum. Open from 11 a.m. to 9 p.m. Monday through Saturday and from 11 a.m. to 7 p.m. on Sunday, it serves what it calls "country food," including beef burgundy, chicken casserole, lasagne, moussaka, quiche, flan, pies, and vegetarian dishes. Prices range from about £1.50 to £3.50 for most dishes, and you help yourself from the cafeteria-style bar. There's seating outside in warm weather.

There are two pubs in the vicinity of the British Museum where you can grab a pint or a bite to eat. **Museum Tavern,** 49 Great Russell St. (tel. 242-8987), claims to have had Karl Marx as a customer, no doubt after he had spent a few dry hours working on *Das Kapital* in the British Museum's library. It serves the regular pub fare for lunch, including steak-and-kidney pie, a ploughman's lunch of bread and cheeses, salads, and quiche. Not far away is **The Plough,** 27 Museum St. (tel. 636-7964), which has a more modern interior and serves hot bar lunches such as casseroles, pies, sandwiches, and rolls. From noon to 2:30 you can also eat upstairs, with a changing menu that might include liver, steak, lamb cutlets, or sole, and prices starting at about £3.80.

Charing Cross and Soho

Godfather's Warehouse, 146 Charing Cross Rd. (tel. 240-2261), is located at the north end of the street. Decorated with '20s decor and gangster memorabilia, it has pizzas ranging from £2.20 to £3.50. There's also a set pasta menu for £2.70 in which you choose your own pasta and sauce combination. Hours are noon to 3 a.m. Monday through Thursday, closing at 4 a.m. on Friday and Saturday and at midnight on Sunday.

Cranks, 17–18 Great Newport St. (tel. 836-5226), is a sister health-food restaurant to the one described in the Regent Street stroll. It has the same healthy menu, including salads, quiche, hot vegetarian dishes, and desserts. Hours here are 8 a.m. to 7:30 p.m. Monday to Friday and 10 a.m. to 7:30 p.m. on Saturday.

There are lots of places to eat in Soho, many of which are located on Old Compton Street. **Soho Brasserie,** 23–25 Old Compton St. (tel. 439-3758), looks like a Parisian coffeehouse and serves French food. A fashionable watering hole for all the trendy people in Soho, it's open throughout the day from 10 a.m. to midnight, but meals are served only from noon to 3 p.m. and 6 to 11:30 p.m. It's closed Sunday. Included on the menu is fresh fish bought daily from the market, as well as such creative dishes as grilled calves' liver with sage and lemon, terrine of veal and bacon garnished with black and green olives, and saddle of wild rabbit with courgettes and marjoram. Most items range from about £3.80 to £7.

Patisserie Valeria, 44 Old Compton St. (tel. 437-3466), is a small, simple, and very popular coffeeshop, with color provided by the motherly women who preside over the place. There's no menu, but offerings include sandwiches such as ham and cheese, and wonderful cakes and pastries, the specialty of the house. Such temptations as croissants, fresh cream pastries, cakes, and apple pie fill the display case. Fresh cream pastries cost 85 pence to £1.60. Hours are 8:30 a.m. to 7 p.m.; closed Sunday.

Wheeler's, first established in 1856, has several successful fish restaurants in London, including the Wheeler's at 19–21 Old Compton St. Look for the attractive exterior with dragon lamps. Starting out as an oyster bar, Wheeler's now serves a dozen variations of Dover sole beginning at £10, as well as plaice, trout, salmon, halibut, lobsters, scallops, and steak. The interior of the restaurant is comfortable and traditional, with mounted trophy-winning fish decorating the walls. Hours here are noon to 2:30 p.m. and 6 to 11:15 p.m. Monday through Saturday, and noon to 2:30 and 6:30 to 10:30 p.m. on Sunday.

Maison Bertaux, 28 Greek St. (tel. 437-6007), is a tea room and pastry shop which first opened in Soho back in 1871. Open from 9 a.m. to 6 p.m. Tuesday through Saturday and from 9:30 a.m. to 1 p.m. on Sunday, it's closed Monday. Specialties include strawberry tarts and Mont Blancs, which are chestnuts, meringue, and cream. Upstairs are tables and chairs where you can enjoy your dessert with coffee.

Kettners is located at 29 Romilly St. (tel. 437-6437), which is just south of Old Compton Street. Open from noon to midnight daily, this is an upscale hamburger joint with an adjoining champagne bar. Decorated with potted palms and original artwork, it serves a hamburger deluxe for £3.80, as well as pizzas, salads, and sandwiches.

The **French House,** 49 Dean St. (tel. 437-2799), is a Soho institution. Built in the 16th century and bought by a Frenchman in 1914, it served as the unofficial headquarters of the French Resistance during World War II. Today this French-style pub is bare except for old pictures of French personalities, including boxers, stars, and circus performers. Serving champagne, French and Italian wine, vermouth, and Ricardi, it's open from 11 a.m. to 3 p.m. and 5:30 to 11 p.m.

Dog & Duck, 18 Bateman St. (tel. 437-3478), is located on the corner of Frith and Bateman. Your typical neighborhood pub, it's filled with locals and regulars, and records show that it was built around 1774. A place where people come mainly to drink, it serves some sandwiches, rolls, pies, and sausages. Hours are 11:30 a.m. to 3 p.m. and 5:30 to 11 p.m. Monday through Friday; 11:30 a.m. to 3 p.m. and 7 to 11 p.m. on Saturday, and noon to 2 p.m. on Sunday.

COVENT GARDEN

When I first came to London in my student days back in 1974, the city's main fruit, vegetable, and flower market had just been moved from its centuries-old home at Covent Garden to new quarters at Nine Elms. Everyone in London was grumbling about it, saying how Covent Garden had been robbed of its character and raison d'être. Indeed, when I came back a few years later to write an article on one of Covent Garden's new businesses, the area still seemed rather forgotten and forlorn, and people were still grumbling about the loss of the fruit and flower market.

No longer. In 1980 the charming market building, which had been erected back in the 1820s, reopened as an exciting, renovated complex with shops, boutiques, and cafés. Although some people still complained, saying it was somehow too artificial and too expensive, through the years the new complex has gained acceptance even among the diehards. Known simply as the Market, it is recognized today as one of the most exciting shopping areas of London.

With the opening of the Market, the surrounding area, known as Covent Garden, received a much-needed shot in the arm. Long Acre, Neal Street, James Street, and others have witnessed a boom in popularity and growth, and Covent Garden is now a very trendy address to have. In fact, rents have

Liza Doolittle also sold flowers here

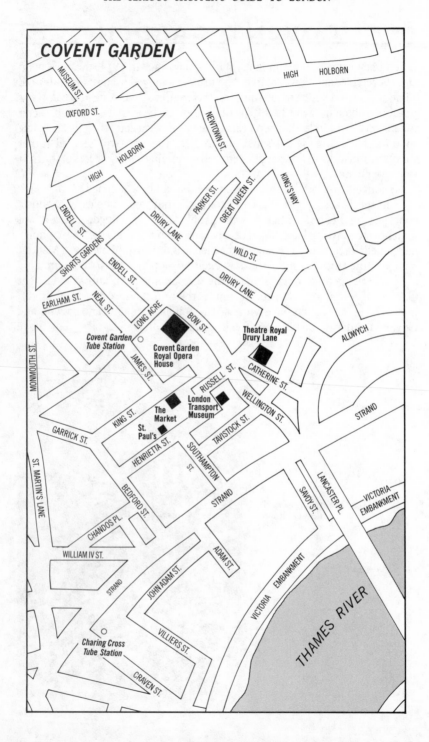

escalated so much in the past few years that new shops, particularly the avant-garde, tend to open and shut with the frequency of a fish's mouth out of water. All of this, however, just adds to the excitement, since one can actually witness—as though it were a living thing—how much Covent Garden changes and grows with each ensuing year.

Covent Garden is a young people's place, crowded with clothing boutiques, specialty shops, restaurants, cafés, and bars. The square surrounding the Market, called the Piazza, has a decidedly carnival-like atmosphere, with open-air stalls selling antiques or crafts and with street performers who give shows regularly throughout the day. Sitting at an outdoor café on the Piazza, you can listen to musicians or watch jugglers, mime artists, magicians, or dancers. If you want, you can even come here early in the evening, since shops in the Market are the only ones in London to stay open until 8 p.m. six nights a week.

The new look at Covent Garden

A COVENT GARDEN STROLL

Because Covent Garden is an area rather than a street, I've designed this stroll to take you crisscrossing through its most important shopping streets. In case you want to mark it beforehand on your map, this tour begins at Covent Garden tube station and proceeds to Long Acre, Neal Street, Floral Street, and James Street before taking you to the Market, after which you can continue down King Street to New Row and Leicester Square.

Emerging from the deep elevator shaft that brings you up from the Covent Garden underground train, you should turn left outside the station where you'll find yourself immediately upon Long Acre. Right in front of you is our first shop, the **Covent Garden General Store,** filled with gift items, china, glass, toys, gag gifts, teas, Crabtree & Evelyn preserves, soaps and toiletries, and Bendicks chocolates. One section of the store is devoted to its "British Shop," where you can buy T-shirts, posters, and other souvenirs.

If you head east on Long Acre (to the left as you exit the General Store), two shops worth noting are **Connections for Men,** 55-56 Long Acre, a men's trendy clothing shop with the French Connection label, and **The Glasshouse,** 65 Long Acre, an exciting shop selling contemporary glass art with an open studio where you can watch glassmakers at work.

Backtracking and walking west on Long Acre, you'll find **Blazer,** 36 Long Acre, a men's store selling the English version of the preppy and traditional Ivy League look in clothes. **Arkitect,** meanwhile, is at the other end of the spectrum, with unique and out-of-the-ordinary clothing designed by Simon Abihssira. Located on Langley Court just off Long Acre, this tiny shop has dressed celebrities such as Bruce Springsteen and the Eurythmics.

Falkiner, 117 Long Acre, is a stationery shop that sells fine writing papers (handmade, Japanese, marbled—you name it) and pens, ink, nibs, and even turkey quills. Both the **Warehouse,** 24 Long Acre, and **Woodhouse,** 138 Long Acre, are young men's clothing stores with several locations in London, while **Stanfords,** 12–14 Long Acre, specializes in the most up-to-date maps and charts and in travel guides.

Returning to Covent Garden tube station, take the road that runs north alongside the Covent Garden General Store. Called Neal Street, it turns into a pedestrian lane with lots of interesting specialty shops. At the corner of Neal and Shelton Streets is **Harvey's Auctions,** which has an auction every Wednesday starting at 10:30 a.m. and sells inexpensive antique and secondhand furniture, ceramics, and pictures and prints. The **British Crafts Centre,** on the corner of Neal and Earlham Streets, is a gallery showing contemporary jewelry, glass, pottery, weavings, tapestries, basketweaving, wood-carvings, and other crafts by British artists. Exhibitions change frequently so there are always new items on display.

Clothkit, 39 Neal St., is a unique store selling colorful coordinated knitwear, along with kits complete with cloth, matching thread, buttons, and instructions for making clothes for yourself and your children. There are sample fashions you can try on for size, and the kits are designed for those with little or no sewing experience. **The Coppershop,** 48 Neal St., sells exactly what its name says, all made in Britain, and ranging from copper bracelets and earrings to spirit warmers, coal boxes, watering cans, and pans. **Astrohome,** 47–49 Neal St., is a hi-tech furniture and housewares store with products that are sleek and minimalist in design. You can try on everything from bowler hats to berets and tweed caps at the **Hat Shop,** 58 Neal St., which has a fun selection of relatively inexpensive men's and women's hats. **Natural Leather,** 62 Neal St., has leather bags, jackets, and clothing, while **World Services,** 68 Neal St., is a men's trendy clothing store which opened in 1986 and sells an exclusive line of fashions made by tailors in London's East End. Styles are reminiscent of the 1960s but have touches of contemporary flourishes, and prices are astonishingly reasonable, with suits going for less than £200 and poplin shirts for less than £38.

Retrace your steps back down Neal Street, pass the Covent Garden tube station, and take James Street heading south. On your left side will be **Connections,** 12 James St., with women's clothes carrying the French Connection label. You'll then come to Floral Street, which has several interesting clothing shops, including **No? Yes!** for women and **Paul Smith** for men. Paul Smith is an English fashion designer who creates English classical clothing with a twist. At 29 Floral St. is **Atissu,** a women's tailor shop opened in 1986 by two ambitious young women who will whip up one of your own creations or one chosen from their own patterns.

Back on James Street, **David Mellor,** at no. 26, is a kitchenware shop with virtually everything you might need in the kitchen, including its own cutlery and Wedgwood china designed specifically for David Mellor. The **Poster Shop,** 28 James St., has a selection of contemporary posters, most of them taken from museum or gallery exhibitions. **Patricia Roberts,** 31 James St., is a designer sweater shop, where you can purchase a ready-made sweater, yarn and a pattern for a Patricia Roberts sweater you can make yourself, or simply yarn for your own design.

James Street runs into the Piazza and the Market. Stretching around the Market is a **flea market,** held daily from about 9 a.m. to 4 or 5 p.m. Antiques are sold on Monday, general goods (including clothing) are sold Tuesday through Friday, and crafts are for sale on Saturday and Sunday. This is a good market for browsing, particularly if you don't have time to visit any of London's other markets, and be sure to wander around to the stalls on the Piazza's south side.

In **The Market** itself are more than 40 shops, restaurants, and cafés grouped around two indoor courtyards. Many of the shops are branches of successful larger stores found elsewhere. **Thornton's** is a confectionary shop selling handmade chocolates and is well known for its toffee, while **Covent Garden Kitchen Supplies** sells everything you need for cooking, including unusually shaped cookie tins, Sabatier knives, and Le Creuset sauce pans. **Ferns** is the place to buy exotic-sounding coffee beans, while **Culpeper** will supply you with herbs, soaps, sachets, and lotions. The **Body Shop** also sells body products and is one of an extremely successful chain store with more than 70 locations in the United Kingdom.

Edwina Carroll has two shops in the Market, one for women, with a small but interesting collection of clothing, jewelry, and accessories, and the other for children, with clothes and toys. More fashions are on display at **Hobbs,** with its casual wear and shoes; **S. Fisher,** with its sweaters and fashionable versions of hunting, shooting, and fishing wear; and at **Whistles,** with inexpensive designer clothes from Britain, the continent, and Japan. Stop by the **Ticket Shop** to pick up your tickets for theater, concerts, and sporting events. **Eric Snook** sells novelties, toys, and gifts, while **The Doll's House** sells miniature houses and everything to go in them. It will even make houses to order. **Pollock's Toy Theatres** is a sister shop to the one located at Pollock's Toy Museum (described in the Tottenham Court Road stroll), selling a smaller selection of cut-out theaters and toys. The **Cabaret Mechanical Theatre** is a crafts shop selling handmade automata, mainly from wood. Since this shop is so unique it's difficult to explain exactly what they sell — you'll just have to drop in and see for yourself. Connected to the shop is a museum with 50 automata on display.

If you haven't gotten sidetracked into spending your entire day at the Market, leave by its west side and take King Street to New Row where you'll find several more interesting shops. **Moss Bros.,** located on the corner of New Row and Bedford Street, is a small, family-owned department store founded in 1860. Selling fashionable clothing, riding wear and saddlery, and kilts, it is perhaps best known for its rental clothing. Going out for a very special occasion but forgot your tux or evening gown? You can rent one here: strapless gowns average £45 and a white tuxedo rents for £20. And I'm sure you'll rest easier knowing that if the occasion ever arises, you can even rent a kilt.

Naturally British, 13 New Row, sells handcrafted goods made in the United Kingdom, including toys, jewelry, wool sweaters, soaps and marmalades, while **The Scottish Merchant,** 15 New Row, has both traditional knitwear such as fishermen's ganseys as well as unique designer sweaters. **Arthur Middleton,** 12 New Row, is one of London's largest dealers in antique scientific equipment, with a large stock of telescopes, polished brass sextants, microscopes, com-

Handcrafted items are among the gift pickings at Naturally British

passes, globes, and more. Established in 1840, **Thomas Bland & Sons,** at 21–22 New Row, sells sporting shotguns, rifles, handguns, and all the necessary accessories.

Before leaving New Row, stop by **Drury Tea & Coffee Co.** at no. 3 to buy your beans or leaves. Then, if it's not too late and you're thinking you might like to go to the theater that night but don't yet have tickets, head farther west to Leicester Square where you'll find the **Half Price Ticket Booth.** Open Monday to Saturday from noon to 2 p.m. for matinees and 2:30 to 6:30 p.m. for evening performances, it sells tickets at half price for that day's performances only and solely to personal callers.

SIGHTSEEING SUGGESTIONS

In the Piazza surrounding the Market are two sights worth seeing, St. Paul's and the London Transport Museum. **St. Paul's,** built by architect Inigo Jones and completed in 1638, was constructed as economically as possible and was designed using a barn as a model. Note its overhanging eaves and the Tuscan portico.

The **London Transport Museum** (tel. 379-6344) shows the history and development of nearly two centuries of public transport in London, beginning with the Shillibeer horse-drawn omnibus used around 1830. Seating 22 passengers, this omnibus started with service every three hours. Also on display are other horse-drawn carriages, street cars, trams, buses, trains, and public transport memorabilia. There's a gift shop with souvenirs and books, and hours here are 10 a.m. to 6 p.m. daily, with last admittance at 5:15 p.m.

Due for completion sometime in 1987 is **Victoria and Albert's Theatre Museum,** on Russell Street, which will commemorate the history of theater in London. More information on this newest of London's sights can be obtained from the tourist office.

LUNCHEON SPOTS AND DRINKING ESTABLISHMENTS

There are several places to eat and drink right in the Market itself. Among them is **Bar Creperie** (tel. 836-2137), open from 10 a.m. to 11:30 p.m. daily. With seating outside from which you can watch the Piazza performers, it serves crêpes starting at £3.10 with such fillings as ham and cheese or chicken and asparagus. Try **Cranks** (tel. 379-6508), open from 10 a.m. to 8 p.m. Monday through Saturday, for health foods and behind-the-counter options like quiche, pizza by the slice, salads, or desserts. There isn't much seating here, but if the weather is warm you might want to buy something and take it out onto the Piazza to eat. The **Crusting Pipe** (tel. 836-1415) serves wines as well as hearty meals of grilled sirloin steak for £6, charcoal-grilled rib of beef for £5.75, a plate of roast beef for £3.30, and daily specials. A specialty of the house is sinful chocolate mousse. Hours are 11:30 a.m. to 3 p.m. and 5:30 to 11 p.m.

For more formal dining, one of the best restaurants in Covent Garden is the **Neal Street Restaurant,** located at 26 Neal St. (tel. 836-8368). Opened in 1971, this Terence Conran establishment serves unhurried meals from a small but imaginative menu that changes to include seasonal choices like mushrooms or truffles, prawns with bacon, smoked eel, or veal medallions with walnut sauce. The average cost of dinner without wine runs about £25 per person and it's best to make reservations, especially for lunch. Hours here are 12:30 to 2:30 p.m. and 7 to 11 p.m.; closed both Saturday and Sunday.

Smith's, 33 Shelton St. (tel. 379-0310), is located at the corner of Shelton and Neal Streets and is located in the basement of Smith's Gallery. With its cool stone floors and whitewashed walls, this trendy and popular restaurant is open from noon to midnight Monday through Saturday, with last orders taken at 11:15 p.m. It has a great pre-theater set menu served from 6 to 8 p.m. costing £7.60, as well as daily specials beginning at £5 and a vegetarian dish of the day for £4.30. The regular menu includes such choices as fish, poultry, steaks, and salads, and the wine list has 36 wines from Europe and even a few from California.

Inigo Jones, 14 Garrick St. (tel. 836-6456), is named after the famous architect, although this building was not designed by him. Rather, it was erected in 1864 as a studio and workshop for stained glass and retains such original features as its brick walls and stained-glass windows. Open from 12:30 to 2:30 p.m. Monday through Friday and from 5:30 to 7 p.m. Monday through Saturday for the pre-theater crowd, it offers a daily lunch special for approximately £15.50 and three-course meals with choices for appetizer and main course for about £17.80. The à la carte menu changes every three to four months but may include such inventions as filet of lamb with curry sauce and braised cabbage or baked veal sweetbreads in thin pastry with wild mushrooms and walnut-butter sauce.

London's oldest restaurant, **Rules,** 35 Maiden Lane (tel. 836-5314), was established in 1798 and since then has played host to such customers as Charles Dickens, Charlie Chaplin, Graham Greene, Laurence Olivier, Buster Keaton, Clark Gable, and even royalty. Open from 12:15 to 2:30 p.m. and 5:30 p.m. to midnight every day except Sunday, it's decorated with prints donated by artists who have eaten here and *Vanity Fair* caricatures. With a somewhat cluttered but very cozy and warm atmosphere exemplified by a friendly staff, it serves traditional English food. Specialities include grilled calves' liver, rack of lamb, venison, steak-and-kidney pie, and roast ribs of beef with Yorkshire pudding, and most dishes cost less than £10. There are also game birds offered at various times of the year, including grouse, partridge, and pheasant.

Also serving English food is **Porters,** 17 Henrietta St. (tel. 836-6466), a fun, informal restaurant with a mock old-fashioned setting in which you half expect some robust barmaid to start shouting and a bartender with rolled-up sleeves to start whistling tunes. Decorated with Covent Garden memorabilia, its specialities are English pies, including shepherd's, steak-and-kidney, beef-and-chili, lamb-and-apricot, and turkey-and-chestnut pies, all around £3.80. There are also various hot or cold puddings starting at £1.50 and a large range of beers, lagers, spirits, wines, and cocktails. Open hours are noon to 3 p.m. and 5:30 to 11:30 p.m. closing on Sunday at 10:30 p.m.

A faithful reproduction of the New York Joe Allen, London's **Joe Allen,** at 13 Exeter St. (tel. 836-0651), draws a large pre- and after-theater crowd as well as lunchtime faithfuls. If you want to come here for lunch or dinner, therefore, it's usually best to make reservations a few days in advance. However, because it's open from noon to 1 a.m. Monday through Saturday and until midnight on Sunday, it's a good place to come for a meal in the middle of the afternoon when many other restaurants are closed. Located in a basement whose brick walls are covered with theater posters, it serves American-style food including salads starting at £3.30, chili for £3.80, barbecued ribs for £6, sirloin steak for £9.30, and halibut for £7. Daily specials are written on chalkboards, and the atmosphere is informal and noisy.

Le Café des Amis du Vin, 11–14 Hanover Pl. (tel. 379-3444), is located in a small side street between Long Acre and Floral Street. Open from noon to 11:30 p.m. Monday through Saturday, it has tables outside and resembles a French sidewalk café. With a large selection of French wines, it serves daily set meals for around £7, as well as à la carte selections such as calves' liver, quiche, omelets, grilled sausages from Toulouse, French black pudding and, grilled andouillette.

One of London's best vegetarian restaurants, **Food for Thought,** 31 Neal St. (tel. 836-0231), is so popular that it isn't unusual to see people queued up outside its front door. In fact, one of the drawbacks to this establishment is that there isn't enough seating to accommodate all the people who want to eat here. The food is imaginative and superb, and there's a daily changing menu posted outside the front door. Dishes may include pinto-bean casserole with carrots and onions, stir-fried veggies and rice, various quiches, and salads. Most dishes are under £4 and hours here are noon to 8 p.m. Monday through Friday.

Neals Yard Bakery & Tea Room, 6 Neals Yard (tel. 836-5199), is located in a small courtyard near Neal Street. Part of a cooperative that includes an apothecary with back-to-nature remedies and herbs, the bakery serves hot vegetarian food beginning at noon and closes at 8 p.m. (except on Wednesday when it closes at 3:30 p.m. and on Saturday when it closes at 4:30 p.m.). It's closed all day on Sunday. Selections at the food counter include a hot vegetarian dish of the day, quiche, pizza, cheese-and-mushroom croissants, bean burgers, soups, and salads, all for less than £2. There's also a large selection of cakes and breads. A tea room is located up on the first floor over the bakery, where you can eat what you've purchased downstairs and drink herbal tea.

In the basement of the Covent Garden General Store, 111 Long Acre, is a restaurant called **Green & Pleasant** (tel. 240-7781) which has a salad bar and serves sandwiches, quiche, cakes, and desserts. American owned and operated, it's open from 10:30 a.m. to 11 p.m. Monday through Saturday and from noon to 6 p.m. on Sunday.

Pubs and Pub Lunches

Lamb & Flag, 33 Rose St. (tel. 836-4108), is one of the most renowned pubs in Covent Garden, not only because it is one of the oldest wooden buildings around, built in 1623, but also because the poet Dryden was mugged just outside. He dubbed the pub "The Bucket of Blood," but today there isn't much intimidating about the business people in suits who drink here. With the usual pub hours of 11 a.m. to 3 p.m. and 5:30 to 11 p.m. Monday through Saturday and noon to 2 p.m. and 7 to 10:30 p.m. on Sunday, it serves a light snack of a ploughman's lunch with English cheeses.

The **Crown & Anchor,** 22 Neal St. (tel. 836-5649), is conveniently located on the corner of Neal and Shelton Streets and draws a big after-work crowd that often spills into the outdoors. It serves bar snacks such as sandwiches from 80 pence, steak-and-kidney pie for 70 pence, and baked potato with cheese from 60 pence.

Salisbury, 90 St. Martin's Lane (tel. 836-5863), is a flamboyantly decorated Edwardian pub with cut-glass mirrors, etched windows, art nouveau light figures and statues, and hand-carved mahogany panels and columns. Customers, too, sometimes border on the flamboyant, attracting both a gay and heterosexual crowd. The food changes daily but may include quiche, spaghetti, beef curry and rice, or steak-and-kidney pie.

AFTERNOON TEA

Although it's located about a ten-minute walk or so from the Market, **The Waldorf,** on Aldwych (tel. 836-2400), has one of the most elegant settings in London for afternoon tea and has weekend tea dances. Held in the pleasant Palm Court with its high ceiling and potted palms, afternoon tea here includes sandwiches, toasted English muffins, scones with jam and clotted cream, fruit cake, French pastries or cakes, and choice of teas. On Friday, Saturday, and Sunday from 3:30 to 6:30 p.m. traditional tea dances are held, for which the total price is £10.50. During the rest of the week tea time costs £8.20.

KING'S ROAD

Originating as little more than a pathway for farmers traveling between their homes and their fields, King's Road gained entry into history books when it was appropriated by King Charles II as his own private road. The official records say that the road was necessary as a route to Hampton Court, but the fact that the road was also a shortcut to the home of Nell Gwynne, an actress and the king's mistress, was undoubtedly an added appeal. At any rate, you had to have special permission to travel on "The King's Private Road" back in those days, and royal guardsmen patrolled both day and night. Although the road was opened to the public in 1830, the name stuck so that today it's still known as King's Road.

King's Road is located in Chelsea, which in the late 1800s became known as an artists' colony, followed by a new generation of the avant-garde after World War II. In the 1970s, King's Road became the center of the universe for punk fashion and the outrageous. Teenagers with spiked hair and safety pins stuck through their earlobes roamed the street, buying clothes designed to shock. New shops sprang into existence, and on Saturday King's Road was one of *the* places to parade and be seen.

Things have quieted down since then, and a lot of punk and avant-garde fashions have resurfaced in areas like Kensington and Camden Lock. King's Road and Chelsea are witness to a new generation of punks, who have been joined by the "Sloane Rangers," a totally British version of the American preppy. Punks, Sloane Rangers, tourists, and the rest are all drawn to King's Road and nearby Sloane Street, with shops ranging from trendy boutiques to indoor antique markets. Saturday is still the best day to come.

A KING'S ROAD STROLL

This stroll begins on Sloane Square, which you can reach by taking the underground to Sloane Square station. The largest store on the square is **Peter Jones,** a department store most noted for its linen, lighting fixtures, and antiques. On the opposite side of the square is **David Mellor,** a kitchenware shop with virtually everything you need to make a gourmet meal. Across the street from David Mellor is **Pandora,** 54 Sloane Square, a treasure trove of secondhand designer clothes for women. In business for 40 years, it sells fashion from all the big, established names, including Saint Laurent, Chloé, Emanuel, Jean Muir, Valentino, Jaeger, Giorgio Armani, and many more.

Running north from Sloane Square is Sloane Street, which stretches all the way to Knightsbridge. The **General Trading Company,** 144 Sloane St., is located just off Sloane Square and is one of London's most beautiful shops. Occupying four large Victorian houses, it specializes in household merchandise, including china, glass, kitchenware, linen, gifts, toys, and antique and repro-duction furniture. This is where a lot of Sloane Rangers have their wedding lists, a smart move if you ask me.

Jane Churchill, 137 Sloane St., has fabrics, linen, lampshades, cushions, and other accessories, all designed in-house and fashioned in the English country look. Across the street at 149 Sloane St. is **Cobra & Bellamy,** which specializes in 1920s and 1930s decorative objects, art deco and art nouveau jewelry, and costume jewelry from the 1920s to the 1960s.

Returning to Sloane Square and heading west on King's Road, you'll pass Blushes where you can stop for breakfast or lunch, Pizza Hut and the shoe shop **Russell & Bromley.** On a side street called Blacklands Terrace, you'll see **John Sandoe,** a small bookshop packed with hardback and paperback books dealing with decoration, architecture, art, and fiction. It has a good children's section downstairs in the basement.

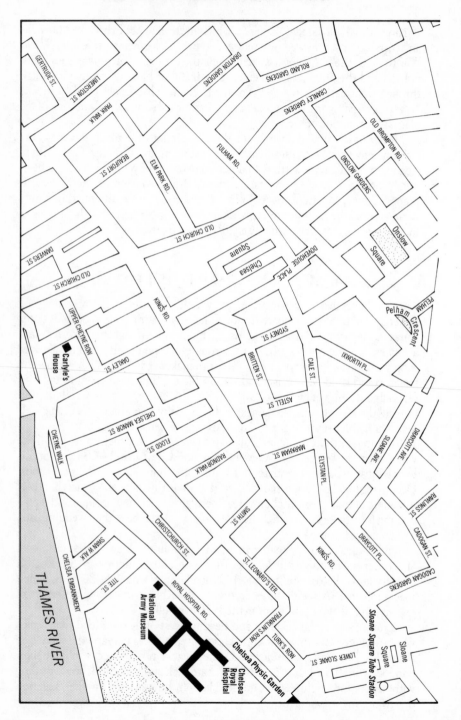

GREAT SHOPPING STROLLS: KING'S ROAD

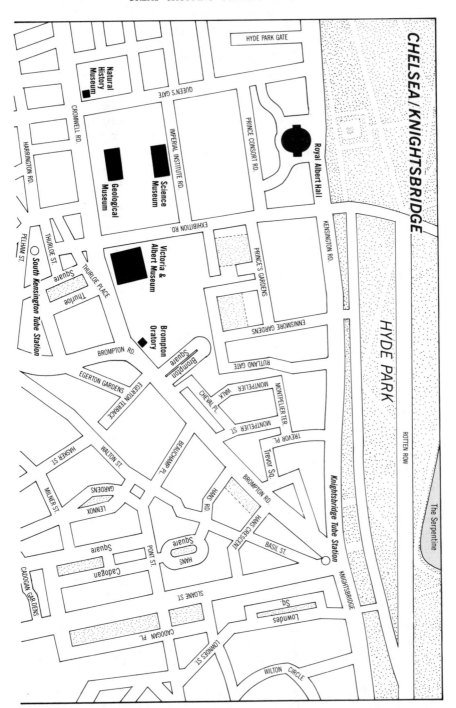

Back on King's Road is **Next,** at no. 72. Part of an innovative group of chain stores, this one deals in women's clothing and home furnishings. A bit farther down the road at 76–78 King's Rd. is another Next, this one selling fashionable clothing for young men. If you're interested in women's lingerie, Next at 102 King's Rd. sells very feminine underclothing.

More women's fashion can be found in some chain stores: **Hobbs,** at 84 King's Rd., **Benetton,** at no. 94; **Wallis,** at no. 96; and **Monsoon,** at no. 33D. **Woodhouse,** 124A King's Rd., sells trendy clothing for men, while English designer **Katharine Hamnet** sells her fashionable wear next door. **Fiorucci,** 126 King's Rd., is an Italian fashion store with fun casualwear for both men and women. **012,** at 132 King's Rd., is Benetton's clothing store for children.

Meanwhile, on the left side of the street is **Take Six,** at 69 King's Rd., a chain store of clothing for young men. **Jones,** 71 King's Rd., sells trendy English designer clothes for men and women, while **Review,** at no. 81, sells unisex clothing at very reasonable prices.

Antiquarius, 135 King's Rd., is an indoor antique and bric-a-brac market with more than 150 stalls selling old clocks, jewelry, china, silver, prints, books, brass, and '20s and '30s period clothing. It's open every day except Sunday from 10 a.m. to 6 p.m. Located in the same building as Antiquarius is **David Fielden,** who makes evening and bridal dresses to measure using silks and exotic lace, and **Edina Ronay,** who designs her own hand-knit sweaters and women's clothing.

Academy, 188A King's Rd., is an interesting clothing store that promotes and highlights young British fashion designers. Every six months this boutique completely alters its image, changing its interior as well as its designer lines and giving new designers a chance to show their stuff. **Habitat,** 206–222 King's Rd., is a furniture and housewares store belonging to the Terence Conran group of stores.

If you want to see one of the original punk stores, stop by **Boy,** 153 King's Rd., which opened in 1976 and sells clothing designed by Murray Blewitt. Much of the clothing has "Boy" written all over it, can be worn by both males and females, and is inexpensive, with lots in the £20 to £30 range. The **Reject Shop,** 234 King's Rd., is where young Londoners come to furnish their first apartments and is filled with moderately priced furniture and housewares. Next to the Reject Shop is **Sydney Street,** where at no. 121, you'll find **Richard Draper** with its own sheepskin products, including coats and boots.

Chenil Galleries, 181–183 King's Rd., is another antique market on King's Road, this one selling art deco and art nouveau objects, books, carpets, dolls and toys, furniture, glass, jewelry, paintings, porcelain, prints, silver, and scientific instruments. Pruskin Gallery, for example, sells art deco and art nouveau objects, including some furniture, lamps, glassware, silver, clocks, jewelry, and statues. Prices are high, but so is the quality.

Givans Irish Linen, 207 King's Rd., carries bed and table linen, duvet (comforter) covers, placemats, bathrobes, and handkerchiefs, and caters to what it delicately calls the "carriage class," meaning the upper crust of society. **Tiger-Tiger,** 219 King's Rd., is a small shop with an interesting selection of children's toys, including dolls, dollhouses, puppets, crib toys, building blocks, party treats, and stuffed animals. It specializes in traditional rather than gimmicky toys, with handcrafted British toys receiving top priority.

The **Chelsea Antique Market,** 245–253 King's Rd., is yet a third antique market on this road. Calling itself the oldest indoor market in all of London, it opened in the mid-1960s and today sells a rather eclectic mix of junk and treasure, with items cheaper than the two antique markets mentioned earlier. Stop here if you're interested in hand-knitted sweaters, glass, used clothing, old records and sheet music, original movie posters, prints, or jewelry.

Jeremy, 255 King's Rd., is an antique shop located in an old house. Opened in 1946, it carries 18th-century and early-19th-century French and English works of art and furniture. If your tastes run along more contemporary lines, stop by **Designers Guild,** which sells fabrics and wallpaper at 277 King's Rd. and furniture and accessories at no. 271. **Osborne & Little,** 304 King's Rd., also sells fabrics and wallpaper, with lovely patterns designed in France as well as in-house, while **Liberty,** 340A King's Rd., carries a selection of fabrics chosen from the famous Liberty department store on Regent Street.

Arcade Jewelry, 309A King's Rd., specializes in original costume jewelry from the Victorian period to the 1950s, with most pieces ranging from £10 to £100. Two shops are located at 313 King's Rd.: **Chelsea Rare Books** and the **Beaufort Gallery.** Browsing is encouraged, so take your time look-

Oh, Boy, it's outrageous!

ing at English literature books from the 18th and 19th centuries, second-hand books, old prints, maps, and watercolors. **Stephen King,** 315 King's Rd., sells men's designer wear in unusual prints and fabrics, while **Rococo,** 321 King's Rd., is a trendy confectionary. Its specialties are its Dragées, bittersweet chocolates in a candy shell. It also sells traditional chocolates, truffles, pralines, and marzipan.

On the right side of the street just before it snakes off to the left is **Eat Your Heart Out,** 360 King's Rd., selling secondhand clothes and objects from the 1920s to the 1950s. Around the bend on the left side of the street is another secondhand clothing store, **20th Century Box,** with bow ties, collars and collar studs, waistcoats, dress shirts, and clothing from the '50s and '60s. **Review,** 398 King's Rd., sells trendy British fashion for women, with designs that are simple but can be dressed up with the right accessories. **Liberated Lady,** 408 King's Rd., sells tight-fitting, slinky cocktail dresses. Many of the store's customers are models and aspiring actresses who want to be noticed, and prices are very reasonable—the average price of a dress runs about £60.

Worlds End, 430 King's Rd., is on the right side of the street just past the bend in the road. A small shop, it's easy to overlook, but a telltale sign is the large clock with hands that turn forever backward. All the clothes here are by Vivienne Westwood, a designer who came to the fore during punkdom in the 1970s. Her creations used to be quite controversial but are now a part of fashion shows from Tokyo to Paris. One of her latest designs has brought back the crinoline.

Worlds End is also the name of this area of King's Road, but it's not quite the end of the world it used to be. If you walk ten minutes farther west, you'll come to **Furniture Cave,** 533 King's Rd., a warehouse-like building filled with antique decorative furniture from all over the world. Approximately 20 dealers are located here, selling everything from original and reproduction pine furniture to Oriental objects, English antiques, and art deco. The constantly changing stock and large selection make this a great place to browse. From here you can either take a bus back to Sloane Square or walk to the nearest underground station, Fulham Broadway.

SIGHTSEEING SUGGESTIONS

Carlyle's House, 24 Cheyne Row, Chelsea (tel. 352-7087), was the home of Scottish writer Thomas Carlyle, who lived here from 1834 until his death in 1881. The house, dating from the early 18th century, is one of the oldest houses in Chelsea and still looks as though Carlyle departed only yesterday. Scattered throughout the house are his personal relics, manuscripts, and other artifacts of the Victorian era. This museum is open only from April to the end of October and hours are 11 a.m. to 5 p.m. Wednesday through Sunday.

The **Chelsea Royal Hospital,** Royal Hospital Road, was founded by King Charles II in 1682 as a home for retired soldiers and was designed by the famous architect Christopher Wren. A newer part houses a small museum with prints, uniforms, and items relating to the history of the hospital. Hours are 10 a.m. to noon and 2 to 4 p.m. Monday through Saturday, and 2 to 4 p.m. on Sunday.

Also located on Royal Hospital Road is the **National Army Museum** (tel. 730-0717), open from 10 a.m. to 5:30 p.m. Monday through Saturday and from 2 to 5:30 p.m. on Sunday. This museum follows the history of the British army from 1485 to the present, with exhibits also on the Indian army and colonial forces. Included are weapons, uniforms, armor, pictures, maps, models of campaigns, and other items relating to army history.

And finally, a third attraction on Royal Hospital Road is the **Chelsea Physic Garden,** a good place to unwind and relax after a day of shopping and sightseeing. An old botanical garden, it dates from 1673. It's open from mid-April to mid-October only on Sunday, Wednesday, and bank holiday Mondays from 2 to 5 p.m.

LUNCHEON SPOTS AND DRINKING ESTABLISHMENTS

Oriel (tel. 730-2804) is located right on Sloane Square not far from the underground station. Open from 8:30 a.m. daily with last orders taken at 11:30 p.m., this French-style café offers a changing menu of the day for about £10, as well as snacks that include an avocado-and-prawn salad, croque monsieur, or calves' liver with onions. Most people, however, come here to drink. Coffee is 60 pence, and a glass of house wine is £1.70. There's seating outside during fine weather.

The **General Trading Company,** 144 Sloane St. (tel. 730-0411), has a pleasant café in its basement. Under the same management as the famous bakery Justin de Blank, it has a greenhouse-like atmosphere as well as outdoor seating in a little patio. In addition to breakfasts, it serves a changing lunch menu and an afternoon tea. It's open from 9 a.m. to 5:15 p.m. Monday through Friday, closing at 1:45 p.m. on Saturday.

Chelsea's only department store, **Peter Jones,** on Sloane Square (tel. 730-3434) has three food-and-beverage outlets. A coffeeshop on the fifth floor serves cakes, pastries, sandwiches, salads, quiche, and frozen-yogurt sundaes. The Crock Pot on the fourth floor serves two daily lunch specials, while the Restaurant offers a salad bar for £9.60, a lunch of the day for £8.80, and other dishes such as honey-and-clove baked ham. From 2:45 p.m. it serves afternoon tea, which costs £2.40 and includes two scones with whipped cream and preserves.

Blushes, 52 King's Rd. (tel. 589-6640), is a trendy café with blushing-pink tablecloths, potted palms, cane chairs, and music with the latest pop tunes. A bar is located in the basement, and in nice weather tables are set up outside on the sidewalk where you can observe humanity parading by. Open from 9:30 a.m. for breakfast, from 11 a.m. to 3 p.m. for lunch, and from 5:30 p.m. to midnight for dinner, it offers a menu of chicken Kiev, veal Cordon Bleu, lamb cutlets, sirloin steak, Dover sole, huge salads, and more, with most dishes ranging from about £6 to £8. Chalkboards announce daily specials, and wine starts at £1.30 for a glass.

The **Pizza Hut,** 56 King's Rd. (tel. 581-5517), serves what you're used to back home, including its various styles of pizza, pasta, and a salad bar. Small pizzas for one person start at £2.90. Hours are 11:30 a.m. to midnight daily, and from noon to 3 p.m. weekdays the management promises it can serve a small vegetarian or supreme pan pizza within ten minutes—or your next pizza is free. Obviously, this is the place to go if you're in a hurry.

The **Chelsea Kitchen,** 98 King's Rd. (tel. 589-1330), looks like the kind of diner you find in small and big towns across America. It serves hearty dishes at affordable prices, and service is quick. Although the menu changes daily, it usually includes a selection of salads, omelets, puddings, soups, and such main courses as spaghetti, liver, roast chicken, or steak-and-kidney pie. Most dishes are less than £2, and hours here are 8 a.m. to 11:45 p.m. Monday through Saturday and noon to 11:30 p.m. on Sunday.

If you're looking for a pub lunch or a pint, a convenient place to stop is the **Chelsea Potter,** at 119 King's Rd. (tel. 352-9479). It's open from 11 a.m. to 11 p.m. Monday through Saturday, although it can't serve alcohol from 3 to 5:30 p.m. Sunday hours are noon to 2 p.m. and 7 to 10:30 p.m. Huge windows make this pub bright inside, and there are tables outside in the summer. Hot food is served throughout the day and might include such items as lasagne, a ploughman's lunch of bread and cheeses, chili con carne, or sandwiches. Most dishes are around £3.

The **Pheasantry,** 152 King's Rd., is a 400-year-old building that used to be a hunting lodge, turning later into a ballet school and then—or so the story goes—a brothel. At any rate, today the old building houses a chic brasserie, a pasta restaurant, and a cocktail bar. **Chelsea Brasserie** (tel. 351-3084) is located on the ground floor and also has seating outside in the forecourt terrace. Dishes here include chicken, veal, duck, steak, medallions of pork, and seafood, with most items ranging from about £7 to £9. There's also a vegetarian lasagne and a vegetarian stir-fry dish, both for less than £4. **Mama Bellini** (tel. 351-7994) is located up on the first floor. With its classical music and greenery, it provides a relaxing setting for a meal of pasta. Especially recommended is its alle vongole, spaghetti served with three different kinds of clams, white wine, tomatoes, and secret ingredients, for £3.80. There are also various kinds of fettuccine, lasagne, ravioli, and salads, and the management reckons that most people spend about £10 average for a meal with wine. Hours for both are 12:30 to 3 p.m. and 6:30 to 11 p.m., with slightly shorter hours on Sunday.

If you're looking for a good ole American hamburger, **Henry J. Bean's,** at 196 King's Rd. (tel. 352-9255), claims to serve exactly that. American owned, it also offers potato skins, nachos, chili, hot dogs, and daily specials, with most prices under £4. Great pluses to this place are its Happy Hour, from 5:30 to 7 p.m. Monday through Friday, when cocktails are offered for half price, and its garden seating out back away from traffic noises. It's open from 11:30 a.m. to 11:45 p.m. Monday through Saturday and from noon to 10:30 p.m. on Sunday.

Dan's, 119 Sydney St. (tel. 352-2718), is a small and intimate restaurant serving a changing and select menu. Open from 12:30 to 2:30 p.m. Monday through Friday and from 7:30 to 11:15 p.m. Monday through Saturday, it offers a daily lunch menu with meat dishes for around £5.50, with items that might include fish, veal, or beef. A set dinner menu is available for about £14.80. Try to get a seat at the back of restaurant, where its conservatory setting includes a removable ceiling.

The **Veritable Crêperie,** 329 King's Rd. (tel. 352-3891), serves all kinds of crêpes and galettes starting at about £2.50. A galette, in case you didn't know, is a specialty of Brittany and is a very thick pancake made with buckwheat flour from China. There are about 40 toppings to choose from, along with salad, beer, coffee, or wine. It's open from noon to midnight every day.

If you end your stroll around Worlds End, a convenient place to stop for nourishment is **La Nassa,** 438 King's Rd. (tel. 351-4118). An Italian restaurant with a strong emphasis on seafood, it's small and cozy and is open daily from noon to 2:30 p.m. and 7 to 11:30 p.m. Pasta dishes include fresh homemade pasta stuffed with cheese and spinach and served in a tomato cream sauce for £3.10, as well as a combination dish with three types of pasta and sauces. Seafood selections include sole with prawns, sautéed scampi, sole in orange-and-butter sauce, and baby squid cooked in white wine.

KNIGHTSBRIDGE

No one knows exactly how Knightsbridge got its name, but the most romantic version tells of two knights on their way to the Crusades who got into an argument, fought, and slew each other atop an ancient bridge. Well, if there ever was a bridge, it's long been replaced by the crush of stores that line Brompton and Fulham Roads. I imagine that if such a scenario were played out today, it would occur in someplace like Harrods—no doubt during one of its annual sales.

After the West End, Knightsbridge has what is probably the largest concentration of stores in London. Most of the chain stores have branches here, and shops that are successful elsewhere have also found Knightsbridge fertile grounds for launching a second shop. If you've toured the stores of the West End, therefore, you'll find a repeat of many of the shops here.

Located southwest of the West End, Knightsbridge can be broken into two distinct areas, Brompton and Fulham Roads, which I cover in two separate strolls. Because Brompton is home to Harrods, one of the world's most famous department stores, as well as charming Beauchamp Place with its many boutiques, it can easily take up a day of shopping. If your time is short, however, and you like to walk, you can easily combine Brompton and Fulham into a single shopping tour. In addition to Harrods, Brompton has primarily clothing boutiques, with a sprinkling of jewelry and shoe shops. At the end of Fulham are a number of antique shops.

BROMPTON ROAD AND
BEAUCHAMP PLACE

If you arrive in Knightsbridge via underground, take the exit that reads "Knightsbridge," which will bring you above ground right in front of **Harvey Nichols.** A department store filled primarily with designer wear, this is one of the loveliest places in town to shop for clothes by Chloé, Sonia Rykiel, Jaeger, Krizia, Edina Ronay, Cacharel, Alexon, Burberry, Windsmoor, Liz Claiborne, and more. Even if you can't afford to shop here, it doesn't cost anything to look at their interesting window displays.

Across the street from Harvey Nichols is Hyde Park Hotel, a good place for afternoon tea. If you continue walking on Knightsbridge Road in the direction of Hyde Park Corner, you'll find **Lucienne Phillips** at 89 Knightsbridge, a shop specializing in British designer clothes and run by the lively and enthusiastic Ms. Phillips herself. **Bradleys,** 83–85 Knightsbridge, is a lingerie shop with a large selection of underclothing, nightwear, and swimming suits.

Backtracking your steps past Harvey Nichols, you'll find Sloane Street to your left, which has a number of fashionable clothing shops. **Browns,** 6C Sloane St., carries clothes of the world's top designers, including Bill Blass, Jean-Paul Gaultier, Jean Muir, Perry Ellis, and many others. Joseph Ettedgui has several shops on Sloane Street, including **Joseph Pour La Maison** at no. 16, **Joseph Tricot** at no. 18, and **Joseph Pour La Ville** at no. 166. There's a **Kenzo** boutique with expensive wear for women at 17 Sloane St., and if you're interested in Japanese fashion there are two designers you should check out—**Yohji Yamamoto,** 6 Sloane St., and **Issey Miyake,** 21 Sloane St.

Laura Ashley fans will be glad to know that there's a shop carrying her home furnishings at 183 Sloane St., while right around the corner at 7–9 Harriet St. there's a Laura Ashley with a comprehensive selection of clothing for women and little girls. More children's clothes can be found at **La Cicogna,** 6a Sloane, which deals in Italian designer clothes for little ones, and **Please Mum,** 22 Sloane St., with expensive clothing imported from Italy and France. Other boutiques on Sloane Street include **Chanel,** with its fashion and perfume at no. 31; **Cecil Gee,** 190–192 Sloane St., with well-tailored, classical clothing for men and women; **Bendicks,** 195 Sloane St., with its tempting handmade chocolates; and **Descamps,** 197 Sloane St., which specializes in beautiful linen from France.

Return to Harvey Nichols, but this time turn left at the intersection and you'll find yourself on Brompton Road. Incidentally, odd-numbered shops are located on the left side of the street, while the even-numbered ones are on the right.

Starting on the left side of the street, you'll find **Lucy's** at 5–7 Brompton Rd., a women's clothing shop with evening wear imported mainly from France and Italy. A few shops down is **Wallis,** 9–13 Brompton, a chain store of women's clothing with a good selection of working and party clothes that closely imitate designer wear without the high price tag.

Issey Miyake: Unique and expensive

Also to your left is **Brompton Arcade,** a short mall with a dozen or so shops, including **Joseph Bis** with fashionable clothing, a herbal cosmetics shop, and the **Italian Paper Shop** with its hand-marbled Italian papers and paper products.

There's a **Benetton** at 23 Brompton Rd., one of many in London of this Italian chain store with casual wear in bright, solid colors. **Fior,** 27 Brompton Rd., carries fun costume and paste jewelry. Stop here for fake diamond and emerald rings beginning as low as £15, brooches, chains, bracelets, necklaces, and watches. At 33 Brompton Rd. is a **Next** boutique with clothing for women, followed by **Charles Jourdan** at 39–43 Brompton Rd., a famous name in clothes, shoes, perfume, and accessories for men and women. Beside the shoe chain store, Russell & Bromley, is **Loewe,** 47–49 Brompton, selling Spanish-made leathergoods such as luggage, handbags, and briefcases, in addition to perfume, clothing, and gift accessories.

Passing shoe shops Rayne and Bally, you'll come to **Kutchinsky,** 73 Brompton Rd., which deals in British-made jewelry, all of which carries the Kutchinsky mark. There's also an in-house designer who will custom-make jewelry. Working clothes and casual wear for young women are found in abundance at **Miss Selfridge,** 75 Brompton Rd., while men's suits and shirts are sold at **Cecil Gee,** 83–85 Brompton Rd.

So far we've covered shops only on the left side of the street, but there are

several shops on the right side clamoring for attention. Of particular note is the **Scotch House,** 2 Brompton Rd., the largest of three Scotch Houses in London. The company was founded more than 100 years ago and opened its Knightsbridge shop at the turn of the century. This is the place to come for Scottish merchandise, especially tartans. There's even a Tartan Room with more than 300 tartans to choose from. If you have Scottish ancestry but don't know your tartan, there's a big book that matches names with patterns. Other items in the store include Burberry raincoats, kilts, sweaters, and gifts, and there's also a children's clothing department.

Farther down on the same side of the street is **Fiorucci,** at 48 Brompton Rd., with fun, bright casual wear, followed by **Chinacraft** with its comprehensive range of china and crystal. If you're looking for inexpensive cosmetics or need a prescription filled, there's a large **Boots** pharmacy at 72 Brompton Rd.

Next comes **Harrods,** on the left side of the street. It's hard to miss this giant, since it takes up one whole block and looks more like some important Parliament building rather than a department store. But, then, this isn't just any department store. Notice the royal warrants listed on its façade—Harrods serves as suppliers of provisions and household goods to the Queen; as outfitters to the Duke of Edinburgh; as suppliers of china, glass, and fancy goods to the Queen Mother; and as outfitters and saddlers to the Prince of Wales. Take your cue from the royal family and enter Harrods' hallowed halls.

My favorite is the food halls. They are absolutely beautiful and seem to stretch on forever. Altogether there are 18 different departments for food alone, including sections for cheeses, meats, chocolates, gourmet items, breads, and

Sausages in a row at Harrods Food Hall Charcuterie

wines. The cheese department offers 500 different cheeses, while the bakery has 130 different types of bread.

But don't forget the other approximately 230 departments. With more than 15 acres of total selling space, Harrods probably has more under one roof than any other store in London. As one Londoner quipped when I told her I was writing a shopping guide, "Why don't you just tell them to go to Harrods?" While it may be true that one can find most everything in Harrods, it doesn't offer the wide assortment of, say, walking sticks that you'd find in a specialty shop specializing in canes. Besides, who would want to miss out on all those tiny, centuries-old shops for which London is legendary? Visit Harrods for the experience of it, but be prepared to get lost. It's a huge place, with restaurants, a tourist information desk and theater ticket booth, travel agency, hairdressers, a dry cleaners, a 24-hour photographic-development service, kennels, and even a funeral service. After seeing some of the prices here, you may need it.

Back in the real world and perhaps in need of money, you'll find an American Express on the right side of the street at 78 Brompton Rd. Clothing stores follow, including **Lanvin,** at 88 Brompton Rd., with classic, well-tailored styles for men, and **Jaeger,** at 96–98 Brompton Rd., with British-designed clothes for men and women.

Jumping over to the left side of the street you'll find more chain-store outlets. **Mothercare,** 143–154 Brompton, has everything under the sun for mothers, mothers-to-be, infants, and children. **Austin Reed,** 163–169 Brompton Rd., carries the same merchandise as its Regent Street store, namely suits, shirts, and other clothing for men and fashion for women. **High & Mighty,** 177 Brompton

Every fish seller should dress like this

Rd., caters to big and tall men who otherwise have trouble finding clothes that fit. If you're on the lookout for famous-name china at discount prices, make a point of stopping off at the **Reject China Shop,** 183 Brompton Rd., which carries dinnerware in fine bone china. Around the corner on Beauchamp Place are three other Reject China Shops, where you can find crystal, silverware, earthenware, figurines, and gift ideas. Be sure to pick up a store guide listing the locations and specialties of each shop.

Beauchamp Place is a short street with lots of shops lining both sides. Too bad it isn't made into a pedestrian lane—there's too much traffic whizzing by. To minimize the risk of being mowed down, let's cover shops on the left side first and then cross over to the other side as we work our way back to Brompton Road.

Janet Reger designs lingerie, using only silk. Her shop here at 2 Beauchamp Pl. is the ultimate for underclothing and nightwear, and many of her customers are men buying pretty underthings for the women in their lives. Silk pajamas cost £385, but you can spend up to £1,000 for a hand-painted nightdress and negligee combination.

Adele Davis sells traditional and conservative-looking clothing for women, while British fashion designer **Caroline Charles** showcases her evening wear and well-tailored outfits for women in her own shop named after her. **Whistles** caters to young, style-conscious women with interesting fashions at reasonable prices, and at **Paddy Campbell** you'll find the classic, traditional English look in women's wear. If money is no object, drop into **Bruce Oldfield** at 27 Beauchamp Pl. A top designer in evening wear and ladies' fashions, Oldfield creates dresses that are draped in interesting ways and which are often featured in such fashion magazines as *Vogue.*

When the coast is clear, cross the street and enter **Spaghetti,** 32 Beauchamp Pl. All the clothes here are by designer Nadia La Valle and include whimsical evening wear with lots of sequins. You can also have clothes custom-made here, including wedding dresses. **Jasper Conran** is the son of furniture-store magnate Terence Conran and has made a career of his own as a fashion designer. His new shop at 37 Beauchamp Pl. carries a good selection of his women's clothes, with a well-designed store to match. **Deliss** makes made-to-order boots and shoes in all variations of leather, as well as snake, lizard, crocodile, water buffalo, elephant, and ostrich. **Ken Lane** has a wonderful selection of costume jewelry, with fake-pearl necklaces and fake-diamond rings and necklaces.

The **Map House** specializes in antique maps, antique engravings, and some globes. Its prints, which start at a couple pounds, cover topographical, legal, sporting, and botanical subjects. **Monsoon** is a chain store with brightly colored ethnic clothing, much of it imported from India, while the **Beauchamp Place Shop** stocks a selection of British and European designer clothes for women. The look here is very classic and very English. **Valbridge** is the place to go for women's shirts, with approximately 15 different kinds of pure-silk blouses in 50 different colors, as well as a huge range of striped or solid-colored cotton shirts. If you don't find what you want, they'll even custom-make shirts. **Crochetta**

Flamboyant style at Spaghetti

specializes in hand-knitted sweaters, with unique designs incorporating such interesting things as leather, ribbons, sequins, and other materials. If you buy a sweater here, you're not likely to encounter someone else wearing the same thing.

Before continuing your stroll down Brompton Road you may want to look for nearby Montpelier Street, where you'll find the auction house of **Bonhams.** Auctioneers since 1793, it holds sales throughout the year, with special annual sales in crafts and Lalique. Other auctions are held several times weekly for such items as furniture, silver, carpets, watercolors, and jewelry. Stop by to see what's in the showroom, or check the *Daily Telegraph* on Monday.

Earle D. Vandekar, 138 Brompton Rd., is a family-owned antique shop established in 1913. It carries primarily ceramics, including English, continental, and Oriental. **John Keil,** 154 Brompton Rd., deals in fine English furniture from the 18th and 19th centuries, while **Alistair Sampson,** 156 Brompton Rd., specializes in 17th- and 18th-century English pottery and stocks country furniture, English brass, and decorative items. **Crane Kalman Gallery,** 178 Brompton Rd., is an art gallery selling mostly 20th-century British art with approximately six exhibitions a year. Represented are such artists as L.S. Lowry, Henry Moore, Ben Nicholson, Winifred Nicholson, and Sir Matthew Smith.

Sightseeing Suggestions

The **Apsley House,** located just east of Hyde Park corner tube station at 149 Piccadilly (tel. 499-5676), has already been described in the Piccadilly stroll but is also easily accessible from Knightsbridge. It was built in the 1770s and was acquired by the Duke of Wellington in 1817. With its paintings, silver, porcelain, and furniture, it's an interesting example of the life of the upper classes during the Regency period. It's closed on Monday and Friday but open the rest of the week from 10 a.m. to 5:30 p.m., except on Sunday when it's open from 2:30 to 6 p.m.

Hyde Park, which stretches south from Marble Arch to Hyde Park Corner and connects with Kensington Gardens to the west, was once the private hunting forest of Henry VIII. In 1625 the park was opened to the public and its Rotten Row (originally the "Route de Roi") became a favorite path for riders on horseback, as it still is today. Separating Hyde Park from Kensington Gardens is the **Serpentine Lake,** constructed in 1730 by Queen Caroline.

The **Brompton Oratory,** Brompton Road (tel. 589-4811), is a Roman Catholic church built in Italian baroque style. Opened in 1884, it was created by members of the Oxford Movement, Victorian intellectuals who converted to Catholicism. Its nave is the third widest in England after Westminster Cathedral and York Minster, and its organ has nearly 4,000 pipes. It's open daily from 7 a.m. to 8 p.m. and the closest underground station is South Kensington.

Also close to the South Kensington tube station and not far from Brompton Road are several great museums. The **Victoria and Albert Museum,** Cromwell Road (tel. 589-6371), is one of my favorite museums of all time and surely ranks as one of the best in the world in decorative and applied arts. Even people who normally shun museums should find sections of the Victoria and Albert fascinating, whether it be the furniture from various periods (including art deco), ceramics, Indian or Oriental arts, drawings, and paintings, or the National Art Library with one of the greatest collections of artists' illustrated books in the world. My favorite departments are the jewelry section displaying tiaras, rings, brooches, and necklaces set with huge diamonds, sapphires, and other precious stones, and the dress collection depicting how clothing has changed over the past 500 years. Even the building housing the museum is an exhibit in its own right, a fine Victorian monolith with parts dating back to the mid-19th century. Hours are 10 a.m. to 5:30 p.m., 2:30 to 5:30 p.m. on Sunday. Note that the Victoria and Albert is closed on Friday.

Just west of the Victoria and Albert are three more museums, all with the same hours: 10 a.m. to 6 p.m. Monday through Saturday and 2:30 to 6 p.m. on Sunday. The **Natural History Museum** (tel. 589-6323) has exhibitions of plants and animals with departments in zoology, entomology, paleontology, mineralogy, and botany. Especially popular are the displays covering dinosaurs, whales, and the evolution of man.

The **Geological Museum** (tel. 589-3444) tells the story of our planet Earth and also has a stunning collection of gemstones, while the **Science Museum** (tel. 589-3456) illustrates the history and development of science and industry.

Included are exhibits on cars, trains, space, medicine, agriculture, microprocessor technology, computers, nuclear physics, and a children's gallery with many working demonstrations.

Luncheon Spots and Drinking Establishments

If you're loaded down with parcels and can't walk another step, Harrods has five restaurants and five snack or bar areas. If you want formal dining, try the **Georgian Restaurant** on the fourth floor. A carvery, it serves a £13 lunch which includes a starter, a main course with choice of ribs of beef, roast lamb, fish filet, and others, and a cold buffet. It also offers a grand buffet for tea for £6.30. The **Green Man,** located in the basement of Harrods, is a pub serving lunch from 11:45 a.m. to 2:45 p.m. Traditional pies served with a chef's salad start at £4.

Another department-store restaurant is **Harveys at the Top,** located on the fifth floor of Harvey Nichols. It serves breakfast from 9:30 to 11:15 a.m. and lunch from 11:45 to 2:30 p.m., after which it serves an afternoon tea. There's an outside terrace where you can eat during warm weather, and the lunch menu includes Dover sole, poached salmon, grilled sirloin steaks, and daily specials from around £5. A cold buffet of roasted meats and quiche is offered for £7.60. If you want to come here for afternoon tea, you can have two scones with strawberry jam, clotted cream, and a pot of tea for £3.25.

In the basement of Joseph Pour La Maison, 16 Sloane St. (tel. 235-9869), is **L'Express Café** with a chic and sleek black-and-white interior. Open from 9:30 a.m. to 6 p.m. Monday through Saturday, it has a snack menu with such items as club sandwiches for £6.50, salads also for £6.50, and desserts like white-chocolate mousse with dark-chocolate sauce or chocolate truffle cake. There are also daily lunch specials and wine is served by the glass.

On Beauchamp Place are several fashionable restaurants where Sloane Rangers like to stop for a tête-a-tête over lunch. **Ménage à Trois,** 15 Beauchamp Pl. (tel. 589-4252), is so popular you need to book a reservation to eat here. Even Princess Di has been seen in this innovative restaurant specializing in one-course meals. Discarding the conventional three-course meal, this restaurant offers customers the opportunity to compose their own meals from a wide range of starters which can be eaten in any order or quantity. The menu is quite large and includes caviar, oysters, lobster cocktails, salads, pastas, seafood, and vegetarian dishes; most items fall between £4.50 and £6. Especially popular is Josephine's Delight, which includes creamed eggs with caviar, smoked salmon mousse with Scottish smoked salmon, and scallop mousse with diced scallops. Hot Pastry Parcels contain seafood or cheeses. Hours here are 11:30 a.m. to 3 p.m. and 7 p.m. to 12:15 a.m. Monday through Saturday.

San Lorenzo, 22 Beauchamp Pl. (tel. 584-1074), is also so popular that it requires a reservation. Filled with the trendy, this Italian restaurant has a menu that changes daily but always includes a selection of pastas and fish. Meals run about £20 per person, and hours are 12:30 to 3 p.m. and 7:30 to 11:30 p.m. Monday through Saturday.

If crowded, trendy restaurants don't appeal to you or you can't get a

reservation, **Sonny's Gourmet,** 39 Beauchamp Pl. (tel. 581-7012), is a modestly priced take-out place with seating for about 20 people. It has a small selection of sandwiches, homemade soup, quiche, and salads, as well as gâteau and cream cakes. It's open from 8:30 a.m. to 8 p.m. Monday to Saturday and from 10 a.m. to 5 p.m. on Sunday.

Richoux, 86 Brompton Rd. (tel. 584-8300), is a pâtisserie offering sandwiches, Welsh rarebit, vegetarian dishes, salads, fish and chips, chicken curry, English pies, and more, with most items less than £5. It also serves an afternoon tea for £4 with scones. Hours are 9 a.m. to 7 p.m. every day except Sunday when it opens at 10 a.m. and Wednesday when it closes at 8 p.m.

St. Quentin, 243 Brompton Rd. (tel. 589-8005), is a charming little French restaurant with fresh flowers on each table. The best deals are the set daily specials, which cost £10.50 for lunch and £14.20 for dinner. Hours here are 11 a.m. to 3 p.m. and 7 to 11:30 p.m. on Sunday, open the rest of the week from noon to 3 p.m. and 7 p.m. to midnight.

Not to be confused with St. Quentin is **Grill St. Quentin,** 136 Brompton Rd. (tel. 581-8377). A newer establishment sporting the bare, minimalist look, it's located in the basement and offers quick service with French food at reasonable prices. Open from noon to 3 p.m. and 7 p.m. to midnight daily, it serves filet steak, lamb cutlets, Dover sole, veal chop, couscous from North Africa, and duck, with main courses averaging about £7. There's a separate wine bar where a glass of house wine starts at £1.40.

If you spent all your pounds on shopping, don't despair. Scrape together all your pence and you'll be able to afford at least a salad, soup, or dessert at **The Stockpot,** 6 Basil St. (tel. 589-8627). Located just off Sloane Street kitty-corner from Yohji Yamamoto, this simple restaurant with wooden booths and chairs offers a wide variety of inexpensive dishes. The menu changes daily but may include spaghetti, grilled minute steak, trout, omelets, chicken Kiev, beef Stroganoff, or pork chop and apple sauce. Most main courses cost between £1.40 and £2.70, with wine by the glass available for 85 pence. It's open from 8 a.m. to 11 p.m. Monday to Saturday and from noon to 10 p.m. on Sunday.

Next door is **Basil's Wine Bar,** 8 Basil St. (tel. 581-3311), located in the basement of the Basil Street Hotel. Candles stuck in old wine bottles give this friendly establishment a warm, cozy glow. More than 200 kinds of wine from all over the world are on the wine list, with about 20 wines offered by the glass. Wine by the glass starts at £1.25. Food counters are laid out with tantalizing hot and cold dishes. The selection changes daily, but there's always at least one pasta dish, a beef dish, vegetarian selection, six different kinds of salads, and cheeses, with most dishes less than £3. It's closed on Sunday but open from noon to 3 p.m. Monday through Saturday and from 5:30 to 11 p.m. Monday through Friday.

Pubs and Pub Lunches

The Gloucester, 187 Sloane St. (tel. 235-0298), offers hot food with waitress service in a room at the back of the pub. Filled with shoppers and tourists, it's

open from 8 a.m. to 8:30 p.m. throughout the day for food. Recommended are the steak-and-kidney pie with potatoes and two vegetables for £3.30, the ham with mixed salad and coleslaw for £5, or the roast beef with mixed salad and coleslaw for £5.70.

The **Crown & Sceptre,** 132 Brompton Rd. (tel. 589-1615), observes the usual pub hours for serving alcohol but stays open throughout the day for coffee and tea. It offers hot food for both lunch and dinner, which may include steak pie, lasagne, salads, quiche, and other daily specials. Most dishes run about £3.30.

Bunch of Grapes, 207 Brompton Rd. (tel. 589-4944), is a Victorian-style pub established in 1875. Only a few minutes' walk from Harrods, it features etched-glass mirrors, wooden screens, ornamental carving, and ceiling fans. Hot fare is served for lunch, while cold dishes are available for lunch or dinner. The menu changes daily but may include steak-and-kidney pie, curries, casseroles, or chili con carne.

The **Enterprise,** 35 Walton St. (tel. 584-8858), is a neighborhood pub located on quiet Walton Street. It offers homemade food "like Mom used to make." The menu varies but might include a quiche, steak-and-kidney pie, and a ham or a roast. Prices for dishes are generally less than £3.

Afternoon Tea

In addition to **Richoux, Harveys at the Top,** and the **Georgian Restaurant,** described above, other places serving tea include the **Terrace Bar,** located on the fourth floor of Harrods. Tea time is between 3:30 and 4:30 p.m., except Wednesday when it's until 6 p.m. and Saturday when it's until 5:30 p.m.; the price is £7 for finger sandwiches, scones, and tea.

An elegant and relaxed setting for afternoon tea is offered by the **Park Room** of the Hyde Park Hotel on Knightsbridge Road (tel. 235-2000). With views of Hyde Park, it serves tea to the accompaniment of a piano from 3:45 to 6 p.m. Monday through Friday and 4 to 6 p.m. on weekends. For £7.40 you receive an assortment of finger sandwiches, toasted English muffins, and scones with Devonshire clotted cream and jams, homemade cakes and pastries, and tea.

Bendicks, 195 Sloane St. (tel. 235-4749), is famous for its chocolates but there's a small tea room here as well where you can enjoy coffee or a meal. Afternoon tea is served from 3 p.m. and includes scones and a choice of pastry or cake from the trolley for £5.20. You can also come here for breakfast, snacks, or lunch. Hours are 8:30 a.m. to 7:30 p.m. Monday through Saturday (to 8:30 p.m. on Wednesday) and 10:30 a.m.. to 6:30 p.m. on Sunday.

FULHAM ROAD

Fulham Road is essentially a continuation of Brompton Road. Beginning in an area known as South Kensington near the South Kensington tube station, it winds toward the southwest through Chelsea all the way to Putney and close to the River Thames.

If you're exploring Fulham as a continuation of the Brompton stroll, simply follow Brompton Road as it swings to the south through a residential area until it abruptly ends and becomes Fulham Road. If you're arriving by underground at the South Kensington station, take the Pelham Street exit, turn left out of the station, and follow Pelham Street to its end. To the left is the last stretch of Brompton Road, with such trendy clothing shops as **Plantation,** at 270 Brompton Rd., which showcases the fashions of Japanese fashion designer Issey Miyake, and **Katharine Hamnet,** at 264 Brompton Rd.

At the junction of Brompton and Fulham Roads is the **Conran Shop,** the most exclusive of the Conran group of stores, which includes Habitat and Heals. Named after owner Terence Conran, who personally selects everything in this store, the Conran Shop sells everything for the well-designed, elegant home, including furniture, fabrics, lighting, bed linen, bathroom accessories, kitchenware, china, and cutlery. Everything is very modern, and prices are high.

Walking down Fulham Road, you'll see **Whittards** on the left at 111 Fulham Rd., which recently celebrated its 100th anniversary of selling tea leaves and coffee beans. Clothing for men by Japanese fashion designer Rei Kawakubo is on display at her shop **Comme des Garçons,** followed by the **Watch Gallery** at 129 Fulham Rd. with wristwatches by Cartier, Rolex, Ebel, Hublot, Heuer, and others. **Oggetti,** 133 Fulham Rd., is a gift shop in which everything for sale has been selected on the basis of its artistic design. There are Braun alarm clocks, sleek pocket knives, scissors, letter openers, lighters, coffee pots, wallets, pens, and chess sets, to name just a few of the items on display.

Divertimenti, 139–141 Fulham Rd., sells cooking utensils and tableware, while **J.K. Hill,** 151 Fulham Rd., is a crafts shop displaying the talents of 180 potters. For sale are such handmade pottery as earthenware dishes, jewelry, tea pots, vases, lamp bases, figures, and bowls. **Ritva Westenius** has a shop at 153C Fulham Rd. and is best known for her re-creations of the Edwardian look and for her hand-beaded dresses and wedding gowns. **Laura Ashley** sells her home furnishings and women's and children's pretty dresses and pinafores at 157 Fulham Rd.

Pelham Galleries, 163–165 Fulham Rd., is the first of many antique shops on Fulham Road, several of which are introduced toward the end of this stroll. Dealing in continental and English furniture and works of art, Pelham Galleries also has stock that includes some early musical instruments, clocks, and Oriental lacquerware. **Souleiado,** 171 Fulham Rd., specializes in fabrics and accessories from southern France that are made from original wood blocks more than 200 years old. Designs are as bright and sunny as the part of the world from which they come. In addition to its shop on South Molton Street, **Butler & Wilson** has another jewelry shop at 189 Fulham Rd. It sells costume jewelry only, primarily paste jewelry with a glittering glass cut to look like diamonds.

Across the street from Butler & Wilson is **Monsoon,** a women's boutique specializing in ethnic clothing, mainly from India. Next to Monsoon is the **Constant Sale Shop,** which belongs to a group of stores that includes Basile,

Armani, Krizia, Katharine Hamnet, Valentino, and Comme des Garçons—and which receives the end of the lines from each of these stores, selling them at greatly discounted prices. Sorry, fellows, this shop sells women's clothes only. **Tatters,** 74 Fulham Rd., sells off-the-peg and made-to-measure wedding dresses, ballgowns, and cocktail and dinner dresses, 90% of which are designed in-house. Two shops in one are at 78 Fulham Rd.: **Night Owls** has lingerie and beachwear, and **Great Expectations** has designer maternity clothes.

After walking past Sumner Place and Brompton Hospital, on your right side you'll find **Argenta** at 82 Fulham Rd., which sells contemporary silver jewelry from Denmark as well as the exclusive work of British goldsmiths. After Argenta **Michael Lipitch,** at 98 Fulham Rd., is the first of several antique shops. It carries top-quality English furniture, prints, and watercolors from the 18th century. Don't let its small appearance deceive you—altogether there are five floors of showrooms.

Clifford Wright, 104–106 Fulham Rd., specializes in 18th-century and early Regency furniture, gilt furniture, and 18th-century mirrors. Also dealing in 18th-century English furniture is **Richard Courtney,** 112–114 Fulham Rd., this time specializing in early walnut furniture from the Queen Anne period. Finally, one more store with fine 18th-century English furniture is **Apter-Fredericks,** 265–267 Fulham Rd., which has been a family business since it first opened in 1946.

Divertimenti: Good browsing for cooks

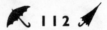
Sightseeing Suggestions

The **Brompton Oratory,** the **Victoria and Albert Museum,** the **Natural History Museum,** the **Geological Museum,** and the **Science Museum** are all close to Fulham Road and the South Kensington tube station. For more information on these attractions, turn to the Brompton stroll sightseeing section.

Luncheon Spots and Drinking Establishments

Walton's (tel. 584-5297) is located on the corner of Walton Street and Draycott Avenue, not far from the Conran Shop. With its elegant dining hall and low lighting, it offers a pleasant respite from the traffic of Fulham Road. Of great value is its set lunch for £12, which gives a choice of an appetizer, principal dish, and dessert. The main menu offers seafood, veal, lamb, calves' liver, and chicken selections. Hours are 12:30 to 2:30 p.m. and 7:30 to 11:30 p.m. Monday to Saturday. Hours are slightly shorter on Sunday: 12:30 to 2 p.m. and 7:30 to 10:30 p.m.

Not far away is Pond Place, where at no. 2A you'll find **Drakes** (tel. 584-4555). Located in a basement, this English restaurant with heavy wooden ceiling beams, brick floor, and open wine cellar looks as though it belongs in a baron's rustic country home. Chefs prepare trout, game pie, venison, rack of lamb, or fish behind a wall of glass, so you can watch them at their work. I recommend one of the one-course lunches, which might typically be a club sandwich, vegetable tartlet, or a shoal of shellfish. Prices start at around £5 and include a glass of wine and coffee. Hours here are noon to 2:30 p.m. and 6:30 to 11 p.m. Monday to Saturday and 12:30 to 3 p.m. and 7 to 10:30 p.m. on Sunday.

San Frediano, 62 Fulham Rd. (tel. 584-8375), is a lively, friendly, and popular Italian restaurant. One or more of the several owners are always present, and regular customers are greeted with much fanfare. The food here is creative and interesting, and includes trout, steak, veal escalope, and daily specials. There's a minimum charge of £5, but most meals average £10 to £15. Closed on Sunday, it's open the rest of the week from 12:30 to 2:15 p.m. and 7:15 to 11:15 p.m.

The **Queen's Elm,** 241 Fulham Rd. (tel. 352-9157), is a pub serving hot lunches, with most dishes costing less than £2. The menu changes but may include baked potato with various fillings, shepherd's pie, casseroles, and curries. Live music is provided several evenings during the week.

KENSINGTON

Serving as a thoroughfare during Roman times, Kensington has been bustling ever since. In the 19th century, villas for the rich were built here, followed by apartment blocks constructed in late-Victorian and Edwardian styles. Today these pleasant residential areas intermingle with Kensington's fashion bou-

tiques and antique shops. Young people come to Kensington for its avant-garde fashion and for its two clothing markets, Hyper Hyper and Kensington Market, both of which sell the creations of young, aspiring fashion designers. Antique lovers come for a stroll along Kensington Church Street, a winding lane with a scattering of specialty shops selling everything from antique clocks to old weapons and art deco. Kensington also has its share of chain stores and a couple department stores.

Rather than bask in its past and present glory, however, Kensington has striven to stay abreast of the times by changing its appearance and atmosphere. In the past few years Kensington has been in a state of flux as old establishments shut down and new businesses move in. Buildings have been torn down, Barkers department store expanded and changed its name to House of Fraser, and there's even talk of erecting a new shopping area with a piazza similar to that of Covent Garden. At any rate, Kensington is a shopping area to be reckoned with, giving London's other shopping regions stiff competition.

A KENSINGTON STROLL

Kensington's two most important shopping streets are Kensington High Street and Kensington Church Street. Let's begin this stroll at the closest tube station, High Street Kensington. Passing through a tiny shopping arcade, you'll find yourself on Kensington High Street, a busy road with lots of traffic.

To your left are a string of chain stores, interesting only if you haven't visited them in Knightsbridge or the West End. Go to **Benetton, Next,** or **Woodhouse** if you're looking for trendy and youthful fashion. **C&A** sells reasonably priced clothing for the entire family, while at **Boots** you can pick up inexpensive cosmetics or have a prescription filled. **W. H. Smith** or **Ryman** will supply you with stationery, and at the **Body Shop** is a line of products for your skin, hair, and body. **Mothercare** sells clothing, toys, and products for infants, children, mothers, and mothers-to-be. Two good toy shops are the **Early Learning Centre** at 225 Kensington High St., which specializes in toys for children under 8 years old, and **Young World** at 229 Kensington High St., which has a good selection of children's books as well.

Retrace your steps along Kensington High Street past the tube station, where you'll immediately find **Marks & Spencer** on the right side of the street. This store is a branch of the famous department store located on Oxford Street in the West End. Marks & Spencer is known for its low prices, particularly for clothing and underwear. Next comes **British Home Stores,** a chain of small department stores specializing in clothing for the family and housewares. If you need yet another department store, **House of Fraser** stocks clothing and items for the home, including china, glass, and kitchenware. Formerly called Barkers, it changed its name in 1986 when it expanded and reopened as an almost entirely new store.

If you continue walking toward Kensington Gardens on the right side of the street, you'll come to **Kensington Market,** at 49–53 Kensington High St.

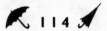
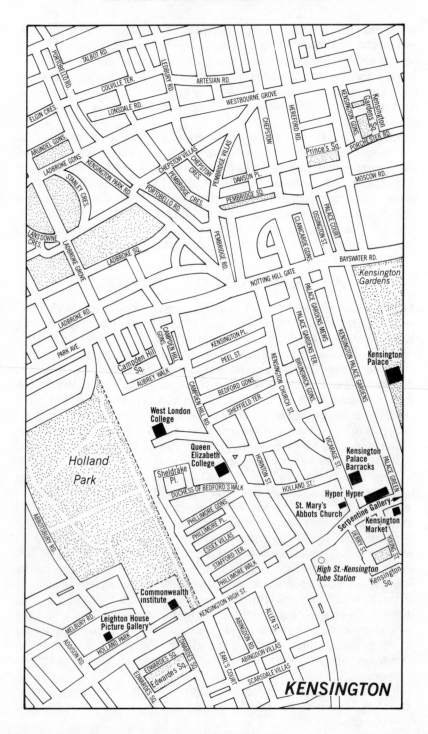

KENSINGTON

Opened in the 1960s, this market with about 90 stalls sells predominantly fashion and accessories for the young. The stallholders here are also young, and many of them design the clothes they sell. Styles range from the outrageous to designer imitations, and most items are original and unusual. If you're looking for a dress made out of a balloon-like stretchy material or clothes of rubber, this is the place for you. Also for sale are secondhand clothes, leather coats and pants, hats, jeans, and T-shirts. The stalls wind throughout an old building in a maze of corridors and it's easy to get lost, but wandering here is akin to being Alice in Wonderland. Lots to see.

Almost directly across the street is **Hyper Hyper,** which is much more upmarket and more expensive. Statues of Greek goddesses mark the entrance to this trendy clothing mecca with its stalls of fashion and accessories by young designers. This is one of the best places in London to see the latest in what's happening in the English fashion scene. Definitely worth a browse even if you don't buy anything.

Upon exiting Hyper Hyper, turn right and you'll find **Che Guevara** next door. On the ground floor is inexpensive casual wear for young people, while the basement is divided into individual stalls with vendors selling jewelry, clothing, and shoes. Then comes **Next,** an innovative chain store selling fashionable and affordable clothing, followed by **Tower Records** with its records and cassettes.

At the next intersection where you'll see St. Mary Abbots Church, turn right onto Kensington Church Street. Our first shop here is **Crabtree & Evelyn,** 6 Kensington Church St., with its beautifully packaged soaps, bath oil, shampoo, jam preserves, mustard, chutney, and toiletry accessories. **Monsoon,**

Hyper Hyper: The name says it all at this avant-garde fashion forum

26–28 Kensington Church St., is a chain store specializing in ethnic clothing for women, with many fashions imported from India.

Continuing uphill on Kensington Church Street, you'll find a number of antique and curio shops. Interspersed with Victorian and Edwardian houses, the shops run the entire stretch of this pleasant, winding street all the way to Notting Hill Gate. Of note are the following shops, listed in the order you'll encounter them.

Raffety, 34 Kensington Church St., deals in 17th- and 18th-century clocks, including wall clocks, longcases, and bracket clocks. **Michael C. German** and **Simon Castle,** 38B Kensington Church St., are two shops in one locale. Although the premises are small, this delightful establishment is packed with antique arms, armor, walking sticks, and treen. *Treen* is a 15th-century word meaning "turned from the tree" and refers to wooden objects ranging from candlesticks to wassail bowls. There are about 500 walking sticks in stock dating from 1680 to 1900, and no two are alike.

Pruskin Gallery, 73 Kensington Church St., specializes in art deco and art nouveau objects and furniture, while **Church Street Galleries,** 77 Kensington Church St., carries 18th-century mirrors and English furniture, especially walnut pieces from the Queen Anne period. **Haslam & Whiteway,** 105 Kensington Church St., has a curious mixture of furniture and objects dating from Gothic Revival through the Arts and Crafts Movement, roughly 1850 to 1920.

Green's Antique Galleries, 117 Kensington Church St., is a curio shop selling an eclectic mix of Victorian and Edwardian jewelry, silver, porcelain, old watches, cigarette cases, and old period clothing. More art deco and art nouveau can be found at **John Jesse & Irini Laski,** 160 Kensington Church St., a small but beautiful shop where top-quality jewelry, bronze and ivory figures, English silver, glass, clocks, and decorative objects are elegantly displayed. **Philip & Bernard Dombey,** 174 Kensington Church St., specializes in French antique clocks from the early 18th century to the end of the 19th century, including mantel, bracket, picture, and carriage clocks.

From here it's only a few minutes' walk to the Notting Hill Gate tube station. If it's a Saturday and still early, you should continue walking north to **Portobello Road,** where you'll find one of London's best and most famous outdoor antique markets.

SIGHTSEEING SUGGESTIONS

Kensington Gardens stretches to the east of Kensington Church Street and offers a pleasant escape from the shopping crowds. On the grounds is **Kensington Palace** (tel. 937-9561), first built in 1605, acquired as a royal residence by King William III and Queen Mary II in 1689 and redesigned by Sir Christopher Wren. Although most of the palace is private, you can visit the State Apartments from 9 a.m. to 4:15 p.m. every day except Sunday when it's open from 1 to 4:15 p.m. On display are the former rooms of William and Mary, along with

On the Portobello Road

furniture and artwork. Especially interesting is Mary's bedroom with its fine 17th-century furniture.

Also in Kensington Gardens is the **Serpentine Gallery** (tel. 402-6075), with exhibitions of contemporary art. Telephone beforehand to inquire about current shows and open hours.

If parks and gardens are your fancy, you might want to take in **Holland Park** also. Here you'll find a formal flower garden with box hedges and statues, and peacocks roam freely throughout the grounds. Unfortunately, there's not much left of Holland House, which was largely destroyed during World War II.

If you're interested in houses, therefore, your best bet is to visit nearby **Leighton House,** 12 Holland Park Rd. (tel. 602-3316), one of London's most unique residences. Although the exterior with its red brick looks like any other house, the interior is a blend of Victorian and Moorish styles, designed by Lord Leighton, who was one of the most successful artists during the Victorian Period. The domed Arab Hall contains 13th- to 17th-century Islamic tiles. Hours here are 11 a.m. to 5 p.m. Monday through Saturday.

Another fascinating home open to the public is the **Linley Sambourne House,** 18 Stafford Terrace (tel. 994-1019). The residence of Edward Linley Sambourne (1845–1910), who was a *Punch* cartoonist, it contains furniture, paintings, and other art from the Victorian period. It's open March through

October only on Wednesday from 10 a.m. to 4 p.m. and on Sunday from 2 to 5 p.m.

Finally, the **Commonwealth Institute,** 230 Kensington High St. (tel. 603-4535), is dedicated to the Commonwealth, with exhibitions on its peoples, cultures, customs, and economics. Each country in the Commonwealth has a display. Hours are 10 a.m. to 5:30 p.m. Monday to Saturday and 2 to 5 p.m. on Sunday.

LUNCHEON SPOTS AND DRINKING ESTABLISHMENTS

Located atop an office building and spreading out over Marks & Spencer, the **Roof Garden** comes as a remarkable surprise. Finished in 1936, it's a rooftop garden with nearly 1½ acres of land. Soil five feet deep supports a Tudor rose garden, a Spanish-style garden, Tudor stone arches, wisteria, sweet peas, fruit trees, and flowers. It's hard to believe you're in the middle of London, not to mention the fact that you're six stories above the ground. A restaurant with large windows and terrace dining serves lunch only, and you have your pick of either a two-course set meal for £10.50 or a three-course set lunch for £12.50. The menu changes daily, but favorites have been breast of chicken with lobster-curry sauce and grilled trout with dill butter. Hours are 12:30 to 3:30 p.m. Monday through Friday, and it's best to make a reservation. You can also come for a Sunday brunch buffet from 12:30 to 4 p.m. Although the address for this restaurant is 99 Kensington High St. (tel. 937-7994), entrance is actually on Derry Street which runs between House of Fraser and British Home Stores. A sign for the restaurant is posted; take the elevator up to the sixth floor.

For more down-to-earth dining, try **Maggie Jones's,** 6 Old Court Pl. (tel. 937-6462). It's located just a minute's walk from the Kensington Church Street and Kensington High Street intersection. A tiny, cozy restaurant serving English food, it looks like a kitchen in a country farmhouse. The decor is rustic with heavy and unfinished wooden tables, wooden booths, and sawdust on the floor. The à la carte menu includes grilled trout, fish pie, steak, steak-and-kidney pie, chicken-and-artichoke pie, rack of lamb, rabbit-and-mustard casserole, duck, and chicken. The average cost of a meal is about £20 per person, but you can eat more cheaply if you opt for one of the set courses for £7.40. It's open from 12:30 to 2:30 p.m. and 7 to 11:30 p.m. Monday through Saturday and from 7 to 11:30 p.m. on Sunday.

The Ark, 35 Kensington High St. (tel. 937-4294), has been serving good French food at modest prices for more than 20 years. Its entrance is just off a tiny side street almost directly in front of Hyper Hyper. With a friendly staff serving such specialties as grilled rainbow trout, roast baby chicken, roast rack of lamb, veal escalope, or peppered filet, it charges about £6 for most courses. A good discovery in the middle of busy Kensington, it's open from noon to 3 p.m. and 7 to 11:30 p.m. Monday through Saturday and from 7 to 11 p.m. on Sunday.

Wheeler's, 17 Kensington High St. (tel. 937-1443), is located across the

street from the Royal Garden Hotel. Part of the Wheeler's seafood restaurant chain which was established back in 1856, its menu includes oysters for about £7.10 per half dozen, lobster dishes starting at £15, scallops, sole, and trout. Hours here are noon to 2:30 p.m. and 6 to 10:45 p.m. every day except Sunday when it's open from noon to 2:30 p.m. and 7 to 10 p.m.

The **Catherine Wheel,** 23 Kensington Church St. (tel. 937-3259), is a Victorian-style pub with a small selection of hot dishes for lunch. The menu varies but may include hot pies, lasagne, salads, quiche, and sandwiches, with most items costing £2 to £3. It's open Monday through Friday from 11 a.m. to 3 p.m. and 5:30 to 11 p.m., on Saturday from 7 to 11 p.m., and on Sunday from noon to 2 p.m. and 7 to 10:30 p.m.

AFTERNOON TEA

The **Garden Café,** located in the Royal Garden Hotel on Kensington High Street (tel. 937-8000), offers a great view of Kensington Gardens. Tea is served from 3 to 5:30 p.m. and you have your choice of just tea and scones for £4.10 or pastries, sandwiches, scones, and tea for £6.30. The Garden Café also serves meals throughout the day and an adjacent bar dispenses cocktails to the thirsty.

PART TWO

THE ULTIMATE LONDON SHOPPING SPREE

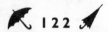

Queen Victoria and the gryphon mark the entrance to the City

CHAPTER IV

LONDON'S SHOPS

The shops below represent the best that London has to offer. If you're making a special trip to a particular store, it's always best to telephone beforehand to make sure the shop has not changed its hours, moved, or shut down. Newer, avant-garde clothing shops have a tendency to open and shut with great frequency, but even centuries-old establishments have been forced to shut their doors, unable to compete with the larger chain stores. Although I've listed examples of goods and their prices for most stores, you should use these only as an example of what's available. Prices do change, and they usually go up instead of down.

ANTIQUES

London would not be the same without its antique shops. After all, what could be more English than Chippendale, Hepplewhite, or Sheraton period furniture? What would London be without its antique flea markets, its elegant, antique furniture shops, its countless family-run businesses spread throughout the city? The fun thing about shopping for antiques in London is that there are objects of desire to suit anyone's budget, whether it's Victorian cutlery for a few pounds or a rare piece of 18th-century English furniture for half a million pounds. Even if you don't end up purchasing very much, you can learn a lot about the history of England and the life of the times by deciphering the form, style, and function of various antiques.

Although antique shops are found in all corners of London, there are several streets with more than their fair share of excellent shops selling a variety of antiques. Among them are Pimlico Road, Bond Street, Kensington Church Street, Fulham Road and New King's Road. Policies on forms of payment vary: many shops do not accept credit cards but will take personal checks once they've cleared the banks. In addition, all the shops listed below will take care of shipping or air-transport arrangements.

If you're an amateur antique buff, it's best either to stick to the reputable dealers listed in this book or to confine your purchases to items you'd be happy with even if they turn out to be fakes. If you don't know what to look for, it could be very difficult to distinguish between a genuine antique and a reproduction piece made to look like an antique. While you shouldn't have any problems in this regard when dealing with members of the British Antique Dealers Association, stallholders at flea markets demand a certain amount of healthy suspicion. I personally found stallholders to be quite honest and often very knowledgeable and engaging, but I still don't know whether that art deco mantel clock I bought is actually more modern than I was led to believe. However, at £30 it was something I decided I couldn't live without regardless of its age.

The shops listed below deal primarily in antique furniture, although many of them also carry decorative objects such as vases, mirrors, candelabras, and other antique items. I've also listed several indoor antique markets open throughout the week where you can look for a wide variety of antiques ranging from walking sticks to paintings and jewelry.

If, however, your interest in antiques goes beyond furniture or markets into specific collector's items, refer to the appropriate category. Antique prints, jewelry, silver, porcelain, portrait miniatures, music boxes, rugs, clocks, and glass, for example, are all important enough to warrant their own headings and are handled later in this book. Similarly, because an antique is defined as anything more than 100 years old, shops selling art deco and art nouveau are listed under their own separate heading. Remember, too, that London's many auction houses have regular sales of antiques in hundreds of categories, from furniture to glass, paintings, carpets, dolls, coins, and more. Refer to the auction section for more information.

Generally speaking, English furniture sold in London's finer shops stems from the 18th century. The 18th century is further divided into various decades and periods, during which times furniture often shared common characteristics. Since furniture is frequently described according to the reigning monarch of the time or by the style of the most famous cabinetmakers, the English have only to recall their history lessons to know what is meant by Queen Anne or Early Georgian periods. For the rest of us, however, here's a short rundown of the various styles and periods in English furniture starting at the beginning of the 18th century:

1702–1714 (Queen Anne Period): Walnut is the favored wood, with styles distinguished by simple claw-and-ball feet, cabriole legs, and inlay.

1714–1745 (Early Georgian Period): This period incorporates the reign of George I and part of the reign of George II. The Queen Anne style was further elaborated, with more claw-and-ball feet and the use of eagle- or lion-head carvings. Although walnut was still widely used, mahogany was introduced and became very popular.

1745–1770 (Chippendale Period): Named after England's most famous cabinetmaker, Thomas Chippendale, who designed furniture

taken from rococo, revived Gothic, and Chinese sources. Characteristics of furniture from this period include square legs and lavish carvings, with mahogany the predominant wood used. Furniture from the late 1700s is also named after George III, who began his rule in 1760.

1770–1795 (Adam and Hepplewhite Styles): Architect Robert Adam and cabinetmaker George Hepplewhite were inspired by the classics. Mahogany, satinwood, sycamore, and other light woods became fashionable, sideboards were introduced, and French styles were anglicized.

1790–1810 (Sheraton Style): Thomas Sheraton was a furniture designer who published *Cabinet Maker and Upholsterer's Drawing Book.* Inlay was widely used, but carving was done more sparingly. Characteristics of this period include square-backed chairs, drop-leaf sofa tables, and pedestal dining tables.

1811–1820 (Regency Period): Although part of the 19th century, the Regency period is often represented in fine antique shops. Strictly speaking, Regency refers to styles prevalent from 1811 to 1820 when the Prince of Wales was regent. To the annoyance of history-buff sticklers, however, the term today is often loosely applied to mean anything designed between 1800 and the accession of Queen Victoria in 1837. At any rate, the Regency style incorporates Greek, Egyptian, and Chinese motifs, with lots of brass inlay and gilt. Rosewood became a favorite wood.

INDOOR ANTIQUE MARKETS

The indoor antique markets listed below have regular hours throughout the week, making them in many respects just like any store. The difference, however, lies in the variety of items offered, since individual stallholders usually specialize in a certain type of object. Thus you may have as diversified a range of antiques as dolls, jewelry, porcelain, silver, furniture, and paintings, all under one roof. Be aware, however, that stallholders operate independently of one another—most accept credit cards, but some do not.

In addition to the indoor markets listed here, there are a number of antique flea markets in London, each of which is held usually one or two days a week. Because overhead is low, these markets offer some of the best values around, besides being just plain fun. Among the best-known antique markets are Portobello Road, Camden Lock, Camden Passage, and Bermondsey Antique Market. For more information on these flea markets, refer to "Markets," below.

There are also special antique fairs held annually throughout the city. The most famous is the Chelsea Antiques Fair, held two times a year, in March and September, at the Chelsea Old Town Hall on King's Road. At the high end of the market is the Grosvenor House Antiques Fair held in June at the Grosvenor House Hotel on Park Lane. The top dealers display

their best pieces here, and prices are expectedly high. For more information on these and other antique fairs, be sure to pick up a copy of "Events in London," a free pamphlet issued monthly and available at tourist offices. In addition, "Time Out," a weekly magazine that tells of events being staged throughout London, lists antique fairs.

ANTIQUARIUS
135 King's Rd., SW3 (tel. 351-5353)
Underground Station: *Sloane Square*
Hours: *Monday through Saturday from 10 a.m. to 6 p.m.*

This antique market contains more than 150 stalls selling a wide range of goods from clocks and jewelry to china, silver, prints, books, brass, and '20s and '30s period clothing. This is a good place to pick up old lace. The atmosphere here is relaxed and somewhat bohemian. There are also several contemporary fashion stores under the same roof, including an Edina Ronay shop with her handknitted sweaters and a David Fielden shop with his made-to-measure wedding dresses and evening gowns.

BOND STREET ANTIQUE CENTRE
124 New Bond St., W1 (tel. 351-5353)
Underground Station: *Bond Street*
Hours: *Monday through Friday from 10 a.m. to 5:45 p.m., on Saturday to 4 p.m.*

The 44 shops in this antique market on swanky Bond Street are predictably top-scale. Items for sale include antique jewelry, porcelain, silver, watches, portrait miniatures, watercolors, and Oriental objects. A silver candlestick holder from Dublin dating from around 1770 was going for £1,800, but there are plenty of items for much less. It's certainly worth a browse, especially if you're visiting the shops on Bond Street.

THE CHELSEA ANTIQUE MARKET
245–253 King's Rd., SW3 (tel. 352-5689)
Underground Station: *Sloane Square*
Hours: *Monday through Saturday from 10 a.m. to 6 p.m.*

Strictly speaking this market falls more into the flea market category, since most of the items for sale are not old enough to be classified as antiques. It claims to be the oldest indoor market in all of London, and judging by the looks of things, it probably is. Opened in the mid-1960s, its 100 stalls offer a rather chaotic mixture of both junk and treasure, including jewelry, prints, used clothing, records, original movie posters, sheet music, glass, and an assortment of bric-a-brac.

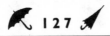
CHENIL GALLERIES
181–183 King's Rd., SW3 (tel. 351-5353)
Underground Station: *Sloane Square*
Hours: *Monday through Saturday from 10 a.m. to 6 p.m.*

Under the same management as both Antiquarius and the Bond Street Antique Centre, Chenil Galleries, in the heart of Chelsea, has dealers specializing in art deco, art nouveau, books, carpets, clocks, dolls and toys, furniture, glass, jewelry, paintings, porcelain, prints, silver, and scientific instruments. The dealers here are reputable and serious, and merchandise is of very good quality.

FURNITURE CAVE
533 King's Rd., SW10 (tel. 352-4229)
Underground Station: *Fulham Broadway*
Hours: *Monday through Saturday from 10 a.m. to 6 p.m.*

Furniture Cave is different from the markets listed so far in that it is basically a huge, warehouse-like building filled with antique and decorative furniture from England, the continent, and even the Orient. About 20 antique furniture dealers are housed here and the stock changes constantly. I find it a great place to browse for items ranging from past centuries to almost yesterday. How about a huge French birdcage costing £3,025? With stock ranging from a mid-Victorian hardwood library stepladder to a French art deco desk carved in the shape of a half moon, you can pick up reproduction and antique pine furniture, pedestals, sofas, tables, cabinets, four-poster beds, and Oriental vases. Only some of the dealers accept credit cards, but most will arrange for the shipment of purchases abroad.

GRAYS ANTIQUE MARKETS
58 Davies St. and 1–7 Davies Mews, W1 (tel. 629-7034)
Underground Station: *Bond Street*
Hours: *Monday through Friday from 10 a.m. to 6 p.m.*

Grays is actually two separate antique markets under the same management. Grays at 58 Davies St. is easily visible from Oxford Street. A 30-second walk around the corner is Grays, at 1–7 Davies Mews.

Together, the Grays markets are among the best and most charming of the indoor antique markets. Both are located in attractive Victorian buildings and a total of 170 stalls sell a variety of top-quality antiques from around the world. For sale are Oriental works of art, jewelry, silver, glass, porcelain, British watercolors, snuff boxes, paperweights, arms and armor, scientific instruments, antiquarian books, watches, clocks, canes, antique lace, Edwardian toys, art deco, and art nouveau. Oriental antiques and arms and armor are especially well represented.

ANCIENT

ALISTAIR SAMPSON
156 Brompton Rd., SW3 (tel. 589-5272)
Underground Station: *Knightsbridge*
Hours: *Monday through Friday from 9:30 a.m. to 5:30 p.m., on Saturday*
by appointment
Credit Cards: *AE, MC, V*

Established in the mid-1960s and catering to a large American clientele, Alistair Sampson specializes in 17th- and 18th-century pottery, English country furniture (especially oak), English brass, needlework, and decorative items. Prices start at around £100 for a piece of pottery, about £1,100 for primitive paintings or 18th-century brass candleholders.

ANTIQUUS
90–92 Pimlico Rd., SW1 (tel. 730-8681)
Underground Station: *Sloane Square*
Hours: *Monday through Friday from 10 a.m. to 5:30 p.m. (on Thursday*
to 8 p.m.), on Saturday to 1 p.m.
Credit Cards: *None*

The shop's premises here are strikingly beautiful, with brick walls, wooden floors, subdued lighting, and classical music playing inobtrusively in the background. One look around tells you that the objects on display are both expensive and exclusive. Specializing in European works of art and pictures from the classical period to 1600, this shop sells furniture, paintings, pottery, early Christian crosses, Roman sculptures, Greek helmets dating from about the 5th century B.C., textiles, tapestries, and Renaissance jewelry. A 17th-century walnut Umbrian table was priced at £16,500.

CHRISTOPHER GIBBS
118 New Bond St., W1 (tel. 629-2008)
Underground Station: *Bond Street*
Hours: *Monday through Friday from 9:30 a.m. to 5:30 p.m.*

This is not the kind of place where you just drop in. Customers tend to be millionaires, many of them referred here by museums. Dealing in Greek and Roman antiquities as well as unusual English antiques, owner Christopher Gibbs is recognized as one of the top in his field, selling statues, busts, furniture, and paintings. A cabinet made for Lord Charlemont was listed at £400,000.

ROBIN SYMES
94 Jermyn St., SW1 (tel. 930-5300)
Underground Station: *Piccadilly Circus*
Hours: *Monday through Friday from 10 a.m. to 5:30 p.m.*
Credit Cards: *None*

This small shop on Jermyn Street is the sister shop to the more expensive Robin Symes at 3 Ormond Yard, which sells mainly to museums. The Jermyn Street shop is much more accessible and prices are much more affordable. Roman glasses, for example, range from £220 to £3,300, while Greek pots begin at £275. This shop deals in Greek, Roman, and Egyptian objects, including jewelry, glass, marble sculpture, bronzes, terracotta, and Old Master drawings. I found the Roman jewelry especially interesting, with finger rings beginning at £660.

ENGLISH AND FRENCH

A. & M. OSSOWSKI
83 Pimlico Rd., SW1 (tel. 730-3256)
Underground Station: *Sloane Square*
Hours: *Monday through Friday from 9:30 a.m. to 5:30 p.m., on Saturday from 10 a.m. to 1 p.m.*
Credit Cards: *None*

This shop is slightly different from the rest in that it specializes in 18th-century mirrors and carvings, primarily English in origin. A George III carved-wood and gilt Chippendale mirror dating from around 1760, with the original plate and backboard, costs around £23,200. What makes this shop even more unusual, however, is that the owners are carvers and gilders and will execute commissions designed to look like the real thing. Whether it's a Chippendale-style mirror or a more classical Adam-style mirror, a reproduction costs a fraction of the genuine antique's price. For about £1,540, for example, you can get a pair of wall mirrors hand-carved of pine and gilded with water, the same technique used in the 18th century as opposed to the quicker oil-gilding commonly used today.

APTER-FREDERICKS
265–267 Fulham Rd., SW3 (tel. 352-2188)
Underground Station: *South Kensington*
Hours: *Monday through Friday from 9 a.m. to 6 p.m., on Saturday by appointment*
Credit Cards: *None*

In its present location since 1946, this shop is now in its fifth generation of shopkeepers. It stocks 18th-century fine English furniture, as well as early Regency pieces. Aiming for furniture of high quality and good color, it sells gilt mirrors and decorative objects in addition to its furniture, with a small 18th-century table going for around £3,300.

BOX HOUSE ANTIQUES
105 Pimlico Rd., SW1 (tel. 730-9257)
Underground Station: *Sloane Square*

Hours: *Monday through Friday from 10 a.m. to 5 p.m., on Saturday*
from 10 a.m. to noon
Credit Cards: *None*

Furniture, needlework, samplers, and paintings from the 18th and 19th centuries are represented here. Antiques are primarily English, with a few from other countries as well. The price range is anywhere from £330 up to about £16,500. A pair of 19th-century Chinese chairs, for example, cost £870, while an Edison phonograph was being sold for £750. All items are clearly marked and described.

CHURCH STREET GALLERIES

77 Kensington Church St., W8 (tel. 937-2461)
Underground Stations: *High Street Kensington or Notting Hill Gate*
Hours: *Monday through Friday from 9 a.m. to 6 p.m., on Saturday from*
10 a.m. to 4 p.m.
Credit Cards: *None*

About 60% of what this shop sells goes to the United States, indicating a large American clientele. Specializing in 18th-century English furniture, it carries an especially good stock of Queen Anne walnut furniture, as well as 18th-century mirrors. A small room in the back of the shop is devoted to 18th-century brass candlesticks, ranging in price from £130 for one to £1,650 for an especially fine pair. Expect to pay between £220 and £8,000 for a mirror, while most furniture is priced higher than £1,200. This shop is larger than it looks from the outside, and everything is clearly priced, dated, and labeled.

CLIFFORD WRIGHT

104–106 Fulham Rd., SW3 (tel. 589-0986)
Underground Station: *South Kensington*
Hours: *Monday through Friday from 9:30 a.m. to 5:30 p.m., on Saturday*
from 10:30 a.m. to 1:30 p.m.
Credit Cards: *None*

You'll find 18th-century and early Regency furniture, 18th-century mirrors, and gilt furniture at Clifford Wright. Regency mirrors start at £3,300, but if you want an Adam-style mirror from around 1780, "the sky's the limit." A 1765 George III gilt Chippendale mirror was for sale for £13,750 during my last visit. I also saw a Regency rosewood game table for £6,000, a Regency chandelier for £9,300, and a pair of George III gilt-wood armchairs from about 1780 for £13,750.

GREEN'S ANTIQUE GALLERIES

117 Kensington Church St., W8 (tel. 229-9618).
Underground Station: *Notting Hill Gate*

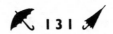
Hours: *Monday through Saturday from 10 a.m. to 5:30 p.m.*
Credit Cards: *MC, V*

This shop could qualify as a bric-a-brac shop; it's filled with the same kinds of things you find at London's weekend flea markets. Cluttered and pleasant, it carries an eclectic mix of Victorian and Edwardian jewelry, silver, porcelain, old clocks and watches, and old clothing. I saw a 1787 snuff box priced at £105, and a 1931 silver tea pot was listed at £550.

HASLAM & WHITEWAY LTD.
105 Kensington Church St., W8 (tel. 229-1145)
Underground Station: *Notting Hill Gate*
Hours: *Monday through Friday from 10 a.m. to 1 p.m. and 2 to 6 p.m., on Saturday from 10 a.m. to 2 p.m.*
Credit Cards: *None*

This is a specialist's shop for furniture and objects dating from around 1850 to 1920—that is, Gothic Revival through the Arts and Crafts Movement. The stock changes constantly but may include chairs, pewter mugs, crumb plates, lamps, and obscure and unique items. A wardrobe by Gordon Russell was priced at £1,100.

HOTSPUR
14 Lowndes St., Belgrave Square, SW1 (tel. 235-1918)
Underground Station: *Knightsbridge*
Hours: *Monday through Friday from 8 a.m. to 6 p.m., on Saturday from 9 a.m. to 1 p.m.*
Credit Cards: *None*

Considered by some to be the best antique dealer in town, Hotspur carries top-quality 18th-century English furniture, all in good enough condition to be displayed in museums. In fact museums have purchased from this well-known shop, and prices here range from £1,100 to more than £250,000. Pieces are elegantly displayed in a beautiful house built during the Regency period, and the service is gracious and friendly. Although it sells mainly furniture, you can also find mirrors, ornamental objects, some prints, and occasionally chandeliers.

JEREMY LTD.
255 King's Rd., SW3 (tel. 352-0644)
Underground Station: *Sloane Square*
Hours: *Monday through Friday from 8:30 a.m. to 6 p.m., on Saturday from 9 a.m. to 5 p.m.*
Credit Cards: *None*

In business since 1946, this shop in an old home sells basically 18th-century and early-19th-century French and English works of art and furniture. Objects are

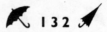
spread spaciously throughout the many rooms, where you may find such antiques as a convex mirror of the Regency period, an Adam-period table with legs culminating in lion heads, or an 18th-century secretary. An early-19th-century French clock with an Egyptian motif in a mahogany case was priced at £13,750, while £20,350 was the asking price for a pair of Regency carved rosewood armchairs.

JOHN KEIL
154 Brompton Rd., SW3 (tel. 589-6454)
Underground Station: Knightsbridge
Hours: Monday through Friday from 9 a.m. to 6 p.m., on Saturday by appointment
Credit Cards: None

Claiming to have the best available in 18th- and 19th-century fine English furniture, it stocks both furniture and mirrors. The top price here is £423,500, but with three floors of merchandise, there's a wide selection to choose from. Established in 1959, it distributes its own catalog twice a year to selected clients, most of whom don't blink an eye at the prices.

LOOT ANTIQUES
76–78 Pimlico Rd., SW1 (tel. 730-8097)
Underground Station: Sloane Square
Hours: Monday through Friday from 10 a.m. to 6 p.m., on Saturday from 11 a.m. to 2 p.m.
Credit Cards: None

Simple elegance is bypassed here in this crowded shop specializing in 18th- and 19th-century decorative furniture, pictures, carpets, and miscellaneous objects. The furniture is mostly from the Victorian period, with lots of inlaid wood or mother-of-pearl and richly colored pieces. The style is overstated but fun, and the atmosphere is laid-back and relaxed. You're welcome to browse to your heart's content, and even though items are clearly marked, the owners are willing to bargain. During my visit I saw a chest with mother-of-pearl inlay for £2,400 and an oval-shaped, marble-topped dining table for £3,850.

MALLET & SON
40 New Bond St., W1 (tel. 499-7411)
Underground Station: Bond Street
Hours: Monday through Friday from 9:15 a.m. to 5:15 p.m.
Credit Cards: None

One of the big names in 18th-century English furniture, Mallet & Son was first established in 1865 in Bath by John Mallet and his son. The store moved to its present address on Bond Street after the turn of the century. It is certainly one of the most elegant antique shops in the world and offers one of the finest

collections under one roof. The antiques are beautifully displayed in about a dozen different rooms, just the way you'd find them in a luxurious 18th-century home. To add to the period effect, lamps are used for lighting rather than overhead spotlights.

All pieces are meticulously restored (as opposed to being left in the condition found), and there are also old items that have been changed for modern use, such as antique vases fashioned into lamps. The shop is especially known for its walnut furniture. Prices for furniture range from about £5,000 to £500,000, but there are small decorative objects on display for £1,100 or less. Furniture on display has included a mahogany bed by Hepplewhite for £53,350 and an 18th-century mirror lavishly decorated with birds and trees for £24,200.

MICHAEL LIPITCH
98 Fulham Rd., SW3 (tel. 589-7327)
Underground Station: South Kensington
Hours: Monday through Friday from 9 a.m. to 6 p.m., on Saturday by appointment
Credit Cards: None

With five floors of showrooms, this shop is one of London's largest and sells 18th-century English furniture. Striving to sell pieces only of top quality in excellent condition, it offers commodes, chairs, sofas, and tables, as well as a range of 18th-century prints and watercolors. Expect to pay more than £1,000 for anything in the store, with most prices much, much higher. For those of you who are interested, the owners have a shop in New York as well.

NORMAN ADAMS
8–10 Hans Rd., SW3 (tel. 589-5266)
Underground Station: Knightsbridge
Hours: Monday through Friday from 9 a.m. to 5:30 p.m., on Saturday by appointment
Credit cards: None

Located across the street from Harrods department store, opposite its west side, Norman Adams looks somberly unpretentious from the outside but houses some of the city's finest 18th-century English furniture, some in its original condition. The staff is knowledgeable and helpful, and some of the pieces are quite rare, fetching upwards of £500,000. The shop prides itself as selling only top-quality merchandise, the trademarks for which are the patina and color of its furniture.

PARTRIDGE
144–146 New Bond St., W1 (tel. 629-0834)
Underground Station: Bond Street

Hours: *Monday through Friday from 9:30 a.m. to 5:30 p.m.*
Credit Cards: AE

Sharing the spotlight with London's top antique dealers is Partridge, founded at the beginning of the 20th century and subsequently passed from father to son to grandson. It occupies the former gallery and showroom built for the Colnaghi fine-arts dealer at the end of the 19th century. Most of its furniture is from the 18th century, each piece qualifying as a collector's item and many ending up in museums. The emphasis is on rare pieces of French and English furniture, worth collectively more than $8 million. In addition to furniture, you'll find silver, bronzes, paintings, decorative objects, and clocks. A beautiful catalog is issued free to customers, with color photographs and descriptions of its best pieces.

PELHAM GALLERIES
163–165 Fulham Rd., SW3 (tel. 589-2686)
Underground Station: South Kensington
Hours: *Monday through Friday from 9 a.m. to 5:30 p.m., on Saturday by appointment*
Credit Cards: None

Established in 1928, this shop describes itself as one of the largest and most serious dealers in town. It carries a wide range of 17th- to 19th-century English and European furniture, as well as such decorative items or smaller objects as antique tapestries, clocks, and Oriental lacquerware. It usually has a few antique musical instruments on hand, such as the 18th-century English harpsichord I saw selling for £26,400. The price range here is from £330 for a decorative object like a snuff box up to £220,000.

RICHARD COURTNEY
112–114 Fulham Rd., SW3 (tel. 370-4020)
Underground Station: South Kensington
Hours: *Monday through Friday from 9:30 a.m. to 5:30 p.m.*
Credit Cards: None

Dealing in 18th-century English furniture, Richard Courtney is especially strong in early walnut furniture from the Queen Anne period. You'll pay about £3,300 for a stool or chair, while larger pieces fetch around £71,500.

STAIR
120 Mount St., W1 (tel. 499-1784)
Underground Station: Bond Street
Hours: *Monday through Friday from 9 a.m. to 5:30 p.m.*
Credit Cards: None

Located in the plush surroundings of Mount Street, Stair is another elegant antique shop selling predominantly English furniture from the 18th century,

along with some smaller items such as mirrors, tea caddies, lamps, and chandeliers. About the lowest you can expect to pay here is £770 for a pair of 1780 English decanters. A color catalog is issued twice annually, and a recent edition revealed such pieces as a well-patinaed mahogany tea table dating from around 1740, a set of six early 18th-century walnut chairs with legs culminating in claw-and-ball feet, and a very rare Chinese coromandel lacquer screen dating from 1706.

Antique musical instruments are among the classic antiques at Pelham Galleries

ORIENTAL

Several shops listed above occasionally carry antiques from the Orient, including **Grays Antique Markets** with its stalls specializing in antiques from Asia. Be sure also to check with **Liberty** department store, which has an Oriental department and often launches special sales on Asian antiques. If you're looking for Oriental porcelain, refer to the "China" section, where you'll find **Earle D. Vandekar**, one of the best antique porcelain shops in town.

JOHN SPARKS
128 Mount St., W1 (tel. 499-2265)
Underground Station: *Bond Street*
Hours: *Monday through Friday from 9:30 a.m. to 5 p.m.*
Credit Cards: *None*

This is undeniably one of the best places to shop for Oriental art. Although the stock is very small, the quality is excellent. It sells Chinese works of art, including jades, porcelains, and works on silk, and some Japanese antiques. Items date from as early as the 10th century to the 19th century. Prices are expectedly high and pieces are exquisite.

LENNOX MONEY ANTIQUES LTD.
93 Pimlico Rd., SWI (tel. 730-3070)
Underground Station: *Sloane Square*
Hours: *Monday through Friday from 9:45 a.m. to 6 p.m., on Saturday from 11 a.m. to 1 p.m.*
Credit Cards: *None*

In an entirely different vein, this delightful store concentrates on items made in colonies of the British Empire that show a marked English influence. On display, for example, may be a rosewood balloon-back chair commonly found in England in the mid-1800s—except that this one from India boasts an elaborately carved eagle on the railing below the seat. As one staff member explained, its customers are "looking for something a bit quirky." Most objects date from the 17th to 20th centuries and are largely from the Orient and India. Unlike many antique shops, the front door is unlocked and casual browsing is actively encouraged. Items for sale have included a pair of Chinese damascened metal moon-shaped flasks from the 18th century priced at £1,540, an Indian marble tray inlaid with mother-of-pearl and made in Agra in the 19th century selling for £350, and a Regency mahogany breakfast table priced at £2,150.

SCIENTIFIC INSTRUMENTS

ARTHUR MIDDLETON
12 New Row, Covent Garden, WC2 (tel. 836-7042)
Underground Station: *Leicester Square*
Hours: *Monday through Friday from 9:30 a.m. to 6:30 p.m., on Saturday from 11 a.m. to 5:30 p.m.*
Credit Cards: *AE, DC, MC, V*

Since this shop does not encourage browsing, you may have to content yourself with looks at the fascinating objects on display in its windows. Those who are serious collectors of antique scientific instruments, however, will find this a wonderful little shop for hand-held and tripod-mounted telescopes, polished-brass sextants, microscopes, compasses, surveying theodolites and levels, barometers, scales, antique globes, medical instruments, and more. Most instruments date from the 19th century and are in good working order, both optically and mechanically. Hand-held compasses start at £70, hand-held telescopes at £93, and a huge globe made in London in 1854 was listed at £16,500.

TREVOR PHILIP

75A Jermyn St., SWI (tel. 930-2954)
Underground Station: Piccadilly Circus or Green Park
**Hours: *Monday through Friday from 9 a.m. to 6 p.m., on Saturday from
10 a.m. to 4 p.m.***
Credit Cards: *AE, DC, MC, V*

Specializing in antique medical, scientific, and marine instruments, Trevor
Philip prides itself in stocking items hard to find anywhere else and sells what it
calls "gifts for the man who has everything." Every item has been meticulously
labeled with the date it was made and the function it performs, a necessity for
some of these rare pieces. In stock are usually 18th-century microscopes,
protractors and sextants, compasses, antique scales used for coins, Victorian
and Edwardian gold and silver pens and pencils, and clocks.

On display during my visit, for example, was a rare and important candle
clock from 1795. As for medical instruments, former catalogs have listed such
items as a dental hygiene kit with three silver items hallmarked for the year
1791, a field surgeon's kit dating from the early 19th century, a silver-plated ear
trumpet from the mid-19th century, a bleeding set from the mid-19th century,
and a post-mortem kit from circa 1860. Prices in the store start at around £80 for
the Victorian or Edwardian pens, with most objects under £500.

ARMS AND ARMOR

During the Middle Ages a choice of a certain type of armor and weaponry
could mean the difference between life and death. Learning about various
weapons available, therefore, was part of any young man's training in
arms. As interest in weaponry grew beyond that of survival into one of
collecting, copies of armor and arms were manufactured to keep up with
the demand. Some of these Victorian reproductions were so well executed
that they have become worthy collectibles themselves.

London has several dealers in antique arms and armor. A convenient
place to begin a perusal is in **Grays Antique Markets**, described in the
"Antiques" section, where several stallholders sell arms and armor from
Japan, the continent, and England. In addition, **Holland & Holland**,
listed in the "Guns" section, stocks a selection of antique guns and swords
beginning at £165.

MICHAEL C. GERMAN & SIMON CASTLE

38B Kensington Church St., W8 (tel. 937-2771)
Underground Station: *High Street Kensington*
**Hours: *Monday through Friday from 10 a.m. to 5 p.m., on Saturday to 3
p.m.***
Credit Cards: *AE, DC, MC, V*

This small shop manages to pack in a large selection of antique weaponry, armor, walking sticks, and treen (carved wooden objects, from candlestick holders to wassail bowls). Its arms date from about 1640 to 1860 and include wheel locks, flintlocks, and percussions. There are also swords and daggers from around the world and both original and copied suits of armor.

While you're here, don't neglect the wonderful collection of about 500 walking sticks, dating from around 1680 to 1910. The vast majority of them are Victorian. No two are alike and they come from all over the world, including Japan, where they used to be made with ivory handles. Prices for canes start at £50.

PETER DALE
11 Royal Opera Arcade, Pall Mall, SW1 (tel. 930-3695)
Underground Station: *Piccadilly Circus*
Hours: *Monday through Friday from 9 a.m. to 5 p.m., on Saturday by*
   appointment
Credit Cards: *AE, DC, MC, V*

This shop has been selling antique weaponry in the Royal Opera Arcade for 25 years, with stock dating from about 1500 to 1900. Included are pistols, fowling pieces, rifles, swords, daggers, pole arms, rapiers, armor, helmets, gauntlets, and crossbows. A Victorian officer's saber may start at about £220, but most items average between £500 and £1,000. All weaponry is cleaned so that it will last a couple more centuries without restoration and everything sold comes with a certificate authenticating its age.

ART DECO AND ART NOUVEAU

The market for art nouveau and art deco is flourishing. Bronzes and ivory figures, Lalique glass, Liberty jewelry, silver art nouveau picture frames, Georg Jensen silver tableware and flatware from the 1920s and 1930s—all have boomed in popularity and worth. Prices have risen dramatically in just the past decade, especially for art deco. As one dealer told me, "Ten years ago you couldn't give away the stuff. Now it's a hot commodity." The result is that people who used to buy art deco in a small way at low prices now find the cost prohibitive. Collecting art nouveau and art deco has become an expensive business.

Art nouveau is defined as a style of decoration and architecture of the late 19th and early 20th century, characterized by the use of flowing, sinuous lines. Art nouveau to me is epitomized by the image of a lithe and slender nymphet, her hair swirling down to her feet. Such a motif was often used in posters, lamp bases, and on picture frames.

ART DECO & ART NOUVEAU

In contrast, **art deco** features geometrical designs, straight lines, and angles. Its name derives from the Exposition Internationale des Arts Décoratifs et Industriels Moderns, an exposition held in Paris in 1925. To my eye, art deco is more reserved than art nouveau, sometimes even resembling Japanese stark simplicity in its design.

At any rate, London is a good place to look for art deco and art nouveau, and even though prices are high for top-quality items, there are plenty of smaller objects that cost much less in England than they would in the United States. A good place to look for inexpensive art deco items and '40s and '50s plastic are at **flea markets**, particularly Portobello Road near Ladbroke Grove station and in the Old Stables in Camden Town. Refer to the "Markets" section for more information. Other places you should try include **Chenil Galleries**, described in the "Antiques" section and auction houses. **Bonhams**' annual Lalique auction draws bidders from around the world.

The shops listed below sell a variety of art deco and art nouveau. In addition to these, refer to the "Jewelry" section for shops selling exclusively jewelry, and to the "Art Galleries" section for information on **Grosvenor Gallery**, which sells original paintings, drawings, graphics, and posters.

EDITIONS GRAPHIQUES
3 Clifford St., W1 (tel. 734-3944)
Underground Station: *Piccadilly Circus or Green Park*
Hours: *Monday through Friday from 10 a.m. to 6 p.m., on Saturday to 2 p.m.*
Credit Cards: *AE, DC, MC, V*

Located just off Bond Street, this shop deals primarily in art nouveau and art deco graphics, drawings, and paintings, and in sculptures. It also stocks some furniture, lamps, jewelry, glass, ceramics, posters, and silver, all dating from about 1880 to 1930. Small pictures range from £33 to about £13,200, while sculptures begin at £110 and go all the way to £22,000.

GALERIE 1900
267 Camden High St., Camden Town, NW1 (tel. 485-1001)
Underground Station: *Camden Town*
**Hours: *Monday through Saturday from 10 a.m. to 5:30 p.m., on Sunday
    from 11 a.m. to 5:30 p.m.***
Credit Cards: *AE, DC, MC, V*

Specializing in objects dating from the turn of the century to 1940, Galerie 1900 is a shop located in the heart of the Camden Town flea market, making it a good place to stop off if you're here for the weekend. Prices range from £100 to £1,000 for such items as pictures, jewelry, glass, pewter, china, and furniture. The average price is about £300.

Curvaceous art nouveau at Galerie 1900

JOHN JESSE & IRINA LASKI
160 Kensington Church St., W8 (tel. 229-0312)
Underground Station: Notting Hill Gate
Hours: Monday through Friday from 10 a.m. to 6 p.m., on Saturday
from 11 a.m. to 5 p.m.
Credit Cards: AE, DC, V

This shop is a beautiful showcase for art nouveau and art deco from Europe, England, and the United States. Items are elegantly displayed and are of top quality. Included are bronze and ivory figures, English silver, glass, lamps, clocks, pictures, ceramics, some furniture, and even an occasional stained-glass window. Liberty, Georg Jensen, and Lalique are all represented. Silver items begin at about £200, while paste and Bakelite jewelry start at £52. The VAT is deducted right in the store—they trust customers to send the forms back after passing through Customs.

PRUSKIN GALLERY
73 Kensington Church St., W8 (tel. 937-1994)
Underground Station: High Street Kensington or Notting Hill Gate
Hours: Monday through Friday from 10 a.m. to 6 p.m.
Credit Cards: AE, MC

One of the leading art deco and art nouveau shops in London, this gallery always has furniture on display, along with art deco bronze figures. Bronzes range from about £1,650 to £2,750. Pruskin has another shop in the Chenil Galleries, 183

King's Rd. (tel. 352-9095), which has less furniture and more decorative objects. Here you'll find lamps, glassware, silver, clocks, jewelry, and statues, along with watches of the period. Prices are high, but so is the quality.

TADEMA GALLERY
10 Charlton Pl., Islington, N1 (tel. 359-1055)
Underground Station: Angel
Hours: Tuesday through Saturday from 10 a.m. to 5 p.m.
Credit Cards: AE, MC, V

Located just off Camden Passage where an antique flea market is held on Wednesday and Saturday, Tadema Gallery sells decorative art of the 20th century, including paintings, jewelry, and some bronzes, glass, furniture, and ceramics. The paintings are hung gallery style in the basement. The jewelry ranges from German Jugendstil to art nouveau and art deco, including Liberty jewelry produced from 1895 to 1915. A Liberty amethyst ring was priced at £1,400, while gold necklaces start at £770 and silver ones at £250. If it doesn't have to be Liberty—other jewelry is available beginning at about £30. The shop is also starting to stock decorative objects from the '50s. The price of the VAT is deducted directly in the shop, and customers are trusted to send back the form after passing through Customs.

ART GALLERIES

The art market in London is alive and well, particularly for works by the Old Masters. Because collecting in England has remained uninterrupted by revolutions or social upheavals through the centuries, dealers have developed an expertise rarely matched in the rest of the world, passing on their knowledge from generation to generation. London is undoubtedly one of the best places in the world for Old Master dealers.

An enthusiasm for contemporary art, on the other hand, has been slower in coming. Although London has seen a great upsurge in contemporary and modern galleries in recent years, the popularity of the market lags behind that in the United States. In fact, Americans are among the most prevalent buyers in London's galleries. They've found that there are some very good buys here, particularly in limited-edition prints of young artists.

Most of London's art galleries are centrally located in the West End close to the major auction houses. Bond Street is the favored area of dealers in the Old Masters, while nearby Cork Street has an extraordinary number of contemporary galleries. Remember, too, to check the auction houses for their regular sales of art. While it's true that one of Manet's impressionist paintings sold at Christie's for a cool £7.7 million in 1986, there are plenty of paintings and prints sold at prices normal folks can

afford. In addition, be sure to check with the tourist office about seasonal fairs and markets. The Royal Academy of Arts, for example, holds a summer exhibition of graphics, paintings, and sculpture by contemporary artists at reasonable prices.

In addition to the galleries listed below, the "Prints" section of this book lists shops selling antique prints, particularly illustrations for books and prints of botanical and architectural scenes. Shops selling antique books and maps also often have prints for sale.

For more information on London's art galleries, be sure to pick up a copy of "Galleries," published monthly with a rundown of current exhibits. More than 350 galleries are listed, along with maps showing locations. You can pick up a copy of this valuable booklet at many of the galleries around town.

OLD MASTERS

ARTHUR ACKERMANN & SON
3 Old Bond St., WI (tel. 493-3288)
Underground Station: *Piccadilly Circus or Green Park*
Hours: *Monday through Friday from 10 a.m. to 5:30 p.m., on Saturday from 10:30 a.m. to 1 p.m.*
Credit Cards: *AE, V*

Established in 1783, this gallery is one of London's finest for English prints and paintings of sporting scenes, most of which date from 1750 to 1860. Marine, botanical, and some landscape prints and paintings are also represented. About two to four special exhibitions are held annually, but the main sporting exhibition takes place every year in October. There's also a special Christmas exhibit. Although prints sometimes start as low as £110, a more realistic starting figure is around £500. Paintings generally range from £2,200 to £100,000. Catalogs are available for special exhibitions for around £5.50, the proceeds of which go to charity.

THE FINE ART SOCIETY
148 New Bond St., WI (tel. 629-5116)
Underground Station: *Bond Street*
Hours: *Monday through Friday from 9:30 a.m. to 5:30 p.m., on Saturday from 10 a.m. to 1 p.m.*
Credit Cards: *None*

The Fine Art Society was founded in 1876 and is one of Bond Street's finest institutions. Specializing in British and European art from 1800 to 1940, it has several thousand pieces of artwork on hand and a small number of contemporary pieces. Although it's sometimes possible to pick up something in the £500 range, a more realistic figure would be several thousand pounds or higher.

ART GALLERIES

Approximately 12 to 15 exhibitions are held annually based on various themes and featuring paintings, furniture, and decorative objects. Former exhibitions, for example, have centered on sculpture of Britain between the World Wars, artwork depicting great cities of the 19th century, and Orientalist painters of the 19th century. A recent showing took a look at Scottish interiors from the Age of Enlightenment through Victorian and Edwardian times and included furniture, works of art, and pictures.

LEGER GALLERIES
13 Old Bond St., WI (tel. 629-3538)
Underground Station: *Piccadilly Circus or Green Park*
Hours: *Monday through Friday from 9:30 a.m. to 5:30 p.m.*
Credit Cards: *AE, DC*

Specializing in English paintings, watercolors, and Old Masters from the 18th and 19th centuries, Leger Galleries was established in 1892. Included in its stock are works by Gainsborough, Raeburn, Reynolds, Rowlandson, Stuart, Turner, and Zoffany. Two exhibitions are held yearly: from May to July is a special exhibit on oils, while November to December features watercolors. In between exhibitions the gallery has a permanent display.

P. & D. COLNAGHI
14 Old Bond St., WI (tel. 491-7408)
Underground Station: *Piccadilly Circus or Green Park*
Hours: *Monday through Friday from 9:30 a.m. to 6 p.m., on Saturday during exhibitions only from 10 a.m. to 1 p.m.*
Credit Cards: *None*

One of the oldest names on Bond Street, Colnaghi was established in 1760 and features Old Master Prints, paintings, and watercolors. Included are English paintings, drawings, and watercolors, as well as European sculpture, furniture, and works of art. Approximately six exhibitions are launched every year and last approximately one month. Themes of former exhibitions have included a British view of sporting life, English drawings and watercolors, and Old Master drawings.

THOMAS AGNEW & SONS
43 Old Bond St., WI (tel. 629-6176)
Underground Station: *Piccadilly Circus or Green Park*
Hours: *Monday through Friday from 9:30 a.m. to 5:30 p.m. (to 6:30 p.m. on Thursday)*
Credit Cards: *None*

Agnew opened its gallery on Old Bond Street in 1876 and is still housed in a grand Victorian building on the site of the house where Laurence Sterne, author of *Tristram Shandy*, died a pauper's death in 1768. It specializes in Old Masters

and watercolors, but has contemporary works of art by modern English painters as well. Also in stock are drawings, prints, and sculpture. Exhibitions are held every month, with January and February slated for its annual English watercolor exhibition.

WILDENSTEIN
147 New Bond St., W1 (tel. 629-0602)
Underground Station: Bond Street
Hours: Monday through Friday from 10 a.m. to 5:30 p.m.
Credit Cards: None

With galleries also in New York City, Buenos Aires, and Tokyo, Wildenstein deals in impressionist and Old Master paintings and drawings from both England and the continent. It stages two exhibitions a year, one in June or July and one in autumn.

WYLMA WAYNE
17 Old Bond St., W1 (tel. 629-4511)
Underground Station: Piccadilly Circus or Green Park
Hours: Monday through Friday from 10:30 a.m. to 6 p.m.
Credit Cards: AE

As the only American-owned gallery in London, Wylma Wayne is something of an upstart on Bond Street. It's named after Ms. Wayne, who opened her gallery here in 1981. She specializes in Rembrandt etchings, and her collection is impressive. She also has some Albrecht Dürer woodcuts.

MODERN AND CONTEMPORARY

BROWSE & DARBY
19 Cork St., W1 (tel. 734-7984)
Underground Station: Piccadilly Circus or Green Park
Hours: Monday through Friday from 10 a.m. to 5:30 p.m., on Saturday
*   from 10:30 a.m. to 1 p.m.*
Credit Cards: None

English contemporary art is the emphasis of this gallery, along with 19th- and 20th-century English and French paintings, drawings, and sculpture. Most pieces date from about 1870 to 1950. The starting price for contemporary pictures is about £300. The gallery holds a major exhibition in June and July and smaller exhibitions monthly.

CHRISTIE'S CONTEMPORARY ART
8 Dover St., W1 (tel. 499-6701)
Underground Station: Green Park

Hours: Monday through Friday from 9:30 a.m. to 5:30 p.m., on Saturday from 10 a.m. to 4 p.m.
Credit Cards: AE, DC, MC, V

If you're just starting to look for artwork to furnish your home or office, or you're looking for a special but affordable gift, this gallery is a good place to begin your search. It specializes in original prints at reasonable prices by artists from around the world. Prices begin at £50 for a small etching or lithograph. Many more prints are available for around £100. All the work in stock, which includes original prints, etchings, screenprints, and lithographs, is on display in its gallery. You can also order prints through the catalog, which is issued free 10 to 12 times yearly.

Founded in 1972 as a subsidiary of Christie's International, the auction house, Christie's Contemporary Art became an independent public company in 1985. In addition to galleries in New York and Tokyo, it recently opened a second gallery in London at 17 Princes Arcade (tel. 439-1472), where you can see original limited-edition prints of Picasso, Henry Moore, Miró, Matisse, and others.

CRANE KALMAN GALLERY
178 Brompton Rd., SW3 (tel. 584-7566)
Underground Station: Knightsbridge
Hours: Monday through Friday from 10 a.m. to 6 p.m., on Saturday to 4 p.m.
Credit Cards: AE, MC, V

Established more than 30 years ago, this gallery deals primarily in 20th-century British paintings, along with some sculptures. It also represents some European 20th-century painters. It stocks works by British artists Henry Moore, L. S. Lowry, Ben Nicholson, and Sir Matthew Smith, to name only a few. It holds about six exhibitions a year, and prices start at around £400.

FRANCIS KYLE GALLERY
9 Maddox St., W1 (tel. 499-6870), just off Regent Street
Underground Station: Oxford Circus
Hours: Monday through Friday from 10 a.m. to 6 p.m., on Saturday from 11 a.m. to 5 p.m.
Credit Cards: AE, DC, MC, V

This small, contemporary gallery features works by living artists. As one staff member explained, "We try to keep them alive by showing their work." The gallery has a good eye for spotting little-known artists who later move on to bigger and better things. British, European, and American artists are featured, and different exhibitions are staged monthly. Former shows have featured the works of Adrian George, Paul Gell, and Gerald Mynott. A poster is issued for each of its exhibitions for £5, a good souvenir if you can't afford the real thing. There are also calendars for £9.30.

GROSVENOR GALLERY
48 South Molton St., WI (tel. 629-0891)
Underground Station: Bond Street
Hours: Monday through Friday from 10 a.m. to 5:30 p.m.
Credit Cards: None

You could easily overlook this first-floor gallery located on fashionable South Molton Street off Oxford Street. It stocks mainly original art deco and art nouveau and also deals in Italian futurism and Russian constructivism. Its pieces consist of original posters, paintings, lithographs, drawings, and illustrations used in advertising. It stages exhibitions infrequently, but you can call to make an appointment to see its stock. Prices range from about £270 to £100,000 and more. Former exhibitions have showcased the talents of Mucha and Erté, and depicted European art of the '60s.

KNOEDLER GALLERY
22 Cork St., WI (tel. 439-1096)
Underground Station: Piccadilly Circus or Green Park
Hours: Monday through Friday from 10 a.m. to 5:30 p.m., on Saturday to 1 p.m.
Credit Cards: None

This small gallery represents approximately 20 artists, primarily British and American, including David Hockney, Gillian Ayres, Stephen Buckley, Anthony Caro, Frank Stella, and Helen Frankenthaler. Exhibitions are staged once a month.

MARLBOROUGH FINE ARTS
6 Albemarle St., WI (tel. 629-5161)
Underground Station: Green Park
Hours: Monday through Friday from 10 a.m. to 5 p.m., on Saturday to 12:30 p.m.
Credit Cards: None

With approximately eight exhibitions a year, this gallery features selected Old Masters; impressionist and 20th-century paintings, drawings, watercolors, and sculpture; and 20th-century photographs. It acts as agents for Andrzej Jackowski, John Piper, Henry Moore, Edward Seago, and Oskar Kokoschka.

MARLBOROUGH GRAPHICS GALLERY
39 Old Bond St., WI (tel. 629-5161), on the fourth floor
Underground Station: Green Park or Piccadilly Circus
Hours: Monday through Friday from 10 a.m. to 5 p.m., on Saturday by appointment
Credit Cards: Would rather not, but has on occasion accepted AE

Affiliated with Marlborough Fine Arts described above, this gallery specializes in original, limited-edition prints, including etchings, screenprints, and litho-

graphs. In stock are prints by Frank Auerbach, R. B. Kitaj, Kokoschka, Moore, Ben Nicholson, Victor Pasmore, John Piper, and others. There are lots of prints in the £200 to £500 range.

RONA GALLERY
1–2 Weighhouse St., W1 (tel. 491-3718), off Duke Street
Underground Station: Bond Street
Hours: Monday through Saturday from 10:30 a.m. to 5:30 p.m.
Credit Cards: None

"Rona" stands for Registre des Artistes Naïfs and this gallery is unique in that it features the work of naïve British and international artists. The term *naïve* refers to self-taught artists whose paintings often feature bright colors, objects out of proportion, and uninhibited interpretations of the world. Most of the pieces here are contemporary, but the gallery stocks some 18th- and 19th-century British primitives as well. I personally find this gallery fascinating and well worth a visit. Most artwork ranges from about £260 to £1,000.

PICCADILLY GALLERY
16 Cork St., W1 (tel. 629-2875)
Underground Station: Piccadilly Circus or Green Park
Hours: Monday through Friday from 10 a.m. to 5:30 p.m.
Credit Cards: None

This gallery features exclusively the works of British artists. All the work is figurative, with a surreal emphasis. Represented are Eric Holt, Michael Murfin, Graham Ovenden, John Morley, Adrian Berg, Timothy Dickinson, and Graham Arnold. Prices range from about £130 to £10,000.

SERPENTINE GALLERY
Kensington Gardens, W2 (tel. 402-6075)
Underground Station: Lancaster Gate, South Kensington, High Street Kensington, or Knightsbridge
Hours: Daily during exhibitions from 10 a.m., closing at 4 p.m. November through February and at 6 p.m. March through October
Credit Cards: None

Run by the Arts Council of Great Britain, this gallery features contemporary art by rising young artists. It allows installment payments. Another such gallery run by the Arts Council is the ICA Gallery, The Mall, SW1 (tel. 930-3647). It's best to call beforehand to find out what's being exhibited.

TRYON GALLERY
23–24 Cork St., W1 (tel. 734-6961)
Underground Station: Piccadilly Circus or Green Park
Hours: Monday through Friday from 9:30 a.m. to 5:30 p.m.
Credit Cards: None

Specialists in paintings depicting sporting, wildlife, or natural history scenes, this gallery features artists both past and present from around the world. Prints start as low as £15.

WADDINGTON GALLERIES
4 and 31 Cork St., W1 (tel. 439-1866); and 2, 11, and 34 Cork St.,
   W1 (tel. 437-8611)
Underground Station: *Piccadilly Circus or Green Park*
Hours: *Monday through Friday from 10 a.m. to 5:30 p.m., on Saturday*
   to 1 p.m.
Credit Cards: *None*

Waddington has five showrooms on Cork Street. The gallery at no. 4 features graphics, while the one at no. 31 has prints. The other three have changing exhibits of paintings, sculpture, and art. Waddington deals primarily in modern and contemporary art beginning at the turn of the century, but has some impressionist work as well. Exhibited have been the works of Klee, Matisse, Miró, Moore, Picasso, Ben Nicholson, William Turnbull, Georges Braque, Milton Avery, Jean Dubuffet, Victor Pasmore, R. B. Kitaj, Andy Warhol, and many others too numerous to mention.

ASTROLOGER / PSYCHIC

MYSTERIES
9–11 Monmouth St., WC2 (tel. 240-3688)
Underground Station: *Covent Garden or Tottenham Court Road*
Hours: *Monday through Saturday from 10 a.m. to 6 p.m.*
Credit Cards: *MC, V*

Opened in 1981, Mysteries sells psychic, mystical, and spiritual books and equipment and offers psychic consultations on the premises. Books cover everything from acupuncture and tarot readings to witchcraft and occultism. Basic readings of tarot, palmistry, psychometry, numerology, or graphology last about 30 minutes and cost £9.30. More in-depth readings lasting an hour cost £16.50. You can also have your astrology done through a computer for £5.50. If you want to stock up on your equipment, you can purchase tarot decks, crystal balls, pendulums, a pyramid energy kit, and more, including incense and cassettes.

AUCTIONS

Auctions are not the formidable, exclusive affairs that Hollywood movies would lead you to believe. The fact is, auctions are open to everyone. Not

only that, they're fun and they're worth going to even if you're not interested in buying anything. They also qualify as one of the cheapest forms of entertainment around—unless, that is, you're swept up in the drama of it and can't refrain from bidding. You should never, however, bid a considerable sum on an item you haven't inspected closely before the sale. If it's broken, has missing parts, or is even a fake, you're stuck with it. The auctioneer is not responsible.

The three big names in auction houses are Christie's, Sotheby's, and Phillips, all located in the West End. They dominate the world market and are the only truly international companies in their field. All three have huge branches in New York, and all three had their beginnings as far back as the 18th century. Their big boom, however, didn't come until the past three decades. In 1960 Sotheby's consisted only of its auction house in London with a small office in New York and employed fewer than 100 people. By 1980 Sotheby's had expanded into six auction rooms in England alone, had offices or auction houses in 17 foreign countries, and employed more than 1,000 people. Both Christie's and Phillips experienced similar success.

Together with another well-known company called Bonhams, these auction houses sell about everything imaginable in the antique world. Auctions are held for furniture, fine art, Oriental art, furs, carpets, silver, jewelry, crystal, china, clocks, coins, wine, dolls, scientific instruments, stamps, silver, miniature portraits, arms and armor, and countless other collectibles. If you collect something specific, therefore, it's worth contacting the auction houses to inquire about scheduled sales. They may even issue catalogs on a subscription basis that will tell you of sales and items being sold for the coming year. Sotheby's, for example, issues special-interest catalogs on everything from jewelry to Japanese works of art.

In addition to the big auction houses there are smaller ones that sell ordinary household goods and furniture. There are also special-interest auctioneers selling stamps, coins, silver, and other collector's items.

To find out what's going on in the auction world, check with the publication "What's On & Where to Go," available at most newsstands. It tells the time of the sale and what's being sold. In addition, weekly auction schedules are published in the *Daily Telegraph* on Monday. Some auction houses such as Christie's and Sotheby's close down during August and September, while others remain open.

At any rate, the procedure at all auction houses is basically the same. All have a viewing period for a day or more prior to the actual auction. That means you can inspect beforehand items that interest you, checking for defects. Auction houses also issue catalogs on each auction with descriptions of the items being sold, known defects, and how much they are expected to bring in. You can buy a catalog at the auction house's information desk, which is usually just inside the front door. And finally,

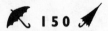
people in the know advise prospective buyers to make a personal note of the maximum amount they're prepared to pay. It's easy to get caught up in the excitement of an auction and end up paying far more for an item than originally intended.

As for the actual bidding procedure, that may differ from house to house. Christie's, for example, has initiated a new practice in which all potential bidders register and receive a card with a number on it. To bid, you simply hold up your card. Other auction houses may still use the nod, the raised hand, or other methods for indicating bids. You can also bid on an item even if you're unable to attend the auction, and if no one goes higher than your bid the item is yours. Ask at the information desk where you can leave your bid.

Once you've bid successfully for an item, you'll pay for it immediately after the sale or before you leave. Most auction houses add a buyer's premium, an extra 10% to 15% charge on the hammer price for each purchase. Unless it's an antique, they will also add the VAT. None of the auction houses listed below accepts credit cards, so if you intend on making a major purchase it's best to clear your form of payment with the cashier beforehand, preferably at the time of the viewing a few days before. Personal checks must first be cleared through the banks. And be sure to pick up your purchase as soon as possible. A storage charge will be levied for any goods left more than a few days or a week after the auction. The major houses will arrange for shipping.

BONHAMS
Montpelier Street, Knightsbridge, SW7 (tel. 584-9161), off Brompton Road
Underground Station: Knightsbridge
Hours: Open for viewing Monday through Friday from 9 a.m. to 5:30 p.m. (until 7 p.m. on Tuesday). Sales are generally held Tuesday through Friday starting at 10 a.m.

Bonhams opened its first gallery in 1793 and remains a family-run business. Unlike other auction houses, it is open the whole year, with up to seven auctions held weekly. Items regularly sold include silver, furs, watercolors, drawings, European oil paintings, antique furniture, jewelry, and objects of virtu. There are also periodic sales held for prints, 20th-century paintings and graphics, books and manuscripts, Oriental carpets, Oriental ceramics, and works of art. Yearly sales are held for crafts and Lalique. Catalogs, ranging from about 90 pence to £5, are available for each sale, and monthly schedules are handed out free.

In addition to its Montpelier Galleries, Bonhams has a second auction house at 65–69 Lots Rd., SW10 (tel. 352-1380), where less expensive items and bric-a-brac are sold. Furniture and carpet sales are held weekly on Tuesday

beginning at 10 a.m., while general ceramics and pictures are auctioned off fortnightly. Viewing times are on Saturday from 10 a.m. to 1 p.m. and on Monday from 9 a.m. to 7 p.m. Most items sell for less than £100. A Victorian ebonized and gilt-painted spoon-back chair with a rush seat, for example, was listed in a recent catalog at £30 to £50 as the expected price.

CHRISTIE, MANSON & WOODS

8 King St., St. James's, SW1 (tel. 839-9060), just off St. James's Street
Underground Station: Green Park
Hours: Open for viewing Monday through Friday from 9:30 a.m. to
4:30 p.m. Sales are usually held twice a day, at 10:30 or 11:30 a.m.
and at 2:30 p.m. Times may vary, so check beforehand.

Perhaps because of its New York branch, Christie's is probably the best known of the auction houses. It's been featured in movies and television programs, and is in the news whenever there's a record sale. In 1986, for example, a Manet painting sold at Christie's for a record £7.7 million, almost double what it was expected to bring and the most ever paid for an impressionist painting. Although the bidding does reach unimaginable sums, there's plenty sold at prices normal folks can afford.

James Christie held his first sale in London in 1766. Today Christie's has almost 60 offices in 20 foreign countries. Christie's specializes in antiques of every kind and in works of art, including Old Masters, English watercolors and drawings, prints, and modern paintings. It also holds regular auctions for wines. As much as two-thirds of the lots sold go for less than £1,100. A Chinese black-lacquer low table, for example, with a rectangular top designed with a coromandel panel of figures in a pavilion with a lake in the distance, was listed in a recent catalog at £400 to £600 as the expected price.

Christie's is closed all of January, August, and most of September. Catalogs are available for all sales with prices varying according to the size. Christie's also publishes a magazine called *Christie's International Magazine*, with an annual subscription rate to the United States of $40 for ten issues. It has photographs of items being sold at various Christie's around the world, including New York, Geneva, Amsterdam, and England. It also tells of future sales and gives a calendar of Christie's events.

In addition to its King Street location, Christie's has another auction house in South Kensington at 85 Old Brompton Rd., SW7 (tel. 581-7611), which opened in 1975. In contrast to most other auction houses, there's no buyer's premium charged here. Items sold include many collector's items such as dolls, textiles, photography, toys, and scientific instruments, as well as such things as furniture, watercolors and drawings, old and modern jewelry, books, Oriental works of art, and much more. Viewing hours here are 9 a.m. to 5 p.m. Monday through Saturday (open late on Monday until 7 p.m.)

HARVEY'S AUCTIONS
14 – 18 Neal St., Covent Garden, WC2 (tel. 240-1464), at the corner of Neal and Shelton Streets
Underground Station: Covent Garden
Hours: Viewing hours are 9:30 a.m. to 3:30 p.m. on Tuesday. Sales are held every Wednesday beginning at 10:30 p.m.

Harvey's sells inexpensive antiques, general furniture, ceramics, silver, pictures, prints, and odds and ends, and considers itself an auction house for everyone. Its sales and viewing room is located in a large basement room and resembles the site of a secondhand store, with low prices to match. There's a lot in the under-£50 range and you might be able to pick up a real bargain here. A catalog is available for each sale for £1. Unfortunately it doesn't list any expected prices, but examples of recent items for sale have included a Japanese Noritake green- and gilt-bordered tea set of 25 pieces, a lady's fur coat, and a Victorian mahogany oval drop-leaf dining table on baluster turned legs.

HATTON GARDEN AUCTIONS
Hatton Garden, EC1 (tel. 242-6452)
Underground Station: Farringdon or Chancery Lane
Hours: Viewing is on Friday from 9 a.m. to 4:30 p.m. Sales are held on Thursday at either 1:30 or 3 p.m.

This specialty auction house sells either jewelry or silver on Thursday afternoon. Although buyers are usually in the trade, the general public can also bid on items.

PHILLIPS
Blenstock House, 7 Blenheim St., W1 (tel. 629-6602), just off New Bond Street
Underground Station: Bond Street
Hours: Viewing hours are Monday through Friday from 9 a.m. to 4:30 p.m. Sales are held daily, usually beginning at 10 or 11 a.m.

A spokesman at Phillips told me his auction house held more sales per week than any other auction house. Most auctions fall in a middle price range, although finer sales are held every once in a while as well. Sales are held every week for antique and modern furniture, glass and objects, works of art, carpets, ceramics (including Oriental, English, and continental), stamps, silver, and collector's items. In addition, specialized sales are scheduled periodically for such items as arms and armor, art nouveau, coins and medals, books, boxes and miniatures, clocks, furs, jewelry, lace and textiles, musical instruments, Oriental carpets, and fine art, including Old Masters, Victorian, modern continental and British prints, and impressionist works. There have been collector's sales of sporting items, 20th-century war memorabilia, rock'n'roll memorabilia, lead soldiers and figures, toys, and postcards and cigarette cards.

Phillips encourages newcomers and is happy to answer any questions. Prices range from under £100 for collectibles to six-digit figures. Catalogs are issued for each sale, with the price dependent on size. A year's subscription to a catalog on scientific instruments to be sent to the United States, for example, costs £20. Other Phillips auction houses in London are Phillips West 2, 10 Salem Rd., W2 (tel. 221-5303), with weekly sales on Thursday for furniture and decorative objects, and Phillips Marylebone Auction Room, Hayes Place, Lisson Grove, NW1 (tel. 723-2647) with sales on Friday for ordinary household goods, furniture, and occasionally pianos.

SOTHEBY'S

34–35 New Bond St., WI (tel. 493-8080)
Underground Station: Bond Street
Hours: Viewing hours are Monday through Friday from 9 a.m. to
    4:30 p.m. Sales are held most weekdays; times vary.

Founded in 1744, Sotheby's is perhaps the biggest auction house in London. Almost everything imaginable in fine arts and antiques is sold here, including Old Masters, impressionist works, prints, photographic images, arms and armor, clocks, art nouveau and art deco, ceramics and glass, jewelry, silver, portrait miniatures, Oriental works of art, antiquities, coins, books, sporting guns, and collector's items. Every sale has its own catalog, usually available a month in advance, listing prices the sale objects are expected to bring, shortcomings, and repairs that have been made. Sotheby's is closed all of August and part of September and during the Christmas holidays.

AUTOGRAPHS

MAGGS BROS. LTD.

50 Berkeley Square, WI (tel. 499-2007)
Underground Station: Green Park
Hours: Monday through Friday from 9:30 a.m. to 5 p.m.
Credit Cards: MC, V
Overseas Information: Catalogs issued frequently; mail order possible to
    anywhere in the world; shipping services.

A family-run business since the 19th century when the Maggs family first began buying and selling antiquarian books, this delightful, old-fashioned shop dealing in rare books also sells autograph letters and historical documents. The staff is knowledgeable and very helpful. American, British, and European autographs are for sale.

Catalogs are issued frequently and mail orders are taken from anywhere in the world. Recent catalogs have listed a document signed during his presidency by

John Quincy Adams for £440, a signed photograph of Sarah Bernhardt for £190, an autograph envelope addressed to her father by Charlotte Brontë for £300, and an autograph note by Sir Winston Churchill for £630. Other autographs that have been offered for sale include those of Mark Twain, Charles Darwin, Degas, Arthur Conan Doyle, Dumas, Queen Elizabeth I, Ulysses S. Grant, T. E. Lawrence ("Lawrence of Arabia"), Jenny Lind, David Livingston, Maria Theresa, Henri Matisse, Monet, Napoléon I, Florence Nightingale, George Orwell, William Penn, F. D. Roosevelt, George Bernard Shaw, Dylan Thomas, Leo Tolstoy, Jules Verne, Queen Victoria, Virginia Woolf, Yeats, and many, many more.

SOTHERAN'S
2–5 Sackville, Piccadilly, W1 (tel. 734-1150)
Underground Station: Piccadilly Circus
Hours: Monday through Friday from 9 a.m. to 5:30 p.m.
Credit Cards: AE, DC, MC, V

Founded in York in 1761 and established in London in 1815, Sotheran's is one of London's oldest and most famous bookshops. With its old, glass-enclosed bookcases along the walls, it has a delightful Old World feel to it, somehow just right for a bookstore. In addition to its rare books, maps, and prints, Sotheran's also has an autograph letters department, with a room devoted solely to the display of autograph letters, inscribed books, illuminated manuscript leaves, and historical documents.

Recent catalogs have listed autograph letters of Charles Dickens for £570, Sir Arthur Conan Doyle for £380, Thomas Hardy for £649, and Rudyard Kipling for £370.

AUTOMOBILES

Sorry, folks, but you won't be able to walk into a car dealership in London and buy a Rolls-Royce or Jaguar on a whim. I checked with several dealers of luxury cars and they all told me the same thing: that they were not allowed to sell cars—used or new—to American visitors.

Several reasons were given. For one thing, there are different automobile specifications; for example, British cars are built the steering wheel on the right side. In general, American regulations are apparently much tougher, and many foreign cars do not meet them.

The main reason, however, is one of economics. According to a spokesman in the legal department of the British Motor Agents Association, there are quota restrictions on the import of British vehicles to the United States, in part to protect our own auto industry. But even more revealing is the fact that the restriction against selling cars in London to American buyers is a company one. Jaguar prohibits its British dealers

from dealing directly with Americans, because that would be undercutting its U.S. dealers who are trying to sell Jaguars in America.

There is, however, a way to pick up your new British car in England, but it takes some advance preparations. That is, you must go through a dealer in the United States, who will then take care of all the arrangements for you. After paying a deposit and ordering the type of car you want, all you have to do is arrive at the car factory in Great Britain on a prearranged pickup day.

If you're buying a Jaguar, you'll probably have to pick the car up at the factory in Coventry unless you make special arrangements for the car to be driven to London. Rolls-Royces can be picked up at a special London showroom on Conduit Street, which is just off Bond Street. At any rate, because company policies can change, check with your local dealer about the specifics of ordering a British car.

BAGPIPES

BILL LEWINGTON
144 Shaftesbury Ave., W1 (tel. 240-0584)
Underground Station: *Leicester Square*
Hours: *Monday through Saturday from 9 a.m. to 5:15 p.m.*
Credit Cards: *AE, DC, MC, V*

This musical-instrument shop specializes in bagpipes, brass, and woodwinds. It sells a variety of bagpipes from different countries, including four kinds of Scottish bagpipes. The lowest prices for bagpipes are for those made in Pakistan, which cost £120. Scottish bagpipes start at about £380, £580 for those that are handmade.

BATHROOM ACCESSORIES

If you're looking for the normal bathroom accessories such as soap dishes, towel racks, towels, and the like, department stores are good places to begin your search. Towels are also sold at many of London's linen shops, which are listed in this book under a separate heading. If, however, you're looking for bathroom fixtures and accessories that are a bit out of the ordinary, try the two shops below.

BONSACK
14 Mount St., W1 (tel. 629-9981)
Underground Station: *Bond Street*
Hours: *Monday through Friday from 9:30 a.m. to 5:30 p.m.*
Credit Cards: *AE, DC*

Its location on fashionable Mount Street tells you that this is no ordinary bathroom store. Bonsack is the ultimate in bathroom decor, providing customers with everything from apple-shaped tubs with leaf-shaped headrests to its famous Moon bath, the first of Bonsack's luxury baths to rise to fame during a major London exhibition in 1967. Baths can be made with lion-claw feet, with overhead shower canopies, or with whirlpools or air streams. You can also purchase your basin, toilet, bidet, and such bathroom accessories as taps and fittings, chandeliers, crystal lights, mirrors, powder jars, tissue holders, perfume bottles, soap dishes, soaps, towels, and even bathrobes. If you want, you can have an entire bathroom custom-made for you, right down to the bathroom fixtures. Delivery time for custom orders generally takes four months. Prices here start at about £3,300 for a bathtub, going all the way to £44,000 for complete bathroom facilities.

SITTING PRETTY
131 Dawes Rd., SW6 (tel. 381-0049)
Underground Station: *Fulham Broadway*
Hours: *Monday through Friday from 10:30 a.m. to 4 p.m., on Saturday from 11 a.m. to 3 p.m.*
Credit Cards: *None*

Sitting Pretty specializes in antique and reproduction Victorian bathroom accessories, including tubs, basins, bidets, brass taps, and wooden seats. The cost of a wooden seat, stained and varnished, is £79 in oak or mahogany. You can also purchase do-it-yourself kits for wooden toilet seats for £54. Seats can also be decorated with family crests, special patterns, or whatever you wish.

BEAUTY SALONS AND HAIRDRESSERS

MEN'S AND WOMEN'S

THE CADOGAN CLUB
182 Sloane St., SW1 (tel. 235-3814)
Underground Station: *Knightsbridge*
Hours: *Monday through Friday from 9 a.m. to 6 p.m., on Saturday to 1 p.m.*
Credit Cards: *AE*

Popular with the well-heeled middle-aged who are drawn to Sloane Street and Knightsbridge because of the fashionable shops, the Cadogan Club offers hairdressing, manicures, pedicures, facials, waxing, eyelash and brow tinting, and will even apply your makeup. Although it's safest to make an appointment, they'll take you without one if they have an empty slot. Haircuts for men start at £13.75, while a cut and blow-dry treatment for women starts at £27.50.

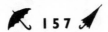

BEAUTY SALONS & HAIRDRESSERS

ESSANELLE
Fourth floor of D. H. Evans department store, 318 Oxford St., W1
(tel. 629-8800)
Underground Station: Bond Street or Oxford Circus
Hours: Monday through Saturday from 9:30 a.m. to 6 p.m. (on Thursday
to 8 p.m.)
Credit Cards: AE, DC, MC, V

All major department stores in London have hairdressing and beauty salons and are probably better equipped to take in off-the-street traffic than other salons. This one in D. H. Evans has a large staff and caters to workers in the vicinity, shoppers, and tourists with little time on their hands. Prices are very reasonable, starting at £7.65 for men's or children's shampoo and haircut, and at £13.65 for women's. Perms start at £28.50, pedicures are £11.50, and manicures are £5.50

GLEMBY INTERNATIONAL
Third floor of Selfridges department store, 400 Oxford St., W1
(tel. 629-1234)
Underground Station: Marble Arch or Bond Street
Hours: Monday through Saturday from 9 a.m. to 6 p.m. (on Thursday to
7:30 p.m.)
Credit Cards: AE, DC, MC, V

An American company, Glemby has salons in several department stores. The salon in Selfridges has a staff available especially for drop-ins, making this a good bet if you hate committing yourself to appointments. It has a gamut of services, including facials, makeup lessons, eyebrow tints and reshaping, body scrubs, massage, hair removal, tanning services, manicures, and pedicures. If you feel like splurging, you can treat yourself to a five-hour luxury service which includes steambath, massage, facial, manicure, pedicure, shampoo, cut, and even refreshments, all for £49. Otherwise, haircuts start at £13.50 for women and £4.50 for men. Permanents start at £27.50, a half-hour facial costs £7.60, a 20-minute massage costs £8.80, and a bikini wax costs £5.

Another Glemby is located in Harvey Nichols department store in Knightsbridge (tel. 235-5000). It's open Monday through Saturday from 9:30 a.m. to 6 p.m. (on Wednesday to 7 p.m.) Its prices are slightly higher; women's haircuts cost £19, men's cuts cost £11.50, and permanents start at £38.50. It also offers facials, eyebrow and eyelash tinting, massage and steambaths, waxing, manicures, pedicures, ear piercing, and electrolysis.

MICHAELJOHN
23A Albemarle St., W1 (tel. 629-6969)
Underground Station: Green Park
Hours: Monday through Saturday from 8:45 a.m. to 6 p.m.
Credit Cards: V

With a salon also in Beverly Hills, Michaeljohn has a steady and faithful clientele and will take appointments up to two months in advance. For simple haircuts, you can often be fitted in within 30 minutes without an appointment, but for coloring or perms you should book ahead. Prices vary according to who cuts your hair, ranging from £27.50 to £41 for women and £24.75 to £33 for men for a shampoo and cut. Permanents start at £38.50. If you want your nails done, complete with tips and acrylic, it will cost £38.50. You can have your nails silk-wrapped for £33. Michaeljohn also puts out a full line of beauty products, including shampoo, conditioner, scalp treatment, hairdressings, sculpture lotions, and mousse.

MOLTON BROWN

58 South Molton St., WI (tel. 629-1872 for women's cuts, 493-5236 for men's)
Underground Station: Bond Street
Hours: Monday to Friday from 10 a.m. to 5:30 p.m., on Saturday from 9 a.m. to 4:30 p.m.
Credit Cards: AE, MC, V

Molton Brown is known for products made of natural ingredients, free from fragrance, artificial coloring, or animal extracts. Its camomile or rosemary shampoo costs £4 for 300 milliliters, while its seaweed antistatic setting lotion costs £3.80 for the same amount. Other products include magnolia bath milk and lotion, sun lotions, and facial cleansers, toners, and moisturizers. They also sell Molton Browners, which are pliable, soft hair rollers that can be twisted and coaxed into producing a number of different hair styles. You can also buy combs, hair jewelry, headbands, and other hair accessories. For men there are shaving sets and aftershave lotion.

If you want to come here for treatment, haircuts for women start at £17.50 and go up to £32 for cuts by top stylists. Men's cuts start at £18. Other services are eyebrow reshaping and tinting, manicures, and pedicures.

SISSORS

46 King's Rd. (tel. 589-9471) and 69 King's Rd. (tel. 351-3339), Chelsea, SW3
Underground Station: Sloane Square
Hours: Monday through Saturday from 10 a.m. to 6:30 p.m.
Credit Cards: None

These two hair salons on King's Road cater primarily to young people, giving them everything from traditional bobs to more far-out creations. Prices start at £14 for a cut, and permanents and coloring treatments are also available. Walk-ins are welcome.

TAYLOR OF OLD BOND STREET

74 Jermyn St., SWI (tel. 930-5321)

BEAUTY SALONS & HAIRDRESSERS

Underground Station: Piccadilly Circus or Green Park
Hours: Monday through Saturday from 8:30 a.m. to 6:30 p.m.
Credit Cards: AE, DC, MC, V

This salon is named for its prior location on Bond Street, where it first opened in 1854. The salon was founded by the present owner's great-grandfather, who gained a reputation with his botanical extract for treatment of the scalp and hair. Its hair products and toiletries are still going strong, with shampoos, conditioners, and holding lotions available for several hair types, all using herbal ingredients. Its Herbal Mousse for £4.30 is nonsticky and antistatic. Skin oils, called Aromatherapy, are available for £4.30 in various scents. Foaming bath gel with scents of rose, gardenia, lily of the valley, or others also costs £4.30. Other products that also make good gifts include English lavender soaps, shaving sets, shaving brushes, and a sandalwood shaving cream.

A man's cut and shampoo costs £15, while a woman's cut only is £12. A face massage is £16.50 and permanents start at £25.

VIDAL SASSOON—WOMEN'S
60 South Molton St., WI (tel. 491-8848)
Underground Station: Bond Street
Hours: Monday through Wednesday from 9 a.m. to 5 p.m., Thursday
**   through Saturday beginning at 8:30 a.m. and closing at 7 p.m. on**
**   Thursday, at 6:30 p.m. on Friday, and at 5:30 p.m. on Saturday**
Credit Cards: AE, DC, MC, V

When I got my hair cut here, I felt like I was getting the royal treatment. My hair was first studied to see which type of cut would be best; that was followed by meticulous trimming and styling. Although I dropped in without an appointment, I was able to get a haircut within 30 minutes. Afternoons are usually fully booked, but morning appointments are generally easier to get. Prices for a cut start at £21.75, going up to £29 for a cut by a top stylist. You can also buy Vidal Sassoon's products here.

Other women's salons are at 44 Sloane St. (tel. 235-7791) and at 130 Sloane St. (tel. 730-7288). If you're not picky about your hair, you might also consider letting students at Vidal Sassoon's training school practice with your mane. Haircuts for both men and women are given Monday through Friday at 9:30 a.m., 11:30 a.m., and again at 1:30 p.m. The cost is only £3.80. For more information, call 629-4635. The school is located at 56 Brook St. in the same building as the men's salon.

VIDAL SASSOON—MEN'S
56 Brook St., WI (tel. 493-5428)
Underground Station: Bond Street
44 Sloane St., SWI (tel. 235-1957)
Underground Station: Knightsbridge

The men's version of Vidal Sassoon is stylish and trendy, with cuts starting at £16.50. Other services include beard trims, manicure and hand massage, restructurizing, permanents, and coloring. All products used in salon may be purchased at the reception desk.

YARDLEY
33 Old Bond St., WI (tel. 629-9341)
Underground Station: Piccadilly Circus or Green Park
Hours: Monday through Friday from 9 a.m. to 5:30 p.m.
Credit Cards: AE

Best known for its soaps, perfumes, aftershave lotions, and other beauty products developed since the company first opened as a perfumery in 1770, Yardley also has a beauty salon for women. No haircuts are given, but you can come here for facials, makeup lessons, eyebrow shaping, and wax treatments. A full facial with a toning mask, makeup, and eyebrow "tidying" costs £16.50. A full leg wax costs £18.50, while either a bikini wax or an underarm wax costs £6.30.

MEN'S HAIRDRESSERS

GEO. F.B. TRUMPER
9 Curzon St., WI (tel. 499-1850)
Underground Station: Green Park
Hours: Monday through Friday from 9 a.m. to 5:30 p.m., on Saturday to 1 p.m.
Credit Cards: AE, DC, MC, V

Trumper was established as a perfumer and barbershop in 1875 by Geo. F. Trumper. He made his perfumes, toilet waters, and pomades in vaults underneath his Curzon Street shop, and it wasn't long before his oils and essences became popular with the royal court. Today Trumper still produces handmade perfumes and soaps, and the hairdressing salon is one of the most traditional around, with its original dark-wood and glass fittings. Barbers here charge £10.50 for a cut and shampoo, and you can also have your face massaged and your nails buffed.

Trumper's products are also for sale, including colognes, aftershaves, skin balms, hairdressings, shampoos and hair conditioners, soaps, brushes, and shaving kits. If you're interested only in its products, Trumper has another shop at 20 Jermyn St. (tel. 734-1370) with an amazing selection of shaving kits and products.

TRUEFITT & HILL
23 Old Bond St., WI (tel. 493-2961)
Underground Station: Piccadilly Circus or Green Park

Hours: *Monday through Friday from 9 a.m. to 5:30 p.m., on Saturday to 12:30 p.m.*
Credit Cards: None

Established in 1805 as a perfumer and hairdresser, this male bastion on fashionable Bond Street is a delightful, old-fashioned salon. Its entertaining staff makes it a good place to pick up the local news, and it's fitted with art nouveau–style lamps and quietly whirring ceiling fans. Customers are generally decked out in suits and ties, fitting for a hairdressers that has a royal warrant to the Duke of Edinburgh. A cut and shampoo here costs £13, a shave costs £7.50, a face massage is £6.50, and a manicure is £6. The shop also sells a variety of toiletries for men, including soaps, cologne, shaving kits, hairbrushes, and shoe horns.

BOOKS

Living up to its long literary history, London is a mecca when it comes to bookstores and shops. The fact that we share a common language makes London especially happy hunting grounds, whether it's antiquarian, secondhand, specialist, or Penguin pocketbooks you're looking for.

In addition to the bookstores listed below, check the museum shops for books in specialized fields. The British Museum in particular publishes an outstanding collection of books on everything from coins to antiquities to architecture and art. It even produces a catalog with listings of British Museum publications. If you're looking for travel guides and can't find what you need in one of the stores below, refer to Stanfords in the "Map" section of this book. Specializing in maps and charts, it has a strong travel-guide section as well. Books on design, graphics, and interior design can be found in the Design Centre, listed under the "Gifts" section.

CONTEMPORARY AND SPECIALIST

COLLET'S INTERNATIONAL BOOKSHOP
129–131 Charing Cross Rd., WC2 (tel. 734-0782)
Underground Station: Tottenham Court Road
Hours: *Monday through Friday from 10 a.m. to 6:30 p.m., on Saturday to 6 p.m.*
Credit Cards: MC, V

Collet's is one of the best places in London for books on left-wing politics and sociology, including publications from and about the Third World. It has a large Russian department, featuring books written in Russian and books in English about Russia. Collet's also has foreign-language books and books on how to teach English as a foreign language. Other departments cover international fiction, travel guides, feminist history and fiction, art publications, and best-sellers. There's also a record department of folk music.

COLLET'S PENGUIN BOOKSHOP
64–66 Charing Cross Rd., WC2 (tel. 836-6306)
Underground Station: Leicester Square
**Hours: Monday through Friday from 10 a.m. to 6:30 p.m., on Saturday
    to 6 p.m.**
Credit Cards: MC, V

This is Collet's shop for both new and secondhand Penguins and for bestselling paperbacks from other publishers. There's a monthly catalog for Penguin books available, and you can order by mail.

FOYLES
113–119 Charing Cross Rd., WC2 (tel. 437-5660)
Underground Station: Tottenham Court Road or Leicester Square
**Hours: Monday through Saturday from 9 a.m. to 6 p.m. (on Thursday to
    7 p.m.)**
Credit Cards: None

In 1904, at the age of 19, William Foyle founded a book-selling business. Today Foyles calls itself "The World's Greatest Bookshop." It has more than 30 departments spread over five floors, with subjects ranging from books on advertising and ballet to entomology and stamps. Particularly strong departments include books on technology, medicine, drama, and music. Other departments carry books on travel, foreign languages, art, birds, Celtic subjects, coins, children's literature, cooking, criminology, embroidery, farming, heraldry, genealogy, photography, poetry, wines, and witchcraft—to name only a few. The main complaint most people have against Foyles is that it's difficult finding anything. The bookstore sprawls in all directions in a maze of various rooms on different floors. The book you want is probably there—if only you can find it.

In addition to its contemporary books, Foyles also has a rare-books collection, for which a free catalog is issued about three times a year. In one recent catalog, a 17-volume set of poems by Robert Browning published in 1889–1894 was listed at £1,150, while a first edition of Thomas Chippendale's *The Gentleman and Cabinet-Maker's Director*, published in 1754, was priced at £4,000.

HATCHARDS
187 Piccadilly, W1 (tel. 439-9921)
Underground Station: Piccadilly Circus or Green Park
**Hours: Monday through Friday from 9 a.m. to 5:30 p.m., on Saturday to
    5 p.m.**
Credit Cards: AE, MC, V

Booksellers since 1797 and moving to its Piccadilly location back in 1801, Hatchards is one of the most famous names in the bookstore business and has royal warrants as booksellers to the royal family. It specializes in new titles and in

Bow windows and a handsome portico make a great frontispiece for fine books

some older ones that are still popular. Although the store is fairly large and is elegant for a bookstore (notice the quaint bow windows), it is not at all intimidating. It offers traditional service and personal attention, without a trace of snobbery. "We're happy to see anyone who wants to read come through the door, whether they're a duchess or a chambermaid," said one enthusiastic staff member.

Hatchards specializes in the latest books in fiction, art, cooking, gardening, and ornithology, and it claims to have the largest paperback department in central London. Other departments include biography and memoirs, history, travel, architecture, sports and pastimes, the performing arts, and children's books. Hatchards has several branches in London: at Harvey Nichols department store in Knightsbridge, at 390 Strand (tel. 379-6264), and at 150–152 King's Rd. (tel. 351-7649).

HEYWOOD HILL
10 Curzon St., W1 (tel. 629-0647)
Underground Station: *Green Park*
Hours: *Monday through Friday from 9 a.m. to 5:30 p.m., on Saturday to 12:30 p.m.*
Credit Cards: *None*

Your first impression upon entering this cluttered, book lover's haven is that the books are taking over. They're stacked everywhere, piled precariously on tables, on the floor, and on the shelves. Lest you fear that it's all chaos, however, be assured that the staff knows their books. They can advise, encourage, and match books up with delighted readers. Without a doubt, this is a bookstore for writers and for people who love to read.

Founded in 1936 by Heywood Hill and his wife, the shop originally sold new and secondhand books. It soon became somewhat of a haunt for leading literary figures, including Evelyn Waugh, Nancy Mitford, and Anthony Powell. During World War II, Mitford, a prolific and provocative journalist, worked in the shop.

Today Heywood Hill keeps up the tradition, specializing in literary works. In contrast to some bookstores, the staff here actually reads the books and is very knowledgeable. In addition to fiction, the store also carries books on architecture and natural history. There's a good children's department that even has some children's books from Victorian times.

PLEASURES OF PAST TIMES
11 Cecil Court, WC2 (tel. 836-1142)
Underground Station: *Leicester Square*
Hours: *Monday through Friday from 11 a.m. to 2:30 p.m. and 3:30 to 5:45 p.m., and on the first Saturday of the month from 11 a.m. to 2:15 p.m., otherwise by appointment.*
Credit Cards: *None*

David Drummond's small and interesting shop revels in the performing arts, with books on the theater, musicals, and even the circus. He also carries memorabilia and items pertaining to the performing arts, including posters, autographs, postcards, and old programs. As Drummond himself said, "I can provide things for people whether they're mad about Gilbert and Sullivan or Conan Doyle."

JOHN SANDOE
10–11 Blacklands Terrace, SW3 (tel. 589-9473), just off King's Road
Underground Station: *Sloane Square*
Hours: *Monday through Saturday from 9:30 a.m. to 5:30 p.m.*
Credit Cards: *None*

This small, personable bookshop is packed with hardback and paperback selections in fiction, decoration, architecture and art, history, biography, travel, and cooking. It has a good children's section in its basement.

ZWEMMER LTD.
24 Litchfield St. and 80 Charing Cross Rd., WC2 (tel. 836-7049); and 72 Charing Cross Rd., WC2 (tel. 240-1559)

Underground Station: *Leicester Square*
Hours: *Monday through Friday from 9:30 a.m. to 6 p.m., on Saturday to 5:30 p.m.*
Credit Cards: *AE, MC, V*

Zwemmer Ltd. has three bookshops in close proximity, each dealing in a different subject. The shop on Litchfield Street specializes in books on fine art, sculpture, and arts and crafts, while the Zwemmer at 80 Charing Cross Rd. deals in books on cinematography, photography, graphic design, art technics, fashion, calligraphy, typography, and illustration.

At 72 Charing Cross Rd. is Zwemmer's O.U.P. Bookshop, which carries only books from the Oxford University Press. The subjects here are mainly academic, along with educational and reference books and smaller selections of novels, poetry, and paperbacks.

SECONDHAND

Though it's unlikely you'll find any buried treasures in London's second-hand bookshops, you will find used books at greatly discounted prices. Paperbacks are often listed for less than £1, and hardbacks are not much more.

ANY AMOUNT OF BOOKS
62 Charing Cross Rd., WC2 (tel. 240-8140)
Underground Station: *Leicester Square*
Hours: *Daily from 10:30 a.m. to 7:30 p.m.*
Credit Cards: *MC, V*

Known for its low prices and fast turnover, this secondhand book shop specializes in art and literature. In addition, antiquarian books and first editions sometimes pass through its doors. Paperbacks start at 45 pence, with the rarest books costing up to £330.

HENRY PORDES BOOKS
58–60 Charing Cross Rd., WC2 (tel. 836-9031)
Underground Station: *Leicester Square*
Hours: *Monday through Saturday from 10 a.m. to 7 p.m.*
Credit Cards: *None*

Boasting a good stock of general-interest books, this shop carries secondhand books, out-of-print titles at half the price originally charged, and modern first editions. About 90% of the books in the store were published in the United Kingdom. A small number of antiquarian, leather-bound books are usually available. Prices here start at 55 pence, going up to £330 for antiquarian editions.

READS

48A Charing Cross Rd., WC2 (tel. 379-7669)
Underground Station: *Leicester Square*
Hours: *Monday through Saturday from 9 a.m. to 10 p.m., on Sunday from noon to 8 p.m.*
Credit Cards: *AE, DC, MC, V*

This shop has shelves so high that you need stepladders to reach the top ones. Musty-smelling and crowded, it has lots of books, but finding what you want may be a problem. It's best to come with an open mind and simply browse. Used paperbacks of fiction cost £1.30, hardbound fiction costs anywhere from £2.50 to £4.50, and first editions run £11 to £22.

SKOOB BOOKS

15 Sicilian Ave., Holborn, WC1 (tel. 404-3063), just off Southampton Row
Underground Station: *Holborn*
Hours: *Monday through Saturday from 10:30 a.m. to 6:30 p.m.*
Credit Cards: *AE, MC, V*

One of London's best—if not *the* best—secondhand bookstores, Skoob carries general-interest books, with a large selection of used academic books, including literature, technical, and medical books. There are lots under £5.

ANTIQUARIAN

If you're looking for a specific title, the search can present a real challenge. That, however, is part of the fun for most collectors of antiquarian books. In London, there are a great number of shops selling fine and rare books, and who knows what you might discover as you browse your way through them. Most antiquarian bookshops are located on tiny Cecil Court, a narrow pedestrian lane just off Charing Cross Road. Shops here are small and friendly, staffed by people who have a passion for what they sell.

ALAN BRETT LTD.

24 Cecil Court, WC2 (tel. 836-8222)
Underground Station: *Leicester Square*
Hours: *Monday through Saturday from 9:30 a.m. to 5:30 p.m.*
Credit Cards: *AE, DC, V*

This small shop sells primarily books printed before 1850, mainly of topographical subjects. It also carries maps and prints that were printed before 1850, with a large selection of *Vanity Fair* prints starting at £5.50. Illustrated books are usually available as well.

BELL, BOOK AND RADMALL

4 Cecil Court, WC2 (tel. 836-5888)

Underground Station: *Leicester Square*
Hours: *Monday through Friday from 10 a.m. to 5:30 p.m.*
Credit Cards: *AE, DC, MC, V*

The speciality here is first-edition literature printed in the late 19th and 20th centuries, including works of fiction, poetry, and drama. Both American and English titles are represented, and prices range from £5.50 to £600. You can order by mail from catalogs produced three to four times a year.

BERNARD QUARITCH LTD.
5-8 Lower John St., Golden Square, W1 (tel. 734-2983)
Underground Station: *Piccadilly Circus*
Hours: *Monday through Friday from 9:30 a.m. to 5:30 p.m.*
Credit Cards: *None*

Established in 1847 and named after its founder, Bernard Quaritch is one of the largest dealers in rare books in the world. It carries early printed books and manuscripts (in 1978 it sold a copy of the Gutenberg Bible to the University of Texas for $2.4 million), as well as antiquarian books covering natural history, science, medicine, technology, travel, philosophy and human sciences, and the arts. English literature of all periods is strongly represented, and there are also illustrated and children's books. Altogether there are nine different departments, each headed by a specialist in the field. About ten catalogs are published annually, each focusing on the stock of a single department. Most of the business trade is by mail. Prices start at about £110, going up to £10,000. Prices can, however, be much higher. One manuscript from medieval times recently sold for £8 million.

CHELSEA RARE BOOKS
313 King's Rd., SW3 (tel. 351-0950)
Underground Station: *Sloane Square*
Hours: *Monday through Saturday from 10 a.m. to 6 p.m.*
Credit Cards: *AE, DC, MC, V*

The ground floor of this shop sells rare and secondhand books, while the basement is devoted to a gallery of English prints and watercolors. Books in stock include 18th- and 19th-century English literature, illustrated children's books, and travel and art books. There's a small selection of first editions as well, but the greater part of the shop's stock consists of secondhand books of general interest. The average price of a secondhand book here is £2.70. The staff is very friendly and accessible.

FROGNAL RARE BOOKS
18 Cecil Court, WC2 (tel. 240-2815)
Underground Station: *Leicester Square*
Hours: *Monday through Friday from 10 a.m. to 6 p.m.*
Credit Cards: *MC, V; U.S. dollars also accepted*

This shop carries a general stock, with a slant toward history books published from the 16th through the 19th centuries and toward works of literature from the 19th century up to the 1930s. Books on theology, art, and law are also in stock. In addition, this shop usually has a few books with fore-edge paintings, which means that the pages have gilt edges; if you look at the edges of the closed book opposite its binding, you'll find that the gilt edges come together to form a picture. The top prices for books here are £5,500, but some titles are available for £11.

Chelsea Rare Books also carries prints and secondhand volumes

H. M. FLETCHER
27 Cecil Court, WC2 (tel. 836-2865)
Underground Station: Leicester Square
Hours: Monday through Friday from 10 a.m. to 5:30 p.m.
Credit Cards: MC

This shop specializes in books printed before 1500, which are mostly in Latin or Greek and are known as incunabula. Prices for these can easily cost £22,000 but there are also all sorts of secondhand books, some available at 20 pence.

MAGGS BROS. LTD.
50 Berkeley Square, W1 (tel. 499-2007)
Underground Station: Green Park
Hours: Monday through Friday from 9:30 a.m. to 5 p.m.
Credit Cards: MC, V

The Maggs family has been buying and selling antiquarian books since the mid-1800s, moving to its present location on tree-shaded Berkeley Square in 1939. A delightful establishment with a helpful staff and five floors of antiquarian books, it became royal booksellers to the Queen in 1982 and over the years has been booksellers by appointment to George V, the late Prince of Wales, and the kings of Portugal and Spain.

Maggs's books cover a wide range of subjects, including English literature, travel, military and naval history, and works on history and theology published before 1660. There's also a department dealing with autographs. Maggs publishes a variety of catalogs, each covering different departments. Mail orders make up a large part of the business here, going "to all obscure areas of the world." Prices range from about £65 all the way to £7,700 for rare books of the 15th and 16th centuries.

As a bit of a sidelight, you might be interested in knowing that the old house Maggs occupies is supposedly haunted. The story goes that a young woman became distraught when her parents disapproved of her lover. To end her sorrow, she reputedly threw herself out of an upper-story window of the house, impaling herself on the pointed gate below. Today she coexists with all those books, no doubt finding comfort in the fact that some of them date from her time.

PETER STOCKHAM AT IMAGES
16 Cecil Court, WC2 (tel. 836-8661)
Underground Station: Leicester Square
Hours: Tuesday through Friday from 11 a.m. to 6 p.m., and on the first Saturday of the month from 11 a.m. to 2 p.m.
Credit Cards: None

Children's and illustrated books are the specialty here, including both new, secondhand, and antiquarian books. Most are English books published in the 18th through 20th centuries. Altogether about 10,000 children's books are in stock, packed ceiling to floor. A lot of passersby stop in to inquire whether the shop carries a book they remember from childhood and would like to own again. Books start at £1.50 and go up into the thousands, but the average prices fall between £4.50 and £160.

REG AND PHILIP REMINGTON
14 Cecil Court, WC2 (tel. 836-9771)
Underground Station: Leicester Square
Hours: Monday through Friday from 10 a.m. to 5 p.m.
Credit Cards: None

If you're interested in antiquarian and secondhand books written about voyages, travels, and natural history, this shop is worth your time. It's here that I found editions of travel books by Isabella Bird, a remarkable woman who

traveled in Japan in the late 1800s. In stock are both contemporary books and those written since the 15th century, and the shop carries maps and prints, as well. Secondhand books range from about £2.50 to £550.

SOTHERAN'S
2–5 Sackville, W1 (tel. 734-1150)
Underground Station: Piccadilly Circus
Hours: Monday through Friday from 9 a.m. to 5:30 p.m.
Credit Cards: AE, DC, MC, V

Sotheran's publishes about five or six catalogs yearly listing its antiquarian books in stock. Established in 1815, this well-known and old-fashioned bookshop has been in its present location about 50 years and still has its old, glass-enclosed bookcases along the walls. The staff is friendly and outgoing. The stock includes out-of-print and antiquarian books, antiquarian prints and maps, and autographs. The shop can also obtain any book that is currently in print.

Recent catalogs have listed the following works for sale: Lawrence Durrell's *Prospero's Cell*, a first edition of a guide to Corsica published in 1945 and priced at £46; a first edition of Oscar Wilde's *A Woman of No Importance*, published in 1894 and priced at £195; Sir Winston Churchill's first book, *The Story of the Malakand Field Force*, published in 1898 and priced at £437; and the fourth collected edition of Shakespeare, printed in 1685 and priced at £3,135. In other words, there are books in all price ranges.

BOOTS

Refer to the "Shoes" section of this book for shops that sell handmade boots.

BRASS RUBBINGS

LONDON BRASS RUBBING CENTRE
St. James's Church, Piccadilly, W1 (tel. 437-6023)
Underground Station: Piccadilly Circus
Hours: Monday through Saturday from 10 a.m. to 6 p.m., on Sunday
from noon to 6 p.m.
Credit Cards: None

You needn't have prior experience to make your own brass rubbings at this center, located under St. James's Church. Altogether there are about 70 brass reliefs, all reproductions of famous works of art from around England. Most of the reliefs are of saints and knights, including one of St. George and the Dragon taken from a woodcut from 1590. Sizes range from about typing-paper dimen-

sions up to seven feet and range in price from 60 pence to £11. Included in the price are all the materials necessary to make your brass rubbing, as well as instructions from the staff. If you'd like a brass rubbing but are too lazy to make one yourself, ready-made ones are available for about double the price of the do-it-yourself versions. This is a great activity for older kids, and the finished products make nifty souvenirs and gifts.

CANES

Refer to the "Walking Sticks" section for information regarding canes.

CARPETS

Shops selling carpets are listed under "Rugs."

CHINA

It's probably no surprise to hear that china comes originally from China. A type of porcelain was being produced in China as early as the 8th century, appearing in its present form sometime around 1300. In any case, Chinese porcelain began arriving in Europe in appreciable quantities during the Middle Ages. So great was the desire to possess this exotic ware that European potters began imitating the product without knowing what materials were used by the Chinese.

It wasn't until shortly after 1700, however, that Europeans had any great success in producing porcelain, a type of ware known as "true porcelain." A factory in Germany was the first to manufacture the porcelain, soon followed by factories in Vienna and later by firms in France.

England's first porcelain factory, however, didn't start production until 1743. Famous names during those early years include Chelsea, Bow, and Derby, with factories located in London, Bristol, Worcester, and Liverpool. Soaprock became a favored substance of English potters throughout the 18th century. Then around 1800, Josiah Spode is said to have revolutionized china production by introducing bone ash to his porcelain, thereby creating bone china. Allowing firing at a much higher temperature than true porcelain, bone ash produced a lighter, white china that was more durable and less expensive. Today bone china is widely produced in England.

One of the most famous names in English china is Wedgwood. Josiah Wedgwood, born in 1730, can be credited with changing the entire course of the European pottery industry. Born the last of 12 children, he belonged

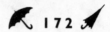
to the fourth generation of a family of potters. Through many years of experiments he developed techniques for high-fired earthenwares and stonewares. He became famous for his creamwares (a creamy white earthenware covered with a transparent glaze), his basaltes (a dense, black stoneware, popular for vases), and his jasperware (a fine stoneware almost indistinguishable from unglazed porcelain).

Interestingly enough, Josiah Wedgwood never produced porcelain. He did, however, make his wares cheaply by large-scale manufacture, and so they became affordable to many people who could never buy them before. Today antique Wedgwood pieces fetch high prices, but the masses are still catered to with a large production of china, particularly tableware.

Other famous china brands found in shops throughout London include Spode, Minton, Royal Crown Derby, Royal Worcester, Aynsley, and Coalport, all of which had their beginnings in the 1700s. Also popular is Royal Doulton, produced by a company founded in 1815.

Shops selling china in London usually offer a wide variety of table china, and most offer porcelain figures, porcelain flowers, crystal, and cutlery as well. All the shops listed here will mail your purchases from their shop, and they will also take mail orders in case you decide to add to your collection or pattern after you've returned home. In addition to these shops, several of the stores listed under "Gifts" carry a small selection of chinaware. For antique porcelain and pottery, don't forget to check for sales at London's auction houses.

ANTIQUE

ALISTAIR SAMPSON
156 Brompton Rd., SW3 (tel. 589-5272)
Underground Station: *Knightsbridge*
Hours: *Monday through Friday from 9:30 a.m. to 5:30 p.m., on Saturday by appointment*
Credit Cards: *AE, MC, V*

I already listed Alistair Sampson in the "Antiques" section, but it's worth mentioning this shop again for its pottery. It specializes in 17th- and 18th-century English pottery, with prices starting at £100.

THE ANTIQUE PORCELAIN CO.
149 New Bond St., WI (tel. 629-1254)
Underground Station: *Bond Street, Piccadilly Circus, or Green Park*
Hours: *Monday through Thursday from 9:30 a.m. to I p.m. and 2 to 6 p.m., on Friday to 5 p.m.*
Credit Cards: *None; U.S.-dollar traveler's checks and cash accepted*

**Elegant china and crystal for the table
at Fortnum & Mason**

Located up on the first floor, this shop deals in porcelain from the time it was first produced in Europe through the 18th century. Its specialty is 18th-century European porcelain, including figures, plates, cups, and saucers. There's also some French furniture of the 18th century, gold boxes, and scent bottles. Prices for porcelain start at £1,100, which is the bottom price for some of the porcelain figures.

EARLE D. VANDEKAR
138 Brompton Rd., SW3 (tel. 589-8481)
Underground Station: *Knightsbridge*
Hours: *Monday through Friday from 9:30 a.m. to 5:30 p.m.*
Credit Cards: *AE, DC, V*

Established in 1913, this family business happens to have one of the largest selections of antique porcelain and pottery in London. The stock includes English, continental, and Oriental pieces, most produced before 1830. Particularly good is its range of Oriental porcelain, which was made especially for export to the European market in the 18th century. Oriental pieces range from about £600 to £70,000. A Chinese soup tureen decorated with a European coat-of-arms, for example, was priced at £70,000. If you're looking for antique dinner and dessert services, they range in price from £6,500 to £40,000, depending on the number of people it serves and the extent of decoration.

Earle D. Vandekar: Antique porcelain and pottery

MODERN AND CONTEMPORARY

In addition to the shops listed below, department stores also have chinaware. Harrods, Selfridges, and Peter Jones all have large china and crystal departments. For modern pottery produced by Britain's many fine artists, refer to the "Crafts" section of this book.

CHINACRAFT
130 New Bond St., WI (tel. 499-5816)
Underground Station: Bond Street
Hours: Monday through Saturday from 9 a.m. to 6 p.m. (on Thursday to 7:30 p.m.)
Credit Cards: AE, CB, DC, MC, V

With 40 stores throughout the United Kingdom, Chinacraft is one of the largest chains specializing in fine British bone china. It also carries crystal, cutlery, porcelain figurines, and silver and silver-plated tea and coffee sets. Its catalog, available for £3.80, is excellent, with color photographs of its pieces, short biographies of the various companies represented, and prices for items in stock. Although the list is long, it should be noted that Chinacraft carries Wedgwood,

CHINA

Royal Doulton, Royal Crown Derby, Royal Worcester, Minton, Spode, Aynsley, Coalport, Royal Copenhagen, Haviland, Herend, Limoges. Its crystal collection includes Waterford, Lalique, Stuart Crystal, Royal Brierly, Baccarat, and St. Louis.

Wedgwood's Columbia Powder Ruby tableware, first introduced in 1920, costs £353 for one five-piece place setting. If that's too expensive, Wedgwood's April Flowers pattern is available for £25 for one five-piece place setting. In addition to the address given above, Chinacraft can also be found in London at 198 Regent St., 71 Regent St., 7/11 Burlington Arcade, 50 Brompton Rd., 556 Oxford St., 1/3 Beauchamp Pl., 74 Southhampton Row, and 98 The Strand. Ask at your hotel for the one nearest you.

GEORG JENSEN
15 New Bond St., W1 (tel. 629-3622)
Underground Station: *Piccadilly Circus or Green Park*
Hours: *Monday through Friday from 9:15 a.m. to 5:30 p.m., on Saturday from 10 a.m. to 1 p.m.*
Credit Cards: AE, DC, MC, V

This shop sells only products from Denmark, all made by Georg Jensen, Royal Copenhagen, or Holme Gaard. Particularly popular are the porcelain figurines by Royal Copenhagen, each painted by hand, which start at £44. Royal Copenhagen also issues an annual collector's plate at Christmas which costs £29. Other items for sale include Georg Jensen's watches, silver jewelry, and cutlery, as well as glassware by Holme Gaard.

GERED
158 Regent St., W1 (tel. 734-7262)
Underground Station: *Oxford Circus or Piccadilly Circus*
173–174 Piccadilly, W1 (tel. 629-2614)
Underground Station: *Green Park*
Hours: *Monday through Friday from 9 a.m. to 5:30 p.m., on Saturday to 1 p.m., for both stores*
Credit Cards: AE, DC, MC, V

As members of the Wedgwood Group, these two Gered stores stock a complete range of Wedgwood china, including Jasper, porcelain figurines, and Wedgwood jewelry. Other names in china are represented as well, including Coalport, Spode, Royal Doulton, Minton, and Royal Crown Derby, but there's no question as to who's the boss around here. Wedgwood's five-piece place settings cost £58 for Osborne, £80 for Dark Blue Runnymede, £51 for Cavendish, and £47 for Amherst, to name just a few of the more popular patterns. Wedgwood porcelain figurines range in price from £41.50 to £74.90. A sister shop to Gered is Wedgwood at Oxford Circus, listed under its own name.

An English classic

LAWLEYS
154 Regent St., WI (tel. 734-3184)
Underground Station: *Piccadilly Circus*
Hours: *Monday through Saturday from 9 a.m. to 5:30 p.m. (on Tuesday from 9:30 a.m., and on Thursday to 9 p.m.)*
Credit Cards: AE, DC, MC, V

A landmark on Regent Street for more than 60 years, Lawleys is a bit contemptuous of the upstart Reject China Shop next door. It claims to offer better and more knowledgeable service, and its wares are tastefully and pleasantly displayed. It carries nearly all the popular makes of English china, including Wedgwood, Aynsley, Royal Worcester, Spode, Minton, Royal Doulton, and Royal Albert. It also carries Waterford crystal. Each manufacturer issues its own brochure with prices of its pieces. Aynsley's brochure, for example, lists its plain, white Golden Crocus pattern with a simple gold trim at £30.75 for a five-piece place setting.

REJECT CHINA SHOP
134 Regent St., WI (tel. 434-2502)
Underground Station: *Piccadilly Circus*

Hours: *Monday through Saturday from 9 a.m. to 6 p.m. (on Thursday to 7 p.m., on Sunday from 10 a.m. to 6 p.m.)*
Credit Cards: AE, CB, DC, MC, V

With prices that are as much as half what the same items would cost in the United States, the Reject China Shop offers more than just china, and there's very little offered today that qualifies as a factory reject. Although Reject China Shop began as a discount store for manufacturers who wanted to get rid of factory seconds and damaged stock, the stock offered today is perfect and is of the same quality you'd find in department stores. You won't find any chipped or damaged pieces here. Instead, you'll find fine pieces offered for about 10% less than in London's stores. Annual sales offering even additional bargains are held in January and August. There's a mail-order catalog and items can be shipped from the shop.

Price lists are displayed throughout the store and give both the local price and the price without the VAT for those taking goods out of the country. To qualify for a VAT refund, store policy dictates that you must spend more than £65. At any rate, all items are available by the piece, the place setting, or the entire set. The list of brands carried is quite exhaustive and includes products from around the world. Among them are Mikasa, Villeroy & Boch, Spal, Noritake, Denby, Aynsley, Paragon, Royal Albert, Royal Worcester, Spode, Portmeirion, St. Louis, Baccarat, Boehm, Lalique, Waterford, Lenox, Limoges, and Coalport — almost everything except Wedgwood.

There's another Reject China Shop outlet in Knightsbridge. Actually it's three shops close together, each specializing in different items ranging from china to crystal to silverware, figurines, and Caithness paperweights. Addresses for these shops are 183 Brompton Rd., 33–35 Beauchamp Pl., and 56–57 Beauchamp Pl.

THOMAS GOODE

19 South Audley St., W1 (tel. 499-2823)
Underground Station: *Bond Street, Green Park, or Marble Arch*
Hours: *Monday through Friday from 9 a.m. to 5 p.m. (on Tuesday from 9:30 a.m.), on Saturday from 9:30 a.m. to 1 p.m.*
Credit Cards: AE, DC, MC, V

With more than 150 years of experience dealing in fine English china, Thomas Goode can also boast holding royal warrants as suppliers of china and glass to the Queen, the Queen Mother, and the Prince of Wales. The front door of this fine red-brick Victorian house is guarded by ceramic elephants made by Minton in 1870 for the Goode family's display at the Paris World's Fair. Pass through its Victorian mechanical doors and you'll find yourself in an elegant shop with a large and varied selection of china, crystal, housewares, and gifts.

It carries china by Herend, Minton, Royal Crown Derby, Royal Doulton,

Haviland, Villeroy & Boch, Coalport, Wedgwood, Royal Worcester, and Spode, to name a few; and crystal by Baccarat, St. Louis, Cristal de Sèvres, Royal Brierley, Waterford, Stuart, and Atlantis. Also on display are chandeliers, clocks, silver, cutlery, lamps, cork placemats, cloisonné, photo frames, and even gifts for children, including a ten-piece Wedgwood Peter Rabbit tea set for £31.80. Be sure to pick up the store's catalog, which costs $4 if it's sent to the United States but is given out free in the shop. It lists prices and tells how to order by mail. VAT refunds are given only on purchases over £50.

WEDGWOOD AT OXFORD CIRCUS
270 Regent St., WI (tel. 734-5656)
Underground Station: Oxford Circus
Hours: Monday through Friday from 9 a.m. to 5:30 p.m. (on Thursday to
**   6:30 p.m.), on Saturday to 5 p.m.**
Credit Cards: AE, DC, MC, V

This shop is the sister shop to Gered listed earlier and carries much of the same merchandise. In addition to an exhaustive range of Wedgwood china, it also carries china from such manufacturers as Royal Worcester, Royal Doulton, Coalport, Spode, and Minton. It also stocks figurines by Royal Doulton, Hummel, Coalport, and Wedgwood. The price for Wedgwood figures ranges from £27.45 to £93.50. Caithness paperweights cost £10 to £47.

If you're looking for a gift or souvenir, the Wedgwood jewelry collection offers jasper and black basalt cameos decorated with classical motifs designed by 18th-century artists. Cameos are available as brooches, pendants, rings, earrings, cuff links, and tie tacks. You can also buy jasper plates, teapots, cups and saucers, boxes, candy trays, and other items. Wedgwood also issues commemorative plates for Christmas and other special occasions.

CIGARS

In addition to the two shops listed below, Dunhill, listed under "Tobacconists," has a large selection of cigars. Remember that U.S. Customs limits you to 100 cigars on your personal exemption and that none of them can be from Cuba unless you purchase them in Cuba itself. London's shops sell almost exclusively Cuban cigars, and when I asked one employee what Americans did when they walked into his cigar shop, he replied, "They cry." Another cigar seller told me he sometimes sold cigars stripped of their Cuban labels to Americans who wanted to smuggle them back. I have a feeling this is pretty common practice, but I wouldn't encourage you to take the risk.

CIGARS

DAVIDOFF
35 St. James's St., SW1 (tel. 930-3079)
Underground Station: Green Park
Hours: Monday through Saturday from 9 a.m. to 6 p.m.
Credit Cards: AE, DC, MC, V

This sparkling, modern showroom in the heart of St. James's specializes in Havana cigars, with the price per cigar ranging from £3.50 to £13. They also carry Jamaican, Honduran, Danish, and Dutch cigars, and stock all the accessories for smokers, including humidors, cigar cutters, ashtrays, pipes, and tobaccos.

ROBERT LEWIS
19 St. James's St., SW1 (tel. 930-3787)
Underground Station: Green Park
Hours: Monday through Friday from 9 a.m. to 5:30 p.m., on Saturday to 12:30 p.m.
Credit Cards: AE, DC, MC, V

Founded in 1787, Robert Lewis is probably the oldest cigar merchant in the country. From 1900 until shortly before his death, Winston Churchill had an account and purchased all his cigars here. Run by friendly and courtly gentlemen, the shop has a pleasant, old-fashioned interior. Havana cigars are the specialty here, but the shop also has a house brand. Other products sold include some pipes and tobacco, Turkish cigarettes, humidors, and snuff. Single cigars range in price from £2.20 to £14.

Winston Churchill purchased all his cigars at Robert Lewis

CLOCKS

England has produced some of the best clockmakers in the world, and in London's antique shops you can find everything from longcases to bracket and carriage clocks. All the shops listed below sell antique clocks, accept mail orders, and will undertake shipping arrangements. Another shop dealing in antique clocks is **Keith Harding**, listed in the "Music Boxes" section.

If you're interested in modern clocks, refer to the "Jewelry" section, where you'll find **Garrard**, which sells both modern and antique clocks, and **Mappin and Webb**, which carries a selection of reproduction carriage clocks. In addition, **Asprey**, listed in the "Gifts" section, has a unique range of modern clocks.

BUSHE ANTIQUES
52–53 Camden Passage, Islington, N1 (tel. 226-7096)
Underground Station: *Angel*
Hours: *Tuesday through Saturday from 9:30 a.m. to 6 p.m. (on Wednesday from 8:30 a.m.)*
Credit Cards: *AE, DC, MC, V*

This small shop abounds in English longcases and in ornately decorated French mantel clocks dating from about the mid-18th century to the late 19th century. Among its stock are boulle clocks (decorated with tortoiseshell inlaid in brass) and skeleton clocks. About 50 longcases are usually in stock, ranging in price from £1,100 to £10,000, along with 200 French mantel clocks priced between £450 and £3,800. The shop also carries some Swiss music boxes starting at £2,200. All items sold from the store have been restored and come with a one-year guarantee.

PHILIP & BERNARD DOMBEY
174 Kensington Church St., W8 (tel. 229-7100)
Underground Station: *Notting Hill Gate*
Hours: *Monday through Friday from 10 a.m. to 4 p.m., on Saturday to 2 p.m.*
Credit Cards: *AE, DC, MC, V*

Dealing in French antique clocks from the early 18th century to the end of the 19th century, this shop is a good source for French mantel, bracket, picture, and carriage clocks. Prices range from £650 to £11,000.

RAFFETY
34 Kensington Church St., W8 (tel. 938-1100)
Underground Station: *High Street Kensington*
Hours: *Monday through Friday from 10 a.m. to 5 p.m., on Saturday to 1 p.m.*
Credit Cards: *AE, DC, MC, V*

Offering repair services as well, Raffety sells 17th, 18th-, and some 19th-century English clocks, including wall clocks, longcases, and bracket clocks. It also has a small selection of barometers, some scientific instruments, and watches. Bracket clocks here start at £550.

STRIKE ONE
51 Camden Passage, Islington, N1 (tel. 226-9709)
Underground Station: *Angel*
Hours: *Monday through Saturday from 9 a.m. to 5 p.m.*
Credit Cards: *AE, DC, MC, V*

An enthusiastic dealer in clocks for 20 years, owner John Mighell sells primarily English longcases, bracket, and wall clocks, along with lantern clocks, French carriage clocks, Vienna regulators, and English barometers. The majority of his stock is in the £650 to £11,000 range, and everything sold has been completely overhauled and is guaranteed worldwide for one year. Each customer receives a book on how to set up his clock, and Mighell even has a list of clockmakers across the United States who can repair antique clocks. If Strike One doesn't have what you want, Mighell will find it for you.

Time ticks on . . . in London too

CLOTHING

Selecting the shops and boutiques for this clothing section was by far my most formidable task. After all, just a short stroll down any of London's major shopping streets will tell you that London is literally packed with clothing shops, which means that one has to be selective when it comes to choosing stores. In addition, I'll wager that almost every visitor who shops in London buys at least one article of clothing.

Admittedly, there are many fine shops I had neither the time nor the space to investigate. I am confident, however, that the selection of shops below are among the best the city has to offer. The range is wide, from the traditional and classical cuts of Jaeger, Paddy Campbell, and Laura Ashley to the unique designer wear of Jasper Conran, Katharine Hamnet, and Bruce Oldfield. I've also included a large selection of shops with clothing by foreign designers, primarily French, Italian, and Japanese.

If you're visiting London primarily for its clothing stores, it's worth it to plan your trip around the annual sales. Probably 90% of the clothing stores have two big sales a year, generally right after Christmas or in January and again sometime in summer, usually in July or August. Savings can be substantially more than 50% off the regular price, with many items going for next to nothing. All the Londoners I know wouldn't dream of buying designer clothes unless they're on sale.

THE BIG STORES

In addition to the stores listed here which carry almost exclusively clothing, London's department stores are also excellent places to shop for men's, women's, and children's clothing. Most of them carry name-brand clothing of famous fashion houses as well as concessions of designer wear. My favorites are **Harvey Nichols** and **Selfridges**, while **Marks & Spencer** has unbeatable prices on everything from underwear and sweaters to coats and casual wear. **Dickens and Jones** has recently switched its emphasis almost entirely to clothing. If you're looking for inexpensive, functional children's clothes, try **British Home Stores**. Even **Liberty**, known most for its wonderful fabrics, and **Fortnum & Mason**, famous for its food hall, have clothing sections. And of course, who hasn't heard of London's biggest department store, **Harrods**. For more information on these and other department stores, refer to the "Department Stores" section.

AQUASCUTUM
100 Regent St., W1 (tel. 734-6090)
Underground Station: *Piccadilly Circus*
Hours: *Monday through Saturday from 9 a.m. to 5:30 p.m. (on Thursday to 7 p.m.)*
Credit Cards: *AE, DC, MC, V*

Perhaps best known for its raincoats, Aquascutum, established in 1851, has a wide range of men's and women's clothes as well. The clothes are dependably top quality, with classic styles that can be worn season after season without becoming dated. The stock ranges from sportswear and knitwear to suits, blouses, dresses, and accessories, including luggage, mufflers, and umbrellas. Men's long-sleeved cotton dress shirts range from £41 to £49.50, while a woman's classically cut black dress suit is priced at £236.

As for its raincoats, Aquascutum has years of specialty experience. In fact, the shop first opened as a showroom for waterproof wool coats, and the store's name comes from the Latin word meaning "watershield." Aquascutum raincoats have accompanied British soldiers in the Crimean and First and Second World Wars. Today there are many variations of the raincoat available for both men and women, from trenchcoats to dress coats and overcoats. Men's trenchcoats with either button or zip-out liners cost £374, while a man's dress coat with a zip-out liner and hidden buttons costs £280. In the women's department, trenchcoats with zip-out liners begin at £297. Petite sizes for both men and women are available.

AUSTIN REED

103 Regent St., WI (tel. 734-6789)
Underground Station: *Piccadilly Circus*
Hours: *Monday through Saturday from 9 a.m. to 5:30 p.m. (on Thursday to 7 p.m.)*
Credit Cards: *AE, DC, MC, V*

Known for its classic styles, Austin Reed also has remarkably reasonable prices. Beginning as a small shirt and hosiery shop and expanding into men's clothing more than 60 years ago, the store now carries a woman's collection called Options, shoes, luggage, perfume, hats, ties, jewelry, and other accessories in addition to a wide range of men's fashions. It's a good place to shop for traditional business clothes. A men's classic check wool suit costs £214, while a men's dress overcoat in wool is priced at £175. A three-piece pinstripe suit starts at £148. In the women's department, a chalk-striped work dress is priced at £115, while a red double-breasted long coat is £145. Throughout the store are forms you can fill out to be put on the mailing list for catalogs. In addition to the Regent Street location, there is another Austin Reed at 163–169 Brompton Rd. (tel. 734-6789).

BURBERRYS

18–22 Haymarket, SWI (tel. 930-3343); and 165 Regent St., WI (tel. 734-4060)
Underground Station: *Piccadilly Circus*
Hours: *Monday through Saturday from 9 a.m. to 5:30 p.m. (on Thursday to 7 p.m.).*
Credit Cards: *AE, DC, MC, V*

Raincoats are the specialty of Burberrys, with dozens of styles to choose from. Men's single-breasted raincoats range from about £160 to £250, while double-breasted ones run £210 to £434 depending on whether they're lined. Women's raincoats begin at £155, with a silk coat priced at £467. You can even buy children's raincoats here, starting at £93.50. Burberrys also has a large selection of sweaters, casual wear, golf and tennis clothes, scarves, handbags, luggage, umbrellas, and men's and women's fashions. A woman's lambswool knitted skirt is priced at £43.50, while a man's double-breasted gray flannel suit costs £275.

C & A
505 Oxford St., W1 (tel. 629-7272)
Underground Station: Marble Arch
Hours: Monday, Tuesday, and Saturday from 9:30 a.m. to 6 p.m.,
Wednesday through Friday to 8 p.m.
Credit Cards: AE, MC, V

This is the London flagship store for this Dutch-based company specializing in affordable clothing for the entire family. Three floors offer working, party, and casual clothes, in addition to nightwear, stockings, socks, ties, belts, purses, hats, shoes, and other accessories. Most of the women's dresses are made of polyester, which is certainly a much better material than it used to be, and most prices range from £22 to £60. A department called Clock House carries modern styles for young women. Men's suits are very good bargains, beginning at £65 for polyester-wool blends. Other C & A stores in London are at 200 Oxford St. (tel. 629-7272) and 160 Kensington High St. (tel. 937-6362).

FENWICK
63 New Bond St., W1 (tel. 629-9161)
Underground Station: Bond Street
Hours: Monday through Saturday from 9:30 a.m. to 6 p.m. (on Thursday
to 7 p.m.)
Credit Cards: AE, MC, V

Fenwick is actually a small department store selling primarily women's clothing, accessories, and cosmetics. It's especially popular with working women who stop off for a quick look at the fashions or to buy a new bottle of nail polish. It also has a small men's section, a Glemby hair salon, and some selections in women's designer clothes, including Jaeger and Nicole Farhi. A Nicole Farhi green wool duster is priced at £197, with a matching straight skirt priced at £79. The staff is pleasant and helpful, a continuation of the store's tradition that began when it opened in 1891 with a policy that clerks should not speak to customers unless first spoken to. The policy proved so successful that a rival establishment put out a sign reading "We, too, have the new non-speaking type of shop assistant."

JAEGER
204–206 Regent St., WI (tel. 734-8211)
Underground Station: Oxford Circus
Hours: Monday through Saturday from 9:30 a.m. to 5:30 p.m. (on Thursday to 7 p.m.)
Credit Cards: AE, DC, MC, V

A British company established before the turn of the century and famous for using natural fibers, Jaeger is known for classic, elegant cuts in unusual and exclusive fabrics. Most of the clothes are British designed and British made, but Jaeger also carries French and Italian designs made especially for them. There are lots of separates in a full range of solid colors. A woman's purple-and-black sweater priced at £60, for example, can be combined with various skirts for around £70. Full-length wool dresses begin at £130, while a woman's beige-and-white Prince of Wales check linen jacket is priced at £152. The men's shop, in the basement, has trousers from £70 and suits from £197.

Other Jaeger shops can be found at 148 Regent St. (tel. 734-8211), 96–98 Brompton Rd. (tel. 584-2814), 145 King's Rd. (tel. 352-1122), 184 Kensington High St. (tel. 937-8211), and 163 Sloane St. (tel. 235-2505). Jaeger clothes are also featured in Harrods, Harvey Nichols, Selfridges, and Fenwick.

Jaeger: Traditional British elegance

LILLYWHITES
Piccadilly Circus, SW1 (tel. 930-3181)
Underground Station: Piccadilly Circus
Hours: Monday through Saturday from 9:30 a.m. to 6 p.m. (on Thursday
   to 7 p.m.)
Credit Cards: AE, DC, MC, V

The largest sporting goods and sportswear store in town, Lillywhites is where
you shop for track suits, cricket footwear, rugby shirts, ski wear, tennis and
running shoes, as well as all the equipment needed for fishing, ice skating, golf,
skiing, tennis, riding, squash, and other sports. Reebok tennis shoes start at
£41.75 and rugby shirts range from £20 to £33.

MOSS BROS.
21-26 Bedford St., WC2 (tel. 240-4567)
Underground Station: Leicester Square or Covent Garden
Hours: Monday through Saturday from 9 a.m. to 5:30 p.m. (on Tuesday
   from 9:30 a.m., and on Thursday to 7 p.m.)
Credit Cards: AE, DC, MC, V

A family business since its founding in 1860, Moss Bros. is a friendly, relaxed,
and slightly old-fashioned department store, delightfully off the beaten path. It
specializes in men's and women's clothes, riding clothes and saddlery, ski wear,
and kilts. It even has a clothing rental service, where you can rent tuxedos,
evening dresses, and kilts. Its fashion departments carry Aquascutum, Christian Dior, Jaeger, Planet, Windsmoor, Alexon, and shoes by Church's and
Bally. Men's suits range from about £155 for a polyester-rayon mix to £467 for a
wool, double-breasted suit by Ungaro.

If you find yourself invited to an important function but don't have the proper
clothing, evening gowns rent for an average of £45, all of them designed
in-house and most of them strapless. A man's double-breasted dinner suit,
including shirt, bow, and cumberbund, rents for £33. Rental clothes are often
for sale at excellent prices.

THE SCOTCH HOUSE
2 Brompton Rd., Knightsbridge, SW1 (tel. 581-2151)
Underground Station: Knightsbridge
Hours: Monday through Saturday from 9 a.m.; on Monday, Tuesday, and
   Thursday to 5:30 p.m., on Wednesday to 6:30 p.m., and on Friday and
   Saturday to 6 p.m.
Credit Cards: AE, DC, MC, V

Founded more than 100 years ago and moving to its Knightsbridge location at
the turn of the century, the Scotch House sells Scottish merchandise, namely
woolens, tartans, kilts, scarves, gloves, and hats. It has a children's department
too, with cute plaid skirts and kilts, plaid dresses, cashmere sweaters, and
raincoats. Burberry raincoats, Church's shoes, and sweaters by Ballantyne,

CLOTHING

Pringle, Barrie, and Murray Allen are also for sale. This is the largest shop, with two other locations on Regent Street at no. 84 (tel. 734-5966) and no. 191 (tel. 734-4816).

SIMPSON
203 Piccadilly, W1 (tel. 734-2002)
Underground Station: Piccadilly Circus
Hours: Monday through Saturday from 9 a.m. to 5:30 p.m. (on Thursday to 7 p.m.)
Credit Cards: AE, MC, V

Recently celebrating its 50th year in Piccadilly, Simpson was exclusively a men's store until a few years back. Now it carries a full range of women's fashions as well. It is the international showcase for DAKS clothing for men and women. A woman's DAKS double-breasted jacket costs £160, while a man's double-breasted checked sports jacket is only slightly more at £175. Altogether there are six floors of fashions and accessories, including raincoats, sweaters, luggage, nightwear, casual and tennis wear, hats, umbrellas, and an international designer collection.

FASHIONABLE CHAIN STORES
Men's and Women's

BENETTON
328 Oxford St., W1 (tel. 491-2016)
Underground Station: Bond Street or Oxford Circus
Hours: Monday through Saturday from 9 a.m. to 6 p.m. (on Thursday to 8 p.m.)
Credit Cards: AE, MC, V

Italy's Benetton seems to be taking the world by storm, and London is no exception. There are more than a dozen Benetton shops on Oxford Street alone, and this store is one of the largest. Shops are franchised to individuals who then sell a ready stock of casual clothes in Benetton's trademark bold solid colors of greens, purples, reds, and other easy-to-coordinate wool and cotton separates. A cotton, cable-knit sweater is £47, khaki Bermuda shorts are £30.60, and wool sweaters range from £16 to £65. Shops in other parts of London include those at 23 Brompton Rd. (tel. 589-2123), 129 Kensington High St. (tel. 937-3034), and 94 King's Rd. (tel. 584-2563).

CECIL GEE
190–192 Sloane St., Knightsbridge, SW1 (tel. 235-4433)
Underground Station: Knightsbridge
Hours: Monday through Saturday from 9 a.m. to 6 p.m. (on Wednesday to 7 p.m.)
Credit Cards: AE, DC, MC, V

Cecil Gee stocks clothing mainly for men but has a few women's selections as well. The fashion houses of Hugo Boss, Lanvin, Brioni, and Cerruti are represented here, with men's suits ranging from about £220 to £750. Ties start at £14.20, cotton shirts at £55, and sweaters at £65. Other shops are located at 85 Brompton Rd. (tel. 589-0085), 46 King's Rd. (tel. 589-8269), and 120 New Bond St. (tel. 629-8030).

FIORUCCI
126 King's Rd., SW3 (tel. 584-3681)
Underground Station: Sloane Square
Hours: Monday through Saturday from 10 a.m. to 6 p.m. (on Wednesday to 7 p.m.)
Credit Cards: AE, DC, MC, V

Clothes from this Italian company are fun and casual, and appeal to the young at heart. Prices are moderate, and during my visit I saw tightfitting peach-colored jeans for women priced at £27.50 and tight short skirts of wool and acrylic priced at £24. For the guys, there are sweatshirts, jeans, and jackets, with jean jackets priced at £91.20. Another Fiorucci is located at 48 Brompton Rd. (tel. 584-3683).

HENNES & MAURITZ
261–271 Regent St., W1 (tel. 493-4004)
Underground Station: Oxford Circus
Hours: Monday through Saturday from 10 a.m. to 6:30 p.m. (on Thursday to 8 p.m.)
Credit Cards: AE, MC, V

This Swedish company caters to young shoppers in their teens and 20s and carries clothes under its own label. Styles are flashy and colorful and would appeal to those who like to make their presence known. There are some surprises in style, and bright colors combined with black seem to be especially big. Women's pink-and-black tights of acrylic and wool cost £17.50, while a man's turquoise cotton jacket is £27.50.

NEXT COLLECTION
160 Regent St., W1 (tel. 434-2515)
Underground Station: Oxford Circus or Piccadilly Circus
Hours: Monday through Saturday from 9:30 a.m. to 6 p.m. (on Thursday to 8 p.m.)
Credit Cards: AE, DC, MC, V

If you had invested in the Next concept for stores in the early 1980s, you'd be making quite a bit of money by now. The first store to open up was called Hepworth and was located in Victoria. It sold women's clothes and was so innovative and successful that the company began branching out with shops selling men's clothing, fabrics, and homewares as well. Today, Next stores are

CLOTHING

found throughout London. Next Collection sells both men's and women's fashions, as well as fabrics and wallpaper. With its decor of white walls, pine floors, and a generally trendy appearance, it tries to draw in shoppers who are on Regent Street because of Liberty and Laura Ashley, with styles that are classical but by no means boring. A woman's double-breasted black dress with a revere collar and fitted waist is £66, while men's wool suits range from £132 to £220. Men can even have a suit made here; the cheapest begins at £120 for a wool-and-polyester mix. Other Next Collection stores are at 72 King's Rd. and 33 Brompton Rd.

SAVOY TAYLORS GUILD
93–95 The Strand, WC2 (tel. 836-7881), next to the Savoy Hotel
Underground Station: Covent Garden, Aldwych, or Charing Cross
Hours: Monday through Saturday from 9 a.m. to 6 p.m. (on Thursday to 7 p.m.)
Credit Cards: AE, DC, MC, V

Established in 1905, this is the flagship store for several shops in London and is under the same ownership as Cecil Gee. Its clothes are from European fashion houses. Men's suits range from £269 to £715 and shirts run £32.50 to £82. In the women's department, a sweater of mohair mix with sequins is priced at £357.50. Another shop is conveniently located at 164 New Bond St. (tel. 408-1680).

Women's

HOBBS
17 The Market, Covent Garden, WC2 (tel. 836-9168)
Underground Station: Covent Garden
Hours: Monday through Friday from 10:30 a.m. to 6:30 p.m. (on Friday to 7 p.m.), on Sunday from noon to 5 p.m.
Credit Cards: AE, DC, MC, V

Hobbs is a chain store owned by Marilyn Anselm, who also designs the clothing in her stores. Her style is color-coordinated and loose-fitting casual separates with lots of corduroys, cottons, and wools. She appeals to women from their teens to their 50s and designs a line of shoes as well. A ribbed wool sweater costs £52, black leather boots are £88, and a cream Shetland wool dress is £76. Other shops are at 47 South Molton St. (tel. 629-0750) and 84 King's Rd. (tel. 730-1020).

MISS SELFRIDGE
40 Duke St., W1 (tel. 629-1234)
Underground Station: Bond Street
Hours: Monday through Saturday from 9:30 a.m. to 6 p.m. (on Thursday to 8 p.m.)
Credit Cards: AE, DC, MC

Armies of London's working girls come here to buy office clothes, casual wear, and fun fashions for nights on the town. Prices are moderate and the stock keeps up with the latest fashion trends, offering all kinds of coordinated tops, pants, skirts, coats, dresses, and underclothing, lots of it costing less than £25. A cable polo sweater is £20, a fake fur coat in royal blue is £54, and lambswool leggings are £18. It's often worth stopping here or at their other shop at 75 Brompton Rd. (tel. 584-7814) to find the latest bargains.

MONSOON
33D King's Rd., SW3 (tel. 730-7552)
Underground Station: *Sloane Square*
Hours: *Monday through Saturday from 10 a.m. to 6 p.m. (on Wednesday to 7 p.m.*
Credit Cards: AE, DC, MC, V

A British-owned chain, Monsoon has designs that are conceived in England but made in India and Hong Kong. The style is ethnic, with flowered prints or strong geometric designs. Most of the clothing is color coordinated for mixing and matching; wool sweaters start at £38 and pants and skirts range from £27 to £44. Other Monsoon addresses are 194 Sloane St. (tel. 235-8564), 26–28 Kensington Church St. (tel. 937-4282), 54 Fulham Rd. (tel. 589-9192), and 23 The Market, Covent Garden (tel. 836-9140).

NEXT TOO
327–329 Oxford St., W1 (tel. 491-7930)
Underground Station: *Bond Street*
Hours: *Monday through Saturday from 10 a.m. to 6 p.m. (on Thursday to 8 p.m.)*
Credit Cards: AE, DC, MC, V

Aiming at women in their mid-20s, Next Too carries clothes more casual than Next Collection. "The idea behind the store is to cater to the free spirit," one employee explained, "but the clothes are something you can wear anywhere." Fabrics are soft wale cotton, wool jersey, and a mix of wool and man-made fibers. A black lambswool cardigan costs £39, a black straight skirt is £18, and a Prince of Wales double-breasted check wool jacket is £66. Other Next Too stores: 11 The Strand (tel. 930-0416), 9–10 South Molton St. (tel. 629-0513), and 102 King's Rd. (tel. 225-2352).

TOP SHOP
Oxford Circus, W1 (tel. 636-7700)
Underground Station: *Oxford Circus*
Hours: *Monday through Friday from 10 a.m. to 6:30 p.m. (on Thursday to 8 p.m.), on Saturday from 9:30 a.m. to 6 p.m.*
Credit Cards: AE, DC, MC, V

CLOTHING

Located in the basement of Top Man for men, this sprawling shop has a great selection of inexpensive clothes for young women. I saw lots of fun fashions that appealed to me, from clothing for lounging to dresses for classier occasions. It carries names like Top Notch, French Connection, and Sacha, with most separates in the £25 to £35 range.

WALLIS
215–217 Oxford St., W1 (tel. 437-0076)
Underground Station: Oxford Circus
Hours: Monday through Saturday from 9 a.m. to 6 p.m. (on Thursday to 8 p.m.)
Credit Cards: AE, MC, V

Managed by the British Sears company, Wallis does a good imitation of fashions by European designers, with a selection of working clothes with flair. Originally aimed at women in their 20s, it has since branched out to appeal to women up to their 40s. Coats and raincoats come in petite sizes too. A cashmere-and-blended-wool full-length coat costs £110, while most dresses average £55 to £80. A cream wool gabardine suit with an oversize jacket and straight-cropped skirt is priced at £97. Other Wallis stores are at 96 King's Rd. (tel. 584-0069), 9–13 Brompton Rd. (tel. 584-1368), and 272–274 Oxford St. (tel. 499-1900).

WAREHOUSE
27 Duke St., W1 (tel. 486-5270)
Underground Station: Bond Street
Hours: Monday through Friday from 9:30 a.m. to 5:30 p.m. (on Thursday to 8 p.m.), on Saturday to 6 p.m.
Credit Cards: AE, MC, V

All designs of this successful chain store are styled in-house and carry the Warehouse label. It stocks clothing primarily in solid colors, with lots of separates good for brushing up on wardrobe necessities. Choose a basic color like gold, purple, or turquoise, and then make a whole outfit with a skirt or pants, a cotton top or sweater, and a jacket. A lambswool sweater is priced at £33. There's a large Warehouse at 76 Brompton Rd. (tel. 584-3835), with a smaller branch at 24 Long Acre (tel. 240-8243).

WHISTLES
12–14 St. Christopher's Pl., W1 (tel. 487-4484)
Underground Station: Bond Street
Hours: Monday through Saturday from 10 a.m. to 6 p.m. (on Thursday to 7 p.m.)
Credit Cards: AE, DC, MC, V

Whistles carries its own label and clothes commissioned from young designers in England, the continent, and Japan. It specializes in casual clothes that are fun and boast unusual cuts, principally black, browns, and blues. A white cotton shirt with hidden buttons is £39, a navy sarong wool skirt is £75, and a tight blue denim skirt with a dipped hem is £62. Other shops: 14 Beauchamp Pl. (tel. 581-4830), 27 Sloane Square (tel. 730-9819), and 20 The Market, Covent Garden (tel. 379-7401).

Whistles: A showcase for international designers

Men's

DUNN & CO.

56–58 Regent St., WI (tel. 734-1904)
Underground Station: *Piccadilly Circus*
Hours: *Monday through Saturday from 9 a.m. to 5:30 p.m. (on Thursday to 7 p.m.)*
Credit Cards: *AE, DC, MC, V*

With 108 shops in all of England and four in central London, Dunn & Co. is well known for its hand-woven Harris Tweed jackets, which cost £73 and come in 15 different patterns. Harris Tweed, which is woven on treadle looms by

weavers in Scotland who work out of their homes, is also fashioned into matching caps and hats. Tweed hats range from £11 to £16, while caps are £5.50 to £10. Dunn also sells British-made bowler hats for £46, cotton shirts for £14, and traditional two-piece wool suits beginning at £93.50. Other shops can be found at 54–56 Oxford St. (tel. 636-0128) and 228–229 Piccadilly (tel. 930-3744).

HIGH AND MIGHTY
22–23 Princes St., WI (tel. 409-0400), off Regent Street
Underground Station: Oxford Circus
Hours: Monday through Saturday from 9 a.m. to 5:30 p.m.
Credit Cards: AE, DC, MC, V

High and Mighty caters to big and tall men with a full range of suits, shirts, sweaters, jeans, jackets, and coats. Two-piece suits range from £126.50 to £544, jeans cost about £30, and a black leather jacket is £385. Other shops: 177 Brompton Rd. (tel. 589-7454), 275 High Holborn, WC1 (tel. 405-8566), and 415–417 Oxford St. (tel. 629-1219).

NEXT FOR MEN
427 Oxford St., WI (tel. 491-4168)
Underground Station: Bond Street
Hours: Monday through Saturday from 10 a.m. to 6 p.m. (on Thursday to 8 p.m.)
Credit Cards: AE, DC, MC, V

Next stores carrying clothes exclusively for men have a logo of an "M" with a circle drawn around it. Continuing in the Next concept of merchandising, this is a hip store with fashions for men who are interested in the latest look. Most wool suits are priced under £195, and three-piece suits can be made especially for you for less than £220.

TAKE SIX
362–364 Oxford St., WI (tel. 491-7141).
Underground Station: Bond Street
Hours: Monday through Saturday from 9 a.m. to 6 p.m. (on Thursday to 8 p.m.)
Credit Cards: AE, DC, MC, V

This fashion chain appeals to men under 30, especially those who are buying their first suits. Both English and loose, baggy Italian suits are in stock, ranging in price from about £88 to £155. Shirts are bright and colorful, with most in the £15 to £33 range. Leather jackets are also a hot item, the majority priced around £164. Leather pants are priced at £104. Other Take Six shops are at 162 Oxford St. (tel. 636-2185), 235 Regent St. (tel. 491-7298), 19–21 Kensington

Church St. (tel. 937-4680), 157 Kensington High St. (tel. 937-0929), and 69 King's Rd. (tel. 730-5533).

TOP MAN
Oxford Circus, WI (tel. 629-7179)
Underground Station: Oxford Circus
Hours: Monday through Friday from 10 a.m. to 6:30 p.m. (on Thursday to 8 p.m.), on Saturday from 9:30 a.m. to 6 p.m.
Credit Cards: AE, DC, MC, V

This chain store also appeals to young men in their teens and 20s, with clothes that are zany and fun. Pop music and good, eye-catching window and store displays set the mood. There's a large selection of jackets, from highly visible ones in wild colors of purple and blue starting at £38 to more serious and traditional cuts of Italian or West German design costing £165. On the first floor is a snackshop where you can relax and watch young men deliberate over what to buy.

WOODHOUSE
99 Oxford St., WI (tel. 437-2809)
Underground Station: Oxford Circus to Tottenham Court Road
Hours: Monday through Saturday from 9:30 a.m. to 6:30 p.m. (on Thursday to 8 p.m.)
Credit Cards: AE, DC, MC, V

This men's chain carries primarily Italian-designed clothing, with cuts that are contemporary and smart-looking without a correspondingly high price tag. Suits range from £218 to £385 and carry labels of Giorgio Armani and others. Leather coats start at £247 and shirts with the Woodhouse label cost £36.80. There's also casual wear, such as T-shirts in summer and wool sweaters in winter. More Woodhouse shops are at 138 Long Acre, Covent Garden, WC2 (tel. 240-2008); 8 Sloane St. (tel. 235-1507); 124A King's Rd. (tel. 584-5888); and 141 Kensington High St. (tel. 937-2420).

TRENDY BOUTIQUES AND DESIGNER WEAR
Men's and Women's

ARKITECT
I Langley Court, Covent Garden, WC2 (tel. 240-5071)
Underground Station: Covent Garden
Hours: Monday through Saturday from 10:30 a.m. to 6:30 p.m.
Credit Cards: AE, DC, MC, V

With all clothes designed by Simon Abihssira who also designs his own fabrics, Arkitect is a very trendy shop which has dressed such celebrities as Bruce Springsteen and members of the Eurythmics. Using bold colors and unusual prints, Abihssira designs clothes that are a bit out of the ordinary but that can be worn practically anywhere. Many of the fashions look equally good on women, with shining silk shirts starting at £77, sweaters at £55, and leather or sheepskin jackets and coats ranging from £236 to £1,100.

BOY
153 King's Rd., SW3 (tel. 351-1115)
Underground Station: *Sloane Square*
Hours: *Monday through Saturday from 10 a.m. to 6 p.m.*
Credit Cards: AE, DC, MC, V

Opened in 1976, Boy has been around since the days of punkdom and continues to sell Murray Blewitt's outrageous fashions in tight leggings, miniskirts, T-shirts, and bondage trousers and coats. "Boy" is splashed across many of the garments so there's no mistake where you bought it. Prices start at around £8.80 for a T-shirt with the "Boy" logo and go up to the most expensive item in the shop, a wool coat for £100. There's lots in the £25 to £35 range. Boy also has a booth in Hyper Hyper, described later in this section.

Trend setting at Arkitect

BROWNS
23–27 South Molton St., WI (tel. 491-7833)
Underground Station: *Bond Street*
Hours: *Monday through Saturday from 10 a.m. to 6 p.m. (on Thursday to 7 p.m.)*
Credit Cards: *AE, DC, MC, V*

Without a doubt, Browns is the best and most exclusive place in town for one-stop shopping in designer wear. Located on fashionable South Molton Street, this chic shop sells the creations of almost all the major European and some American designers, including Geoffrey Beene, Bill Blass, Byblos, Comme des Garçons, Jasper Conran, Perry Ellis, Jean-Paul Gaultier, Norma Kamali, Donna Karan, Missoni, Claude Montana, Thierry Mugler, Jean Muir, and Sonia Rykiel. Prices are expectedly high, but so is the quality, and the selection is excellent. Items on the racks have included a man's white viscose T-shirt by Gaultier for £60, a woman's black-and-white dogtooth check wool double-breasted jacket by Comme des Garçons for £340, and a man's double-breasted gray wool flannel suit by Claude Montana for £599. There are people who would kill to shop here during Browns' annual sales, held in January and in July/August and offering unbelievable bargains. Another Browns is at 6C Sloane St. (tel. 491-7833, ext. 240).

Browns: One-stop shopping for designer wear

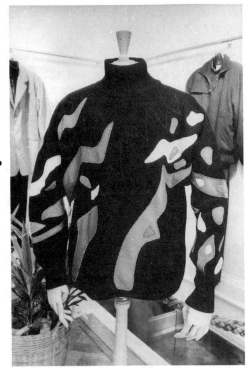

Browns for men too

CACHAREL
103 New Bond St., WI (tel. 629-1964)
Underground Station: *Bond Street*
Hours: *Monday through Saturday from 9:30 a.m. to 6:30 p.m. (on Thursday to 7:30 p.m.)*
Credit Cards: *AE, MC, V*

This French clothing boutique offers a good selection of well-tailored fashions for men, women, and children. Styles are impeccable and always in good taste. Men's suits range from £275 to £330, a woman's red fitted dress is priced at £142, and girls' dresses are £45 to £90.

CHARLES JOURDAN
39–43 Brompton Rd., SW3 (tel. 581-3333)
Underground Station: *Knightsbridge*
Hours: *Monday through Saturday from 10 a.m. to 6:30 p.m. (on Wednesday to 7 p.m.)*
Credit Cards: *AE, DC, MC, V*

Charles Jourdan's London boutique carries clothes for men and women, hand-bags, jewelry, shoes, boots, scarves, ties, belts, and other accessories. Most

shoes are priced £75.90 and up, and there are scarves that make wonderful gifts in the £59 to £147 range.

CHE GUEVARA
36 Kensington High St., W8 (tel. 937-3151)
Underground Station: High Street Kensington
Hours: Monday through Wednesday from 10 a.m. to 6 p.m., on Thursday to 7 p.m., on Friday to 6:30 p.m., and on Saturday from 9:30 a.m. to 6 p.m.
Credit Cards: AE, DC, MC, V

Young casual wear is the ticket here, for jeans, sweaters, pants, and tops going at very low prices. Stretch leggings are £6.50 and cotton jackets are £28.50. In the basement are individual stallholders selling more clothing, jewelry, shoes, and accessories.

CLOTHKITS
39 Neal St., WC2 (tel. 240-7826)
Underground Station: Covent Garden
Hours: Monday through Saturday from 9:30 a.m. to 6 p.m. (on Thursday to 7 p.m.)
Credit Cards: MC, V

Clothkits offers a unique concept, selling both ready-to-wear and kits including fabric for clothing you can make yourself. The kits are designed for those with little or no experience in sewing and have easy-to-follow instructions. For some patterns the cutting lines are printed directly onto the fabric while others come with the fabric already cut out and ready to sew. The materials are bright and cheerful, reminiscent of styles you might find on rosy-cheeked, healthy Scandinavians. The children's clothes are especially precious, with Laplander hats, smocked dresses, dungarees, and Oriental padded jackets. Kits for girl's pinafores cost less than £10 and for men's shirts less than £18. There are samples in the store to try on for size, as well as ready-made selections you can buy off the rack.

CROLLA
35 Dover St., W1 (tel. 629-5931)
Underground Station: Green Park
Hours: Monday through Saturday from 10 a.m. to 6 p.m.
Credit Cards: AE, DC, MC, V

Located in a former apartment of a lady-in-waiting to the royal family in the 19th century, and decorated in ornate stucco, this shop is anything but old-fashioned. Rather, it sells the highly imaginative creations of Scott Crolla, who combs the Far East for rich brocades and tapestries and then incorporates them into unique and interesting jackets, dresses, shirts, slippers, boxer shorts, and ties. Crolla started the craze for floral and chintz trousers which has since

spread around the world. Customers have included Mick Jagger, Elton John, Faye Dunaway, and Tina Turner. Boxer shorts make a great gift at £16, swimming trunks are £27, and colorful, unusual jackets start at £275.

GUCCI
27 Old Bond St., WI (tel. 629-2716)
Underground Station: Green Park or Piccadilly Circus
Hours: Monday through Friday from 9 a.m. to 5:30 p.m., on Saturday to 5 p.m.
Credit Cards: AE, DC, MC, V

Gucci and its famous logo need no introductions for its handsome designs in handbags, luggage, belts, shoes, scarves, jewelry, and men's and women's fashions. The scarves are beautiful, in rich floral designs, ranging from £53.90 to £93.50. Handbags start at £71 for the smallest. An inexpensive gift is a key ring with the Gucci trademark for £11.

HYPER HYPER
26–40 Kensington High St., W8 (tel. 937-6964)
Underground Station: High Street Kensington
Hours: Monday through Saturday from 10 a.m. to 6 p.m. (on Thursday to 7 p.m.)
Credit Cards: *Varies with stallholders*

Opened in 1983, Hyper Hyper is quite simply the best place to go to see the latest in avant-garde fashion by London's youngest designers. Many have started out at stalls here and moved on to bigger and better things. Clothing, jewelry, shoes, hats, and other interesting accessories are on display, each stall completely different from the next. Most items are in the £55 to £130 range. There are two floors of stalls and a restaurant serving snacks.

JANET FITCH
2 Percy St., WI (tel. 636-5631), off Tottenham Court Road
Underground Station: Tottenham Court Road or Goodge Street
Hours: Monday through Friday from 10 a.m. to 7 p.m., on Saturday from 11 a.m. to 5 p.m.
Credit Cards: AE, DC, MC, V

Opened in 1986, this trendy shop in Soho sells what it calls "wearable arts," mainly the unique creations of small manufacturers, students, or single artists. For sale are handmade jewelry, fanciful hat creations, hand-painted ties, hand-printed shirts, hand-knitted sweaters, ceramics, and men's and women's clothing. Owned and managed by former journalist Fitch, the shop itself is light and spacious and does justice to the items displayed. Hand-painted ties and bow-ties range from £25 to £35.

JONES

71 King's Rd., SW3 (tel. 352-6899)
Underground Station: Sloane Square
Hours: Monday through Saturday from 10 a.m. to 6:30 p.m.
Credit Cards: AE, DC, MC, V

This chic boutique sells innovative and popular designs that have a touch of the British classics in them. A man's wool-and-acrylic, baggy, black jacket is priced at £294, leather jackets are £385, and wool sweaters start at £165. A woman's tight-fitting dress by Gaultier that reminds me somehow of a wet suit is priced at £165.

KANSAI

101 New Bond St., W1 (tel. 629-3869)
Underground Station: Bond Street
Hours: Monday through Saturday from 10:30 a.m. to 6:30 p.m. (on
    Thursday to 7:30 p.m.)
Credit Cards: AE, DC, MC, V

All of Kansai's distinctive international collection is here, ranging in color from somber blacks to electrifying hues in clothing by this eccentric Japanese designer. I saw a woman's tailored, two-piece waisted black suit that I wanted instantly, until I found out it cost £770. Sigh! Kansai jackets, as well as beaded sweaters, are priced at £250.

KATHARINE HAMNETT

50 South Molton St., W1 (tel. 629-0827)
Underground Station: Bond Street
Hours: Monday through Saturday from 10 a.m. to 6 p.m. (on Thursday
    to 7 p.m.)
Credit Cards: AE, DC, MC, V

Both men and women can wear Katharine Hamnett's minimalist and unfussy designs. This contemporary British designer uses cottons, silks, and gabardine in solid colors of black, navy, and khaki, switching to light linens and poplins in summer. Prices are reasonable, with shirts starting at £42.90, trousers at £60, and jackets at £132. I saw a practical black Lycra short skirt for £44 and a waisted long-sleeve white poplin shirt with metal stud buttons for £63. Other Katharine Hamnett stores are at 124B King's Rd. and 264 Brompton Rd.

KENSINGTON MARKET

49–53 Kensington High St., W8 (tel. 937-1572)
Underground Station: High Street Kensington
Hours: Monday through Saturday from 10 a.m. to 6 p.m.
Credit Cards: Depends on stallholders, but most don't

Located almost directly across the street from Hyper Hyper, this indoor market has about 90 stalls and tiny rooms spread out like a maze, making it easy to get

lost and spend the rest of your life looking at clothes made of rubber, punk fashions, secondhand clothes, country-western and cowboy wear, and dresses made of a balloon-like substance. Young, avant-garde, and occasionally weird fashion prevails here, some of it quite original. There's lots under £22, and a café and hairdresser's are up on the first floor, but good luck in finding them.

KENZO
27–29 Brook St., W1 (tel. 629-6077)
Underground Station: Bond Street
Hours: Monday through Saturday from 9:30 a.m. to 6 p.m. (on Thursday from 9:45 a.m. to 7 p.m.)
Credit Cards: AE, DC, MC, V

This internationally known designer from Paris has three boutiques in London. His Japanese designs with a French influence make use of natural fabrics in blacks and solid, shocking colors. A pink wool turtleneck costs £64.90, and matching tight pants cost the same price. His other two shops are located at 13 South Molton St. (tel. 493-4420) and 17 Sloane St. (tel. 235-1991).

Kenzo style

LAND & BURR
35 Neal St., Covent Garden, WC2 (tel. 240-8737)
Underground Station: Covent Garden
Hours: Monday through Saturday from 11 a.m. to 7 p.m.
Credit Cards: AE, DC, MC, V

Almost everything in this small, chic shop is designed by either Land or Burr, whose products range from men's, women's, and children's wear to jewelry, hats,

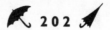
gloves, and bags. Clothes are fairly traditional but often have one feature that saves them from being entirely straight, such as a woman's tailored suit with enormous culottes. Black capes of polyurethane cost £165, while hats range from £45 to £83.

POLO RALPH LAUREN
143 New Bond St., W1 (tel. 491-4967)
Underground Station: Bond Street
Hours: Monday through Saturday from 10 a.m. to 6 p.m. (on Thursday to 7 p.m.)
Credit Cards: AE, DC, MC, V

The fashion dreams of the urban cowboy and cowgirl are fulfilled by this talented American designer, who takes the best in fashion culture from both sides of the ocean. His smartly tailored casual wear includes Scottish hand-knit sweaters, corduroy shirts, jackets, suits, and separates. A woman's navy cashmere cardigan is priced at £319; a man's gray wool, chalk-striped suit costs £500; and women's polka-dot silk pants sell for £210.

REGINE
43–44 New Bond St., W1 (tel. 499-0788)
Underground Station: Bond Street
Hours: Monday through Saturday from 9:30 a.m. to 6 p.m. (on Thursday 10 a.m. to 7 p.m.)
Credit Cards: AE, DC, MC, V

Land & Burr: Traditional but with extra flair

This fashionable boutique carries men's and women's clothing from various well-known designers, including Claude Montana, Missoni, and Erreuno. Women's separates fall into the £220 to £450 range, while men's suits start at £500.

REVIEW

81 King's Rd., SW3 (tel. 352-2920)
Underground Station: Sloane Square
Hours: Monday through Saturday from 10:30 a.m. to 6:30 p.m.
Credit Cards: AE, MC, V

Using exciting fashions from young designers, this unisex clothing shop boasts inexpensive prices as well. Black denim is a favored material, and there's a wide range of men's trousers and '50s-style loose jackets. Sweaters range from £45 to £60.

TRUSSARDI

51 South Molton St., WI (tel. 629-5611)
Underground Station: Bond Street
Hours: Monday through Saturday from 10 a.m. to 6 p.m. (on Thursday
   to 7 p.m.)
Credit Cards: AE, DC, MC, V

In addition to Italian clothing, accessories, and leather goods, this boutique also has a range of gift items, including cigarette holders, pipes, jewelry, watches, perfume, and attractive picture frames made of silver and briar wood. In the clothing section, T-shirts are the cheapest items, beginning at £11, while wool sweaters start at £88. Men's leather pants range from £220 to £450, while sheepskin and leather jackets range from £395 to £1,100. A woman's fitted, sleek leather dress is priced at £550. Leather purses start at £55, while wallets begin at £33.

YOHJI YAMAMOTO

6 Sloane St., SWI (tel. 245-9139)
Underground Station: Knightsbridge
Hours: Monday through Saturday from 9:30 a.m. to 6 p.m. (on
   Wednesday from 10 a.m. to 7 p.m.)
Credit Cards: AE, DC, MC, V

This Japanese designer is keen on the minimalist black look, in a selection of loose-fitting and flowing separates priced mostly from £275 to £330. A cream-colored coat, longer on the left side with fan pleating, is priced at £390. The layout of the shop itself is very interesting, with a high ceiling and huge windows.

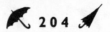
Women's

ACADEMY
188A King's Rd., SW3 (tel. 352-0507)
Underground Station: *Sloane Square*
Hours: *Monday through Saturday from 10 a.m. to 6:30 p.m.*
Credit Cards: AE, DC, MC, V

Promoting the talents of young British designers, this innovative shop completely changes its interior and exterior designs every six months. It also changes the designers it carries, which means that even regular customers will always find something new and exciting. Clothing varies from classic to the avant-garde, and prices range from £45 to £450.

ADELE DAVIS
10 New Bond St., W1 (tel. 493-2795)
Underground Station: *Green Park or Piccadilly Circus*
Hours: *Monday through Friday from 9 a.m. to 5:30 p.m., on Saturday from 10 a.m. to 1 p.m.*
Credit Cards: AE, DC, MC, V

First opened in the early 1940s, Adele Davis is probably the oldest privately owned dress shop on Bond Street. Its European-designed clothing appeals to middle-aged women who are looking for conservative classics. Dresses start at £110, and there are also women's suits, blouses, and coats. There's another Adele Davis at 4 Beauchamp Pl. (tel. 589-1201).

BASILE
21 New Bond, W1 (tel. 493-3618)
Underground Station: *Bond Street, Piccadilly Circus, or Green Park*
Hours: *Monday through Saturday from 10 a.m. to 6 p.m.*
Credit Cards: AE, DC, MC, V

This is the only London shop of this leading Italian manufacturing company, with designs by Luciano Sopriani. Styles are dramatic and well tailored. Dresses average about £400, blouses start at £220, skirts at £170, and jackets at £385.

THE BEAUCHAMP PLACE SHOP
55 Beauchamp Pl., SW3 (tel. 589-4155)
Underground Station: *Knightsbridge*
Hours: *Monday through Friday from 10 a.m. to 6 p.m. (on Wednesday to 6:30 p.m.), on Saturday from 11 a.m. to 6 p.m.*
Credit Cards: AE, DC, MC, V

This beautiful boutique stocks a selection of British- and European-designed clothing by Claude Barthelemy, Paul Costelloe, Cerruti, Rifat Ozbek, Jacques

Azagury, Edina Ronay, and many more. The emphasis is on the classic and simple English look, which is based on understatement in styles that will last a long time. There are lots of long, pleated skirts and unfussy but feminine blouses. Hand-knit cotton sweaters average £165.

BRUCE OLDFIELD

27 Beauchamp Pl., SW3 (tel. 584-1363)
Underground Station: Knightsbridge
Hours: Monday through Friday from 10 a.m. to 6 p.m. (on Wednesday to 6:30 p.m.), on Saturday from 11 a.m. to 6 p.m.
Credit Cards: AE, DC, MC, V

Bruce Oldfield is one of the top names in women's evening wear, and his creations are often featured in *Vogue* and other fashion magazines. His dresses are draped in interesting ways, so that the wearer will stand out from the crowd. Prices start at £275 for day dresses and £750 for sequined evening wear. A long raven-black velvet jacket is priced at £580.

CAROLINE CHARLES

11 Beauchamp Pl., SW3 (tel. 589-5850)
Underground Station: Knightsbridge
Hours: Monday through Friday from 9:30 a.m. to 5:30 p.m. (on Thursday to 6:30 p.m.), on Saturday from 10 a.m. to 4:30 p.m.
Credit Cards: AE, DC, MC, V

Caroline Charles emerged in the 1960s as one of England's most talented designers and today she continues to create sophisticated, ageless, and wearable fashions for women. Light-weight and two-piece wool suits start at £330, while a violet velvet evening dress with a plunging neckline and a skirt full from the hips is priced at £263. Tunic blouses cost £130.

CATHERINE BUCKLEY

302 Westbourne Grove, W11 (tel. 229-8786), just off Portobello Road
Underground Station: Notting Hill Gate
Hours: Saturday from 9:30 a.m. to 6 p.m., Monday through Friday by appointment only
Credit Cards: AE, DC, MC, V

Catherine Buckley has been creating her line of romantic, feminine, and very nostalgic party and wedding dresses for almost a quarter of a century. Various designs are available, from beaded 1920s flapper dresses to Irish crocheted wedding dresses. Clothing can be made to order or bought off-the-peg. Antique lace and net are used for many of the wedding dresses and many of the party dresses are hand-beaded. Ready-made dresses range from £550 to £6,000, and the price for made-to-measure dresses depends on the price of the antique lace. Frilly white blouses start at £214.

CHANEL
26 Old Bond St., WI (tel. 493-5040)
Underground Station: Green Park or Piccadilly Circus
Hours: Monday through Friday from 9:30 a.m. to 5:30 p.m., on Saturday
   from 10 a.m. to 4 p.m.
Credit Cards: AE, DC, MC, V

World-famous Chanel sells its perfumes, cosmetics, women's fashions, and accessories from both this boutique and another shop located at 31 Sloane St. (tel. 235-6631). Both Chanel No. 19 and No. 5 sell for £31 for seven milliliters. A woman's off-white silk suit sells for £1,080, while a ballgown with a taffeta bodice, embroidered cotton skirt, and a tulle underskirt costs £1,540.

CONNECTIONS
12 James St., Covent Garden, WC2 (tel. 836-0522)
Underground Station: Covent Garden
Hours: Monday through Saturday from 11 a.m. to 7 p.m. (on Thursday
   to 8 p.m.), on Saturday from noon to 5 p.m.
Credit Cards: AE, MC, V

Women's clothing with the French Connection label are featured here in a wide range of color-coordinated separates. Straight-legged gray-and-white trousers are priced at £50, with a matching jacket costing £65. A tight, straight miniskirt is £24.

DAVID FIELDEN
137 King's Rd., SW3 (tel. 351-1745)
Underground Station: Sloane Square
Hours: Monday through Saturday from 10 a.m. to 6 p.m.
Credit Cards: AE, DC, MC, V

One of London's top designers for bridal dresses and evening wear, David Fielden uses exotic lace and silks for styles ranging from nostalgic, frothy wedding dresses to slinky evening wear. Prices for his bridal gowns range from about £330 to £1,320, while evening dresses start at £220. There are lots of styles to choose from, and gowns can be made to order from his designs at the same cost as the off-the-peg price.

EDINA RONAY
141 King's Rd., SW3 (tel. 352-1085)
Underground Station: Sloane Square
Hours: Monday through Friday from 10 a.m. to 6 p.m. (on Wednesday to
   7 p.m.), on Saturday from 11 a.m. to 6 p.m.
Credit Cards: AE, DC, MC, V

Edina Ronay designs all the clothes and sweaters she sells in her shop, with prices that are justifiably high. All the sweaters are hand-knit and start at £140. A cream-colored linen jacket is priced at £175, while a matching skirt is £165.

EDWINA CARROLL
16 The Market, Covent Garden, WC2 (tel. 836-9873)
Underground Station: Covent Garden
Hours: Monday through Saturday from 10 a.m. to 6 p.m.
Credit Cards: AE, MC, V

This tiny boutique specializes in hand-knitted British clothes, with prices ranging from about £25 to £220 for most knitwear. The shop's collection represents the personal selection of Ms. Carroll and includes earrings, scent bottles, pottery, and other items as well. Because the shop is tiny, only a few people are allowed in at a time.

GORDON LOWES
179–180 Sloane St., SW1 (tel. 235-8484)
Underground Station: Knightsbridge
Hours: Monday through Friday from 9 a.m. to 5:30 p.m. (on Wednesday to 7 p.m.), on Saturday from 9:30 a.m. to 4:30 p.m.
Credit Cards: AE, DC, MC, V

Hand-knitted British fashions at Edwina Carroll

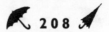
Specializing in the very classic, well-tailored English look, this shop is known for its casual, country styles. It sells Aran hand-knitted sweaters for £88, Austrian clothing by Geiger, Italian coats, and other fashions made mostly from natural fibers. Waterproof cotton jackets by Barbour start at £77.

GREAT EXPECTATIONS
78 Fulham Rd., SW3 (tel. 584-2451)
Underground Station: *South Kensington*
Hours: *Monday through Friday from 10 a.m. to 6 p.m., on Saturday to 5 p.m.*
Credit Cards: *AE, DC, MC, V*

If you're tired of drab, unexciting maternity clothes, this shop up on the first floor will gladden your heart. It sells designer-made maternity wear, mostly of natural fibers, from underclothing to party dresses. Dresses range from £82 to £440.

HACKETT
65A New King's Rd., SW6 (tel. 736-4012)
Underground Station: *Fulham Broadway*
Hours: *Monday through Friday from 10 a.m. to 7 p.m., on Saturday from 9 a.m. to 6 p.m.*
Credit Cards: *AE, MC, V*

The plain, classic look is featured in this shop's tweed jackets, striped shirts, gabardine trousers, and bow ties for women. Popular are the short-sleeve, crew-neck lambswool sweaters for £29 that can be combined with gilt-buttoned cardigans for £42.90 in a style reminiscent of the 1950s. There are some secondhand accessories, including gilt brooches and crocodile handbags.

HARDY AMIES LTD.
14 Savile Row, W1 (tel. 734-2436)
Underground Station: *Piccadilly Circus*
Hours: *Monday through Friday from 9:30 a.m. to 5:30 p.m.*
Credit Cards: *AE, DC, V*

Serving as royal dressmakers to the Queen, this couturier is located on that bastion of men's tailor shops, Savile Row. Established in the 1940s, it charges a starting price of £825 for made-to-measure wedding dresses and gowns. It also produces ready-made dresses beginning at £275. The staff is very obliging and helpful.

ISSEY MIYAKE
21 Sloane St., SW1 (tel. 245-9891)
Underground Station: *Knightsbridge*

CLOTHING

Hours: *Monday through Saturday from 10 a.m. to 6 p.m. (on Wednesday to 7 p.m.)*
Credit Cards: AE, DC, MC, V

This Japanese designer uses silk, cotton, and wool to produce interesting weaves and colors for his unique fashions. He is a master at making a simple cut interesting by adding special touches and is known for his oversize designs. Prices are very high, with trousers or skirts starting at £220. An oversize raincoat of polyester and nylon, amazingly soft to the touch, is priced at £453. Issey Miyake sells his clothes also at Plantation, located at 270 Brompton Rd. (tel. 581-3760).

JASPER CONRAN
37 Beauchamp Pl., SW3 (tel. 589-4243)
Underground Station: Knightsbridge
Hours: *Monday through Friday from 10 a.m. to 6 p.m. (on Wednesday to 6:30 p.m.), Saturday from 11 a.m. to 6 p.m.*
Credit Cards: AE, DC, MC, V

Designing clothes since he was a teenager, Conran opened up his own shop in 1986. The boutique itself is artfully dramatic, powerful yet restrained, reflecting Conran's style in clothes. A woman's gray flannel suit is £292, a white cashmere sweater is £278, and a two-layered silk skirt is £400.

JOSEPH TRICOT
16 South Molton St., W1 (tel. 408-2031)
Underground Station: Bond Street
Hours: *Monday through Saturday from 9:30 a.m. to 6 p.m. (on Thursday from 9:45 a.m. to 7 p.m.)*
Credit Cards: AE, DC, MC, V

Joseph Ettedgui is firmly entrenched in the London market, with a myriad of other shops in addition to this one. The look here is full, loose, and oversize, with many separates in basic colors such as blacks and whites. Knitted hand-framed sweaters start at £97, while a fully lined leather skirt is £203. Another Joseph Tricot is located at 18 Sloane St. (tel. 235-2719). Other Ettedgui shops include Joseph Pour La Ville with women's fashions at 13 South Molton St. and 166 Sloane St., and Joseph Pour La Maison at 16 Sloane St. with its fascinating combination of clothing and well-designed, sleek home furnishings and accessories.

KARL LAGERFELD
173 New Bond St., W1 (tel. 493-6277)
Underground Station: Green Park or Piccadilly Circus
Hours: *Monday through Saturday from 9:30 a.m. to 6 p.m.*
Credit Cards: AE, DC, MC, V

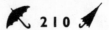
The sales staff assured me that prices for Karl Lagerfeld's distinctive fashions were cheaper here than in the United States and that the shop receives lots of mail-order requests from abroad. Dresses average about £440 to £650 and sweaters start at £155.

LAURA ASHLEY
256–258 Regent St., WI (tel. 437-9760)
Underground Station: Oxford Circus
Hours: Monday through Friday from 9:30 a.m. to 6 p.m. (on Thursday to 7:30 p.m.), on Saturday from 9 a.m. to 6 p.m.
Credit Cards: AE, MC, V

With more than a dozen branches in London alone, and more shops in big cities around the world, Laura Ashley is famous for her pretty, feminine dresses and pinafores that would make even vaudeville actresses look prim and proper. Prices in London are unbelievably low, with long-sleeve, waisted cotton dresses with full skirts priced from £27.50 to £42.90. A two-piece, double-breasted navy wool suit is £126.50. If you're looking for young girls' clothing, sailor dresses start at about £23, jumpers run about £16, and trousers are about £20. Laura Ashley designs all her own fabrics, along with her own line of wallpapers, lamps, curtains, sofas, and other home accessories, all in cheerful florals and prints. The shop above is the largest Laura Ashley shop in the world; other boutiques are located at 7–9 Harriet St. (tel. 235-9797), 157 Fulham Rd. (tel. 584-6939), and High Street Kensington (tel. 938-3751).

Joseph Tricot: Stylish woolens

CLOTHING

Laura Ashley: The queen of British florals and prints

LIBERATED LADY

408 King's Rd., SW10 (tel. 351-3055)
Underground Station: *Sloane Square*
Hours: *Monday through Saturday from 10 a.m. to 6:30 p.m. (on Wednesday to 7 p.m.)*
Credit Cards: *AE, DC, MC, V*

Sexy, daring, slinky cocktail dresses at low prices, popular with young models and aspiring actresses just dying to be discovered. A short and strapless metallic purple dress costs £55, the average price for most dresses here. There are also lace gloves, underwear, patterned tights, belts, and other accessories to brighten up your wardrobe.

LUCIENNE PHILLIPS

89 Knightsbridge, SW1 (tel. 235-2134)
Underground Station: *Knightsbridge*
Hours: *Monday through Saturday from 9:30 a.m. to 6 p.m. (on Wednesday to 7 p.m.)*
Credit Cards: *AE, DC, MC, V*

Run by the lively and enthusiastic Ms. Phillips, this boutique has a varied selection of fashions by both well-known and little-known designers, including

Jean Muir, Janet Alexander, Penny Green, Anna Cloonan, Jasper Conran, Betty Jackson, and Victor Edelstein. Prices are expectedly high, and there's a large selection of evening wear. A black beaded dress by Jasper Conran is £715.

LUCY'S
107 New Bond St., WI (tel. 629-2161)
Underground Station: Bond Street
Hours: Monday through Friday from 9:30 a.m. to 6 p.m. (on Thursday to 7 p.m.), on Saturday to 5:30 p.m.
Credit Cards: AE, MC, V

Specializing in evening wear from France, Italy, England, and Germany, Lucy's has everything from subdued to elaborate, from floor-length gowns to short strapless dresses, at prices reaching above £5,000. There are also day dresses, such as a white sweater dress with black dots going for £132. Another Lucy's is located at 5–7 Brompton Rd. (tel. 581-1277).

NORMAN HARTNELL
26 Bruton St., WI (tel. 629-0992), off Bond Street
Underground Station: Bond Street
Hours: By appointment only: Monday through Friday from 9:30 a.m. to 5 p.m.
Credit Cards: AE, DC, MC, V

Norman Hartnell first opened his shop in the 1920s and became famous for his solid-sequin dresses. He designed the wedding dresses for both the Queen and Princess Margaret, and also the Queen's coronation dress. Since his death in 1979, his house continues as a first-rate couturier and carries both off-the-peg and made-to-measure creations by several well-known designers, including Victor Edelstein.

NO? YES!
38 Floral St., Covent Garden, WC2 (tel. 836-8220)
Underground Station: Covent Garden
Hours: Monday through Friday from 11 a.m. to 6:30 p.m. (on Thursday to 7:30 p.m.), on Saturday to 6 p.m.
Credit Cards: AE, MC, V

Designer Sue Jenkyn-Jones creates all the clothes for the NO? YES! label, with fun fashions that are a cut above other boutiques in the area. Wool jersey dresses are £93.50, and trousers run from £55.

PADDY CAMPBELL
8 Gees Court, WI (tel. 493-5646)
Underground Station: Bond Street

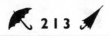
Hours: Monday through Friday from 10 a.m. to 6 p.m. (on Thursday to 7 p.m.), on Saturday from 10:30 a.m. to 5:30 p.m.
Credit Cards: AE, MC, V

The well-tailored, classic English look prevails in fashions from this shop, with lots of wools, linens, and natural fabrics. Businesswomen will find lots to choose from: for example, a white linen suit priced at £182, tweed jackets at £160, and matching skirts at £97. Another Paddy Campbell is at 17 Beauchamp Pl. (tel. 225-0543).

PAPIER-MÂCHÉ
14 Endell St., Covent Garden, WC2 (tel. 240-6624)
Underground Station: Covent Garden
Hours: Monday through Friday from 10:30 a.m. to 7 p.m. (on Thursday to 8 p.m.), on Saturday from 11 a.m. to 6 p.m.
Credit Cards: AE, MC, V

This tiny, trendy boutique sells a small selection of chic women's clothes and a few designs by Williwear for men. The style is nonchalant and primarily loose and baggy, with shirts starting at a low £31.90. Women's jackets are priced at £120.

REVIEW
398 King's Rd., SW10 (tel. 351-7908)
Underground Station: Sloane Square
Hours: Monday through Saturday from 10:30 a.m. to 6:30 p.m.
Credit Cards: AE, MC, V

This trendy, spacious boutique sells Williwear and British-designed clothing that is simple and casual but can be dressed up by adding the right accessories. There are straight and tight dresses, leggings, skirts, and shirts, mostly in dark colors like gray, navy, black, or brown. A sweatshirt-like dress with a zippered neck is priced at £45.50.

RITVA WESTENIUS
153C Fulham Rd., SW3 (tel. 581-3878)
Underground Station: South Kensington
Hours: Monday through Saturday from 10 a.m. to 6 p.m.
Credit Cards: MC, V

Ritva Westenius is known for her re-creations of the Edwardian look in wedding dresses and ballgowns and for her exquisite hand-beaded dresses. If you like silk, Victorian ruffles, ribbons, satin, leg-of-mutton sleeves, and flowing, lace-trimmed skirts, you'll find a variety of styles to choose from for your own made-to-measure dress or gown. Prices range from £275 to £2,750, depending on the complexity of the style you choose. The styles are so reminiscent of the past that everyone will think you're wearing grandmother's wedding dress.

ROLAND KLEIN
26 Brook St., WI (tel. 629-8760)
Underground Station: *Bond Street*
Hours: *Monday through Friday from 10 a.m. to 6 p.m. (on Thursday to 7 p.m.), on Saturday to 5:30 p.m.*
Credit Cards: *AE, DC, MC, V*

The showcase of Roland Klein's elegant but never-overstated dresses, separates, and evening wear. Fabrics are mainly of natural fibers: linen and cotton in summer and jersey and silk in winter. Day dresses start at around £220, while evening dresses average £380. A black-and-white-check linen duster is priced at £328.

SAINT LAURENT
113 New Bond St., WI (tel. 493-1800)
Underground Station: *Bond Street*
Hours: *Monday through Saturday from 9:30 a.m. to 6 p.m. (on Thursday to 7 p.m.)*
Credit Cards: *AE, DC, MC, V*

Prices are cheaper here than in the United States: blazers average £440, wool dresses start at £220, and silk ones at £450. Another women's boutique is located at 37 Brompton Rd. (tel. 584-0561), while men's clothing is sold at shops at 135 New Bond St. (tel. 493-0405) and 35 Brompton Rd. (tel. 584-4993).

SPAGHETTI
32 Beauchamp Pl., SW3 (tel. 584-0631)
Underground Station: *Knightsbridge*
Hours: *Monday through Friday from 9:30 a.m. to 6 p.m., on Saturday from 10 a.m. to 6 p.m.*
Credit Cards: *AE, DC, MC, V*

Nadia La Valle's unique evening wear stands out among the more traditional shops on Beauchamp Place. Her flamboyant style includes lots of sequins and hand-embroidered silks. £660 is the starting price for most of her short strapless dresses or long gowns, and she will also make clothes to measure, doing a swift business in wedding dresses which begin at £2,200.

TATTERS
74 Fulham Rd., SW3 (tel. 584-1532)
Underground Station: *South Kensington*
Hours: *Monday through Friday from 10 a.m. to 6 p.m., on Saturday to 5 p.m.*
Credit Cards: *AE, DC, MC, V*

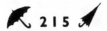
Specializes in exquisite ballgowns and wedding, cocktail, and dinner dresses. About 90% of the fashions are designed in-house and make rich use of such fabrics as velvets, taffetas, brocades, and silks. You can buy right off the peg or have one of the shop's designs custom-made to your exact measurements. Wedding dresses run £330 to £1,650, while ballgowns cost £500 to £1,100. A sashed, blue satin full skirt is £627. It's worth it to keep an eye open for the annual sales in January and July, when the store's samples are sold "dirt cheap."

**Even the bride wore...
Tatters**

WORLDS END
430 King's Rd., SW10 (tel. 352-6551)
Underground Station: *Sloane Square*
Hours: *Monday through Saturday from 11 a.m. to 6 p.m.*
Credit Cards: *None*

Vivienne Westwood began her career designing outrageous clothing at the height of the punk era in the 1970s. She has now settled down to more wearable designs and has given shows around the world. Her London shop is small and easy to miss—look for the clock on the front facade that spins madly backward. Her clothes are hard to describe and change with the seasons, so it's best to come by yourself. One of her latest looks has brought back crinolines, which begin at £27.50. A scoop-neck T-shirt is £33.

The clock spins backwards at avant-garde fashion designer Vivienne Westwood's World's End

ZANDRA RHODES
14A Grafton, WI (tel. 499-6695 or 499-3596), off Bond Street
Underground Station: Green Park or Piccadilly Circus
Hours: Monday through Friday from 9:30 a.m. to 6 p.m., on Saturday to 5 p.m.
Credit Cards: AE, DC, MC, V

English designer Zandra Rhodes gained fame when she began making hippie-style clothes for the affluent, and past clients have included Bianca Jagger and Lauren Bacall. Her creations today are very imaginative, original, and fantasy-provoking—some of them are veritable works of art. A recent knee-length black silk dress, for example, has a flourish of gold-threaded chains patterned into the neckline, making additional jewelry superfluous; it costs £476. Sweat-shirts are £110, but most items in the shop range from £220 to £600.

Men's

More men's fashions can be found under "Tailors," since many of these shops carry a selection of ready-made suits and shirts in addition to their made-to-measure suits.

AIREY & WHEELER
129 Regent St., WI (tel. 734-1008)
Underground Station: Piccadilly Circus
Hours: Monday through Friday from 9 a.m. to 5:30 p.m., on Saturday to
   I p.m.
Credit Cards: MC

Established in 1883, this shop specializes in tropical clothing, including safari suits, lightweight suits, sun hats, swimwear, and casual wear. Cotton safari jackets start at £35, while half-sleeved cotton shirts start at £17. You can also have a safari suit made to measure, beginning at £379. Another shop is located at 44 Piccadilly (tel. 734-8618).

BLAZER
36 Long Acre, Covent Garden, WC2 (tel. 379-6258)
Underground Station: Covent Garden
Hours: Monday through Saturday from I0 a.m. to 6:30 p.m. (on
   Thursday to 8 p.m.)
Credit Cards: AE, DC, MC, V

Good for the English version of the preppy, traditional, Ivy League look, with lots of blazers, sweaters, socks, trousers, and casual clothing. Blazers average £110, striped cotton shirts are £33, and silk ties are £18. Blazer is also located at 90 New Bond St. (tel. 409-2841).

CONNECTIONS FOR MEN
55–56 Long Acre, Covent Garden, WC2 (tel. 379-6560)
Underground Station: Covent Garden
Hours: Monday through Saturday from I I a.m. to 7 p.m. (on Thursday
   to 8 p.m.), on Sunday from noon to 5 p.m.
Credit Cards: AE, MC, V

This is the French Connection shop for men, with trendy, oversize jackets, loose trousers, and chunky sweaters. Accessories include watches, sunglasses, socks, and shoes. Trousers cost around £38, while summer jackets start at £44.

EBONY
45 South Molton St., WI (tel. 629-4721)
Underground Station: Bond Street
Hours: Monday through Saturday from I0:30 a.m. to 6 p.m. (on
   Thursday to 7 p.m.)
Credit Cards: AE, DC, MC, V

A men's shop for the flamboyant, Ebony has put clothes on Elton John, members of Duran Duran, and Ringo Starr. According to the sales staff, customers are affluent, theatrical, and looking for something out of the ordinary, something with flair. As one clerk said, "We dress businessmen by day who

are lunatics at night." The shop specializes in stage wear, with imports from France and Italy. It also has its own label. Prices range from £44 for something in denim to £1,320 for a hand-painted suede jacket.

HACKETT
65B New King's Rd., SW6 (tel. 731-2790)
Underground Station: Fulham Broadway or Parsons Green
Hours: Monday through Friday from 10 a.m. to 7 p.m., on Saturday
   from 9 a.m. to 6 p.m.
Credit Cards: AE, MC, V

All the clothes in this shop are manufactured in England and reflect the restrained, refined taste of traditional English style. In stock are knitwear, ties, suits, trousers, hats, and casual wear. Moleskin trousers (great in cold climates) cost £42.90. Two-piece suits average £247.

HUDSON & HUDSON
6 Shorts Gardens, Covent Garden, WC2 (tel. 836-6495), off Neal Street
Underground Station: Covent Garden
Hours: Monday through Saturday from 11 a.m. to 6:30 p.m.
Credit Cards: AE, DC, MC, V

Opened in 1985, this tiny boutique with a pebble flooring is the showcase for designer Stuart Hudson. His clothes are fun, consisting mainly of baggy trousers and billowing shirts, a cross between Japanese and Italian styles. All fabrics are English, are nice blends of colors, and tend to be fine wools in winter and linen and cotton in summer. Prices represent one of the best values in town, with tops priced at £49.50 and trousers beginning at £44.

JONES
129 King's Rd., SW3 (tel. 352-5323)
Underground Station: Sloane Square
Hours: Monday through Friday from 10 a.m. to 6:30 p.m., on Saturday
   from 9:30 a.m. to 6 p.m.
Credit Cards: AE, DC, MC, V

The casual wear sold here is along classical, preppy lines of the best caliber. There's a lot of variety as well, ranging from leather jackets starting at £330 to striped cotton shirts by Paul Smith for £42.90.

KEY LARGO
2 Bow St., Covent Garden, WC2 (tel. 240-7599)
Underground Station: Covent Garden
Hours: Monday through Saturday from 10 a.m. to 6 p.m.
Credit Cards: AE, DC, MC, V

CLOTHING

The specialty here is hand-framed sweaters made in the Midlands, for £53. You can even have one especially made with your own message, name, company logo, or whatever for £60 (production takes four weeks). Also for sale are American leather jackets, Italian and French designer shirts, swimming trunks, and trousers.

LANVIN
108 New Bond St., W1 (tel. 499-2929)
Underground Station: Bond Street
Hours: Monday through Saturday from 9:30 a.m. to 6 p.m. (on Thursday to 7 p.m.)
Credit Cards: AE, DC, MC, V

Lanvin from Paris is a gentleman's clothing store, where well-tailored shirts start at £77, suits start at £450, trousers at £88, and silk ties at £33. An especially good gift is a limited-edition tie for £77—there are only two made of each design. Another Lanvin is located across from Harrods at 88 Brompton Rd. (tel. 581-4401).

[ixi:z]
St. Christopher's Pl., W1 (tel. 493-9169)
Underground Station: Bond Street
Hours: Monday through Saturday from 10:30 a.m. to 6 p.m. (on Thursday to 7 p.m.)
Credit Cards: AE, MC, V

With stock consisting mainly of T-shirts and sweatsuits, the Japanese clothes sold here are affordable and casual. Colors are bright, happy ones—sea green, yellow, blue, pink—and are often worn by women as well. Cotton T-shirts are £17.50; sweatshirts are £38.

PAUL SMITH
43–44 Floral St., Covent Garden, WC2 (tel. 379-7133)
Underground Station: Covent Garden
Hours: Monday through Saturday from 10 a.m. to 6 p.m. (on Thursday to 7 p.m.)
Credit Cards: AE, DC, MC, V

English designer Paul Smith creates classical clothing with a twist. Fabrics range from the usual to the loud and are put together in an unusual way, with long-sleeve cotton shirts costing £60 and suits ranging from £275 to £500. Paul Smith sells to other shops in 22 countries around the world and even has four shops in Japan.

STEPHEN KING
315 King's Rd., SW3 (tel. 352-5733)

Underground Station: *Sloane Square*
Hours: *Monday through Saturday from 10 a.m. to 6 p.m.*
Credit Cards: *AE, DC, MC, V*

A very stylish shop selling loose-fitting men's clothing. The fabrics have unusual, beautiful color combinations. Shirts start at £50, jackets at £110, and trousers at £82. Another Stephen King is located at 53 Monmouth St. (tel. 240-7577) in Covent Garden, WC2.

WORLD SERVICES LTD.
68 Neal St., Covent Garden, WC2 (tel. 836-0809)
Underground Station: *Covent Garden*
Hours: *Monday through Saturday from 11 a.m. to 7 p.m.*
Credit Cards: *AE, DC, MC, V*

Opened in 1986, World Services is different from other shops in that all its clothes are made in London. Designs are made by East End tailors according to shop owner Chris O'Reilly's specifications, using only natural fabrics. Styles are reminiscent of the 1960s, with highly inventive and contemporary touches. Although presently the shop sells only men's clothing, women's fashions are on the agenda. Striped poplin shirts start at £38, silk shirts are £50, and suits range from £165 to £275.

SHIRTS

Although shirts are sold in most of the shops listed above, London has a fleet of shops specializing in bespoke (made-to-order) and ready-made shirts. Unless otherwise stated, shops below deal in men's shirts only.

COLES
131 Sloane St., SW1 (tel. 730-7564)
Underground Station: *Sloane Square*
Hours: *Monday through Friday from 9:30 a.m. to 6 p.m. (on Wednesday to 7 p.m.), on Saturday to 5:30 p.m.*
Credit Cards: *AE, DC, MC, V*

Shirtmakers since 1878, Coles carries men's, women's, and children's shirts, from the basic, classical striped shirt to its own exclusive range. Ready-made shirts for men include dress shirts for £69 and poplin shirts for £40. Women's silk shirts are £93 and poplin shirts are £42. Children's shirts are £24.75. Made-to-measure shirts start at £76.50.

HARVIE & HUDSON
77 and 96–97 Jermyn St., SW1 (tel. 839-3578)
Underground Station: *Green Park and Piccadilly Circus*
Hours: *Monday through Saturday from 9 a.m. to 5:30 p.m.*
Credit Cards: *AE, DC, MC, V*

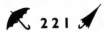

CLOTHING

Pinstripes dominate Coles Ltd.'s windows

Men's bespoke shirts here range from £60 to £105 and take two to four weeks to make. Off-the-peg shirts cost £48.95. Also in stock are ties, suits, sweaters, and robes.

HAWES & CURTIS
2 Burlington Gardens, W1 (tel. 493-3803)
Underground Station: Green Park or Piccadilly Circus
Hours: Monday through Friday from 9 a.m. to 5:30 p.m., on Saturday to
   1 p.m.
Credit Cards: AE, DC, MC, V

Under the same company as Turnbull & Asser and with a royal warrant to the Duke of Edinburgh, Hawes & Curtis offers bespoke shirts beginning at £71.50 and ready-made cotton shirts starting at £45. Ready-made shirts are also available at an additional shop at 23 Jermyn St. (tel. 734-1010).

HILDITCH & KEY LTD.
37 Jermyn St., SW1 (tel. 734-4707)
Underground Station: Green Park or Piccadilly Circus
Hours: Monday through Saturday from 9:30 a.m. to 6 p.m. (on Thursday
   to 7 p.m.)
Credit Cards: AE, DC, MC, V

Hilditch & Key: Shirtmakers since 1899

This shop sells ready-made shirts for women starting at £42.90 and for men at £49. Made-to-measure shirts cost £76.50 each, with a minimum order of six shirts required. Founded in 1899, the company has two other locations, at 73 Jermyn St. (tel. 930-5336) and 87 Jermyn St. (tel. 930-4126), with men's shirts only.

JAMES DREW
3 Burlington Arcade, W1 (tel. 493-0714)
Underground Station: Green Park or Piccadilly Circus
Hours: Monday through Friday from 9 a.m. to 5:30 p.m., on Saturday to 1 p.m.
Credit Cards: AE, DC, MC, V

Armed with a royal warrant and with frequent advertisements in the British edition of *Vogue* magazine, James Drew is a women's shop specializing in shirts, with handmade silk shirts from £130 and cotton ones from £55. Also in stock are jackets, separates, and cashmere sweaters. You can also order a complete made-to-measure outfit.

NEW & LINGWOOD
53 Jermyn St., SW1 (tel. 499-5340)

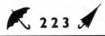
Underground Station: *Green Park or Piccadilly Circus*
Hours: *Monday through Friday from 9 a.m. to 5:30 p.m., on Saturday from 10 a.m. to 3 p.m.*
Credit Cards: *AE, DC, MC, V*

In 1865 Miss New and Mr. Lingwood founded the business that still bears their names. Men's bespoke shirts here range from £71 to £110, while ready-made ones start at £44. Poulsen shoes are also sold here; made-to-measure pairs start at £440.

SULKA
19 Old Bond St., W1 (tel. 493-4468)
Underground Station: *Green Park or Piccadilly Circus*
Hours: *Monday through Friday from 9:30 a.m. to 6 p.m., on Saturday from 10 a.m. to 5 p.m.*
Credit Cards: *AE, DC, MC, V*

Men's bespoke shirts here start at £110 and take approximately six weeks to complete. Sulka is also famous for its silk ties, which begin at £16.50. Other products include dressing gowns, smoking jackets, nightclothes, and boxer shorts. If you want to go all out, buy your man a dressing gown embroidered with 18-karat-gold thread for £2,750.

TURNBULL & ASSER
71–72 Jermyn St., SW1 (tel. 930-0502)
Underground Station: *Green Park*
Hours: *Monday through Friday from 9 a.m. to 5:30 p.m., on Saturday to 4 p.m.*
Credit Cards: *AE, DC, MC, V*

First opened in 1885 when Reginald Turnbull and Ernest Asser began making hunting wear for the aristocracy, this shop is one of the best-known shirtmakers in the world and supplies the Prince of Wales with his shirts. Men's bespoke shirts start at £82.50, while ready-made ones start at £55. It also sells silk ties, bathrobes, pajamas, and sweaters hand-framed in two and four ply.

VALBRIDGE
60 Beauchamp Pl., SW3 (tel. 589-7939)
Underground Station: *Knightsbridge*
Hours: *Monday through Saturday from 9:45 a.m. to 5:30 p.m.*
Credit Cards: *AE, DC, MC, V*

Valbridge stocks an incredible range of women's shirts, from classics to baggy styles, from frilly blouses to dress shirts and camisoles. There are 20 different styles of silk shirts alone, including 15 different types of silk in 50 different colors, ranging in price from £22 to £132. The even-larger stock of cotton shirts ranges in price from £16.50 to £66. With so many styles and sizes to choose from, you'll probably find what you want. If not, you can have them made to your size for about £15 more than the ready-made price, though a minimum order of three shirts is required. There's also a smaller selection of shirts for men.

Turnbull & Asser, world-famous shirtmakers

WOOLENS

One of the best buys in England is its sweaters, including lambswool, cashmere, and hand-knitted traditional woolens. Cashmere is made of goat hair from Kashmir, while lambswool comes from young lambs. Although many of the shops listed above also deal in sweaters, the boutiques below specialize in woolens, often at better prices.

BERK
46-50 Burlington Arcade, WI (tel. 493-0028)
Underground Station: Green Park or Piccadilly Circus
Hours: Monday through Friday from 9 a.m. to 5:30 p.m., on Saturday to 4:30 p.m.
Credit Cards: AE, DC, MC, V

Claiming to have the largest stock of cashmere in the world, Berk certainly has a wide range to choose from, including its own label of long-sleeve V-neck

sweaters costing £76.75 for the women's version and £98.75 for the men's. It also carries sweaters with crew necks, scoop necks, turtlenecks, and cowl necks, as well as cashmere cardigans, skirts, and capes. Berk has other locations in Burlington Arcade, as well as 176 Regent St. (tel. 734-7654) and 61 Brompton Rd. (tel. 589-8000).

CROCHETTA
68 South Molton St., W1 (tel. 493-1500)
Underground Station: *Bond Street*
Hours: *Monday through Saturday from 9:30 a.m. to 6 p.m. (on Thursday to 7 p.m.)*
Credit Cards: *AE, DC, MC, V*

"Women's fantasy sweaters" best describes the unique stock here, creations that include feathers, sequins, satin, beads, and other materials used in the designs. Prices range from £66 to £275 for these hand-loomed and handmade sweaters. There's another Crochetta at 61 Beauchamp Pl. (tel. 589-1266).

MOUSSIE
109 Walton St., SW3 (tel. 581-8674)
Underground Station: *South Kensington*
Hours: *Monday through Saturday from 10 a.m. to 6 p.m.*
Credit Cards: *AE, MC, V*

All the sweaters here are made of natural fibers and are hand-knitted in cottage industries around the country according to the specifications of Moussie. If you see a design you like but none of the sizes fit, you can have one made up at no extra charge. Women's sweaters start at around £132, while children's sweaters range from about £44 to £55.

N. PEAL
37–40 Burlington Arcade, W1 (tel. 493-5378)
Underground Station: *Green Park or Piccadilly Circus*
Hours: *Monday through Friday from 9 a.m. to 5:30 p.m., on Saturday to 4:30 p.m.*
Credit Cards: *AE, DC, MC, V*

Women's cashmere sweaters, in all colors and many price ranges. Classic, simple styles start at £107, while designer sweaters go up to £770. Cashmere scarves and mufflers start at £19.25. A men's shop is located at 54 Burlington Arcade.

PATRICIA ROBERTS
31 James St., WC2 (tel. 379-6660)
Underground Station: *Covent Garden*
Hours: *Monday through Saturday from 10 a.m. to 7 p.m.*
Credit Cards: *AE, DC, MC, V*

This bright and cheerful boutique sells ready-made Patricia Roberts sweaters starting at £330. It also sells specially dyed yarn and Patricia Roberts patterns in case you want to make the sweaters yourself, or you can simply buy the colorful yarn for your own creations. Shetland yarn costs £1.20 for 28 grams, while angora is priced at £7.65 for 20 grams. Another shop is located at 236 Brompton Rd.

RIES WOOLS OF HOLBORN
242–243 High Holborn, WCI (tel. 242-7721)
Underground Station: Holborn
Hours: Monday through Friday from 8:30 a.m. to 6 p.m., on Saturday
from 10 a.m. to 4 p.m.
Credit Cards: AE, MC, V

For people who want to make it themselves, this yarn shop stocks 300 qualities of yarn from 15 different companies in 2,500 shades. It costs approximately £18.70 to knit a woman's wool sweater with Rowan yarn.

S. FISHER
22–23 and 32–33 Burlington Arcade, WI (tel. 493-4180)
Underground Station: Green Park or Piccadilly Circus
Hours: Monday through Friday from 9 a.m. to 5:30 p.m., on Saturday to
4:30 p.m.
Credit Cards: AE, DC, MC, V

A family business for more than four decades, S. Fisher sells men's and women's cashmere, lambswool, and Shetland wool sweaters. Cashmere sweaters start at £87.50 for women and £96.25 for men. Its boutique at 18 The Market in Covent Garden (tel. 836-2576) also sells fashionable versions of hunting, shooting, and fishing wear.

THE SCOTTISH MERCHANT
16 New Row, Covent Garden, WC2 (tel. 836-2207)
Underground Station: Leicester Square
Hours: Monday through Friday from 10:30 a.m. to 6:30 p.m. (on
Thursday to 7 p.m.), on Saturday to 5:30 p.m.
Credit Cards: AE, MC, V

A great place for traditional knitwear, including Shetlands and fishermen's ganseys, and for beautiful designer sweaters. All are hand-knitted or hand-framed by British designers and come in gorgeous colors. Prices range from about £33 for a hand-framed Channel Island gansey up to £220 for designer wear. In addition to its men's and women's sweaters, it also carries gloves, hats, scarves, blankets, and shawls.

SCOTTISH WOOLENS
193 Regent St., WI (tel. 437-5751)

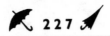
Underground Station: *Oxford Circus or Piccadilly Circus*
Hours: *Monday through Saturday from 9:30 a.m. to 6:30 p.m. (on Thursday to 7:30 p.m.)*
Credit Cards: AE, DC, MC, V

Part of a chain offering inexpensive designer and classic knitwear for women, with lots of young, colorful styles. Cashmere sweaters start at £43.95. Other shops include 141 Regent St. (tel. 437-4735) and 273 Oxford St. (tel. 629-3381).

W. BILL
28 Old Bond St., W1 (tel. 629-9565)
Underground Station: *Piccadilly Circus or Green Park*
Hours: *Monday through Friday from 9 a.m. to 5:30 p.m., on Saturday to 4 p.m.*
Credit Cards: AE, DC, MC, V

Woolen specialists since 1846, this family business stocks cashmere, lambswool, and Shetland sweaters for men and women, as well as Aran knits, kilts, capes, tweed skirts, and tweed by the yard. Women's lambswool sweaters start at £38.40, while cashmere sweaters are around £102. A man's V-neck cashmere sweater is £132. Kilts are priced at £35.

WESTAWAY & WESTAWAY
65 Great Russell St., WC1 (tel. 405-4479), across from the British Museum
Underground Station: *Tottenham Court Road or Holborn*
Hours: *Monday through Saturday from 9 a.m. to 5:30 p.m.*
Credit Cards: AE, DC, MC, V

Turning 50 years old in 1987, this firm offers great prices on lambswool, Shetland, and cashmere sweaters, all with traditional, classical cuts. Women's Shetland pullovers start at a low £15.40, while lambswool crew-neck cardigans are only £25.80. Also for sale are Burberry raincoats, Harris Tweed jackets, kilts, and tartans. If you're interested in more designer-style sweaters, be sure to visit the company's new shop down the street at 92–93 Great Russell St. (tel. 636-1718), where a mohair, silk, and cotton combination sweater will cost around £68.75.

DISCOUNT DESIGNER WEAR

The shops here sell designer wear at greatly reduced prices, either because they act as clearance houses for end of the lines or because they sell secondhand clothes in excellent condition that may have been worn only once. After all, some women wouldn't *dream* of wearing the same Christian Dior dress two years in a row.

THE CONSTANT SALE SHOP
56 Fulham Rd., SW3 (tel. 589-1458)
Underground Station: South Kensington
**Hours: Monday through Saturday from 10 a.m. to 6 p.m. (on Wednesday
 to 7 p.m.)**
Credit Cards: AE, DC, MC, V

Opened in 1986, this shop belongs to a parent company that owns designer
shops of Ungaro, Basile, Armani, Krizia, Valentino, and others, and therefore
has dibs on ends of the lines from these famous designer houses. Savings are from
60% off the original price, with most separates between £60 and £100. Women's
clothing only.

THE DRESSER
39–41 Sussex Pl., Hyde Park Estate, W2 (tel. 724-7212)
Underground Station: Lancaster Gate
**Hours: Monday through Friday from 11 a.m. to 6:30 p.m., on Saturday
 to 6 p.m.**
Credit Cards: MC, V

Men's and women's designer clothes less than a year old and straight from the
cleaners. The stock changes rapidly but may include designs by Jean-Paul
Gaultier, Saint Laurent, Katharine Hamnett, Jasper Conran, or Comme des
Garçons. There's lots in the £25 to £35 range, and you'll find shoes, belts, ties,
handbags, jumpers, raincoats, suits, and costume jewelry.

THE FROCK EXCHANGE
450 Fulham Rd., SW6 (tel. 381-2937)
Underground Station: Fulham Broadway
Hours: Monday through Saturday from 10 a.m. to 5:30 p.m.
Credit Cards: None

Deals in women's clothes from well-known designers and has carried clothing by
Ungaro, Zandra Rhodes, Bruce Oldfield, Gucci, Kenzo, Yohji Yamamoto,
Katharine Hamnett, Caroline Charles, Belleville Sassoon, Jean Muir, Betty
Jackson, Armani, and many more. Most of the customers are aged 18 to 35, who
go crazy over prices two-thirds the original. Designer day dresses start at about
£44, while a Ted Lapidus three-piece woman's suit was recently priced at £120.

THE NOUVEAUX PAUVRES
62 New King's Rd., SW6 (tel. 736-2401)
Underground Station: Parsons Green
Hours: Monday through Saturday from 10 a.m. to 6:30 p.m.
Credit Cards: AE, MC, V

Carries a constantly changing stock of designer samples. Only women's clothing is sold, and has included fashions by Jasper Conran, Armani, Naf-Naf, Ken Williams, Tom Bell, and others. The stock is comprised of casual wear and day and evening dresses, with lots priced between £25 and £50.

PAMELA
93 Walton St., SW3 (tel. 589-6852)
Underground Station: *South Kensington*
Hours: *Monday through Friday from 10 a.m. to 5 p.m., on Saturday to 1 p.m.*
Credit Cards: *AE, DC, MC, V*

Classical designer wear by Saint Laurent, Lanvin, Louis Féraud, Zandra Rhodes, Christian Dior, and others. Only women's clothing is sold, and no garment is more than two years old. A recent visit turned up a Christian Dior two-piece suit for £123 and a Saint Laurent blouse for £49.

PANDORA
54 Sloane Square, SW1 (tel. 730-5722)
Underground Station: *Sloane Square*
Hours: *Monday through Friday from 10 a.m. to 5 p.m.*
Credit Cards: *None*

If only this store could talk. It's been selling secondhand women's designer clothes for the past 40 years and has seen more Saint Laurent, Chloé, Emanuel, Valentino, Armani, and other creations march by than we can ever imagine. The shop buys designer clothes from individuals and then sells them on a commission basis. The stock is large, primarily traditional, and includes cocktail dresses, day dresses, suits, skirts, blouses, furs, coats, raincoats, capes, and summer clothing year round for people going to Australia. A Valentino two-piece wool suit is priced at £220, cocktail dresses start at £55, and an Emanuel evening cape is £137.

PERIOD AND SECONDHAND

BLAX
8 and 11 Sicilian Ave., Holborn, WC1 (tel. 404-0125), off Southampton Row
Underground Station: *Holborn*
Hours: *Monday through Friday from 11 a.m. to 6:30 p.m., on Saturday from noon to 6:30 p.m.*
Credit Cards: *None*

The shop at no. 8 sells women's period clothing from the late 1920s to the early 1950s. Some is the original stock, such as a recent windfall discovery of women's

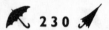
suits dating from the late 1930s and priced at £50. If a line proves especially popular, Blax will commission companies to make faithful and excellent reproductions. The men's shop at no. 11 sells original and reproduction suits, jackets, vests, coats, shoes, ties, and hats ranging from homburgs to felts.

CUBA
56 New Oxford St., WCI (tel. 580-7740)
Underground Station: *Tottenham Court Road*
Hours: *Monday through Saturday from 11 a.m. to 7 p.m.*
Credit Cards: *None*

This shop sells an impressive range of '40s and '50s original fashions and accessories. Ladies' party dresses start at about £16.50, men's dress suits start at £50, and men's white cotton shirts dating from the '20s through the '40s are about £15. Also in stock are shoes, cravats, cricket trousers, and corny ties.

EAT YOUR HEART OUT
360 King's Rd., SW3 (tel. 352-3392)
Underground Station: *Sloane Square*
Hours: *Monday through Saturday from 11 a.m. to 6 p.m.*
Credit Cards: *None*

Sells secondhand clothing and objects dating from the 1920s through the 1950s, lots of junk but some interesting finds as well. Bowler hats are £22, cravats are £3, waistcoats are £6, and tweed jackets start at £13. Men's white nightshirts from Holland are £13, and are popular today with young women.

Eat your heart out for the 1920s through 1950s

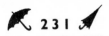

CLOTHING

HILLS DRESSWEAR
15 Henrietta St., Covent Garden, WC2 (tel. 240-1939)
Underground Station: Covent Garden
Hours: Monday through Saturday from "about lunchtime" to 6 p.m.
Credit Cards: None

This delightful shop is run by an equally delightful proprietor whose father started the business 50 years ago. It's packed with period evening wear for gentlemen dating from the '20s and later, all cleaned and pressed. For sale are the kinds of garments you wish some ancient uncle had bequeathed you—a collapsible opera hat (priced at £71), full-tail morning and dress coats, single-breasted and double-breasted dinner suits dating from 1915 and onward, and more. Nothing is marked, but you can be assured of fair deals with most prices ranging from £55 to £150.

JOHN BURKE & PARTNERS
20 Pembridge Rd., W11 (tel. 229-0862)
Underground Station: Notting Hill Gate
Hours: Daily except Thursday and Sunday from 9 a.m. to 5 p.m.
Credit Cards: MC

This 30-year-old shop sells a delightful jumble of secondhand clothing and is run by equally delightful older gentlemen who enjoy talking to customers. "Everyone knows us," said one of the men. "We've been here such a long time. They just call us 'the funny shop.'" The atmosphere is timeless: shelves are piled high with musty hatboxes, hats, old shoes, books, odds and ends, and clothing. Bow ties are £2, ties are £4.50, and there are even silk cumberbunds. There are also military uniforms and caps, the uniforms going for £11 to about £33. This is a good shop to visit if you're on your way to Portobello Road market nearby.

LUNN ANTIQUES
86 New King's Rd., SW6 (tel. 736-4638)
Underground Station: Parsons Green
Hours: Monday through Saturday from 10 a.m. to 6 p.m.
Credit Cards: AE, DC, MC, V

This shop specializes in antique lace since 1750 and carries antique and reproduction pillow cases, sheets, tablecloths, and clothing as well. Irish crocheted jackets dating from 1910 start at £88, while reproduction white nightgowns cost £35. There are also shawls made from antique lace, original Edwardian high-neck blouses, and '20s beaded dresses. Catalogs are available.

20TH CENTURY BOX
357 King's Rd., SW3 (tel. 351-0724)
Underground Station: Sloane Square
Hours: Monday through Saturday from 11:30 a.m. to 6 p.m.
Credit Cards: None

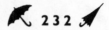
A jumble of '50s and '60s waistcoats, dress shirts, dinner suits, tailcoats, bow ties, collars and collar studs, and more, but primarily clothes for guys. Shirts and waistcoats start at £4.50, but the most you'll pay in this shop is £30, for a tailcoat.

CHILDREN'S CLOTHING

Several shops I've already listed above carry children's clothing, including **Burberrys**, the Scotch House, C & A, Cacharel, Clothkit, Laura Ashley (especially at its Harriet Street store), **Coles**, and **Moussie**. In addition, be sure to check the children's section of department stores. **Marks & Spencer, Littlewoods**, and **British Home Stores** provide the basics in children's wear at very low prices.

EDWINA CARROLL
26 The Market, Covent Garden, WC2 (tel. 836-0955)
Underground Station: Covent Garden
Hours: Monday through Saturday from 10 a.m. to 6 p.m.
Credit Cards: AE, MC, V

In addition to her women's clothing boutique in the Market, Edwina Carroll also has a children's version, with adorable clothing and cuddly toys she has personally selected. Sizes run from the newborn to about 7 years old. Brightly colored Shetland sweaters start at £20, and stuffed animals start at £6.

LA CIGONA
6A Sloane St., SWI (tel. 235-3845)
Underground Station: Knightsbridge
Hours: Monday through Saturday from 9:30 a.m. to 6:15 p.m. (on
Wednesday to 7:15 p.m.)
Credit Cards: AE, DC, MC, V

If you want to go all-out, this is certainly a place that's easy to do it. It sells Italian designer wear for children from the time they're born until they're about 14 years old, giving them time to get used to wearing Armani jackets or Valentino jeans. Enrico Coveri sweatsuits cost £74, sporty jackets cost about £62, and party dresses of silk run about £165. If you're undaunted by those prices, consider a bridesmaid dress for more than £1,500 or christening sets costing more than £2,500.

MOTHERCARE
461 Oxford St., WI (tel. 629-6621)
Underground Station: Marble Arch
Hours: Monday through Saturday from 9 a.m. to 6 p.m. (on Thursday to
7:30)
Credit Cards: AE, MC, V

There are 24 Mothercare shops in London alone, attesting to this chain's immense popularity. It carries just about everything needed, from maternity clothes to nursery furniture, prams, toys, and baby and children's wear. Clothes are durable and reasonably priced: for example, lots of dresses are priced between £5 and £10. Two other locations include 120 Kensington High St. (tel. 937-9781) and 145–147 Brompton Rd. (tel. 584-1397)

PLEASE MUM
22 Sloane St., SW1 (tel. 235-5303)
Underground Station: *Knightsbridge*
Hours: *Monday through Saturday from 9:30 a.m. to 6 p.m. (on Wednesday to 7:30 p.m.)*
Credit Cards: AE, DC, MC, V

Another expensive clothing store, with imports mainly from France and Italy. Most garments cost between £80 and £200, though you can certainly spend more. Boys' suits start at around £200. You can spend more than £400 on a precious party dress, but at that price you may decide your child isn't precious enough. A 2-year-old's silk outfit costs £196 and sweaters start at about £88.

ZERO FOUR
53 South Molton St., W1 (tel. 493-4920)
Underground Station: *Bond Street*
Hours: *Monday through Saturday from 10 a.m. to 6 p.m. (on Thursday to 7 p.m.)*
Credit Cards: AE, V

Italian designer wear for the under-fourteen-year-olds

Catering to children from birth to about 14 years of age, this boutique on fashionable South Molton Street lives up to the neighborhood image with stylish Italian and French casual wear. There are preppy-looking sweaters, jackets, sweatshirts, and hand-smocked dresses. Track suits from France are priced at £44.

012
22 South Molton St., W1 (tel. 409-1599)
Underground Station: Bond Street
Hours: Monday through Saturday from 10 a.m. to 6 p.m. (on Thursday to 7 p.m.)
Credit Cards: AE, MC, V

Not to be outdone, 012 is Benetton's chain of children's clothing. Its trademark is its colorful and cheerful clothing, with sizes that fit from about 18 months to 12 years old. Corduroy trousers start at £17.50 and wool sweaters at £18.50. Other 012 shops are at 131 Kensington High St. (tel. 937-2960), 32 New Bond St. (tel. 499-8439), and 132 King's Rd. (tel. 589-2376).

COINS

GLENDINING & CO.
7 Blenheim St., W1 (tel. 493-2445)
Underground Station: Bond Street
Hours: Sales are held on Wednesday once or twice a month. Viewings are held on Monday and Tuesday from 9 a.m. to noon and 1 to 4 p.m. during auction weeks.
Credit Cards: None

This auction house deals specifically in coins and medals and has one or two auctions a month except during the months of January and August. There's a 10% buyer's premium, and a year's subscription to their coin catalog costs £13.

In addition to this auction house, be sure to contact the major houses listed in the "Auctions" section of this book for their periodic sales of coins.

KNIGHTSBRIDGE COINS
43 Duke St., St. James's, SW1 (tel. 930-7597)
Underground Station: Green Park or Piccadilly Circus
Hours: Monday through Friday from 10:15 a.m. to 5:30 p.m.
Credit Cards: None

Specializes in Great Britain and American coins from Elizabeth I to today. It also does evaluations and buys, sells, and trades.

SPINK & SON
5 King St., SW1 (tel. 930-7888)

Underground Station: *Green Park*
Hours: *Monday to Friday from 9:30 a.m. to 5:30 p.m.*
Credit Cards: *None*

Spink is London's foremost coin dealer, handling everything from antique Greek coins to English coins and medals. It also has bullion coins. In addition, coin auctions are held about six times a year. Catalogs are issued for the auctions, and Spink also publishes a numismatic magazine ten times a year.

COSMETICS

If you're looking for the most comprehensive selection of cosmetics under one roof, **Selfridges** has one of the largest cosmetic departments in the country, followed by **Harrods** at a close second. For inexpensive and everyday makeup, try **Boots** pharmacy and **Fenwick** department store.

THE BODY SHOP
13 The Market, Covent Garden, WC2 (tel. 836-5113)
Underground Station: *Covent Garden*
Hours: *Monday through Saturday from 10 a.m. to 8 p.m., on Sunday from 11:30 a.m. to 6:30 p.m.*
Credit Cards: *MC, V*

The most successful health-and-beauty chain store in England, the Body Shop offers a great selection of makeup, lotions, shampoos, soaps, and other products at low prices. All products are biodegradable, are tested without cruelty to animals, and contain natural ingredients such as aloe, jojoba, cucumber, or orange blossom. Products start at small sizes (great for traveling), including hair conditioner for 90 pence, milk baths at 75 pence, and aloe lotion at 92 pence. Glycerine soaps of various fruit scents are £1, while gift packs of creams, soaps, and various toiletries are priced under £8. In the cosmetics section are eyeshadows, pencils, blushes, lipsticks, foundations and powders, most priced under £2. There are also products for men and sun lotions. Other Body Shops are at 54 King's Rd. (tel. 584-0163), 203 Kensington High St. (tel. 937-1890), and 32–34 Great Marlborough St. (tel. 437-5137).

CHARLES H. FOX LTD.
22 Tavistock, Covent Garden, WC2 (tel. 240-3111)
Underground Station: *Covent Garden*
Hours: *Monday through Friday from 9:30 a.m. to 1 p.m. and 2 to 5 p.m.*
Credit Cards: *MC, V*

A specialist in theatrical makeup, right in the heart of theater land. Colors range from flamboyant to barely noticeable, and there's even a makeup designer who will make up your face (makeup lessons run around £30). Kryolan Brandel,

Leichner, Max Factor, and Stargazer are some of the brands carried, with lots under £5. If you're desperate for special film blood, you can get it here for £3.85, while nose putty costs £2.20. There are also the usual powders, eyeshadows, blushers, lipsticks, and brushes.

CRAFTS

If you are especially interested in seeing and learning about contemporary British artists' work in ceramics, glass, wood, textiles, and other materials, the **Crafts Council** at 12 Waterloo Pl., SW1 (tel. 930-4811), is the best place to start. The council was established to promote crafts and artists, and is located just a few minutes' walk from Piccadilly Circus. It's open Tuesday through Saturday from 10 a.m. to 5 p.m. and on Sunday from 2 to 5 p.m. There's a small gallery with regularly changing exhibitions, as well as a library with 18,000 slides along with an index of artists, just in case you want to commission someone to do a special piece.

The Crafts Council also puts out a pamphlet listing more than two dozen crafts galleries and shops in London, several of which are listed below. The council also maintains a small **Crafts Council Shop** in the Victoria and Albert Museum, with a selection of jewelry, ceramics, glass, and other crafts.

In addition to the shops and galleries listed below, the **Designers Guild,** listed under "Fabrics," has a selection of crafts such as pottery, and **Naturally British,** listed under "Gifts," has a great selection of handmade British products. For galleries dealing exclusively in jewelry, refer to the "Jewelry" section of this book.

Another fertile ground for crafts is the **Chelsea Crafts Fair,** held annually in October at the Chelsea Old Town Hall, King's Road. More than 200 exhibitors display ceramics, blown glass, knitwear, furniture, jewelry, toys, textiles, and much more. Contact the tourist information center for this and other crafts fairs.

BRITISH CRAFTS CENTRE
43 Earlham St., Covent Garden, WC2 (tel. 836-6993), on the corner of Neal and Earlham Streets
Underground Station: Covent Garden
Hours: Monday through Friday from 10 a.m. to 5:30 p.m., on Saturday from 11 a.m. to 5 p.m.
Credit Cards: AE, MC, V

Displaying the work of artists belonging to the Crafts Council, this gallery is one of the best in London to see a variety of crafts, including glass, pottery, jewelry, woodcarvings, basketweaving, tapestries, and more. Prices range from about £8 for earrings and go up to several hundred pounds for hand-woven carpets and furniture.

CRAFTS

CABARET MECHANICAL THEATRE
33–34 The Market, Covent Garden, WC2 (tel. 379-7961)
Underground Station: Covent Garden
Hours: *Daily from 10 a.m. to 7 p.m.*
Credit Cards: AE, DC, MC, V

This unique shop sells handmade automata, all crafted in England. Most pieces are of wood and range in price from about £16.50 to £175. There are donkeys that eat corn, stick figures that dance, and much more. Good gifts for the person who has everything.

THE CRAFTSMEN POTTERS SHOP
William Blake House, 7 Marshall St., W1 (tel. 437-7605)
Underground Station: Oxford Circus or Piccadilly Circus
Hours: *Monday through Saturday from 10 a.m. to 5:30 p.m.*
Credit Cards: AE, DC, MC, V

Founded in 1956, this potter's co-op is bright and airy and has both pottery and ceramics for sale, starting at about £5 and going up into the hundreds.

CRANE GALLERY
171A Sloane St., SW1 (tel. 235-2464)
Underground Station: Knightsbridge or Sloane Square
Hours: *Monday through Friday from 10 a.m. to 6 p.m., on Saturday to 4 p.m.*
Credit Cards: AE, MC, V

This gallery deals in antique folk art, including 19th-century primitive paintings, country furniture, quilts, decoys, pottery, weather vanes, and other crafts, from both America and England. Prices start at about £35 for pottery or brass items.

COLERIDGE
192 Piccadilly, W1 (tel. 437-0106), in the Princes Arcade
Underground Station: Piccadilly Circus or Green Park
Hours: *Monday through Friday from 10 a.m. to 6:15 p.m., on Saturday to 5 p.m.*
Credit Cards: AE, DC, MC, V

This beautiful shop sells a wonderful array of glass art, from paperweights to one-of-a-kind glass sculptures that can cost several thousand pounds. There are some delicately shaped scent bottles starting at £17, and there's lots to choose from in the £50 to £150 range, including both modern and abstract, and functional and decorative pieces.

THE GLASSHOUSE
65 Long Acre, Covent Garden, WC2 (tel. 836-9785)
Underground Station: Covent Garden

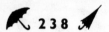
**Hours: Monday through Friday from 10 a.m. to 5:30 p.m., on Saturday
from 11 a.m. to 4:30 p.m.**
Credit Cards: DC, MC, V

First opened in 1969, the Glasshouse is a contemporary studio where you can
watch glassblowers at work and shop for glass art. Prices start at about £16 for
paperweights. There are also candlesticks, plates, bowls, goblets, vases, cups,
and many other transparent pieces of art.

J. K. HILL
151 Fulham Rd., SW3 (tel. 584-7529)
Underground Station: South Kensington
Hours: Monday through Saturday from 10 a.m. to 6 p.m.
Credit Cards: AE, DC, MC, V

Changing displays showcase the wares of 180 potters. Pieces are primarily
functional, and include jewelry, tea pots, mugs, bowls, plates, vases, lamp
bases, figures, and more. Porcelain earrings start at £5, while square earthenware dishes are priced at £38 each.

CRYSTAL AND GLASS

Britain was one of the leading manufacturers of glass in the 18th and early
19th centuries. The development of lead glass allowed for greater refrac-
tive power, permitting construction of a wide variety of objects. Crystal,
which is a high-quality clear and colorless glass, still enjoys widespread
popularity throughout the United Kingdom and Ireland.

Most of the well-known china shops in London sell crystal as well.
Chinacraft, for example, sells Waterford, Edinburgh, Royal Brierley,
Stuart, Lalique, Saint Louis, and Baccarat crystal; while the **Reject China
Shops** stock Atlantis, Baccarat, Caithness, Kosta Boda, Lalique, Orre-
fors, and Waterford, to name only a few. Two other good shops for crystal
are **Thomas Goode** and **Lawleys.** Refer to the "China" section for
information on these stores.

For contemporary blown glass, refer to the "Crafts" section. If you're
looking for antique glass two excellent stores are listed below.

HOWARD PHILLIPS
11A Henrietta Pl., W1 (tel. 580-9844)
Underground Station: Bond Street
Hours: Monday through Friday from 9:30 a.m. to 5:15 p.m.
Credit Cards: None

A foremost dealer in antique glass, covering about 3,000 years of glass history.
The oldest pieces are Phoenician, and the collection includes Egyptian,
Roman, Byzantine, Turkish, Italian, Russian, Austrian, Norwegian, and Eng-

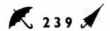
lish glass, up to about 1830. Prices range from about £50 to six-digit figures. Glass from this shop has ended up in the White House.

W. G. T. BURNE
11 Elystan St., SW3 (tel. 589-6074)
Underground Station: South Kensington
Hours: Monday through Friday from 9 a.m. to 5 p.m. (on Thursday to
   1 p.m.), on Saturday to 12:30 p.m.
Credit Cards: None

Old English and Irish glass from the late 17th century to the 1870s. The staff is very friendly and accommodating and happy to show visitors their wine glasses, bowls, wine decanters, chandeliers, and lusters (candlesticks with glass pendants). More than 200 wine decanters are in stock, ranging in price from £65 to £220.

DEPARTMENT STORES

You can find virtually everything in London's department stores, making them good for one-stop shopping if your time is limited or if the weather is foul. Several of them are famous for certain goods or departments, such as Liberty for its fabrics and Fortnum & Mason for its food hall. All the larger department stores will refund VAT (usually for purchases totaling £50 or more) and will ship your purchases directly from the store. Department stores are also well known for their fabulous sales, which unfortunately can also be frustrating experiences due to the huge crowds. Most department stores, including Harrods and Selfridges, have their annual sales in January and July.

ARMY & NAVY
101–105 Victoria St., SW1 (tel. 834-1234)
Underground Station: Victoria
Hours: Monday through Thursday from 9 a.m. to 5:30 p.m. (on Tuesday
   from 9:30 a.m.), on Friday and Saturday to 6 p.m.
Credit Cards: AE, DC, MC, V

Contrary to what the name may lead you to believe, this is not an outlet for army and navy surplus but rather a full-scale, regular department store. Because it's so far removed from the mainstream of London's shopping regions, it's hardly ever crowded, even at Christmastime. It has a strong sports department, including sportswear, as well as a good toy section. Other departments sell clocks, electrical appliances, hats, jewelry, stationery, linens, crystal, and china. There's a restaurant on the second floor, and other services include a beauty salon and florist shop. Women's fashion includes clothing by Jaeger, Alexon, Windsmoor, Mondi, and Country Casuals.

BRITISH HOME STORES
252–258 Oxford St., W1 (tel. 629-2011)
Underground Station: Oxford Circus
Hours: Monday through Saturday from 9 a.m. to 6 p.m. (on Thursday to 8 p.m.)
Credit Cards: MC, V

British Home Stores is a chain of small department stores known for its low prices for clothing, toiletries, and everyday needs and lighting. They are directed more toward local residents than to tourists. Another British Home Store is located at 99–105 Kensington High St. (tel. 937-0919)

D H EVANS
318 Oxford St., W1 (tel. 629-8800)
Underground Station: Oxford Circus
Hours: Monday through Friday from 9:30 a.m. to 6 p.m. (on Thursday to 8 p.m.), on Saturday from 9 a.m. to 6 p.m.
Credit Cards: AE, DC, MC, V

Dan Harries Evans came to London from Wales in 1877 with £400 in his pocket. His ambition was to create the most prestigious department store in London, and within two years the 22-year-old had acquired 320 Oxford St. and two assistants. By the turn of the century, he had a staff of 350 and three floors of goods.

Today, D H Evans's gleaming art deco façade is a familiar landmark on Oxford Street and offers eight floors of shopping. Its biggest departments include fashions, cosmetics, home furnishings, and sports. It boasts a large cafeteria on the sixth floor called River Restaurant, a coffeeshop in the basement, and a good hair salon called Essanelle on the fourth floor.

DEBENHAMS
334–338 Oxford St., W1 (tel. 580-3000)
Underground Station: Oxford Circus or Bond Street
Hours: Monday through Saturday from 9:30 a.m. to 6 p.m. (on Thursday to 8 p.m.)
Credit Cards: AE, DC, MC, V

Renovated in 1986, Debenhams is big on home furnishings and clothing. The clothing tends to be conservative and simple, the women's dresses made mainly from synthetic materials and starting at a low £20. Of note are the china and crystal departments, with names like Wedgwood, Royal Doulton, and Royal Worcester, and the home appliance department. Other departments sell cosmetics and perfume, shoes, lingerie, jewelry, and linen.

DICKENS & JONES
224 Regent St., W1 (tel. 734-7070)

Underground Station: *Oxford Circus*
Hours: *Monday through Saturday from 9:30 a.m. to 6 p.m. (on Thursday to 7:30 p.m.)*
Credit Cards: *AE, DC, MC, V*

Dickens & Jones changed its image recently to one selling almost exclusively fashion, and its goal is to offer the largest selection of clothing in London. It certainly offers a great selection, from casual wear to sportswear and elegant evening wear. Designer names and collections include Gloria Vanderbilt, Paul Costelloe, Escada, Louis Féraud, Alexon, Country Casuals, Jaeger, Planet, Viyella, Windsmoor, Aquascutum, and Burberry. Included are petite and oversize clothing sections, as well as a large shoe department. Men's fashions are in the basement. Services include two restaurants, two coffeeshops, a juice bar, and an Essanelle beauty salon. The minimum purchase for a VAT refund is £75.

FORTNUM & MASON
181 Piccadilly, W1 (tel. 734-8040)
Underground Station: *Piccadilly Circus or Green Park*
Hours: *Monday through Saturday from 9 a.m. to 5:30 p.m.*
Credit Cards: *AE, DC, MC, V*

So beautiful is its food hall that I could write pages and pages on Fortnum & Mason alone. Its food hall is probably the most elegant in the world, with counters of tempting chocolates and confectionary, cheeses, preserves, biscuits, wines, and teas. It's especially famous for its food hampers, filled with such delectables as preserves, sauces, nuts, mustard, honey, tea, and spices, several of which can even be sent to the United States and make great gifts. For more exotic dining, you can also buy smoked salmon, caviar, Blue Stilton cheese (made especially for Fortnum & Mason starting at £7), hams, and fruit tea.

Fortnum & Mason has been selling food ever since 1707 when it first opened as a grocery. William Fortnum was a footman in the royal household of Queen Anne, and the store has been royal purveyors of food ever since. If you're anywhere near the store at the striking of the hour, pause to look at the famous clock on the façade which was installed in 1964. It shows Mr. Fortnum and Mr. Mason in miniature as they emerge and bow to each other as 17 bells peal the hour.

In addition to food, the store also sells clothing, luggage and handbags, jewelry, china and glass, and antique furniture. Its Fountain Restaurant, with an entrance on Jermyn Street, stays open until midnight Monday through Saturday, while the St. James's Restaurant on the fourth floor offers formal dining. The store produces a beautiful catalog, available for £1.

HARRODS
Knightsbridge, SW1 (tel. 730-1234)
Underground Station: *Knightsbridge*

Hours: Monday through Friday from 9 a.m. to 5 p.m. (on Wednesday to 7 p.m.), on Saturday to 6 p.m.
Credit Cards: AE, DC, MC, V

Love it or hate it, Harrods is one of the largest and most famous department stores in the world. Founded 137 years ago by tea merchant Henry Charles Harrod who started out with a grocery shop, Harrods today is a monolith, covering about 4½ acres of land. It has 230 different departments, five restaurants, four snackbars, its own pub, kennels, a funeral service, a tourist information desk, a theater ticket agency, hair salons, and a pharmacy. Harrods hold four royal warrants, employs 4,000 people, and averages about 50,000 customers per day.

Its fashions alone are divided into 34 departments. Designer names include Dunhill and Louis Féraud for men and Jean Muir, Nicole Farhi, Viyella, Windsmoor, Paul Costelloe, Alexon, Norman Hartnell, Missoni, Jasper Conran, and Perry Ellis for women. Way In carries trendy and fashionable wear. Harrods is also well known for its food halls, with 18 departments in all. There are 163 different brands of whisky, 500 kinds of cheeses, and 130 different types of bread. The food halls are truly wonderful and well worth a browse, simply for the experience.

Perhaps because of the store's high visibility, no one who has been to Harrods is without an opinion. Some Londoners tell me it's still the best department store in town—others think it's too large and impersonal. Some people report they've had great difficulty trying to return goods. Important to Americans is the fact that Harrods requires a minimum purchase of £100 before it will give a VAT refund. Harrods issues three catalogs a year, which vary in price from about £2 to £6 and are filled with goods you can order by mail.

HARVEY NICHOLS
109 Knightsbridge, SW1 (tel. 235-5000)
Underground Station: Knightsbridge
Hours: Monday through Saturday from 9:30 a.m. to 6 p.m. (on Wednesday to 7 p.m.)
Credit Cards: AE, DC, MC, V

Arguably the most elegant and luxurious department store in London. Renowned for its innovative window displays, it carries a marvelous selection of designer clothes. I agree with one native shopping enthusiast who told me that if she could afford them, she would buy all of her clothes here. It stocks Jaeger, Edina Ronay, Nicole Farhi, French Connection, Cacharel, Alexon, Burberry, Windsmoor, Liz Claiborne, Chloé, J. Tiktiner, and Sonia Rykiel, to name only a few. Everything in the store is of impeccable taste, with smaller china, linen, and gift departments offering quality rather than quantity. Facilities include waitress service at Harveys at the Top on the fifth floor, a coffeeshop in the basement, and a Glemby hair and beauty salon.

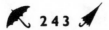

The clock depicting Mr. Fortnum
and Mr. Mason, royal purveyors
of food since 1707

HOUSE OF FRASER
63 Kensington High St., W8 (tel. 937-5432)
Underground Station: *High Street Kensington*
Hours: *Monday through Saturday from 9 a.m. to 6 p.m. (on Thursday to 6:30 p.m.)*
Credit Cards: *AE, DC, MC, V*

Formerly known as Barkers, this department store underwent extensive expansion in 1986 and reopened under the name of House of Fraser. It has the usual fashion department with names like Jaeger, Windsmoor, and Viyella, as well as departments selling cosmetics, fashion accessories, kitchenware, china, and glass. Services include two restaurants and Essanelle beauty salon.

JOHN LEWIS
Oxford Street, W1 (tel. 629-7711)
Underground Station: *Oxford Circus or Bond Street*
Hours: *Monday through Saturday from 9 a.m. to 5:30 p.m. (on Thursday to 8 p.m.)*
Credit Cards: *Only its own*

Based on the store's slogan "Never Knowingly Undersold," John Lewis will refund the difference if you buy something here and then find the same item cheaper elsewhere. The fabrics department is good and extensive, and the lighting, home furnishings, and appliance sections are also well known. It features one restaurant and one coffeeshop.

LIBERTY
Regent Street, W1 (tel. 734-1234)
Underground Station: Oxford Circus
Hours: Monday through Saturday from 9:30 a.m. to 6 p.m. (on Thursday to 7 p.m.)
Credit Cards: AE, DC, MC, V

Founded in 1894, Liberty is a pure joy. From its half-timbered façade facing Great Marlborough Street to its interior oak paneling and balustrade, Liberty is one of London's great shopping experiences. It's famous for fabrics, with brightly colored Varuna wool averaging £17 per meter and cottons costing about £8.75. Liberty scarves are also gorgeous, the long silk ones starting at £28.50. Liberty has also been associated with jewelry, in particular for its styles during the art nouveau period. Today it carries only a limited amount of its own original

The wood-paneled interior is part of the pleasure at Liberty's

Carnival time at Liberty's

jewelry, but it stocks some French and American original costume jewelry as well. Liberty also has a fine Oriental department, a large selection of Oriental carpets, modern and antique furniture, glass and china, and designer fashions. There's a restaurant on the fourth floor and a coffeeshop in the basement.

LITTLEWOODS
207 Oxford St., WI (tel. 437-1718)
Underground Station: Oxford Circus
508 Oxford St., WI (tel. 629-7847)
Underground Station: Marble Arch
Hours: Monday through Saturday from 9:30 a.m. to 6 p.m. (on Thursday to 7:30 p.m.)
Credit Cards: AE, MC, V

Almost dwarfed by the other large department stores on Oxford Street, Littlewoods is a chain store with the second-largest catalog company in the country. It's a small store dealing in moderately priced goods, primarily clothing, plus luggage, hosiery, and shoes. Its styles lean toward the conservative and practical; women's dresses, made mostly of polyester and acrylic, range from a low £13 to £25. Men's three-piece wool suits with the Dormeuil label start at £120.

MARKS & SPENCER
458 Oxford St., WI (tel. 935-7954)
Underground Station: Marble Arch or Bond Street
Hours: Monday through Saturday from 9 a.m. to 6 p.m. (on Thursday to
    7:30 p.m.)
Credit Cards: Only its own

This flagship for Marks & Spencer is so packed and crowded, it looks like it's having a special sale even when it isn't. That's because prices here are some of the best in town. It's great for clothing, with wool sweaters of the "fishermen's look" going for £22, fully lined wool skirts starting at £30, and men's two-piece wool suits from Italy starting at £98.95. It's especially known for its underclothes, and even Margaret Thatcher revealed in an 1986 interview that she bought her underwear here. All the clothes bear the brand name St. Michael, 90% of which is made in Britain. The only drawback about shopping at Marks & Spencer is that there are no fitting rooms so you can't try garments on. You can return them if they don't fit, but your time may be too costly for that. The flagship store is presently undergoing remodeling, due for completion sometime in 1988. Another Marks & Spencer is located at 113 Kensington High St. (tel. 938-3711).

PETER JONES
Sloane Square, SWI (tel. 730-3434)
Underground Station: Sloane Square
Hours: Monday through Saturday from 9 a.m. to 5:30 p.m. (on
    Wednesday to 7 p.m.)
Credit Cards: Only its own

Belonging to the John Lewis group of stores, Peter Jones is best known for linens, lighting, fabrics, kitchenware, household goods, and home furnishings. It also has an impressive china and glass section, as well as a department of antiques. In addition to its fashions, accessories, and perfumery, it has two restaurants, a coffeeshop, and a hairdressing salon.

SELFRIDGES
400 Oxford St., WI (tel. 629-1234)
Underground Station: Marble Arch
Hours: Monday through Saturday from 9 a.m. to 6 p.m. (on Thursday to
    7:30 p.m.)
Credit Cards: AE, MC, Sears, V

Selfridges gets my vote as one of the best department stores in London. Its staff is friendly and helpful, there's an information desk on the ground floor, and the environment is pleasant for shopping or just browsing. It has one of the largest cosmetic and perfumery departments in Europe, as well as a very good fashions department, with names like Crochetta, Jaeger, Jasper

Conran, Aquascutum, Burberry, Benetton, Frank Usher, Janice Wainwright, Caroline Charles, Paul Costelloe, and Lanvin. Other good departments include those selling glass, china, luggage, toys, and furniture. There are two restaurants, several coffeeshops and snackbars, and a hairdressing salon. There's also a tourist information desk and theater ticket outlet on the ground floor.

The famous ladies around Selfridges equally famous clock

DOLLS AND DOLLHOUSES

The shops listed here specialize in dollhouses and antique dolls for the collector. For inexpensive dolls for children, refer to the "Toys" section of this book. If you're interested in Ann Parker dolls made to resemble such famous English personages as Henry VIII or Queen Victoria, check with Hummel, listed under "Model Soldiers."

THE DOLLS HOUSE
29 The Market, Covent Garden, WC2 (tel. 379-7243)
Underground Station: *Covent Garden*
Hours: *Monday through Saturday from 10 a.m. to 8 p.m.*
Credit Cards: *MC, V*

Stocks dollhouses and all the tiny people, furniture, and accessories to go with them. You can even buy Rover the dog for £8.80. Handmade figures in porcelain are £55, those made of wax are £44, and cloth babies and toddlers are £4.70. Other items include chandeliers for £23, a canteen of silver cutlery for about £44, a violin in a case for £63.25, and Chippendale-style chairs for £55 each. A mousetrap from Taiwan costs 40 pence. There are more than 20 varieties of dollhouses, built in Victorian, Georgian, or Tudor style. A Tudor home with seven rooms and an attic costs £460, while a house made to order costs £330 and up.

THE SINGING TREE
69 New King's Rd., SW6 (tel. 736-4527)
Underground Station: *Fulham Broadway*
Hours: *Monday through Saturday from 10 a.m. to 5:30 p.m.*
Credit Cards: *MC, V*

This shop sells old and new dollhouses, accessories, wallpapers, and dolls for collectors. Approximately 80% of its products are exclusive to the store and are handmade rather than machine-made. There are tiny leather bags that really open, baby carriages with padding and wheels that turn, brass beds, folding ironing boards, five-arm brass chandeliers with real candles, photograph albums with genuine photos reduced in size, and fully jointed miniature teddy bears. Prices start at less than £2 for a set of six books stuck together with real leather. A tray of cakes and brioches costs £6. There are even kits for making your own dollhouse: a four-room Georgian kit costs £73.

YESTERDAY'S CHILD
24 The Mall Antiques Arcade, 359 Islington High St., N1 (tel. 354-1601)
Underground Station: *Angel*
**Hours: *Wednesday from 7:30 a.m. to 3 p.m., on Saturday from 9 a.m. to
    1:30 p.m.***
Credit Cards: *None*

Dealing in antique dolls for more than 15 years, and one of the first shops to open in this arcade near Camden Passage market, this shop specializes in bisque dolls from France and Germany. Most of them date from about 1870 to 1920. There are about 100 dolls usually in stock, and prices start at about £220.

ENAMELS

HALCYON DAYS
14 Brook St., W1 (tel. 629-8811)
Underground Station: *Bond Street*

Exquisite bisque dolls at Yesterday's Child

Hours: *Monday through Friday from 9:15 a.m. to 5:30 p.m., on Saturday from 9:30 a.m. to 4:30 p.m.*
Credit Cards: AE, DC, MC, V

The history of enameling is thousands of years old, but the specific art of enameling on copper achieved its zenith in England from about 1750 to the early part of the 19th century. Halcyon Days revives the art, turning out an extensive collection of contemporary enamel boxes in a myriad of shapes and sizes, thimbles and other sewing accessories, musical boxes, replicas of 17th- and 18th-century boxes, clocks and watches, and commemorative editions. Music boxes start at £143, while most enamel boxes are priced under £50. You can even have a box specially commissioned with a name or picture of your house; these range in price from £60 to £550.

FABRICS

John Lewis and Liberty, both already described in the "Department Stores" section of this book, have large fabric departments. **Liberty** is especially famous for its printed fabrics, with a small specialty shop located at 340A King's Rd. (tel. 352-6581). In addition, **Laura Ashley** carries a selection of cheerful prints, available at its flagship store on Regent Street. Remember that material sold in London is usually by the meter, which equals 3.3 feet.

What made Liberty famous

FOR INTERIOR DESIGN

CHARLES HAMMOND
165 Sloane St., SWI (tel. 235-2151)
Underground Station: *Knightsbridge*
Hours: *Monday through Friday from 9 a.m. to 5:30 p.m.*
Credit Cards: *MC, V*

A pleasant, small shop with an interior designing and decorating staff, it deals in antiques, reproductions, and its own line of in-house fabrics for home decorating. The style epitomizes dignified English country living, and fabric here starts at about £18.50 per meter.

COLEFAX & FOWLER
39 Brook St., WI (tel. 493-2231)
Underground Station: *Bond Street*
Hours: *Monday through Friday from 9:30 a.m. to I p.m. and*
   2 to 5:30 p.m.
Credit Cards: *None*

Colefax & Fowler is famous for its flowered chintzes, all made from original patterns of the late 18th and early 19th centuries. The firm was founded by Sibyl Colefax and John Fowler in the 1930s and was instrumental in shaping public opinion as to what a cozy, country cottage should look like. Its shop, designed in the 1700s, is a showroom for the Colefax & Fowler style, decorated in antiques

FABRICS

just like a country house. Most chintzes range in price from £13.75 to £25 per meter.

DESIGNERS GUILD
277 King's Rd., SW3 (tel. 351-5775)
Underground Station: Sloane Square or South Kensington
Hours: Monday through Friday from 9:30 a.m. to 5:30 p.m. (on
Wednesday from 10 a.m.), on Saturday from 10 a.m. to 4 p.m.
Credit Cards: AE, DC, MC, V

This interior design shop carries fabrics and wallpaper, all created to comple-ment the range of furniture and accessories at its shop next door at 277 King's Rd. The style is light and airy, with lots of pastels and large floral designs. Fabrics and wallpapers are designed in-house, and the starting price for chintz is £14.25 per meter.

JANE CHURCHILL
137 Sloane St., SW1 (tel. 824-8484)
Underground Station: Sloane Square
Hours: Monday through Saturday from 9:30 a.m. to 5:30 p.m. (on
Wednesday to 7 p.m.)
Credit Cards: AE, MC, V

Country fabrics in
a country house setting
at Colefax & Fowler

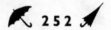

All products are designed in-house and include linen, rugs, cushions, bedroom accessories, tiles, tables, and sofas in addition to its decorating fabrics. In other words, Jane Churchill sells a complete look, all in coordinating and complementing colors and designs. The look is of the classic country estate, and fabrics for drapes and other interior-design uses range from £8.20 to £10.95.

NEXT INTERIOR
72 King's Rd., SW3 (tel. 584-1308)
Underground Station: *Sloane Square*
Hours: *Monday through Saturday from 10 a.m. to 6 p.m. (on Monday from 10:30 a.m., on Wednesday to 7 p.m.)*
Credit Cards: AE, DC, MC, V

Part of the burgeoning chain of Next stores, this shop specializes in home furnishings and fabrics. Styles are traditional English and range from paisley to florals and pastels. Fabrics start at £8.79 a meter.

OSBORNE & LITTLE
304 King's Rd., SW3 (tel. 352-1456)
Underground Station: *Sloane Square*
Hours: *Monday through Friday from 9:30 a.m. to 5:30 p.m., on Saturday from 10 a.m. to 4 p.m.*
Credit Cards: AE, DC, MC, V

With a showroom in New York which opened in 1986 and distribution worldwide, Osborne & Little is well known for its decorating fabrics and wallpapers. Colors are rich and deep, and most of the fabrics are cottons, starting at £11.25 per meter. Silk pastels start at £43 per meter.

SOULEIADO
171 Fulham Rd., SW3 (tel. 589-6180)
Underground Station: *South Kensington*
Hours: *Monday through Friday from 9:30 a.m. to 5:30 p.m., on Saturday from 10 a.m. to 5 p.m.*
Credit Cards: AE, DC, MC, V

Souleiado means "sun shining through after the rain." The name adequately describes the bright and sunny colorful fabrics sold here. They're from southern France, with designs taken from 200-year-old original wooden blocks. The French company supplying the fabric has been in operation for more than two centuries and possesses more than 40,000 block designs from which its present collection is taken. All the fabrics are cotton and are £15.40 a meter.

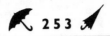

FABRICS

FOR CLOTHING

ALLANS
56–58 Duke St., WI (tel. 629-3781)
Underground Station: Bond Street
Hours: Monday through Friday from 9 a.m. to 6 p.m., on Saturday
   to 1 p.m.
Credit Cards: AE, DC, MC, V

A family shop since it opened here in 1946, Allans specializes in pure fabrics such as wools and silks, including material imported from Italy, France, and Switzerland and wool from England. Silks range from about £22 to £65 a meter, but if you want to go all-out, there's intricate, beaded silk for £550 a meter.

THE FABRIC STUDIO
10 Frith St., WI (tel. 434-2897)
Underground Station: Tottenham Court Road
Hours: Monday through Saturday from 10 a.m. to 5:30 p.m.
Credit Cards: None

This discount fabric shop in the heart of Soho is run by a husband-and-wife team that specializes in cloth that comes from the ends of designer collections. "We don't have masses of any one thing," the husband said, "because designers usually know exactly how much they'll need. It's best to come to this shop with an open mind because we don't have a set stock. But the fabrics will be good because fashion designers wouldn't use bad fabrics for their creations." Fabrics are as much as a third off the original price, with tweeds going for £7 a meter and silk starting at £7.50 a meter. Fabric of Belleville Sassoon was available during my visit, along with a varied assortment of woolens, velvets, jerseys, suedes, leathers, silks, and cottons.

JACOB GORDON LTD.
75 Duke St., WI (tel. 629-5947)
Underground Station: Bond Street
Hours: Monday through Saturday from 9 a.m. to 6 p.m. (on Thursday
   from 10 a.m. to 7 p.m.)
Credit Cards: AE, DC, MC, V

This friendly West End shop specializes in natural fibers and supplies both couturiers and the Royal Opera House with fabrics. It's one of the largest importers in volume of European silks in England, starting at £11 a yard. Cashmere costs £49.50 a yard, wool and angora jersey is £16.50 a yard, and wool antelope, a specialty, is £27.50 a yard.

JASON'S
53 New Bond St., WI (tel. 629-2606)

Underground Station: Bond Street
Hours: Monday through Friday from 9 a.m. to 6 p.m. (on Thursday to 7 p.m.), on Saturday to 1 p.m.
Credit Cards: AE, DC, MC, V

Specializes in silks from Italy, Switzerland, and France and English woolens. It carries silk from the continent that is available in England only in its shop. Fabric ranges in price from £13.20 to £440 per meter.

FLOWERS

If you're looking for a bouquet of flowers to present to a hostess or friend, department stores, underground tube stations, and hotels often have small florist shops that can fulfill your needs. If you're looking for something more special, try the shops below. They deal in both fresh and artificial flowers and plants, and all take care of delivery within London.

FELTON
220–224 Brompton Rd., SW3 (tel. 589-4433)
Underground Station: South Kensington and Knightsbridge
Hours: Monday through Friday from 8:30 a.m. to 5:30 p.m., on Saturday to noon
Credit Cards: AE, MC, V

Established in 1900, this florist shop is dependable for the quality of its flowers. It provides many churches, hotels, and other establishments with arrangements. In addition to fresh flowers, it also sells dried and silk flowers. Silk blooms start at 80 pence apiece. An artificial bonsai maple is priced at £145. They'll deliver in London.

THE FLOWERSMITH
34 Shelton St., Covent Garden, WC2 (tel. 240-6688)
Underground Station: Covent Garden
Hours: Monday through Friday from 10 a.m. to 6 p.m., on Saturday from 11:30 a.m. to 6 p.m.
Credit Cards: AE, DC, MC, V

Unusual flowers and plants from around the world are sold here at reasonable prices. Artificial and dried flowers are also available.

MOYSES STEVENS
6 Bruton St., W1 (tel. 493-8171)
Underground Station: Green Park
Hours: Monday through Friday from 8:30 to 5:30 p.m.
Credit Cards: AE, MC, V

As the royal florists to the Queen, this shop has been selling blossoms for 100 years. They're famous for their elaborate floral arrangements combining fresh flowers with silk blossoms, but they also sell simpler arrangements starting at about £16.50. Dried flowers are £5.50 a bunch.

OASIS ARTIFICIAL FLORA
194–196 Walton St., SW3 (tel. 584-9519)
Underground Station: South Kensington
Hours: Monday through Friday from 10 a.m. to 6 p.m., on Saturday
   from 11 a.m. to 3 p.m.
Credit Cards: AE, V

Seeing is not necessarily believing. You'll have to touch these plants, flowers, and trees to assure yourself they're not real, so convincingly are they made. Real tree stems are used, to which artificial leaves are then grafted. The shop will make trees and plants to your specifications, including shape, dimension, and whether it will be placed inside or out. A six-foot ficus costs about £220 to £330. Flower stems start at about £2 apiece. An artificial bouquet will run about £22.

FOOD

Nothing can beat **Harrods** or **Fortnum & Mason** for one-stop shopping for tea, coffee, chocolate, cheese, jams, and any other English food you can think of. These food halls stock everything from marzipan to caviar, from smoked salmon to chutney. Refer to the "Department Stores" section for more information on both of these famous London traditions. If you're looking for quaint specialist shops selling teas, spices, chocolates, or other food items, read on.

CHEESE

PAXTON & WHITFIELD
93 Jermyn St., SW1 (tel. 930-0250)
Underground Station: Piccadilly Circus
Hours: Monday through Friday from 8:30 a.m. to 6 p.m., on Saturday
   from 9 a.m. to 4 p.m.
Credit Cards: AE, DC, MC, V

London's oldest, most famous, and most charming cheese shop. Established in 1797, it still recalls days of yore with cured hams hanging in the front window and sawdust spread on the floor. As the royal cheesemongers to the Queen Mother, this shop boasts up to 300 different kinds of cheeses from France, Denmark, Germany, Holland, Italy, Switzerland, and of course, England. Their Stilton is the most popular. You can sample before you buy, and most cheeses run below £5 a pound. The shop also sells hams, biscuits, coffee, and tea.

Well, that's what the label says they are at Harrods Food Hall!

CHOCOLATES

BENDICKS
55 Wigmore St., WI (tel. 935-7272)
Underground Station: *Bond Street*
Hours: *Monday through Friday from 9:30 a.m. to 5 p.m.*
Credit Cards: *None*

Bendicks is one of the best-known names in British chocolates. Its specialties are bittermints and mint crisps. Other favorites are rum truffles, creamed chocolates, marzipan, vanilla Fourré, pralines, walnut-topped creams, and tangerine creams. Everything is beautifully packaged. Bittermints come in six quantities, beginning at 200 grams for £3.25. Another Bendicks, located at 195 Sloane St. (tel. 235-4749), is a combination chocolate shop and tea room.

CHARBONNEL ET WALKER
I Royal Arcade, 28 Old Bond St., WI (tel. 491-0939)
Underground Station: *Green Park or Piccadilly Circus*
Hours: *Monday through Friday from 9 a.m. to 5:30 p.m., on Saturday*
   from 10 a.m. to 4 p.m.
Credit Cards: *AE, DC, MC, V*

Not to be outdone is the prestigious Charbonnel et Walker, established in 1875 and possessing a warrant as chocolate suppliers to the royal family.

There's the story of a New York hostess who, upon discovering that her dinner mints were running low, sent her chauffeur flying to London to replenish her supply at Charbonnel et Walker. At any rate, it carries a large variety of chocolates, ranging from those flavored with orange or strawberry to chocolate-covered Brazil nuts or truffles. Prices start at £4.80 for a quarter of a pound. It's famous also for its Boîtes Blanche with a chocolate-lettered message inside. Foiled in gold, ruby, or silver, these chocolates with letters of the alphabet can be arranged in any message you wish to deliver, perfect for anniversaries, birthdays, and other occasions. Prices for these begin at £14.45 for 14 letters. An additional shop is located at 2 Knights Arcade, Brompton Road (tel. 581-3117).

PRESTAT
40 South Molton St., W1 (tel. 629-4838)
Underground Station: Bond Street
Hours: Monday through Friday from 10 a.m. to 6 p.m., on Saturday to 5 p.m.
Credit Cards: AE, DC, MC, V

Handmade chocolates and truffles have been the business of this small shop for the past 60 years. Plain, coffee-, and rum-flavored truffles start at £2.20 for a quarter pound. They also sell chocolate figures of Paddington Bear, starting at £3.50.

ROCOCO
321 King's Rd., SW3 (tel. 352-5857)
Underground Station: Sloane Square
Hours: Monday through Saturday from 10 a.m. to 6:30 p.m.
Credit Cards: AE, DC, MC, V

Opened in 1983 by two young sisters, this avant-garde chocolate shop makes wicked Dragées, bittersweet chocolate enclosed in a candy shell and starting at £1.37 for a quarter pound. Truffles for £8.80 a pound include champagne, cognac, whisky, coffee, orange, rum, and white-chocolate varieties. Traditional chocolates such as caramels, Brazil nuts, marzipan, or rose and violet creams start at £7.15 a pound.

THORNTON'S
2 The Market, Covent Garden, WC2 (tel. 836-2173)
Underground Station: Covent Garden
Hours: Monday through Saturday from 10 a.m. to 7 p.m.
Credit Cards: AE, MC, V

This chain store is famous for its handmade chocolates, which start at £2.20 for a quarter pound of your choice. It also has great toffee, including plain, treacle, or fruit nut, starting at 52 pence a quarter pound. Other shops are located at 353 Oxford St. (tel. 493-7498) and 143 Kensington High St. (tel. 938-3239).

TEA AND COFFEE

The English are famous for their teas and tea time, importing exotic leaves from the Orient to support their pleasurable habit. Perhaps less well known is the fact that London is also a good place for coffee beans. The best shops do their own roasting of coffee beans, often right on shop premises. The resulting smell is glorious, and I wouldn't be surprised if you could get a caffeine high just by stepping into a shop. Most shops selling coffee sell tea as well.

DRURY TEA & COFFEE CO.

3 New Row, Covent Garden, WC2 (tel. 836-1960)
Underground Station: Leicester Square
Hours: Monday through Friday from 8:30 a.m. to 6 p.m., on Saturday
   from 11 a.m. to 5 p.m.
Credit Cards: MC, V

Teas from Ceylon, India, China, and other tea-growing countries start at 85 pence for 125 grams. Coffee beans, ranging from dark roast Honduran to light roast Kenyan, are priced under £4 per pound. There's another shop in Covent Garden at 37 Drury Lane (tel. 836-2607).

FERNS

27 Rathbone Pl., W1 (tel. 636-2237), off Oxford Street
Underground Station: Tottenham Court Road
Hours: Monday through Friday from 8:30 a.m. to 5:30 p.m., on Saturday
   to 1 p.m.
Credit Cards: None

Established in 1893, this shop has an Old World ambience to it and looks little changed over the past 90-some years. Its coffee blends range in price from £2 per half pound for Austrian to £2.57 for decaffeinated beans from Colombia. Teas, which include Orange Pekoe, Darjeeling, Passion Fruit, Formosa Oolong, Earl Grey's, Jasmine Flower, Assam, and Ceylon, range between £1.55 and £1.90 per half pound. The shop also sells all the accompanying paraphernalia, including coffee grinders and decanters. There's another Ferns at 7 The Market, Covent Garden (tel. 379-7659).

H. R. HIGGINS

42 South Molton St., W1 (tel. 629-3913)
Underground Station: Bond Street
Hours: Monday through Wednesday from 8:45 a.m. to 5:30 p.m., on
   Thursday to 6:30 p.m., on Friday to 6 p.m., and on Saturday from 10
   a.m. to 1 p.m. and 2 to 5 p.m.
Credit Cards: MC

**Strictly coffee
at H. R. Higgins**

The smell of coffee wafts so wonderful in this shop that it makes me weak in the knees. The staff is friendly and knowledgeable and will ask you how you want your coffee ground. They can also advise and are happy to do so. Brochures describe the various beans they carry, which come from Colombia, India, Tanzania, Ethiopia, Brazil, Kenya, Java, Costa Rica, and Jamaica. Prices for most beans are between £3.80 and £5 per pound. They sell only coffee and have a royal warrant.

WHITTARDS
111 Fulham Rd., SW3 (tel. 589-4261)
Underground Station: *South Kensington*
Hours: *Monday through Friday from 8 a.m. to 5 p.m., on Saturday from
9 a.m. to 1 p.m.*
Credit Cards: AE, DC, MC, V

Whittards recently celebrated its 100th anniversary as a supplier of teas and coffee. Along its walls are old tea pots and original tea tins from China that were used when the store first opened. Teas from India, Ceylon, Assam, and China range from £3 to £6.80 per pound. Coffee is roasted on the premises each day to ensure freshness and starts at £4.40 per pound.

Hundred-year-old Chinese tea canisters are part of the ambience at Whittards

HERBS, SPICES, MARMALADES, AND MORE

CRABTREE & EVELYN
6 Kensington Church St., W8 (tel. 937-9335)
Underground Station: *High Street Kensington*
Hours: *Monday through Saturday from 9:30 a.m. to 6 p.m. (on Thursday
   to 7 p.m.)*
Credit Cards: *MC, V*

Perhaps better known for its beautifully packaged toiletries, Crabtree & Evelyn also carries biscuits, cookies, English fruit preserves, marmalades, honeys, herbal jellies, preserves, English mustards, chutneys, English sauces, and herbs and spices. A nine-ounce jar of whole-grain mustard costs £1.60, while 10.6 ounces of mango chutney is £2.10.

CULPEPER
21 Bruton St., WI (tel. 499-2406)
Underground Station: *Green Park or Bond Street*
Hours: *Monday through Friday from 9:30 a.m. to 6 p.m., on Saturday to
   5 p.m.*
Credit Cards: *AE, DC, MC, V*

In addition to its soaps, bath preparations, lotions, and powders, Culpeper also has a wide range of spices and herbs, from garam masala to ginger, juniper

The emphasis is on natural ingredients at Culpeper

berries, and curries. Most come in small packets for less than 60 pence. It also sells honeys from around the world, mustard, chutneys, sauces, vinegars, and oils. A real treat are the genuine licorice sticks for 5 pence.

JAMES BODENHAM & CO.
88 Jermyn St., WI (tel. 930-5340)
Underground Station: Green Park or Piccadilly Circus
Hours: Monday through Friday from 9:30 a.m. to 5:30 p.m., on Saturday to 4 p.m.
Credit Cards: AE, DC, MC, V

This newly opened shop on Jermyn Street sells herbs and spices, dried flowers, jams, preserves, honeys, marmalades, fudge sauces, chutneys, vinegars, and mustards. No artificial preservatives or colorings are added. It also sells coffees, teas, and toiletries.

FURNITURE

For antique furniture, consult the "Antiques" section.

ASTROHOME
47–49 Neal St., Covent Garden, WC2 (tel. 240-0420)
Underground Station: Covent Garden, Tottenham Court Road, or Leicester Square

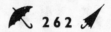
Hours: Monday through Friday from 10 a.m. to 6:30 p.m., on Saturday to 6 p.m.
Credit Cards: AE, DC, MC, V

Sleek, minimalist, and hi-tech are the catchwords for the furniture and household accessories sold here. Lots of metals and tubing are used, and the predominant color is black. A tubular kitchen table without a glass covering costs £179, while a bar with a granite top and fluted aluminum sides is £2,750. Also for sale are chairs, bathroom fixtures, lamps, dishes, desk accessories, kitchenware, and other items.

THE CONRAN SHOP

77 Fulham Rd., SW3 (tel. 589-7401)
Underground Station: South Kensington
Hours: Monday through Saturday from 9:30 a.m. to 6 p.m. (on Tuesday from 10 a.m.)
Credit Cards: AE, MC, V

Sir Terence Conran is credited with introducing simple but original designs in furniture to the English masses with the opening of his Habitat furniture stores. The Conran Shop goes a step beyond, catering to London's more affluent crowd. Sir Terence himself selects the goods for this shop, which has been described by *Harper's* magazine as the most natural place for the well-heeled with a passion for their homes to look for furniture. The service is excellent and goods sold include furniture, fabrics, lighting, floor coverings, bed linen, bathroom accessories, kitchenware, and tableware. The style for furniture draws from the '20s and '30s, with designs that are irreproachably simple. A Thonet art deco–style chair costs £470, while a simple director's chair is £28. In the kitchenware section are useful gadgets, including champagne pliers for £22. A coffee pot replica of the service used on the *Orient Express* train is £71.

It should be noted that plans call for the Conran Shop to move across the street into 81 Fulham St. by the end of 1987.

DRAGONS

23 Walton St., SW3 (tel. 589-3795)
Underground Station: Knightsbridge or South Kensington
Hours: Monday through Friday from 9:30 a.m. to 5:30 p.m., on Saturday from 10:30 a.m. to 4:30 p.m.
Credit Cards: AE, DC, MC, V

This shop specializes in hand-painted children's furniture. All the furniture is made in England and can be custom-painted according to individual wishes. A popular gift is a small wooden chair with a rush seat and painted with the child's name, which starts at £46. In addition to supplying the entire furniture needed for a playroom or a bedroom, this shop also carries children's fabrics, hair brushes, and some toys.

HABITAT
196 Tottenham Court Rd., W1 (tel. 631-3880)
Underground Station: Goodge Street
Hours: Monday from 10 a.m. to 6 p.m., on Tuesday, Wednesday, and Friday from 9:30 a.m., on Thursday from 9:30 a.m. to 7:30 p.m., on Saturday from 9 a.m. to 6 p.m.
Credit Cards: AE, MC, V

Habitat has probably done more to change the way the English think about furniture than any other store. This Terence Conran shop was the first to bring in simple utilitarian designs, with styles that combine English tradition with hi-tech. It's known for the square look in tables, chairs, and sofas, tempered with pastels and floral designs. In addition to its furniture, Habitat sells linen, lighting fixtures, desk accessories, fabrics, carpets, wallpaper, kitchenware, and housewares. A catalog is available for £1.50, and another shop is located at 206–222 King's Rd. (tel. 351-1211).

HEAL'S
196 Tottenham Court Rd., W1 (tel. 636-1666)
Underground Station: Goodge Street
Hours: *Same as Habitat*
Credit Cards: AE, DC, MC, V

Recently acquired by the Habitat group of stores, Heal's is striving to maintain its own identity, offering furniture and accessories slightly more upgrade and more expensive than Habitat. The upholstery is mainly British, but cabinets and wooden furniture come primarily from Denmark, Holland, and Italy. Departments sell children's furniture, linen, bathroom accessories, toys, carpets, curtain fabrics, lamps, china, and kitchenware.

MAPLES
145 Tottenham Court Rd., W1 (tel. 387-7000)
Underground Station: Warren Street
Hours: Monday through Saturday from 9 a.m. to 5:30 p.m. (on Tuesday from 9:30 a.m.)
Credit Cards: AE, DC, MC, V

Everything you need to furnish your home, including sofas, cabinets, dining room tables and chairs, beds, and desks. In addition to its English furniture, goods are imported from Italy, Spain, France, and other continental countries as well. Much of the furniture is modern, but the store tries to cater to various styles in taste ranging from the traditional English to the Middle Eastern preference for gilt. A reproduction antique writing table with a yew finish is priced at £735, while a set of six stickback sidechairs with white finish from Italy is £1,115.

S. & H. JEWELL
26 Parker St., WC2 (tel. 405-8520)

Underground Station: *Holborn*
Hours: *Monday through Friday from 9 a.m. to 5:30 p.m.*
Credit Cards: *None*

Established in 1830, these cabinetmakers now specialize in reproduction English furniture, primarily in Georgian style. They offer bookcases, desks, chairs, tables, china cabinets, wardrobes, and other pieces. Woods used include walnut and mahogany, and a pair of elbow chairs costs £825. The shop also stocks 60- to 80-year-old reproduction furniture that was built to imitate Georgian style.

GAMES

The shop below has games for both adults and children. More children's games can be found in shops in the "Toys" section.

GAMES CENTRE
100 Oxford St., W1 (tel. 637-7911)
Underground Station: *Tottenham Court Road*
Hours: *Monday through Saturday from 10 a.m. to 7 p.m. (on Thursday to 8 p.m.)*
Credit Cards: *AE, DC, MC, V*

All the games people play are stocked here, including a wide assortment of board games, puzzles, children's games, war games, word games, strategy games, playing cards, chess, and computer games. It's a great place for the British version of Trivial Pursuit and Scrabble in different languages (yes, the German Scrabble varies from the English). A good gift is the British Monopoly for £7.65. Or how about Pass Out—whoever remains standing at the end of this adult drinking game wins.

GENEALOGISTS AND HERALDRY

The original purpose of a coat-of-arms in the 13th century was so that heavily armed men in battle could recognize each other even with their visors down. After wars and tournaments in armor were over in the 16th century, these arms were transferred onto gateways of homes, coaches, fireplaces, embroidery, silver, and other personal belongings.

If you are interested in knowing whether your family name entitles you to a coat-of-arms or if you are simply interested in tracing your family roots, the following organizations can put you on the right track.

COLLEGE OF ARMS
Queen Victoria Street, EC4 (tel. 248-2762)
Underground Station: *Blackfriars or Mansion House*
Hours: *Monday through Friday from 10 a.m. to 4 p.m.*
Credit Cards: *None*

The College of Arms has records of all official arms ever given. For a fee of about £82, you can have them conduct research to find out whether your name entitles you to a coat-of-arms. Pedigrees are also on record, and if more detailed research is desired, the College of Arms can recommend genealogists.

SOCIETY OF GENEALOGISTS
14 Charterhouse Buildings, Goswell Road, EC1 (tel. 251-8799)
Underground Station: *Barbican*
Hours: *Tuesday, Friday, and Saturday from 10 a.m. to 6 p.m., on Wednesday and Thursday to 8 p.m.*
Credit Cards: *None*

The Society of Genealogists will undertake genealogical research, but you can expect a delay of about three months before they can get to yours. If you're looking for a specific piece of information that will take only an hour or so, the rate is £10 per hour. If more detailed research about ancestry is required that takes several days, the charge is £79 per day. The society prefers written queries to telephone calls.

GIFTS

Technically speaking, all the shops in this book sell items appropriate for gifts. However, there are some shops in London that are known especially as gift shops, the most exclusive and elegant of which is Asprey. In addition to the shops listed here, those found under "Soaps and Toiletries" and "Perfume" have beautifully packaged products that make great gifts for women. Garrard, a jewelry shop, also has a newly opened gift section with desk accessories, crystal, china, and other items. Chapter II on "Shopping Strategies" has lots of ideas for gifts in all price ranges. Museum shops are also fertile ground for gifts.

All the shops listed below give refunds for VAT, though £50 is usually required as a minimum purchase. Exceptions are the Design Centre, which requires a minimum purchase of £100, and Naturally British, with a minimum purchase requirement of £75.

ASPREY
165–169 New Bond St., W1 (tel. 493-6767)
Underground Station: *Bond Street, Green Park, or Piccadilly Circus*

Hours: *Monday through Friday from 9 a.m. to 5:30 p.m., on Saturday to 1 p.m.*
Credit Cards: *AE, DC, MC, V*

Established in 1781 and moving to its New Bond Street location in 1841, Asprey is the ultimate in gift shops. From its imposing Victorian shopfront to its huge interior gleaming with objects in silver, gold, and precious stones, Asprey is the place to shop if you're trying to make an impression on somebody with a unique and expensive gift. There are 12 departments in all, selling antiques, fine china, leather, silver, books, luggage, jewelry, glass, clocks, watches, and an astounding number of rare and unusual things.

There are sewing kits, corkscrews, swizzle sticks, picture frames, wine decanters, walking sticks, whisky flasks, "mystery clocks" in which the workings of the clock are hidden, silver opera glasses, grape scissors, art deco jewelry, cufflinks, tea and coffee services, and diaries—a list that only scratches the surface. If money is no object, how about a 1924 toiletry set with 28 separate items such as button hooks, shoe horn, mirrors, and brushes, all neatly packed in a crocodile suitcase lined with silk and costing £27,220? A solid-gold toothbrush is £700, an enamel decanter label is £16.50, a gilt swizzle stick is £26, and a Swiss army knife is £8.50. Beautiful catalogs are published once a year from which you can order by mail.

BLEWCOAT SCHOOL
23 Caxton St., SW1 (tel. 222-2877)
Underground Station: *St. James's Park*

A gift from Asprey makes a definite impression

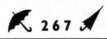
Hours: *Monday through Friday from 10 a.m. to 5:30 p.m. (on Thursday to 7 p.m.)*
Credit Cards: AE, MC, V

This old school is now the property of the National Trust, a conservation organization set up in 1895 to protect stately homes, medieval barns, and other buildings of historical interest. The National Trust maintains a gift shop at Blewcoat School, selling toiletries, children's games, British crafts, pottery, china, glass, tea cosies, cardigans, aprons, jams and preserves, handmade chocolates, and other items.

COVENT GARDEN GENERAL STORE
111 Long Acre, Covent Garden, WC2 (tel. 240-0331)
Underground Station: *Covent Garden*
Hours: *Monday through Saturday from 10 a.m. to midnight, on Sunday from 11 a.m. to 7 p.m.*
Credit Cards: AE, DC, MC, V

This shop has lots of inexpensive gift items, including adult games, gag gifts, teas, Crabtree & Evelyn preserves and toiletries, wicker baskets, chocolates from Bendicks, posters, and greeting cards. Its "British Shop" has souvenirs, including London T-shirts starting at £4.40.

THE DESIGN CENTRE
28 Haymarket, SW1 (tel. 839-8000)
Underground Station: *Piccadilly Circus*
Hours: *Monday and Tuesday from 10 a.m. to 6 p.m., Wednesday through Saturday to 8 p.m., on Sunday from 1 to 6 p.m.*
Credit Cards: AE, MC, V

The Design Centre was set up by the Design Council to promote British design and to inform the public about specific British goods. In addition to its large photographic index of 8,000 products that are British made and approved by the Design Council, the Design Centre also has a shop with a varied inventory of British-made goods. Although the products change constantly, they generally include toys, china and glass, kitchenware, jewelry, sweaters, books on design, and other gift items. During a recent visit I saw paperweights starting at £12.35, scent bottles for £16.45, and very modern clocks with hands made out of colorful paper for £12.

THE GENERAL TRADING COMPANY
144 Sloane St., SW1 (tel. 730-0411)
Underground Station: *Sloane Square*
Hours: *Monday through Friday from 9 a.m. to 5:30 p.m., on Saturday to 2 p.m.*
Credit Cards: AE, DC, MC, V

The General Trading Company describes itself as "London's most fascinating shop." It's also one of the most expensive gift shops around and is a favorite place for Sloane Rangers to have their wedding lists. Occupying four large Victorian houses, the shop sells antique and reproduction furniture, toys, china and glass, kitchenware, linen, stationery, cutlery, and Oriental goods. A carved wood Rajasthan bowl is priced at £82, a late-17th-century pewter charger is £350, initialed Limoges porcelain toothmugs are £9.35, and a set of eight cork tablemats is £35. Catalogs are available for free.

THE IRISH SHOP
11 Duke St., W1 (tel. 935-1366)
Underground Station: Bond Street
Hours: Monday through Saturday from 9:30 a.m. to 5:30 p.m.
Credit Cards: AE, DC, MC, V

Goods from Ireland are sold here, including Belleek china, Aran hand-knitted sweaters, Waterford crystal, Irish linen, and tweeds. A Belleek shamrock basketweave tea pot is £104.80, men's hand-knitted fishermen's cardigans start at £92, and tweed caps are £18.30.

THE LITTLE GALLERY
122 Regent St., W1 (tel. 439-0505 or 439-0498)
Underground Station: Piccadilly Circus
Hours: Monday through Saturday from 9:30 a.m. to 9 p.m., on Sunday
from 10 a.m. to 6 p.m.
Credit Cards: AE, DC, MC, V

This shop specializes in gifts made in the United Kingdom, including British coin pendants, Caithness paperweights, ceramic cottages, cork tablemats and coasters, brass and copper items, handmade pewter tankards, model soldiers, and some crystal and china. There are statues of British characters, such as the lady golfer, the country policeman, or the barrister, starting at £87.95.

NATURALLY BRITISH
13 New Row, WC2 (tel. 240-0551)
Underground Station: Leicester Square
Hours: Monday through Saturday from 10:30 a.m. to 6:30 p.m. (also
open on Sunday in winter)
Credit Cards: AE, DC, MC, V

This gift shop sells crafts handmade in the United Kingdom, including pottery, glass, jewelry, toys, wood and basket ware, clothes and knitwear, ceramics, table linens, homemade preserves, and antique and reproduction Victorian pine furniture. Stuffed toys start at £5.75, hand-painted bone-china brooches are £17.20, Shetland wool sweaters are £69, and Irish tweed caps are £16.45.

OGGETTI

133 Fulham Rd., SW3 (tel. 581-8088)
Underground Station: *South Kensington*
Hours: *Monday through Saturday from 9:30 a.m. to 6 p.m.*
Credit Cards: *AE, MC, V*

This gift shop is filled with an eclectic mix of objects, all selected on the basis of their beautiful design. A Bauhaus chess set, for example, modeled after a set first designed by Joseph Hartwig in 1923, costs £96.40 for the pieces and £48.20 for the board. Slim, sleek lighters by Rowenta start at £28.40, wallets made of sheep or ostrich range from £30 to £148, and modern-looking scissors start at £3.40. Other items include Swiss army knives, Braun alarm clocks, letter openers, business-card holders, and many desk items. Another Oggetti is located on Jermyn Street.

SAVILLE-EDELLS

25 Walton St., SW3 (tel. 584-4398)
Underground Station: *South Kensington or Knightsbridge*
Hours: *Monday through Saturday from 9:30 a.m. to 6 p.m.*
Credit Cards: *AE, DC, MC, V*

**Eclectic modern designs make
perfect gifts at Oggetti**

This shop is in an old town house that still looks like someone's home, with fireplaces that are lit in wintertime. Two floors are filled with gifts and decorative items, including Daum Crystal model cars, Christofle silverware, Lalique glass, bronze statues, Limoges china, umbrellas, walking sticks, and more. A walking stick containing a tiny flask for your favorite whisky is £28, while one with a retractable fishing rod and accessories is £163. Catalogs are available for £1.50.

GUNS AND RIFLES

Only registered dealers in Britain may sell firearms. If you are visiting the country for less than 30 days, you can buy a shotgun without any special license. If you want to buy a rifle, however, the shopkeeper must apply for an export license from the Board of Trade, which may take two or three weeks to process. These restrictions do not apply to antique weaponry; for shops, consult the section on "Arms and Armor."

HOLLAND & HOLLAND
33 Bruton St., W1 (tel. 499-4411), off Bond Street
Underground Station: Green Park or Bond Street
**Hours: Monday through Friday from 9 a.m. to 5:30 p.m., on Saturday
from 9:30 a.m. to 1:30 p.m.**
Credit cards: AE, DC, MC, V

Gun makers since 1835 and royal rifle makers to the Duke of Edinburgh, Holland & Holland produces and sells literally any type of gun, as well as antique arms. Antique swords or guns start at £165, while the company's own Cavalier boxlock gun with 12 bore starts at £4,675. Holland & Holland also stocks a wide range of outdoor clothing and shooting accessories, including waterproof jackets, walking sticks, waterproof boots, cartridge belts, gun-cleaning tool boxes, ear protectors, and whisky flasks.

PURDEY & SONS
57–58 South Audley St., W1 (tel. 499-1801)
Underground Station: Hyde Park Corner, Marble Arch, or Bond Street
Hours: Monday through Friday from 9 a.m. to 5 p.m.
Credit Cards: AE, DC, MC, V

This old firm, established more than a century ago and located on the corner of South Audley and Mount Streets, is one of the finest gunsmiths in the world. Since guns are made by hand, Purdey produces fewer than 100 new ones each year. Prices start at about £18,700 for a hammerless ejector game gun for up to three-inch shells and 12 to 20 gauge. Guns are custom-built to the measurements of its owner. For the hunting enthusiast there is a wide range of clothing and accessories, including waterproof jackets, sweaters, caps and hats, shoes

and boots, shooting sticks (walking sticks with folding seats), cartridge bags, and whisky flasks.

THOMAS BLAND & SONS
21–22 New Row, WC2 (tel. 836-9122)
Underground Station: *Leicester Square*
Hours: *Monday through Friday from 9 a.m. to 4:30 p.m.*
Credit Cards: *MC, V*

Established in 1840, this gun shop sells sporting shotguns, rifles, handguns, and all the necessary accessories. Foreign-made shotguns start at £440, while English shotguns range in price from £1,100 to £20,900.

HATS

Nothing completes, changes, or revitalizes an outfit as much as a hat will, and the English have long been famous for their hats. A good hatter can tell customers which hats are most flattering, hide defects, and enhance facial features. From the top hat to the derby (called a bowler in England), from women's berets to artistic creations, hatters in London offer a delightful assortment of all types of hats in all different price ranges.

Several department stores have a good selection of designer hats, including **Harrods, Harvey Nichols,** and **Selfridges.** In addition to the shops listed below, **Dunn & Co.** in the "Clothing" section carries tweed hats and caps and bowler hats.

BATES
21A Jermyn St., SW1 (tel. 734-2722)
Underground Station: *Piccadilly Circus*
Hours: *Monday through Friday from 9 a.m. to 5:30 p.m., on Saturday from 9:30 a.m. to 4 p.m.*
Credit Cards: *AE*

This tiny hatter's shop is filled with a jumble of hats and hatboxes piled on shelves all the way up to the ceiling. For the past century it has served the needs of the St. James's gentleman, that English breed with the pin-striped suit and ever-present umbrella. All its hats are handmade and include tweed caps and hats, panamas, bowlers, and wide-brimmed felt hats. Tweed caps are £21.45, while felt hats range from £41 to £55. Nestled in among all the hats is a glass case containing a stuffed cat named Binks, who "Strolled in as a kitten June 1921 and passed out Nov. 1st, 1926. Admired and loved by everyone."

DAVID SHILLING
44 Chiltern St., W1 (tel. 935-8473 or 487-3179)
Underground Station: *Baker Street*

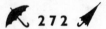
Hours: *Preferably by appointment—Monday through Friday from 9 a.m. to 6 p.m.*
Credit Cards: AE, DC, MC, V

Designer David Shilling creates two collections of women's hats a year. You can either choose from the existing stock, or, if none fits, have one made to your measurements. Shilling, an enthusiastic and outgoing personality who designed everything in his shop down to the wallpaper, suggests at least a half hour be allowed for the whole experience. It's best to call first to make sure he's there, and his creations start at about £220.

THE HAT SHOP
58 Neal St., Covent Garden, WC2 (tel. 836-6718)
Underground Station: Covent Garden
Hours: *Monday through Thursday from 10 a.m. to 6 p.m., on Friday to 7 p.m., on Saturday from 10:30 a.m. to 5 p.m.*
Credit Cards: MC, V

This shop deals in all kinds of inexpensive hats for both men and women in a wide range of colors. Women's berets start at £3.50, men's tweed caps are £12, and bowler hats are £33. There are also some designer hats starting at £80. Sales are held the entire months of August and February. Another shop is located at 9 Gees Court, St. Christopher's Place (tel. 629-1347).

"Maybe I should pop in to Bates and top off my outfit with a hat..."

HERBERT JOHNSON
13 Old Burlington St., W1 (tel. 439-7397), not far from Burlington Arcade
Underground Station: *Green Park or Piccadilly Circus*
Hours: *Monday through Friday from 9 a.m. to 5:30 p.m., on Saturday from 9:30 a.m. to 1 p.m.*
Credit Cards: *AE, DC, MC, V*

This small shop with a lot of personality has a very attentive staff and serves as hatters for the Queen and the Prince of Wales. Established in 1889, it stocks both men's and women's hats. In the men's section are felt hats for £53, panamas starting at £33, tweed caps for £21.50, and handmade riding caps starting at £148. There are also top hats, bowlers, and summer hats. Women's hats start at about £30. Custom-made hats can be ordered for about £10 more, and it takes about four weeks to fill an order.

JOHN BOYD
91 Walton St., SW3 (tel. 589-7601)
Underground Station: *South Kensington*
Hours: *Monday through Friday from 10 a.m. to 5:30 p.m.*
Credit Cards: *AE, DC, MC, V*

John Boyd designs women's hats, many of them ordered especially for Ascot's Day. He also makes hats for royalty. Styles range from the classical to the more

Hats were always in fashion at Herbert Johnson

daring, with prices averaging £88 to £130 for most hats. The minimum purchase for VAT refund here is £100.

KIRSTEN WOODWARD
Unit 26 in Portobello Green Arcade, 281 Portobello Rd., W10
  (tel. 960-0090)
Underground Station: *Ladbroke Grove*
Hours: *Monday through Saturday from 10 a.m. to 6 p.m.*
Credit Cards: *None*

Kirsten Woodward is an up-and-coming young hat designer who handmakes all her hats and who has created hats for Karl Lagerfeld and Princess Di. Her hats have also found their way into Saks in New York and other U.S. department stores.

Her designs tend to be unusual, but there's always a selection of more classical hats as well as turbans. She works with feathers, suedes, velvet, and fake furs, and predominantly black material. As she becomes more successful, she will probably move her shop to more convenient quarters, so it's best to call beforehand. Otherwise the Portobello Green Arcade makes a good stop if you're visiting Portobello Market.

LOCK & CO.
6 St. James's St., SW1 (tel. 930-8874)
Underground Station: *Green Park*
Hours: *Monday through Friday from 9 a.m. to 5 p.m., on Saturday from*
  9:30 a.m. to 12:30 p.m.
Credit Cards: *AE, DC, MC, V*

This charming hatter's shop has been here more than 300 years. In its front window is a display of old hats once produced by the shop, including a Duke of Wellington hat, a police helmet, regimental hats, and top hats. Also in the window is a conformateur, a device formerly used to measure customers' heads. As the shop that supplied Lord Nelson with the hat he wore at Trafalgar, Lock is also credited as being the birthplace of the bowler. Prices begin at £16.50 for straw summer hats. Other men's styles include panamas, homburgs, tweed hats, caps, riding hats, and a variety of felt hats.

HOUSEWARES

Department stores are good places to look for general housewares, especially **Harrods, Selfridges, John Lewis,** and **Peter Jones.** Furniture shops also often carry household goods, particularly **Habitat, Heal's,** and the **Conran Shop.** The **General Trading Company,** in the "Gifts" section, also stocks a wide range of exclusive houseware items suitable for weddings, birthdays, anniversaries, and other special occasions. Kitchen items can be found in stores listed under "Kitchenware."

**Indispensable equipment for the British elements
at Herbert Johnson**

Crowning headgear at Lock & Co.

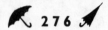
CHRISTOPHER WRAY'S LIGHTING EMPORIUM
600 King's Rd., SW6 (tel. 736-8434)
Underground Station: *Fulham Broadway*
Hours: *Monday through Saturday from 10 a.m. to 6 p.m.*
Credit Cards: *MC, V*

This shop has an amazing variety of lamps and lighting fixtures, making it the best place to go if you're interested in shedding some light on your life. Styles are traditional rather than hi-tech, and there are antique lamps as well as reproduction lamps of brass and hand-blown glass. There are coach lamps, ship lanterns, art deco–style lamps, desk lamps, Tiffany lamps and shades, oil lamps, and Victorian-style lights. Art deco–style leaded-glass wall lamps start at £60, while coach lamps start at £24.75.

THE REJECT SHOP
234 King's Rd., SW3 (tel. 352-2750)
Underground Station: *Sloane Square*
Hours: *Monday through Saturday from 9:30 a.m. to 6 p.m. (on*
Wednesday from 10 a.m. to 7 p.m.)
Credit Cards: *AE, DC, MC, V*

This shop caters primarily to young people buying the basics of their first apartment and includes furniture, dhurries, bed sheets and towels, kitchenware, china, and practical, everyday household items. There's lots priced under £22, and much of it is the same kind of thing you'd find back home. Other Reject Shops are located at 209 Tottenham Court Rd. (tel. 580-2895) and 245–249 Brompton Rd. (tel. 584-7611). Incidentally, Reject Shops have nothing to do with the Reject China Shops.

JEWELRY

Many of the big-name jewelers in the West End sell antique jewelry, admittedly at high prices. If you're interested in Victorian and Edwardian jewelry at lower prices, comb the stalls of the weekend flea markets such as Portobello and the indoor antique markets.

WEST END JEWELERS

BENTLEY & CO.
65 New Bond, W1 (tel. 629-0651)
Underground Station: *Bond Street*
Hours: *Monday through Friday from 10 a.m. to 5 p.m.*
Credit Cards: *AE, DC, V*

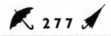
JEWELRY

Bentley specializes in antique estate jewelry, including art deco and unusual signed pieces you won't find elsewhere. It also stocks some Fabergé and other Russian pieces, silver, and pocket watches. An emerald ring dating from about 1880 will fetch about £16,500, while a Victorian diamond brooch may cost around £1,760. Not everything is so expensive, however—earrings start at £55. The staff is friendly and accommodating.

CARTIER
175 New Bond St., W1 (tel. 493-6962)
Underground Station: Green Park or Piccadilly Circus
Hours: Monday through Friday from 9:30 a.m. to 5:30 p.m., on Saturday
    from 10 a.m. to 4 p.m.
Credit Cards: AE, DC, MC, V

Cartier's London boutique sells a wide range of jewelry and accessories, including watches, eyeglasses, perfume, cigarette lighters, scarves, clocks, pens, handbags, and desk items. Most jewelry listed in its catalog is priced over £2,000, such as yellow-gold and diamond heart-motif earrings for £3,560. Watches are usually adorned with diamonds and stones such as sapphires. An 18-karat watch with inlaid sapphire, for example, is £1,830. Women's patterned scarves are £65.

COLLINGWOOD
171 New Bond St., W1 (tel. 734-2656)
Underground Station: Green Park or Piccadilly Circus
Hours: Monday through Friday from 10 a.m. to 5:30 p.m., on Saturday
    to 2 p.m.
Credit Cards: AE, DC, MC, V

Established in 1817, Collingwood carries three royal warrants. Its jewelry ranges from antique to contemporary, including styles designed and made exclusively for Collingwood. A pair of contemporary earrings with diamond, ruby, and emerald settings is priced at £1,450, while a pearl necklace with a ruby, diamond, and pearl drop is £790. Collingwood also stocks traditional and designer watches.

GARRARD
112 Regent St., W1 (tel. 734-7020)
Underground Station: Piccadilly Circus
Hours: Monday through Saturday from 9 a.m. to 5:30 p.m.
Credit Cards: AE, DC, MC, V

Responsible for the upkeep and care of the Crown Jewels, Garrard ranks as one of London's foremost jewelers. Because of its elegant display windows and perhaps because of its reputation, many pedestrians are apt to pass this shop by,

considering it too expensive and too exclusive for mere mortal souls. Too bad! While prices can be exceedingly high, Garrard is much more than a jewelry shop and there's none of the snobbery one might expect. It's true that Prince Andrew bought Sarah her engagement ring here for a cool £25,000, but there's jewelry in many price ranges, including wedding rings for less than £100. Garrard also stocks antique and contemporary silver items, watches, clocks, and many gift items. A special gift section is located on the first floor, and browsing is encouraged. You'll find china, crystal, leather desk sets, pens, lighters, and coffee and tea sets. A silver and briarwood veneer calculator is priced at £91.

MAPPIN & WEBB

170 Regent St., WI (tel. 734-3801)
Underground Station: Oxford Circus or Piccadilly Circus
Hours: Monday through Friday from 9 a.m. to 5:30 p.m., on Saturday to 5 p.m.
Credit Cards: AE, DC, MC, V

Personal service makes shopping here a pleasure. As soon as you enter the door, you're ushered to the jewelry, silver, or watch department and given a comfortable chair and your own sales clerk. Wedding rings start at £75 for an 18-karat gold band, while a ring with sapphire, diamond, and ruby settings may cost upward of £8,000. In the silver department are antique and contemporary pieces. A sterling-silver tea strainer is £115, an exquisite sterling-silver condiment set is £243, and an antique silver-plated butter dish from about 1875 is £132. Mappin & Webb also carries a comprehensive range of watches, including Rolex, Cartier, Ebel, Corum, Longines, Omega, and Heuer. Mappin & Webb even produces its own watches, one a woman's gold-plated quartz watch with crocodile strap priced at £120. Another Mappin & Webb is located at 65 Brompton Rd. (tel. 584-9361).

S. J. PHILLIPS

139 New Bond St., WI (tel. 629-6261)
Underground Station: Bond Street
Hours: Monday through Friday from 10 a.m. to 5 p.m.
Credit Cards: AE, DC, MC, V

Founded in 1869, this shop has one of the finest collections of antique jewelry and silver in the country. Prices are expectedly high, but the atmosphere manages to be both informal and grand at the same time. The silver collection is mainly Georgian, along with reproduction silver imitating older styles.

TESSIERS

26 New Bond St., WI (tel. 629-0458)
Underground Station: Bond Street
Hours: Monday through Friday from 9:30 a.m. to 5 p.m.
Credit Cards: AE, V

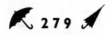
The tiny shop of Tessiers is one of the most quaint and charming shops in all of London, occupying a building constructed in the 1720s. The interior of the shop is just as it was in the middle of the last century, complete with the original gas fittings and mahogany display cases. On the walls are pictures designed with human hair, now a forgotten art.

Tessiers specializes in jewelry from the beginning of the 19th century to the present day, as well as antique and contemporary silver. A recent catalog lists an antique ruby and diamond ring for £5,775; a cultured pearl necklace with diamond center for £935; and an 18-karat, three-colored gold Russian-pattern wedding ring for £250. A four-piece Victorian engraved silver tea and coffee set made in London in 1849 is £5,775.

WARTSKI
14 Grafton St., W1 (tel. 493-1141), off Bond Street
Underground Station: Green Park or Piccadilly Circus
Hours: Monday through Friday from 9:30 a.m. to 5 p.m.
Credit Cards: None

Founded in Wales in 1850, Wartski has royal warrants to the Queen, the Queen Mother, and the Prince of Wales. It has a fantastic collection of antique Russian jewelry and objects, particularly Fabergé. A Fabergé gold photo frame with enamel is priced at £13,200, while a two-colored gold cigarette case is £8,800. Silver Fabergé objects start at £2,200, while Fabergé snuff boxes start at £20,000. There are also 18th-century gold snuff boxes from other European countries, priced under £5,500.

ART DECO AND ART NOUVEAU

All the shops listed in the section "Art Deco and Art Nouveau" carry jewelry in addition to their furniture and decorative objects. **John Jesse & Irina Laski**, for example, has paste clip brooches and Bakelite jewelry starting at £52, while **Tadema** has jewelry ranging from German Jugendstil to Liberty necklaces and rings.

Liberty, famous for jewelry produced around the turn of the century, today sells contemporary jewelry, a few original Liberty pieces, and ethnic jewelry from China, India, Africa, and other countries. There's also a small selection of original costume paste jewelry from the 1920s and 1930s. Two original Liberty brooches were recently on sale for £300 and £495. Refer to the "Department Stores" section for more information on Liberty.

ARCADE JEWELRY
309A King's Rd., SW3 (tel. 352-0239)
Underground Station: Sloane Square

Hours: *Monday through Saturday from 10 a.m. to 6 p.m.*
Credit Cards: AE, DC, MC, V

This tiny shop carries jewelry from the Victorian period through art deco to the 1950s, and specializes in original costume jewelry produced from the '20s to the '50s. Most items are very reasonably priced, from £12 for a tiny brooch to £110 for bracelets and necklaces.

COBRA & BELLAMY
149 Sloane St., SW1 (tel. 730-2823)
Underground Station: Sloane Square
Hours: *Monday through Friday from 10 a.m. to 6 p.m., on Saturday to 4 p.m.*
Credit Cards: AE, DC, MC, V

This wonderful shop specializes in costume jewelry from the early 1920s to the early 1960s. Included is American costume jewelry primarily from the '40s, original art deco and art nouveau pieces, and silver and gilt jewelry designed exclusively for this store. Prices start at less than £10 for crystal earring studs. The shop also sells decorative objects dating from the 1920s, wine decanters, and a range of new black-lacquered furniture designed in-house and influenced by the styles of art deco. Cobra & Bellamy has a concession in Liberty department store too.

MOIRA
22–23 New Bond St., W1 (tel. 629-0160)
Underground Station: Bond Street, Green Park, or Piccadilly Circus
Hours: *Monday through Saturday from 10 a.m. to 5:30 p.m.*
Credit Cards: AE, DC, MC, V

This small family-run business deals in antique Georgian, Edwardian, and art nouveau and art deco jewelry. Most pieces are priced over £500. An art deco onyx-and-diamond platinum pendant is £4,125, while a Victorian 15-karat gold heart locket with a star-set diamond is £159.

VAN PETERSON
117 Walton St., SW3 (tel. 589-2155)
Underground Station: South Kensington
Hours: *Monday through Saturday from 10 a.m. to 6 p.m. (on Wednesday to 7 p.m.)*
Credit Cards: AE, V

In addition to Georg Jensen silver dating from the 1930s, old Rolex and Cartier watches, and modern jewelry, Van Peterson sells original jewelry dating from the 1930s, as well as reproduction art deco pieces. Prices for jewelry start at £20 for a pair of earrings or cuff links.

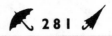
COSTUME JEWELRY

BUTLER & WILSON
189 Fulham Rd., SW3 (tel. 352-3045)
Underground Station: South Kensington
Hours: Monday through Saturday from 10 a.m. to 6 p.m.
Credit Cards: AE, MC, V

A glittering shop filled with a fantastic array of costume jewelry, primarily paste jewelry (which is glass cut to look like diamonds). It also stocks original French, British, and European art deco costume jewelry, as well as agate and Victorian jewelry from Scotland. Art deco earrings start at £66. Butler & Wilson also produces imitation art deco and contemporary paste jewelry at very affordable prices. Paste earrings and bracelets start at £8 and necklaces start at £33. There's also a lot of gilt jewelry. A gilt circular brooch with snake heads is £41, while a pair of gilt, fake pearl, and jet clip earrings is priced at £17.60. Another Butler & Wilson at 20 South Molton St. (tel. 409-2955) sells imitation and contemporary costume jewelry.

FIOR
27 Brompton Rd., SW3 (tel. 589-0053)
Underground Station: Knightsbridge
Hours: Monday through Friday from 9:15 a.m. to 5:30 p.m. (on
Wednesday to 6 p.m.), on Saturday to 4:45 p.m.
Credit Cards: AE, DC, MC, V

Lots of crystal and glittering fake stones are used to make the wide range of costume jewelry including brooches, rings, bracelets, and earrings. A fake diamond-and-emerald ring is priced at £15.40. There are cufflinks starting at £22. A smaller Fior is located at 22 New Bond St. (tel. 491-4119).

KEN LANE
66 South Molton St., W1 (tel. 499-3700)
Underground Station: Bond Street
Hours: Monday through Saturday from 9:30 a.m. to 5:30 p.m. (on
Thursday to 6:30 p.m.)
Credit Cards: AE, DC, MC, V

Ken Lane is the king of fake jewelry. His fake diamonds are made of cut crystal, while his fake pearls are coated with mother-of-pearl. Fake-pearl necklace strands start at £26, clip earrings start at £11, and rings start at £6.50. Other Ken Lane shops are at 30 Burlington Arcade (tel. 499-1364) and at 50 Beauchamp Pl. (tel. 584-5299).

Ken Lane: King of costume jewelry

DESIGNER JEWELRY

Several of the shops listed in the "Crafts" section carry contemporary jewelry. If you're looking for inexpensive, avant-garde jewelry by young designers, check **Hyper Hyper** and the stalls at **Camden Lock flea market.**

ARGENTA
82 Fulham Rd., SW3 (tel. 584-3119)
Underground Station: South Kensington
Hours: Monday through Friday from 9:30 a.m. to 5:30 p.m., on Saturday to 5 p.m.
Credit Cards: AE, DC, MC, V

Argenta carries contemporary jewelry, much of it created of silver and imported from Denmark. In the basement is a gallery displaying the creations of British goldsmiths, all unique to the shop. The staff is friendly and browsing is encouraged. Prices start at about £10 for a pair of earrings.

DETAIL
49 Endell St., Covent Garden, WC2 (tel. 379-6940)
Underground Station: Covent Garden
Hours: Monday through Saturday from 11 a.m. to 7 p.m.
Credit Cards: AE, MC, V

This small shop carries the works of young designers, some very unusual and incorporating such materials as plastic, glass, or brass. Earrings start at less than £4, and the most expensive item in the shop is £165. Most pieces are less than £30.

ELECTRUM
21 South Molton St., WI (tel. 629-6325)
Underground Station: Bond Street
Hours: Monday through Friday from 10 a.m. to 6 p.m., on Saturday to
** 1 p.m.**
Credit Cards: AE, DC, MC, V

This gallery showcases the talents of goldsmiths from around the world and is filled with exciting handmade contemporary jewelry. About 20 artists may be represented at any one time, offering a good variety of unique designs. Prices may start at £10 for ear cuffs, going all the way up to £3,000 for elaborate pieces.

GRIMA
80 Jermyn St., SWI (tel. 839-7561)
Underground Station: Piccadilly Circus or Green Park
Hours: Monday through Friday from 9:30 a.m. to 5 p.m.
Credit Cards: AE, DC, MC, V

The unique architecture of this highly contemporary gallery is an appropriate setting for the expensive and highly original designs produced by Grima. As royal jewelers to the Queen, Grima has also made jewelry for Princess Anne and Princess Margaret. The majority of pieces here are one-of-a-kind, based on the philosophy that the stone itself should dictate the shape of the jewelry. Pieces are nothing short of stunning, with prices starting at about £500 and going up to £75,000.

KUTCHINSKY
73 Brompton Rd., SW3 (tel. 584-9311)
Underground Station: Knightsbridge
Hours: Monday through Saturday from 10 a.m. to 5:10 p.m.
Credit Cards: AE, DC, MC, V

Founded in 1893, Kutchinsky is a family concern. It has its own in-house designer who will custom-make pieces according to customers' wishes. Otherwise, all jewelry sold here is made in Britain and all pieces are signed with the Kutchinsky mark. Although prices are high, the staff is friendly and not at all stuffy. Prices start at about £650, though most pieces are much, much more. An emerald and diamond-cluster ring is priced at £8,990, while 18-karat-gold, diamond, and sapphire cuff links are £4,530. Kutchinsky also carries a large

selection of watches, most encrusted with diamonds and precious stones. A Chopard bangle watch with diamonds and semiprecious stones is £15,950.

KILTS

Several stores listed in the "Clothing" section sells kilts. **Moss Bros.** has a particularly large department of Highland wear, with men's kilts starting at about £148. You can buy an entire Highland outfit for about £385, and there are also kilts for rent. The **Scotch House** has kilts starting at £75. Two other stores selling kilts are **Westaway & Westaway** and **W. Bill.** Refer to the "Clothing" section for more information on these shops.

KITCHENWARE

Department stores carry a wide range of kitchenware and utensils. Several furniture stores also have kitchenware departments, including **Habitat, Heal's,** and the **Conran Shop**. The **General Trading Company,** listed under "Gifts," also carries kitchen items.

THE COPPERSHOP
48 Neal St., Covent Garden, WC2 (tel. 836-2984)
Underground Station: Covent Garden
Hours: Monday through Saturday from 10 a.m. to 6 p.m.
Credit Cards: AE, DC, MC, V

As its name implies, this shop deals in copper, all British-made and consisting mainly of kitchenware. There are saucepans, soup pots, frying pans, omelet pans, Victorian-style pot lids, colanders, kettles, tankards, and spirit warmers. There are also household items such as bed warmers, coal helmets, log carriers, planters, watering cans, and candleholders. A tin-lined Georgian-style kettle is £29.50, while an eight-inch crêpe Suzette pan with a wooden handle is £56.25.

COVENT GARDEN KITCHEN SUPPLIES
3 The Market, Covent Garden, WC2 (tel. 836-9167)
Underground Station: Covent Garden
Hours: Monday through Saturday from 10 a.m. to 8 p.m., on Sunday
   from 12:30 to 5 p.m.
Credit Cards: MC, V

This is a sister shop to the Elizabeth David shop at 46 Bourne St. (tel.730-3123). For the serious cooks there are Sabatier knives, Le Creuset pans, fondue sets, scales, pasta machines, and porcelain bowls. There are kitchen gadgets galore, including egg slicers or wedgers, poultry shears, citrus squeezers, salad

spinners, corkscrews, and trussing needles. Butter stamps start at £2.15 and butter curlers at £3. Scales start at £32.95, while brass weights start at 50 pence for an eighth of an ounce. The shop is also well known for its cake tins shaped in such unusual forms as hearts, Christmas trees, letters of the alphabet, numbers, and more. A catalog is available for £1.50, and sales are held in January and July.

DAVID MELLOR
26 James St., Covent Garden, WC2 (tel. 379-6947)
Underground Station: Covent Garden
Hours: Monday through Friday from 10 a.m. to 6:30 p.m., on Saturday to 6 p.m.
Credit Cards: MC

David Mellor's shop has graters, grinders, cutters, smashers, and everything else you might need in the kitchen. David Mellor is especially famous for his cutlery, which has ended up in many international collections, including the Victoria and Albert Museum and the New York and Philadelphia museums of modern art. Various styles of contemporary cutlery are available, ranging from stainless steel to silver plate. A six-piece place setting starts at £19.90.

Also in the shop are scales, coffee machines, cookbooks, pots, pans, cookie cutters, glassware, bowls, and hand-thrown pottery. David Mellor also has a collection of Wedgwood, designed especially for his shop and available only here. His catalogs show the full range of cookware and utensils, many of which are imported from Germany, Italy, Sweden, France, and other European countries. Another David Mellor shop is located at 4 Sloane Square (tel. 730-4259).

DIVERTIMENTI
139–141 Fulham Rd., SW3 (tel. 581-8065)
Underground Station: South Kensington
Hours: Monday through Friday from 9:30 a.m. to 6 p.m., on Saturday from 10 a.m. to 6 p.m.
Credit Cards: AE, DC, MC, V

Divertimenti has a good selection of practical and gourmet cookware, as well as knife-grinding and copper-retinning services. Its catalog for £2.75 lists a wide range of pots, pans, utensils, gadgets, cutlery, and more. Flan rings start at £1.25, while cookie cutters start at 38 pence. Another Divertimenti is located at 68–72 Marylebone Lane (tel. 935-0689).

LEATHER GOODS

In addition to the shops listed below, **Trussardi**, listed in the "Clothing" section, has a good selection of leather bags, wallets, dresses, pants, jackets, and assorted leather goods. Other clothing shops carrying leather

products include **Gucci** with bags and **Take Six** with leather jackets for men. **Smythson**, listed under "Stationery," stocks a range of leather briefcases, wallets, desk accessories, and leather-bound diaries.

LOEWE
25 Old Bond St., W1 (tel. 493-3914)
Underground Station: Green Park or Piccadilly Circus
Hours: Monday through Saturday from 9:30 a.m. to 5:30 p.m.
Credit Cards: AE, DC, MC, V

Loewe is a Spanish leather shop selling men's and women's fashions, luggage, briefcases, diaries, address books, and perfume. Loewe uses the softest leather and suede, and the colors are beautiful—cornflower blue, rich greens, and a good buttercup yellow. Leather handbags start at about £110. Another Loewe is located at 47–49 Brompton Rd. (tel. 581-4014).

LOUIS VUITTON
149 New Bond St., W1 (tel. 493-3688)
Underground Station: Bond Street, Green Park, or Piccadilly Circus
Hours: Monday through Saturday from 9:30 a.m. to 6 p.m. (on Thursday to 7 p.m.)
Credit Cards: AE, DC, MC, V

Louis Vuitton's famous handbags and luggage have been sold at this fashionable Bond Street address for more than 80 years, proving so successful that a second shop has opened up at 198 Sloane St. (tel. 235-3356). Handbags range in price from £132 to £550, soft luggage ranges from £165 to £650, and hard luggage from £450 to £5,500. There are also accessories such as wallets, key chains, playing cards, photo albums, jewelry boxes, and cigarette holders for sale. A treated-canvas leather-trimmed shoe case for 12 pairs of shoes is £1,100.

NATURAL LEATHER
62 Neal St., Covent Garden, WC2 (tel. 240-7748)
Underground Station: Covent Garden
Hours: Monday through Saturday from 11 a.m. to 7 p.m.
Credit Cards: AE, DC, MC, V

Leather clothing and bags for this shop are made in London from skins imported from various countries. Beautifully crafted leather purses start at £55, a mini-skirt is £44, and a man's leather jacket is £155.

LINENS

Jane Churchill, listed under "Fabrics," carries a range of bed linen, with fitted, single-size percale sheets costing £21.95. In addition, **Lunn An-**

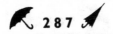
tiques, in the "Clothing" section, stocks antique tablecloths and embroidered sheets and pillowcases. A 19th-century Italian tablecloth with intricate lacework is priced in a recent catalog at £740.

AND SO TO BED
7 New King's Rd., SW6 (tel. 736-9334)
Underground Station: Fulham Broadway
Hours: Monday through Saturday from 10 a.m. to 6 p.m.
Credit Cards: AE, DC, MC, V

The bed linen sold here comes primarily from Italy and France. A set of full-size sheets and pillowcases starts at £65, while queen-size comforters range in price from £110 to £660. Bed linen can also be made to measure in customers' own fabrics.

DESCAMPS
197 Sloane St., SW1 (tel. 235-6957)
Underground Station: Knightsbridge
Hours: Monday through Saturday from 9:30 a.m. to 6 p.m.
Credit Cards: AE, DC, MC, V

Descamps is a French company selling a wide range of bed linen, bathroom towels, comforters, baby linen, and bathrobes. Flat sheets start at £21.

FRETTE
98 New Bond St., W1 (tel. 629-5517)
Underground Station: Bond Street
Hours: Monday through Saturday from 10 a.m. to 6 p.m.
Credit Cards: AE, DC, MC, V

Sheets from Italy are Frette's specialty, in sets consisting of a flat sheet, a fitted sheet, and two pillowcases starting at £110. Handmade sheets are also available. Another Frette is at 84 Brompton Rd. (tel. 589-4630).

GIVANS IRISH LINEN
207 King's Rd., SW3 (tel. 352-6352)
Underground Station: Sloane Square
Hours: Monday through Friday from 9:30 a.m. to 5 p.m.
Credit Cards: AE, MC, V

This small shop carries bed linen, table linen, placemats, towels, duvets (comforters), duvet covers, bathrobes, and handkerchiefs. A linen damask tablecloth measuring 72 inches by 144 inches is £177.50.

THE IRISH LINEN COMPANY
35–36 Burlington Arcade, W1 (tel. 493-8949)

Underground Station: Green Park or Piccadilly Circus
Hours: Monday through Friday from 9 a.m. to 5:30 p.m., on Saturday to 4:30 p.m.
Credit Cards: AE, DC, MC, V

Established in 1875, this shop sells linen for tables and beds. Tablecloths range up to banquet size and come with matching napkins and exquisite embroidery, entirely handmade. Products are primarily at the luxury end of the market, with bed sheets ranging from about £170 for a single to £357 for a king-size. Lunch sets consisting of eight placemats, eight napkins, and a central table runner range from £165 to £440. Handkerchiefs start at £3.25.

THE MONOGRAMMED LINEN SHOP

168 Walton St., SW3 (tel. 589-4033)
Underground Station: South Kensington
Hours: Monday through Saturday from 10 a.m. to 6 p.m.
Credit Cards: AE, DC, MC, V

Anything can be monogrammed in this shop, including towels, dressing gowns, nursery accessories and infants' clothing, sheets, duvet (comforter) covers, and bedspreads. A plain white queen-size sheet with a frilled or scalloped edge costs £29, while a super-king-size Irish linen sheet is £440. The cost of monogramming starts at £3.80 for one or two letters.

THE WHITE HOUSE

51–52 New Bond St., WI (tel. 629-3521)
Underground Station: Bond Street
Hours: Monday through Friday from 9 a.m. to 5:30 p.m., on Saturday to 1 p.m.
Credit Cards: AE, DC, V

This exclusive, spacious shop sells table and bed linen, nightwear, bathroom towels, and nursery accessories. A hand-embroidered linen table set for a dozen diners consisting of placemats and napkins begins at £248, while cotton handkerchiefs begin at £13 for a half dozen. An infant's pure-silk satin wrapping sheet is £64.90, and a woman's silk negligee set from France is priced at £412.

LINGERIE

In addition to the shops listed here, **Marks & Spencer**, in the "Department Stores" section, sells modestly priced underclothing for the whole family, while the **White House**, listed under "Linens," sells exclusive nightwear in silk, satin, and wool.

BRADLEYS

83–85 Knightsbridge, SWI (tel. 235-2902)

LINGERIE

Underground Station: *Knightsbridge*
Hours: *Monday through Friday from 9:30 a.m. to 6 p.m. (on Wednesday to 7 p.m.), on Saturday from 10 a.m. to 5:30 p.m.*
Credit Cards: *AE, DC, MC, V*

A large selection of underclothing, nightwear, and bathing suits is offered by this shop, including robes, tights, and hosiery. Bras from AA to F cups are available, as well as mastectomy bras. Nightgowns range in price from £13 to £650.

JANET REGER
2 Beauchamp Pl., SW3 (tel. 584-9360)
Underground Station: *Knightsbridge*
Hours: *Monday through Friday from 10 a.m. to 6 p.m., on Saturday to 5 p.m.*
Credit Cards: *AE, DC, MC, V*

The ultimate in lingerie, everything in this shop is designed by Janet Reger and is made of silk. Most of the customers are distinguished-looking gentlemen buying presents for the women in their lives. There are slips, bathing suits, robes, underwear, nightgowns, teddies, and negligees. Briefs are £35, negligees start at £275, pajamas average £385, and bra-and-underwear sets average £80.

NEXT
102 King's Rd., SW3 (tel. 225-2354)
Underground Station: *Sloane Square*
Hours: *Monday through Saturday from 10 a.m. to 6 p.m.*
Credit Cards: *AE, DC, MC, V*

Up on the first floor is a full range of feminine, lacy underclothing for women. A cotton vest-and-briefs set is £8.90, silk underpants are £11, and a satin teddy is £21.

NIGHT OWLS
78 Fulham Rd., SW3 (tel. 584-2451)
Underground Station: *South Kensington*
Hours: *Monday through Friday from 10 a.m. to 6 p.m., on Saturday to 5 p.m.*
Credit Cards: *AE, DC, MC, V*

Lingerie and underwear in silk and cotton are sold here, as well as silk and wool nightgowns. Bras start at £11, cotton nightdresses start at £44, and silk nightgowns start at £137. Up on the first floor is a shop called Great Expectations, selling designer maternity clothes.

RIGBY
2 Hans Rd., SW3 (tel. 589-9293), beside Harrods
Underground Station: *Knightsbridge*

Hours: Monday through Saturday from 9 a.m. to 5:30 p.m. (on Wednesday to 7 p.m.)
Credit Cards: AE, DC, MC, V

Rigby specializes in lingerie and special fittings for bras, corsets, and bathing suits. Its staff is fully trained in fitting women who have had operations like mastectomies, and records are kept of customers' sizes so items can be reordered. A large range of sizes is available in bras, girdles, slips, camisoles, knickers, and nightwear, and it carries one of the largest selections of swimwear in town. Made-to-measure bras start at £55.

MAGAZINES

Newsstands at underground stations and train stations sell daily newspapers and selected magazines. Other news agents can be found in hotel lobbies or on central London street corners.

MORONI
68 Old Compton St., W1 (tel. 437-2847)
Underground Station: Piccadilly Circus
Hours: Monday through Saturday from 7:30 a.m. to 7:15 p.m., on Sunday from 8 a.m. to 1 p.m.
Credit Cards: None

This news agent also stocks a wide range of international style and fashion magazines in addition to its daily newspapers in several languages.

NEWSPOINT
104–106 Long Acre, Covent Garden, WC2 (tel. 240-7645).
Underground Station: Covent Garden
Hours: Monday through Saturday from 8 a.m. to 8 p.m., on Sunday from 11 a.m. to 6 p.m.
Credit Cards: None

Packed with fashion and style magazines from England, the continent, America, and Australia, including various national editions of *Vogue*.

THE VINTAGE MAGAZINE SHOP
39–43 Brewer St., W1 (tel. 439-8525)
Underground Station: Piccadilly Circus
Hours: Monday through Saturday from 10 a.m. to 7 p.m., on Sunday from 2 to 7 p.m.
Credit Cards: AE, DC, MC, V

This shop sells both old magazines, old and new posters, photographs of stars and celebrities, Beatles memorabilia, and postcards. The large stock of old magazines is downstairs in the basement and includes back issues of *Life*,

Illustrated London News, Saturday Evening Post, National Geographic, and various newspapers. There are also old fashion magazines, children's comics, movie magazines, and drive-in movie posters from the 1930s. Prices for magazines start at £1 but go up to several hundred pounds for rarer editions.

W. H. SMITH
132 Kensington High St., W8 (tel. 937-0236)
Underground Station: *High Street Kensington*
Hours: *Monday through Friday from 9 a.m. to 6:30 p.m., on Saturday to 6 p.m.*
Credit Cards: *MC, V*

In among the stationery supplies, pens, Filofax folders, and books is a selection of newspapers and magazines, primarily women's fashion publications. There are more than 70 W. H. Smith shops in London alone, with other large stores located at Sloane Square and Brent Cross Shopping Centre.

MAPS

Other shops described elsewhere that carry antique maps are **Alan Brett,** listed under "Books," with maps made before 1850; **Clive A. Burden,** in the "Prints" section, with international maps from the 15th century to the end of the 1800s; and **Sotheran's,** under "Books," with a wide range of antique maps of England, Scotland, Wales, and Ireland.

ANTIQUE

CARTOGRAPHIA
Pied Bull, Bury Place, WCI (tel. 240-5687)
Underground Station: *Holborn*
Hours: *Monday through Saturday from 10 a.m. to 8 p.m.*
Credit Cards: *AE, DC, MC, V*

Cartographia, located close to the British Museum, stocks original maps and prints dating from before 100 years ago, including maps from around the world, maps of English counties, and old globes. Its prints selection includes views of London, as well as botanical, sporting, and caricature prints. Prices range from under £10 up to £5,500.

THE MAP HOUSE
54 Beauchamp Pl., SW3 (tel. 589-4325)
Underground Station: *Knightsbridge*
Hours: *Monday through Friday from 9:45 a.m. to 5:45 p.m., on Saturday from 10:30 a.m. to 5 p.m.*
Credit Cards: *AE, MC, V*

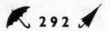
Established in 1907, the Map House has one of the largest stocks of antique maps in London, the majority of which were published between 1470 and 1880. Maps are of all parts of the world as well as of each British county. Prices start at a few pounds and go up to £160,000, with the rare early 16th- and 17th-century maps going for around £5,500. There are also antique atlases and globes, as well as antique prints covering topographical, legal, botanical, and sporting subjects.

O'SHEA GALLERY
89 Lower Sloane St., SW1 (tel. 730-0081)
Underground Station: *Sloane Square*
Hours: *Monday through Friday from 9:30 a.m. to 6 p.m., on Saturday to 1 p.m.*
Credit Cards: *AE, MC, V*

This gallery is a specialist dealer in 15th- to 19th-century maps, sea charts, rare atlases and books, as well as topographical, decorative, natural history, sporting, and marine prints. Maps start at about £15, with the top price reaching £10,000 for a map of the world printed around 1480. Prints start at £6.

CONTEMPORARY

STANFORDS
12–14 Long Acre, Covent Garden, WC2 (tel. 836-1321)
Underground Station: *Covent Garden*
Hours: *Monday from 10 a.m. to 6 p.m., Tuesday through Friday from 9 a.m. to 6 p.m., on Saturday from 10 a.m. to 5 p.m.*
Credit Cards: *MC, V*

Stanfords, established in 1852, bills itself as "The World's Largest Map Shop." Departments stock the latest in British touring maps, worldwide touring and survey maps, world maps, atlases, globes, aeronautical charts, nautical charts, and travel guides. The AA *Illustrated Guide to Britain* is listed at £16.45.

MARKETS

Some of my most pleasant shopping experiences have been at London's lively and bustling street markets, where everything from antiques and collectibles to clothing and vegetables is sold under the sky at makeshift tables and stalls. Some of the markets, particularly those on weekends, have a carnival atmosphere to them, complete with food vendors and hawkers yelling their wares. Bargaining is the rule, and buyers should beware. If it feels like vinyl, it probably is, despite a stallholder's claim that it's genuine leather. If you're looking for bargains in antiques, try to arrive as early as possible, since serious dealers are always the first on the scene and will snap up the best pieces in the wee hours of the morning.

MARKETS

The markets listed here include flea markets, outdoor antique markets, and produce markets. Permanent indoor antique markets open throughout the week are listed under "Antiques," where you'll find information on **Antiquarius, Bond Street Antique Centre, Chenil Galleries**, the **Chelsea Antique Market**, and **Grays Antique Markets.** These markets sell a wide range of antiques, bric-a-brac, and collectibles, including jewelry, silver, china, prints, Oriental objects, art deco and art nouveau, clocks, and more. If you're interested in indoor clothing markets, check the "Clothing" section for **Hyper Hyper** and **Kensington Market** with their many stalls selling young, contemporary fashion.

It's also worth checking to see whether any seasonal markets or fairs are being held in London. The **Chelsea Antiques Fair**, for example, is held twice a year in March and September at the Chelsea Old Town Hall on King's Road. In addition, the **Grosvenor House Antiques Fair**, held in June at the Grosvenor House Hotel on Park Lane, is a showcase for the best antique pieces of the top dealers, many of them hailing from Bond Street. There are also crafts fairs and specialist markets. For more information regarding seasonal markets and fairs, check with such publications as "Time Out," issued weekly and available at newsstands, or with "Events in London," available free at tourist information centers.

BERWICK AND RUPERT STREET

Berwick and Rupert Streets, in the heart of Soho
Underground Station: Oxford Circus or Piccadilly Circus
Hours: Monday through Saturday from 9:30 a.m. to 5 p.m.

This is the West End's only produce market and caters to people who work in the area. For sale are fruits and vegetables, as well as ladies' handbags, clothes, jewelry, and toiletries. It's especially crowded at lunchtime, as office workers pass through during their break. If you have no other opportunity to see London's markets, this one is a *must* and is conveniently located in central London not far from Regent Street's many shops. Most of the action takes place south of Berwick and in the top part of Rupert Street.

BILLINGSGATE

87 West India Dock Rd., E14
Underground Station: Mile End
Hours: Tuesday through Saturday from 5:30 to 8:30 a.m.

This is London's main fish market, where most traders deal wholesale. However, the market is also a public one, so you are perfectly justified in wandering around. Leave your best shoes at home.

CAMDEN PASSAGE

Camden Passage, Islington, N1
Underground Station: Angel

Hours: Wednesday from 7 a.m. to 3 p.m., on Thursday and Saturday from about 8:30 a.m. to 4 p.m.

This market area is small, pleasant, and relaxed, and without the seething crowds that often descend on London's other markets. Antiques are sold on Wednesday and Saturday, while books are sold on Thursday mornings. In addition to the street stalls, there are also a few indoor antique arcades and small permanent shops selling such antiques as clocks, dolls, and art nouveau and art deco.

After exiting from Angel Station, turn right and then turn right again onto Islington High Street, which leads into Upper Street. There you'll see **York Arcade** on the right side, with 12 stallholders selling antiques. Nearby is the **Mall Antiques Arcade**, open every day except Monday. This interesting brick building converted from an old tram shed now houses 35 galleries selling antiques and decorative objects, including clocks, furniture, bronzes, paintings, brass, copper, porcelain, silver, jewelry, and dolls. If you're hungry, there's a trendy and pleasant restaurant up on the first floor serving hot food all day, including vegetarian dishes and salads.

Next comes **Camden Passage**, a narrow street built in the 1760s. Antique shops occupy many of the old buildings now, and it's pleasant strolling from shop to shop and talking to the many street vendors who have set up their wares. The market is good for period and paste jewelry, clothes, bric-a-brac, silver, and odds and ends. I ended up buying a pair of pre–World War II eyeglass frames for £5, reproduction art deco earrings for £4, and a tea cozy for £10. At the end of Camden Passage is the **Georgian Village**, another antique arcade with 70 small shops and stalls.

CAMDEN TOWN

Camden High Street to Chalk Farm Road, NW1
Underground Station: Camden Town
Hours: Saturday and Sunday from 9 a.m. to 5 p.m.

This is one of my favorite markets, an eclectic and vibrant mix of young fashion, bric-a-brac, art deco, and kitsch. The market is a magnet for London's young population, and it's especially crowded on Sunday.

There are several separate markets spread out along Camden High Street. If you're arriving by underground at Camden Town, take a right out of the station onto Camden High Street. To the left you'll see **Inverness**, where a vegetable and fruit market is held on Friday and Saturday. To the right, just beside the station, is the **Electric Ballroom**, an indoor market where young designers sell their own fashion, secondhand clothes, and jewelry. Very much a young person's market, music blasts through loudspeakers above heads that are shaven and hair that is spiked, orange, pink, or blue. An interesting atmosphere and a place where you can pick up some unique and wild items.

Next comes **Camden Market**, where tables and stalls display secondhand clothes, as well as the original creations of young designers, including earrings,

hats, clothing, and accessories. I saw secondhand houndstooth coats going for £35 and handmade hats selling for £6.50

Just before Regent's Canal is the **Camden Lock Antique Centre**, a small indoor market with stalls selling art deco, '50s and '60s items, and decorative objects dating to the 1880s. After crossing the Regent's Canal, to your right is **New Canal Market**, with more bric-a-brac, jewelry, and used clothing, and to your left is **Camden Lock**, the largest market in Camden Town. Camden Lock is a maze of tiny alleys and even tinier stalls selling secondhand goods, handmade originals, home-baked foods, jewelry, shoes, ethnic goods from India, batik silk scarves, ceramics, and other crafts. You can even get your hair cut or your ear or nose pierced. Eventually the alleys lead to a large cobbled courtyard with outdoor cafés. Beside the courtyard is a canal from which you can take a boat to London Zoo (15 minutes) or Little Venice (45 minutes).

One more market worth exploring—if you've still got any energy—is the **Old Stables**, located farther down Chalk Farm Road on the left. The Old Stables gets its name from the fact that during the Victorian period this old brick building used to house sick horses. Today it's a treasure trove for art deco and '40s and '50s kitsch, including old toasters, kitchenware, powder cases, china, clocks, plastic boxes, and collectibles, with lots in the £10 to £30 range. Sunday is the best day to explore this delightful market. From here it's just a few minutes' walk on to Chalk Farm tube station.

CHAPEL MARKET

Chapel Market, off Upper Street, Islington, N1
Underground Station: Angel
Hours: Tuesday, Wednesday, Friday, and Saturday from 6:30 a.m. to 4
   p.m., on Thursday and Sunday from 5 a.m. to noon

Locals come here to buy their vegetables, fruit, eggs, fresh and dried flowers, seafood, kitchenware, plastic housewares, and an occasional shirt or sweater. The market is located just a minute's walk from Angel tube station and is easily combined with a visit to Camden Passage market, described above.

GREENWICH MARKET

Greenwich High Road and Covered Market Square, SE10
Underground Station: Greenwich
Hours: Saturday and Sunday from 9 a.m. to 5 p.m.

The **Greenwich Covered Market** sells crafts, antiques, and clothing. Nearby is the **Greenwich Antique Market**, located almost opposite St. Alfege's Church, with antiques, bric-a-brac, collectibles, and an excellent selection of second-hand and antique clothing. While you're in this part of London, you might want to visit the Cutty Sark Gardens, the National Maritime Museum, and the Greenwich Observatory.

JUBILEE MARKET
Covent Garden Piazza, WC2
Underground Station: Covent Garden
Hours: Monday through Saturday from 9 a.m. to 5 p.m.

Jubilee Market, as well as the Covent Garden outdoor market on the Piazza, specializes in antiques on Monday, general goods and bric-a-brac from Tuesday to Friday, and crafts on Saturday. On antique days you'll find china, jewelry, walking sticks, old eyeglasses, clocks, watches, silver, and glass. Jubilee Market is a covered market located on the south side of the Market in Covent Gardens. Inside the Market itself is a smaller market area called the Apple Market, with antiques sold on Monday and crafts for sale from Tuesday through Saturday. All of these stalls are good for browsing, especially if you have no time to visit London's other outdoor markets.

LEADENHALL MARKET
Leadenhall Street, EC3
Underground Station: Bank or Monument
Hours: Monday through Friday from 7 a.m. to 4 p.m.

This meat, poultry, and fish market is located in a Victorian covered shopping arcade not far from London's business district known as The City. Workers stop off to buy their evening meal.

LEATHER LANE
Leather Lane, EC1
Underground Station: Chancery Lane
Hours: Monday through Friday from noon to 2 p.m.

In the heart of Holborn and The City, this lunchtime market attracts office workers from the vicinity, who stroll through during their lunch breaks. For sale are fruits, vegetables, dried and fresh flowers, sweatshirts, toilet paper, shampoo, handbags, shoes, jewelry, towels, stockings, underwear, bathing suits, and household goods.

NEW CALEDONIAN MARKET
Bermondsey Square, at the junction of Long Lane, Bermondsey Street,
   and Tower Bridge Road, SE1
Underground Station: London Bridge
Hours: Friday only, from 7 a.m. to noon

Also known as **Bermondsey Market**, this market draws antique dealers from around the world, who come here to buy antiques and curios from individual stallholders. It used to be that serious buyers arrived around 3 a.m., scouring the market with flashlights. Now, however, law dictates that bargaining can't start until 7 a.m. At any rate, get there as soon as possible if you're after real bargains. You'll find hundreds of stalls set up in Bermondsey Square, selling silver, glass,

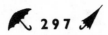
china, dolls, clocks, cutlery, jewelry, some furniture, walking sticks, and Victorian bric-a-brac. Nearby is **Bermondsey Antique Market**, a covered market selling more of the same.

NEW COVENT GARDEN MARKET
Nine Elms Lane, SW8
Underground Station: *Vauxhall*
Hours: *Monday through Friday from 4 to 11 a.m.*

This is where London's main fruit, vegetable, and flower market moved to after leaving the heart of the city at Covent Garden. It doesn't have quite the same atmosphere in its new home, but it sells the same kind of produce wholesale, which means that you have to buy in bulk if you're interested in anything.

PETTICOAT LANE
Middlesex Street, E1, stretching between the Liverpool and Aldgate
*   underground stations*
Hours: *Sunday only, from 9 a.m. to 2 p.m.*

This is one of London's most famous outdoor flea markets and can get quite crowded indeed. It draws some of the most talented street hawkers I've seen anywhere, men who can attract great crowds on the strength of their witty spiels. I saw one man who insisted his gadget encompassed ten tools in one, performing as scissors, a knife sharpener, wire stripper, glass cutter, and more— all for only £5. Another man set up a display of jewelry on a wooden crate, talking up a storm and selling combinations of necklaces, rings, and bracelets for around £2.

Petticoat Lane market stretches the length of Middlesex Street, radiating out into side streets along the way. You won't find any antiques for sale, but there are stalls selling every imaginable household item, along with clothing and accessories. There are bras, brass, ties, watches, shoes, kitchen gadgets, handbags, sweaters, coats, towels, leather jackets, hats, and a jumble of odds and ends. It's a market for common people, those who are looking for bargains in polyester pants or the plastic cheese-and-vegetable grater. For tourists, it's a great place to absorb some local color and is a fun way to spend a fine Sunday morning.

PICCADILLY MARKET
Forecourt of St. James's Church, Piccadilly, W1
Underground Station: *Piccadilly Circus*
Hours: *Friday and Saturday from 10 a.m. to 6 p.m.*

A small outdoor market with crafts of high quality (good hand-knit sweaters), some antiques, and bric-a-brac. It's convenient if you're shopping in the fashionable boutiques of the West End or Jermyn Street.

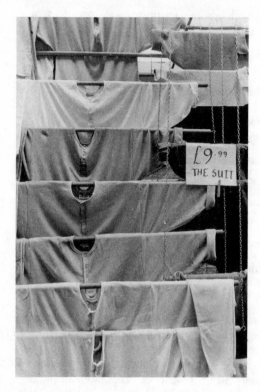

**Window-dressing on
Petticoat Lane**

PORTOBELLO ROAD
Portobello Road, W11
Underground Station: *Notting Hill Gate or Ladbroke Grove*
Hours: *Saturday from 6 a.m. to 5 p.m.*

Despite the claim by some people that Portobello has declined so much into a tourist trap that it's highly overrated, I am of the opinion that Portobello Road remains one of London's best markets and should be high on any visitor's list. There's so much variety and the market itself undergoes so much transformation as you walk its length that it makes for a fascinating day of entertainment. Beginning as an antique market, Portobello then changes into a fruit-and-vegetable market and subsequently dissolves into a chaos of punk and reggae.

Although many of the shops as well as the fruit and vegetable stalls are in operation throughout the week, the best day to come is on Saturday, when antique dealers have also set out their wares. I suggest you start your day from the Notting Hill Gate station, where signs will point you in the right direction. The market itself begins on Portobello Road just past a small street called Chepstow Villas. Here you'll find yourself surrounded by stalls, tables, and indoor arcades, with so much to look at you can't possibly take it all in. There are silver-plated

**Is nothing sacred even to
an East End pigeon?**

English toast holders for around £4, pocket watches, button hooks, pipes, sugar
bowls, canes, and cutlery. In **Roger's Antique Galleries** at 65 Portobello Road I
saw two Wedgwood candlestick holders dating from around 1810 for £148, and a
set of six Victorian knives and forks with mother-of-pearl handles for £65.

Past Elgin Crescent, the market turns into an area of fruits and vegetables.
You'll also notice a distinct West Indies atmosphere, with shops selling ethnic
goods alongside punk fashion. It's a strange combination, this meeting place of
dreadlocks and purple-dyed hair, and is as representative of London today as the
cockney.

Continuing on Portobello Road, you'll soon come to a traffic overpass, which
has an interesting arcade underneath it known as **Portobello Green**. Each of the
small boutiques here sells handmade crafts, including jewelry, glass, and
clothing. At unit 26 is the shop of Kirsten Woodward, a young and creative hat
designer whose work appears often in fashion magazines. Around Portobello
Green are more outdoor stalls selling Victoriana, some art deco, clothing,
crafts, and bric-a-brac. Incidentally, the stalls here are also open on Friday when
a completely different group of antique and curio dealers set up their goods.
From here it's just a short walk to Ladbroke Grove station.

A spread at the Portobello Market

MODEL SOLDIERS

The shops listed here carry collector's model soldiers, some of which contain lead and are unsuitable for children. Although these shops also carry new toy soldiers that are safe for children, shops such as **Hamleys**, listed in the "Toy" section, carry a wider range of inexpensive toy soldiers.

HUMMEL
16–17 Burlington Arcade, W1 (tel. 493-7164)
Underground Station: Green Park or Piccadilly Circus
Hours: Monday through Friday from 9 a.m. to 5:30 p.m.; on Saturday to 4:30 p.m.
Credit Cards: AE, DC, MC, V

In addition to its Ann Parker Dolls, antique dolls, model cars, Beatrix Potter figurines, Hummel figures, and novelties, this souvenir shop also stocks miniature soldiers, especialy 1950s "old Britains" made in lead. A set of four 12th Royal Lancers dating from 1956 costs £110. There are also new miniature soldiers made of white metal that are destined to be tomorrow's collectibles and cost from £6 for a single piece.

UNDER TWO FLAGS
4 St. Christopher's Pl., W1 (tel. 935-6934)
Underground Station: Bond Street

Hours: *Monday through Saturday from 10 a.m. to 5 p.m.*
Credit Cards: *None*

Easily overlooked among all the fashion boutiques on St. Christopher's Place, this small shop specializes in model lead soldiers. Included are "old Britains" which are priced at £88 a set, hand-painted models sold individually, military books and prints, and some toy soldiers suitable for children. They also have kits for constructing and painting your own model soldiers, which begin at £4.35.

MUSEUM SHOPS

A museum shop is good for specialist books and related items that pertain to that museum's displays. Thus the London Transport Museum is a good place to look for books on public transportation methods in olden days, while the British Museum has everything from books on the Elgin Marbles to reproduction Byzantine jewelry.

THE BRITISH MUSEUM SHOP
The British Museum, Great Russell Street, WC1 (tel. 636-1555)
Underground Station: *Tottenham Court Road or Holborn*
Hours: *Monday through Saturday from 10 a.m. to 4:45 p.m., on Sunday from 2:30 to 5:45 p.m.*
Credit Cards: *AE, MC, V*

On guard at Hamley's, the largest toy shop in the world

The British Museum Shop stocks a wide range of books, postcards, posters, and reproduction pieces. A reproduction of an 18th-century enamel box, for example, sells for £57, while an imitation medieval lover's brooch is £19.25. You can even buy a reduced-size replica of the Rosetta Stone for £27.50 or a replica of a bronze Egyptian cat for £70. Altogether there are more than 100 objects and jewelry modeled from treasures in the British Museum, including idols, ancient jewelry pieces, platters, and busts.

The British Museum is also a prolific publisher of books, on subjects ranging from coins and medals to Egyptian, Oriental, Greek, Roman, and prehistoric antiquities. You can purchase books on Egyptian mummies, prehistoric Britain, arts and architecture, and children's books. Catalogs on both publications and museum replicas are available for 50 pence.

LONDON TRANSPORT MUSEUM SHOP
London Transport Museum, Covent Garden, WC2 (tel. 379-6344)
Underground Station: Covent Garden
Hours: Daily from 10 a.m. to 5:45 p.m.
Credit Cards: MC, V

In the corner of the Covent Garden piazza this museum chronicles the history of London's public transportation system and contains a gift shop selling books, posters, and memorabilia. Books include *100 Years of British Electric Tramways* for £10.95, *London's Underground* for £8.95, and *The Golden Jubilee Book* for £6.95 which covers London's buses and underground from 1933 to 1983. There are also model double-decker buses selling for less than a pound, T-shirts, and postcards.

MUSEUM OF MANKIND SHOP
Museum of Mankind, Burlington Gardens, W1 (tel. 437-2224)
Underground Station: Green Park or Piccadilly Circus
Hours: Monday through Saturday from 10:30 a.m. to 12:30 p.m. and 1:30
**   to 4:30 p.m., on Sunday from 3 to 5:45 p.m.**
Credit Cards: AE, MC, V

This small shop carries books relating to peoples and tribes around the world, as well as some postcards and a changing selection of ethnic crafts and jewelry.

THE NATIONAL GALLERY SHOP
The National Gallery, Trafalgar Square, WC2 (tel. 839-3321)
Underground Station: Charing Cross
Hours: Monday through Saturday from 10 a.m. to 5:30 p.m., on Sunday
**   from 2 to 5:30 p.m.**
Credit Cards: MC, V

Since the National Gallery is a museum of European paintings from the 13th to 20th centuries, it probably comes as no surprise to discover that its shop carries color slides, prints, posters, calendars, and bookmarks, all of which show

reproductions of the museum's famous paintings. There are also books relating to the arts and individual artists. Posters start at £7. I'm particularly fond of the museum's Christmas cards, with pictures taken from collections in both the National Gallery and the Tate Gallery. A package of six greeting cards starts at £1.30. You can also have cards specially made with your own greeting and address if you order before December. These start at a cost of £19 for a set of 25.

THE NATIONAL PORTRAIT GALLERY SHOP
2 St. Martin's Pl., WC2 (tel. 930-1552)
Underground Station: Leicester Square
Hours: Monday through Saturday from 10 a.m. to 5 p.m., on Saturday
to 6 p.m., on Sunday 2 to 6 p.m.
Credit Cards: MC, V

This shop sells postcards and posters of famous British men and women, including Anne Boleyn, Lord Byron, Winston Churchill, Charles Dickens, Henry VIII, William Shakespeare, and Virginia Woolf. Posters start at less than a pound. There are also books relating to portraits, such as *Royal Faces*, with portraits of Great Britain's kings and queens through 900 years of history.

THE TATE GALLERY SHOP
Tate Gallery, Millbank, SW1 (tel. 821-1313)
Underground Station: Pimlico
Hours: Monday through Saturday from 10 a.m. to 5:30 p.m., on Sunday
from 2 to 5:30 p.m.
Credit Cards: MC, V

The Tate Gallery is an excellent museum, with works by Picasso, Kandinsky, Miró, Dali, Seurat, Paul Klee, Henri Matisse, Chagall, and such great British artists as George Stubbs and J. M. W. Turner. The gift shop offers reproductions of famous works—posters start at £4.10 and prints at £8.20—plus jigsaw puzzles of famous paintings, calendars, postcards, and books on art and artists.

THE UPSTAIRS GALLERY
Royal Academy of Arts, Burlington House (third floor), Piccadilly,
W1 (tel. 734-7763)
Underground Station: Piccadilly Circus or Green Park
Hours: Monday through Friday from 10 a.m. to 6 p.m., on Saturday
from 11 a.m. to 5 p.m.
Credit Cards: AE, DC, MC, V

This retail gallery sells original lithographs, etchings, oil paintings, water-colors, pen-and-ink drawings, pastels, and some sculpture, all by British contemporary artists or foreign artists living in Britain. Prices are very reasonable, starting at £33 for a limited-edition etching or lithograph. More than 200 artists are represented, including Bernard Dunstan, Elisabeth Frink, Paul Hogarth, John Hoyland, and John Piper.

THE VICTORIA AND ALBERT MUSEUM SHOP
Victoria and Albert Museum, corner of Cromwell and Exhibition Roads,
SW7 (tel. 589-6371)
Underground Station: South Kensington
Hours: Monday through Thursday and Saturday from 10 a.m. to 5:30
p.m., on Sunday from 2:30 to 5:30 p.m.; closed Friday
Credit Cards: AE, MC, V

The Victoria and Albert is one of the world's outstanding museums, with wonderful collections of fine and applied arts from around the world. In the museum shop books mirror the collections on a wide range of subjects, from dolls to English barometers, art, and courtly jewels. There are books on paintings and watercolor, photography, textiles, sculpture, ceramics, architecture, and various countries and their arts.

In a small corner of the shop is the Crafts Council Shop (tel. 589-5070), sponsored by the Crafts Council and featuring crafts by English artists. The crafts shop is so small it makes you wish for more, but included are generally ceramics, glass art, and jewelry. Earrings start at less than £10.

MUSIC BOXES

Music boxes were the rage in the 19th century and were based on a very simple principle. A steel comb, with teeth tuned to the scale in a variety of ways, was plucked by pins projecting from a revolving cylinder. Today these music boxes are highly prized and do not come cheaply. In addition to the store listed below, **Bushe Antiques**, listed in the "Clocks" section, carries a stock of Swiss music boxes starting at £2,200.

KEITH HARDING
93 Hornsey Rd., N7 (tel. 607-6181)
Underground Station: Holloway Road
Hours: Monday through Friday from 9 a.m. to 6 p.m.
Credit Cards: AE, DC, MC, V

This interesting shop sells a unique range of antique clocks and music boxes, some of which deserve homes in museums. Most of the music boxes were made in Switzerland and date from around 1800, with a starting price of £1,100. There are also new music boxes beginning at a modest £16.50.

MUSIC STORES

The stores listed below sell a wide range of contemporary instruments and sheet music. If you're looking for antique musical instruments, check with antique stores. **Pelham Galleries**, listed under "Antiques," for example,

usually has at least one or two early musical instruments on hand, such as the 18th-century English harpsichord I saw selling for £24,000.

If you're interested in bagpipes, refer to **Bill Lewington**, listed under "Bagpipes," a shop that also boasts the largest stock of woodwinds and brass instruments in town.

CHAPPELL
50 New Bond St., WI (tel. 491-2777)
Underground Station: Bond Street
Hours: Monday through Friday from 9:30 a.m. to 6 p.m., on Saturday to 5 p.m.
Credit Cards: AE, DC, MC, V

A Bond Street establishment since 1811, Chappell has an excellent selection of sheet music and books on everything from classical to pop and jazz. Its biggest department is the piano section of grands and uprights, but it also sells electronic keyboards, guitars, violins, brass and percussion instruments, and woodwinds.

FD & H MUSIC
138–149 Charing Cross Rd., WC2 (tel. 836-4766)
Underground Station: Leicester Square or Tottenham Court Road
Hours: Monday through Friday from 9:30 a.m. to 6 p.m, on Saturday to 5 p.m.
Credit Cards: AE, DC, MC, V

This shop stocks a comprehensive supply of musical instruments, including guitars, brass, woodwinds, violins, cellos, drums, and percussion, as well as such accessories as amplifiers and home recording equipment. Established in 1895, it also claims to have the largest selection of sheet music and books in London. Electric guitars start at £97, while acoustic guitars start at £55. In stock are Gibson, Fender, and other well-known names in guitars.

NAUTICAL OBJECTS

CAPTAIN O. M. WATTS
Albemarle St., WI (tel. 493-4633)
Underground Station: Green Park
Hours: Monday through Friday from 9 a.m. to 6 p.m. (on Thursday to 7 p.m.), on Saturday to 5 p.m.
Credit Cards: AE, DC, MC, V

Opened in 1928, this shop was founded by O. M. Watts upon his retirement from the merchant navy. Supplying "Everything for the Yachtsman and his Yacht," the store stocks deck gear such as ladders and

anchors, yacht and dinghy fittings, a wide range of instruments from distress beacons to radars, safety equipment, cabin accessories such as sinks and toilets, electrical supplies such as lights and horns, pumps, sailing clothing, and books. One-piece oilskins start at £32 and to up to £108.95 for those with hoods and lining. An extensive catalog from which you can order by mail from the United States is available for £2.

PENS AND PENCILS

In addition to these tiny shops specializing in pens and pencils, other places to look for writing supplies include stationery shops, department stores, and gift shops.

THE PEN SHOP
27 Burlington Arcade, W1 (tel. 493-9021)
Underground Station: Green Park or Piccadilly Circus
Hours: Monday through Friday from 9:30 a.m. to 5:30 p.m., on Saturday to 4:30 p.m.
Credit Cards: AE, V

This shop is so tiny it's easy to overlook among all the clothing shops in Burlington Arcade. It carries pens ranging in price from £22 to more than £1,000, including Yves Saint Laurent, Mont Blanc, Dunhill, Shaeffer, Elysée, and Parker.

PENCRAFT
119 Regent St., W1 (tel. 734-4928)
Underground Station: Piccadilly Circus
Hours: Monday through Friday from 9 a.m. to 5:30 p.m., on Saturday from 10 a.m. to 5 p.m.
Credit Cards: AE, DC, MC, V

Parker, Shaeffer, Elysée, Mont Blanc, Cross, Waterman, and Lamy are some of the brands sold here. Most ballpoint pens range from £6.50 to £220. Fountain pens start at £6.50 but can go all the way up to £5,500 for those in solid gold.

PHILIP POOLE & CO.
182 Drury Lane, WC2 (tel. 405-7097)
Underground Station: Covent Garden or Holborn
Hours: Monday through Friday from 10 a.m. to 5 p.m., on Saturday from 11 a.m. to 3 p.m.
Credit Cards: None

If you like nibs and ink, you'll find plenty to delight in in this small, quaint shop tucked along a side street in Covent Garden. Hundreds of small, wooden

drawers contain all kinds of nibs. There are even antique nibs for collectors: a box of 50 costs only £3.80. Prices begin at £1 for a wooden penholder and nib, and there are also plenty of calligraphy pens. Accessories include sealing wax, calligraphy paper, and all kinds of inks, including drawing ink, calligraphy ink, ink for dip pens, quick-drying inks, and ink for fountain pens in lots of different colors.

PERFUME

Chemist shops and department stores carry the usual big names in perfume. **Selfridges**, for example, stocks what may well be the most extensive range of perfumes in the world. If you're on the lookout for more unusual English fragrances, the shops listed below are among the best.

FLORIS
89 Jermyn St., SWI (tel. 930-2885)
Underground Station: *Green Park or Piccadilly Circus*
Hours: *Monday through Friday from 9:30 a.m. to 5:30 p.m., on Saturday to 4 p.m.*
Credit Cards: *AE, DC, MC, V*

Established on Jermyn Street in 1730, Floris is a family business that has seen seven generations produce and sell its famous English scents. Holding royal warrants as perfumers to the Queen and as manufacturers of toilet preparations to the Prince of Wales, this elegant shop has selections for both men and women—scents bearing such names as Sandalwood, Wild Hyacinth, No. 89 for Men, Rose Geranium, Edwardian Bouquet, and English Violet. It also stocks both new and antique accessories, including scent bottles, porcelain pillboxes, Lalique glass, manicure sets, and cloisonné vases. Also in stock is soap, bath essence, bath foam, shower gel, bath salt, and talcum powder, all carrying Floris's famous scents.

GEO. F. TRUMPER
20 Jermyn St., SWI (tel. 734-1370)
Underground Station: *Piccadilly Circus*
Hours: *Monday through Saturday from 9 a.m. to 6 p.m.*
Credit Cards: *AE, DC, MC, V*

Established in 1875 on Curzon Street, this men's perfumer has an additional shop in St. James's with a delightful stock of perfumes and shaving accessories. Old favorites in the fragrance department include Wellington, Marlborough, Curzon, and West Indian Limes, and there are also soaps, shampoos, and hair dressings. There's a wide selection of men's shaving sets, which start at about £44 and go all the way to £600 and more for those in ivory or gold.

Luxury soaps, scents, and
toiletries in the luscious
surroundings at Floris

PENHALIGON'S

41 Wellington St., Covent Garden, WC2 (tel. 836-2150)
Underground Station: Covent Garden
Hours: Monday through Friday from 10 a.m. to 6 p.m., on Saturday to 5
   p.m.
Credit Cards: AE, DC, MC, V

Penhaligon's scents are made by hand according to a formula produced by
William Penhaligon, who first opened shop back in 1841 as a barber. Penhaligon's main shop in Covent Garden is exceptionally and conspicuously elegant,
exuding a drawing-room atmosphere complete with wood-paneled walls and
glass-fronted cabinets. In addition to its handmade scents, toilet waters, and
soaps for both men and women, it also sells antique scent bottles, Victorian
silver vinaigrettes and boxes, silver hand mirrors, manicure sets, and dressing
cases. Penhaligon's oldest scent is its Hammam Bouquet, which costs £41.25 for
30 milliliters of its extract. Two other shops are located in the West End at 20A
Brook St. (tel. 493-0002) and 55 Burlington Arcade (tel. 629-1416).

YARDLEY

33 Old Bond St., W1 (tel. 629-9341)
Underground Station: Green Park or Piccadilly Circus
Hours: Monday through Friday from 9 a.m. to 5:30 p.m.
Credit Cards: AE

A traditional English perfumery established in London in 1770, Yardley possesses two royal warrants and is famous throughout the world for its fragrances and soaps. One of its most popular products is its English Lavender, starting at £3.30. Other good gift items include the Yardley Original After Shave and wooden shaving bowls.

PEWTER

Contemporary English tankards and other pewter objects are sold in a number of gift shops, including **Naturally British** and **The Little Gallery**, both listed under "Gifts." Antique pewter is often available in antique shops selling decorative items as well as in the shop described below.

ROBIN MARTIN
44 Ledbury Rd., W11 (tel. 727-1301)
Underground Station: *Notting Hill Gate*
Hours: *Monday through Friday from 10 a.m. to 6 p.m. (sometimes closed during lunch hour), on Saturday to 1 p.m.*
Credit Cards: *None*

Antique continental and English pewter dating from the 17th century to the Victorian period is sold here, including candlesticks, plates, and beer mugs. Prices start at £27.50 for a half-pint beer mug.

Yardley is synonymous with London

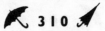
PHARMACIES

Pharmacies in England are called "chemists," and they usually stock a wide range of toiletries, cosmetics, and accessories in addition to pharmaceuticals. If you need a prescription filled late at night, there are chemists that take turns staying open later than usual, though none stays open 24 hours. The local police station can tell you which chemist is scheduled to stay open late.

BOOTS
182 Regent St., W1 (tel. 734-4934)
Underground Station: Oxford Circus or Piccadilly Circus
Hours: Monday through Saturday from 9 a.m. to 5:30 p.m. (on Thursday to 6:30 p.m.)
Credit Cards: AE, MC, V

Boots is one of England's best-known chain stores of chemists, with more than 90 locations in London alone. This shop on Regent Street is one of the largest, with departments in home decor, stationery, housewares, gardening, and even home beer brewing in addition to its cosmetics, perfumes, and toiletries. Along with such names as Chanel, Givenchy, Yardley, and Christian Dior, Boots carries its own small line of products that make great inexpensive gifts for folks back home. A columbine-and-almond-oil face mask in a pretty jar costs £2, while soaps made of natural ingredients like oatmeal and lavender start at £1.20.

Other Boots are found at 151 Oxford St. (tel. 734-4646), 127A Kensington High St. (tel. 937-9533), 122B King's Rd. (tel. 589-0955), 72 Brompton Rd. (tel. 589-6557), and 44 Piccadilly Circus (tel. 734-6126).

D. R. HARRIS & CO. LTD.
29 St. James's St., SW1 (tel. 930-3915 and 930-8753)
Underground Station: Green Park
Hours: Monday through Friday from 8:30 a.m. to 6 p.m., on Saturday from 9:30 a.m. to 5:30 p.m.
Credit Cards: AE, MC, V

This delightful Old World chemist shop stocks a wide range of concoctions, mixtures, and potions you'd never find in pharmacy shops back home. Established in 1790, this family-run chemist is one of London's oldest and still produces most of its own products. Antique cabinets line the wall, along with colored antique bottles. How about trying some of the shop's own The Original Pick-Me-Up, a 130-year-old formula guaranteed to remedy hangovers and lack of energy. You can order it by the glass for £1. If you want to make your eyes sparkle, buy some crystal eye drops, popular among film stars and costing £4.25. Other products include a cucumber-and-rose cleansing cream, almond-oil

soaps, the shop's own cough medicine, bath oils, shampoos, toilet waters, and powders.

JOHN BELL & CROYDON
54 Wigmore St., WI (tel. 935-0055 and 935-5555)
Underground Station: Bond Street
**Hours: Monday through Friday from 9 a.m. to 6 p.m., on Saturday to I
p.m.**
Credit Cards: AE, DC, MC, V

This is the place to come for serious surgical equipment, accessories, and supplies for invalids. Specialists are on hand to advise on everything from orthopedic beds to scales and bed pans. The front of the store is devoted to more ordinary products such as cosmetics, sole inserts for tired feet, health foods, and vitamins.

NEALS YARD APOTHECARY
2 Neals Yard, Covent Garden, WC2 (tel. 379-7222), off Shorts Gardens
Underground Station: Covent Garden
**Hours: Monday through Friday from 10 a.m. to 6 p.m. (on Wednesday to
4:30 p.m.), on Saturday to 5:30 p.m., on Sunday from 11 a.m. to 4
p.m.**
Credit Cards: None

A 130-year-old remedy
for hangovers from
D. R. Harris & Co. Ltd.

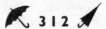

**Neals Yard Apothecary:
Alternative medicines and
natural cosmetics in an
Old World setting**

Opened in the early '80s, this shop dispenses alternative medicines and natural cosmetics free of chemicals, additives, and preservatives. If you have an ailment and wonder which natural ingredients might help, the staff is happy to advise. Basil, for example, is considered useful in treating anxiety, depression, or insomnia, while anis seed can be used against nervous digestion, nausea, and dizzy spells. Wooden shelves contain rows of jars filled with more than 100 different kinds of roots, herbs, leaves, and spices, including sandalwood chips, nettles, plantain, and eucalyptus. Homeopathic remedies are available for about £1.50 for 50 tablets, and the shop carries Bach's flower remedies. The apothecary also produces its own line of shampoos, oils, cleansers, creams, and conditioners. If you are in need of such treatment as acupuncture, massage, aromatherapy, biodynamic therapy, biofeedback, herbalism, shiatsu, or reflexology, Neal's also has "therapy rooms" nearby which offer the services of qualified and experienced therapists.

UNDERWOODS

**75 Queensway, W2 (tel. 229-9266)
Underground Station: Bayswater
Hours: Daily from 9 a.m. to 10 p.m.
Credit Cards: AE, MC, V**

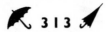
Underwoods is a chain chemist store and its location on Queensway is especially noteworthy for its long hours and Sunday openings. In addition to pharmaceuticals, it also stocks toiletries and cosmetics.

PORCELAIN

(See "China")

PIPES

Shops listed under "Tobacconists" also carry a range of pipes.

ASTLEYS
109A Jermyn St., SW1 (tel. 930-1687)
Underground Station: *Piccadilly Circus*
Hours: *Monday through Friday from 10 a.m., on Saturday from noon to 4 p.m.*
Credit Cards: *AE, DC, MC, V*

This tiny specialist shop deals in briar and meerschaum pipes, plus its own tobacco and cigars. Prices for briar pipes start at £20, while straight-grain handmade briar and block meerschaum pipes begin at £82. Be sure to take a look at the display case of antique English clay pipes dating from about 1590 and retrieved from various spots around London, including the River Thames.

PORTRAIT MINIATURES

LIMNER ANTIQUES
Bond Street Antique Centre, 124 New Bond St., W1 (tel. 629-5314)
Underground Station: *Bond Street*
Hours: *Monday through Friday from 9:30 a.m. to 5:45 p.m., on Saturday from 10 a.m. to 4 p.m.*
Credit Cards: *None*

This stall in the Bond Street Antique Centre specializes in portrait miniatures and usually has about 150 on hand. Most miniatures are British and are all watercolor on ivory, dating from the 17th to the 19th century. Prices begin at £275.

MAURICE ASPREY
41 Duke St., St. James's SW1 (tel. 930-3921)

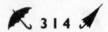
Underground Station: Green Park
Hours: *Monday through Friday from 9:30 a.m. to 5:30 p.m.*
Credit Cards: *AE, DC, MC, V*

In addition to its antique silver, objects of vertu, and jewelry, this shop also sells English portrait miniatures dating from 1730. The stock usually numbers about 25 miniatures, and prices begin at £770.

SIMEON
19 Burlington Arcade, WI (tel. 493-3353)
Underground Station: Green Park or Piccadilly
Hours: *Monday through Friday from 9:45 a.m. to 4:45 p.m., on Saturday to 12:45 p.m.*
Credit Cards: *AE, DC, MC, V*

This antique shop generally has about 45 miniatures at any given time, including those painted on tortoiseshell boxes as well as pendants. Most date from the 1700s to the early 1800s, with prices starting at £165. The shop also stocks Japanese netsuke, Chinese snuff bottles, and antique period jewelry.

POSTERS AND POSTCARDS

London's many **museums** are excellent sources for posters and postcards on a variety of subjects. The Tate Gallery, for example, stocks posters, prints, and postcards taken from paintings by famous contemporary artists, while the London Transport Museum has posters of London's old trams and buses.

If you're looking for contemporary posters of film stars and rock musicians, check with the **Vintage Magazine Shop**, listed under "Magazines." It also stocks Italian posters and original movie posters dating from the 1930s. David Drummond's **Pleasures of Past Times**, described under "Books," carries posters, playbills, and picture postcards relating to the performing arts.

THE POSTER SHOP
I Chalk Farm Rd., NWI (tel. 267-6985)
Underground Station: Camden Town or Chalk Farm
Hours: *Tuesday through Friday from 10 a.m. to 6 p.m., on Saturday and Sunday from 10:30 a.m. to 6 :30 p.m.*
Credit Cards: *MC, V*

Posters here range from £1 to £100 with a large selection to choose from. Following the current craze in exhibition posters, much of its stock consists of posters announcing exhibitions in England, Europe, and the United States, including photography exhibitions. Another Poster Shop, in Covent Garden at 28 James St. (tel. 240-2526), has a slightly smaller stock.

POTTERY

Contemporary pottery can be found in shops listed under "Crafts," while antique pottery and porcelain is available in shops found in the "China" section.

PRINTS

You don't have to spend a lot of money for old prints in London. For less than £10 you can pick up prints of flowers, birds, scenes of London, or political cartoons taken from *Vanity Fair*. In addition to shops listed here, other stores in London carrying old prints include **Alan Brett** and **Sotherans**, listed under "Books," and **Cartographia**, the **Map House**, and **O'Shea Gallery**, described under "Maps."

Contemporary prints, including etchings, lithography, and engravings, are handled in the "Art Galleries" section of this book. Of particular note are **Christie's Contemporary Art** and **Marlborough Graphics Gallery**. Another good place to look for inexpensive lithographs and etchings by contemporary British artists is the **Upstairs Gallery**, listed under "Museum Shops."

THE BEAUFORT GALLERY

313 King's Rd., SW3 (tel. 351-0950)
Underground Station: *Sloane Square*
Hours: *Monday through Saturday from 10 a.m. to 6 p.m.*
Credit Cards: AE, DC, MC, V

This small gallery is located in the basement underneath Chelsea Rare Books. It stocks prints on such subjects as natural history, animals, birds, and flowers, and is especially strong on prints of London scenes. Prices for most prints range from £6.50 to £35. The gallery also sells watercolors dating from the 1800s; most average £85 and cover botanical or landscape subjects.

CLIVE A. BURDEN

13 Cecil Court, WC2 (tel. 836-2177)
Underground Station: *Leicester Square*
Hours: *Monday through Friday from 10:30 a.m. to 5:30 p.m.*
Credit Cards: AE, V

This shop specializes in antique prints that are sold to interior decorators. In stock are natural-history prints dating from 1614 to 1900, maps from around the world, and scenes of country views and London. Prices start at £4 for a small botanical print. The shop also carries *Vanity Fair* caricatures of people from various walks of life, including artists, lawyers, and hunting enthusiasts. If

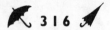
you're looking for an inexpensive gift for a friend or relative who's a doctor, lawyer, or sports fan, these begin at £6.50.

CRADDOCK & BARNARD
32 Museum St., WCI (tel. 636-3937)
Underground Station: Tottenham Court Road or Holborn
Hours: Monday through Friday from 9:30 a.m. to 5:30 p.m.
Credit Cards: None

This tiny gallery not far from the British Museum specializes in 15th- to 20th-century original etchings and engravings, with prices starting at £10. It even carries some Albrecht Dürer engravings and some book impressions by German artist Käthe Kollwitz and etchings by James McNeill Whistler.

THE PRINT ROOM
37 Museum St., WCI (tel. 430-0159)
Underground Station: Tottenham Court Road or Holborn
Hours: Monday through Friday from 10 a.m. to 6 p.m., on Saturday to 4 p.m.
Credit Cards: MC, V

Also located close to the British Museum, the Print Room sells antique English and European prints dating from 1580 to 1870, with subjects ranging from natural history to old scenes of London. A small print of flowers can cost as little as £10.

THE WITCH BALL
2 Cecil Court, WC2 (tel. 836-2922)
Underground Station: Leicester Square
Hours: Monday through Saturday from 10 a.m. to 6 p.m.
Credit Cards: AE, DC, MC, V

Specializing in antique engravings of theatrical interest, this shop covers the range of prints on subjects from music and opera to ballet, dance, and theater. Prices range from £6 to £2,200, though most prints average about £100.

RAINGEAR

London has a reputation for being foggy, soggy, and damp, and the English have learned bravely how to cope with even the foulest of weather. Rare is the day that they venture forth without their umbrellas and their waterproof overcoats, and they demand unfailing excellence from both. If you're looking for quality rainwear, you can hardly do better than London. The two most famous names in raincoats are **Burberrys** and **Aquascu-**

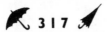
tum. Aquascutum kept soldiers dry during both World Wars, and both produce a wide range of coats in varying prices. Refer to the "Clothing" section for more information on both these stores. If you're on the lookout for heavy-duty rainwear that can withstand the fury of sea squalls, **Captain O. M. Watts**, listed under "Nautical Objects," carries a line of oilskins for deck hands. Waterproof hunting wear is available in several of the shops described in the "Guns" section of this book. Umbrellas are handled in their own section near the end of this chapter.

RECORDS AND CASSETTES

RARE

JAMES H. CRAWLEY
(tel. 807-7760)

This is not a shop but rather a mail-order business for rare and unusual records from the first half of the 20th century. The majority of the records are English and the collection includes a huge selection in 78s for everything from Crosby to Caruso. It costs £5 to be put on the catalog mailing list for one year. Catalogs are issued every two months listing about 400 to 500 largely deleted classical LPs and a couple of thousand 78s. Serious collectors should telephone for more information.

CONTEMPORARY

THE HMV SHOP
363 Oxford St., W1 (tel. 629-1240)
Underground Station: Bond Street
Hours: Monday through Friday from 9:30 a.m. to 6:30 p.m. (on Thursday to 8 p.m.), on Saturday to 6 p.m.
Credit Cards: AE, DC, MC, V

This shop is soon to be overshadowed by a new HMV opening nearby at 150 Oxford St., which will probably be in business by the time you read this. Competition among mega-record stores in London is fierce, with company after company opening bigger and bigger stores. At any rate, HMV has some of the lowest prices, with most records under £6.50. Four floors here offer everything from classical to jazz to pop, along with imports from other countries. Cassettes range from £4.40 to £7.10 and the selection includes music from South America, the Middle East, India, and Europe. Other departments sell compact discs, videos, and books on musicians.

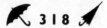
TOWER RECORDS
Piccadilly Circus, W1 (tel. 439-2500)
Underground Station: Piccadilly Circus
*Hours: Monday through Saturday from 9 a.m. to midnight, on Sunday to
    11 p.m.*
Credit Cards: AE, MC, V

This huge record store opened on Piccadilly Circus in 1986 with four floors of records, cassettes, and videos. The classical music section is the strongest, but the store covers almost all spectrums of the music industry, including the latest releases from around the world. Another shop is located at 62–64 Kensington High St. (tel. 938-3511).

VIRGIN MEGASTORE
14–16 Oxford St., W1 (tel. 631-1234)
Underground Station: Tottenham Court Road
Hours: Monday through Saturday from 10 a.m. to 9 p.m.
Credit Cards: AE, DC, MC, V

Virgin Megastore gets my vote as being one of the best record stores in town. Lighted signs make it easy to find the section you want and there are maps to guide you through the two large rooms. There are about 100,000 records and 40,000 cassettes in stock. The store has excellent rock and jazz selections, including works by obscure artists, and also carries sections on African music, reggae, gospel, country, musical soundtracks, soul, nostalgia, and easy listening.

The store is somewhat of a tourist attraction because of its life-size wax figures of such famous musicians as Prince, Rod Stewart, Elvis, Madonna, the Beatles, Michael Jackson, Frank Sinatra, and Dolly Parton. One section of the store sells postcards, posters, T-shirts, and books on musicians. As one employee told me, "I defy anyone to come in with £5 and not spend it."

RIDING GEAR

Horse riding, polo, and fox hunts have long been traditional pursuits of the English, and to serve the needs of the country gentry, very proper and very well-made riding gear has become a specialty of the British. Even cowpokes from Dodge City have heard of the English saddle.

In addition to the shops listed below, **Moss Bros.**, listed in the "Clothing" section, has a department devoted to riding gear and wear. If you want riding breeches and hunting coats custom-made to your measurements, **Bernard Weatherill Ltd.**, **J. Dedge & Sons**, and **Huntsman**, in the "Tailors" section, will undertake orders in riding wear.

GIDDENS
15D Clifford St., W1 (tel. 734-2788)

Underground Station: *Green Park or Piccadilly*
Hours: *Monday through Friday from 9 a.m. to 5:15 p.m., on Saturday from 10 a.m. to 1 p.m.*
Credit Cards: *AE, DC, MC, V*

Giddens is one of the most famous names in riding gear in the world. Since the Gidden family first opened shop in 1806, the company has produced saddles for mounted regiments, police, and royalty throughout the world, including the sultan of Oman. All saddles are made from top-quality hides, are padded with wool, and are built on conventional spring trees. There are saddles for jumping, polo, dressage, and hunting, in all different styles and colors. Prices for saddles range from about £330 for a Rex Stubben to £687 for a Stubben Imperator. The shop also stocks harnesses, bits, stirrups, whips, blankets, grooming accessories, riding hats and gloves, boots, riding wear, racing equipment, and more. Catalogs are available for £2 and mail orders from the United States are accepted.

These boots are made for riding at W & H Gidden, Ltd.

SWAINE, ADENEY, BRIGG & SONS LTD.

185 Piccadilly, W1 (tel. 734-4277)
Underground Station: *Piccadilly Circus or Green Park*
Hours: *Monday through Friday from 9 a.m. to 5:30 p.m., on Saturday from 9:30 a.m. to 5 p.m.*
Credit Cards: *AE, DC, MC, V*

Established in 1750, this prestigious shop caters to the country gentleman, supplying him with riding, polo, and hunting equipment and dressing him for

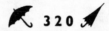
all country occasions. In its riding department are clothing, riding hats, whips, grooming supplies, saddles, and bits. The Chesterford general-purpose saddle is priced at £638, while a balding girth is priced at £41. The company also stocks riding wear for women.

RUGS AND TAPESTRIES

The manufacture of pile carpets in Europe first began in France at the beginning of the 17th century, but it wasn't until 1750 that the technique was introduced into England. At any rate, European carpets dating before 1840 are very rare today and are correspondingly very expensive.

Because they harmonize so well with antique English furniture, Oriental carpets have also always been popular items in British homes. They come in all shapes and sizes, from runners and prayer rugs to large carpets made especially for large European rooms. Very few are antique, and those that remain are too valuable to put on the floor. Most Oriental carpets fall into such categories as Turkish, Persian, Chinese, or Indian, and can be found in many of London's department stores. Liberty, for example, has an exceptional display of silk Persian rugs and tribal kilims. Department stores are also good sources for contemporary rugs, as are furniture stores.

BLACK ORIENTAL CARPETS
96 Portland Rd., W11 (tel. 727-2566)
Underground Station: Portland Road
Hours: Monday through Saturday from 11 a.m. to 6 p.m.
Credit Cards: None

Oriental carpets, embroideries, and brocades are sold in this shop, where rugs start at about £880. If that's too much for you, faithful reproduction carpets made using traditional Oriental weaving techniques are available for £165.

C. JOHN
70 South Audley St., W1 (tel. 493-5288)
Underground Station: Hyde Park Corner, Bond Street, or Marble Arch
Hours: Monday through Friday from 9:30 a.m. to 5 p.m.
Credit Cards: None

This shop specializes in handmade antique carpets from Russia, France, Persia, England, Turkey, and India, as well as tapestries from England, France, and Sweden. It also stocks some textiles. Carpets here begin at £550.

MAYORCAS
38 Jermyn St., SW1 (tel. 629-4195)
Underground Station: Piccadilly Circus or Green Park
Hours: Monday through Friday from 9:30 a.m. to 5:30 p.m., on Saturday

to noon
Credit Cards: None

Antique carpets from France, Holland, Germany, Belgium, and England are sold in this shop, along with cushions, needlework, textiles, and tapestries, including some rare Gothic tapestries. Cushions start at £137, while a framed needlework made in 1610 to cover a Bible is priced at £10,450. An Elizabethan embroidered carpet is priced at £13,750.

S. FRANSES

82 Jermyn St., SW1 (tel. 235-1888)
Underground Station: Piccadilly Circus or Green Park
Hours: Monday through Friday from 9 a.m. to 5:30 p.m., but it's best to make an appointment
Credit Cards: None

This exclusive shop does not cater to off-the-street trade but rather sells to serious collectors who do not flinch at the high prices for Middle Eastern carpets and European tapestries. Since the firm opened in 1909, it has supplied and advised European royalty, governments, museums, and other institutions. Its collection is one of the most extensive in Europe, with more than 500 pieces from almost every continent and period. Included are Eastern and Oriental carpets from the 16th to 20th centuries; early European carpets from England, Ireland, France, Spain, Russia, and Eastern Europe; and antique European tapestries from the 15th century onward. Also in stock are antique textiles and fabrics, decorative needlework, cushions, seat covers, and Aubusson and Savonnerie carpets.

SCOTCH

For those of you unfamiliar with the various kinds of scotch whiskies, malt whiskies are produced from malted barley and blended in onion-shaped pot stills, with each distillation being one charge of the still. Grain whiskies, on the other hand, are made from malted barley and maize and are produced by a continuous distillation process. Blended whiskies are a mixture of the two.

In addition to the shop listed below, check with **Fortnum & Mason**, **Selfridges**, and **Harrods** for selections of malt whiskies.

JOHN MILROY'S SOHO WINE MARKET

3 Greek St., W1 (tel. 437-0893)
Underground Station: Tottenham Court Road
Hours: Monday through Friday from 9 a.m. to 6 p.m., on Saturday from 9:30 a.m. to 5:30 p.m.
Credit Cards: AE, DC, MC, V

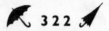
If you're looking for a malt, the original scotch whisky, this is one of the best places to start. Well-known for its single-malt whiskies, it has more than 150 malt whiskies in stock, including old and rare ones 15 and 25 years old. A 25-year-old Macallan is priced at £43.85, while a 25-year-old bottle of Glen Grant is £29.80. Also in stock are grain whiskies, Irish whiskies, blended whiskies, and wines.

SHEEPSKIN PRODUCTS

RICHARD DRAPER
121 Sydney St., SW3 (tel. 351-3527), off King's Road
Underground Station: *Sloane Square*
Hours: *Monday through Friday from 9 a.m. to 5 p.m. (open Saturday in the winter)*
Credit Cards: *MC, V*

All of Richard Draper's sheepskin products are produced in the company's factory in Glastonbury. Sheepskin boots start at £49, while coats begin at £119.

SHOES

There's certainly no lack of shoe stores in London, as a walk down any of the capital's major shopping streets will confirm. Chain stores especially predominate and are found wherever there's a concentration of shops, particularly along Oxford and Bond Street, King's Road, and Brompton Road. Department stores also have wide selections of well-known names in shoes. Clothing stores that carry good selections in shoes include **Hobbs** and **Charles Jourdan**, described in the "Clothing" section. **Lilly-whites,** also listed in the "Clothing" section, carries a wide range of sports shoes from Reebok to golf shoes.

CHAIN STORES

BALLY
116 New Bond St., W1 (tel. 491-7062)
Underground Station: *Bond Street*
Hours: *Monday through Saturday from 9:30 a.m. to 6 p.m. (on Thursday to 7 p.m.)*
Credit Cards: *AE, DC, MC, V*

Bally is a Swiss company internationally known for the good quality of its durable shoes. Styles are conservative and are excellent for working professionals, especially if you're a no-nonsense woman who insists on comfortable

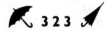
low pumps. Handmade women's shoes are around £100, but less expensive versions produced in England start at around £42.90. Men's shoes range from £60 to £110 and include classic oxfords and loafers.

Other Bally shops are found at 30 Old Bond St. (tel. 493-2250), 246 Oxford St. (tel. 629-6045), 260 Regent St. (tel. 734-2500), 152 Regent St. (tel. 434-1077), 9 Sloane St. (tel. 235-2582), 71–73 Brompton Rd. (tel. 589-9119), 92 King's Rd. (tel. 589-9084), and 127B Kensington High St. (tel. 937-8341).

BERTIE
15 The Market, Covent Garden, WC2 (tel. 836-9147)
Underground Station: Covent Garden
Hours: Daily from 9:30 a.m. to 8 p.m.
Credit Cards: AE, DC, MC, V

Inexpensive women's shoes in bright colors are sold here, designed more for fun and casual wear than for work. Shoes are produced in Italy and sold here starting at about £40. Other shops are located at 48 South Molton St. (tel. 629-9969), 8A Sloane St. (tel. 235-5116), 409 Oxford St. (tel. 629-5833), and 118 King's Rd. (tel. 584-9578).

KURT GEIGER
95 New Bond St., W1 (tel. 499-2707)
Underground Station: Bond Street
Hours: Monday through Saturday from 9:30 a.m. to 6 p.m. (on Thursday
**   to 7 p.m.)**
Credit Cards: AE, DC, MC, V

With concessions in such department stores as Selfridges, Harrods, Liberty, and Dickens & Jones, and with a second shop located at 49 New Bond St., Kurt Geiger is well known for its Italian-designed shoes. Included in the collection are shoes made by Mario Bologna, Pancaldi, Enzo of Roma, Andrea Carrano, Pollini, and Sergio Rossi; most styles are priced over £100 and range from classic to fantasy.

LILLEY & SKINNER
360 Oxford St., W1 (tel. 629-6381)
Underground Station: Bond Street
Hours: Monday through Saturday from 9 a.m. to 6 p.m. (on Thursday to
**   8 p.m.)**
Credit Cards: AE, DC, MC, V

This huge shop has a big selection from both inexpensive and casual footwear to more classical lines from Bally and Roland Cartier. Hard-to-find small and large size are carried, and there's also a children's section. Prices vary wildly, and you get what you pay for.

RUSSELL & BROMLEY
109–110 New Bond St., WI (tel. 629-4001)
Underground Station: Bond Street
**Hours: Monday through Saturday from 9:30 a.m. to 6 p.m. (on Thursday
to 7 p.m.)**
Credit Cards: AE, DC, MC, V

Sturdy, dependable shoes are available in Russell & Bromley in both classical
and trendy styles. Men's brogues range around £100, while women's pumps,
high heels, and sandals range from about £53 to £97. Other shops in the West
End are located at 24–25 New Bond St. (tel. 629-6903) and 494–496 Oxford
St. (tel. 493-3501), with additional shops found at 77 Brompton Rd., 64 King's
Rd., and 81 Knightsbridge.

HANDMADE AND
CUSTOM-MADE SHOES

ALAN MCAFEE LTD.
5 Cork St., WI (tel. 734-7301)
Underground Station: Green Park or Piccadilly Circus
Hours: Monday through Friday from 9:30 a.m. to 5:30 p.m.
Credit Cards: AE, DC, MC, V

Men's classical brogues, oxfords, loafers, and boots are sold here, either from an
existing stock or made to measure. Every customer's size is recorded and kept on
file for easy reordering. Ready-made shoes range between £94 to £132, while
custom-made shoes start at £660. The shop will undertake any style in any color,
including your own design. Branch shops are located at 17 Old Bond St.
(tel. 499-7343), 73 Knightsbridge (tel. 235-7218), and 100 New Bond St.
(tel. 629-7975).

CHURCH'S
163 New Bond St., WI (tel. 499-9449)
Underground Station: Green Park or Piccadilly Circus
**Hours: Monday through Friday from 9 a.m. to 5:30 p.m. (on Thursday to
7 p.m.), on Saturday to 4:30 p.m.**
Credit Cards: AE, DC, MC, V

Producing shoes since the mid-1800s, Church's has a solid reputation for
ready-made men's shoes of excellent quality. If you can't afford to have shoes
custom-made, Church's is the next best thing. English businessmen shop here
for brogues, semi-brogues, oxfords and bookbinders, loafers, and waterproof
casuals. Church's shoes are still made much the same way they were 100 years
ago—eight weeks is required to produce one pair of shoes. The inscriptions
inside the shoe are all handwritten, and only custom-grade leathers are used.
Prices range from about £41 for casual shoes up to £132. Other shops are found at

Burlington Arcade, Jermyn Street, and Brompton Road. At the Brompton Road shop women's shoes are available as well; the women's shoes cater to the middle-aged, with low, sturdy pumps in somber colors.

DELISS
41 Beauchamp Pl., SW3 (tel. 584-3321)
Underground Station: Knightsbridge
Hours: Monday through Friday from 9:30 a.m. to 5:30 p.m. (on Wednesday to 6:15 p.m.), on Saturday from noon to 4 p.m.
Credit Cards: AE

This shop is much newer than the older establishments in the West End and offers lower prices. All shoes are made on the premises, and made-to-measure shoes can be completed within a week. You can choose a style from one of the models in the shop or bring in your own design. Materials range from cow leather to reptile and include whip snake, lizard, crocodile, waterproof buffalo, elephant, and ostrich skin. If you're longing for metallic snakeskin thigh boots topped with bright-blue ostrich feathers, this shop will make your dream come true, and they'll even fix you up with matching handbags and belts. Prices for women's shoes start at £262, while women's ankle boots start at £343. Men's shoes start at £324, while men's ankle boots start at £396. Lasts (made of wood to the exact measurements of your foot) cost extra (£178 for women and £209 for men) and you can either leave them in the shop for future orders or take them home with you.

FOSTER & SON
83 Jermyn St., SW1 (tel. 930-5385)
Underground Station: Piccadilly Circus or Green Park
Hours: Monday through Friday from 9 a.m. to 5 p.m., on Saturday to noon
Credit Cards: AE, DC, MC, V

Founded in 1840, Foster & Son is a well-established shoe- and bootmaker's shop in St. James's. Only men's footwear is made here, and both ready-made and custom-made shoes are available. Ready-made shoes start at £115, while ready-made boots are around £187. Handmade shoes start at £522. Styles include brogues, oxfords, monk shoes, chukka boots, riding boots, and hunting boots. Also sold are hide suitcases starting at £577 and attaché cases.

HENRY MAXWELL & CO.
11 Savile Row, W1 (tel. 734-9714)
Underground Station: Piccadilly Circus
Hours: Monday through Friday from 9 a.m. to 1 p.m. and 2 to 5:45 p.m.
Credit Cards: AE, DC, MC, V

Founded in 1750 and possessing a royal warrant as bootmakers to the Queen, this shop handmakes made-to-measure shoes and boots for both men and

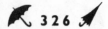
women. "Virtually anything" can be made, including various styles of hunting and riding boots. Boots take approximately three months to complete and begin at £612 for ankle boots and £921 for riding boots. Shoes start at £456. These prices are exclusive of VAT. A small selection of ready-to-wear shoes are available starting at £101.75, as well as leather bags and attaché cases.

LOBB
9 St. James's St., SW1 (tel. 930-3664)
Underground Station: Green Park
Hours: Monday through Friday from 8:30 a.m. to 5:30 p.m.
Credit Cards: None

I love the smell and atmosphere of this bootmaker's shop, with its strong scent of leather and its workshop right on the premises where you can watch masters at their craft. It gives you the feeling that little has changed over the years. As royal bootmakers to the Queen, the Duke of Edinburgh, and the Prince of Wales, Lobb exerts a lot of time and effort in making its women's and men's shoes and boots, generally between six and ten months for a customer's first pair of footwear and about three months for subsequent pairs. Wooden lasts are made for each customer and are kept in stock for ten years. Styles either follow the customer's own designs or are made from the shop's models which include a full brogue derby, perforated oxford, the kangaroo laceless shoe, monk, ladies' strap jodhpurs, polo boots, and a wide range of women's pumps. Shoes start at £686 plus VAT, while boots average £900.

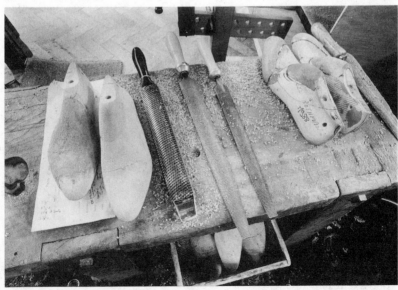

Tools of the trade at royal bootmakers J. Lobb, creators of footwear that lasts

MANOLO BLAHNIK
49–51 Old Church St., SW3 (tel. 352-8622)
Underground Station: *South Kensington*
Hours: *Monday through Friday from 10 a.m. to 6 p.m., on Saturday*
from 10:30 a.m. to 5:30 p.m.
Credit Cards: *AE, MC, V*

Italian designer Manolo Blahnik creates women's shoes that dominate the pages of British fashion magazines. His exclusive shop displays a small selection of handmade shoes. Generally only a dozen or so pairs are made of each design, which means you're unlikely to encounter someone else wearing your shoes. Popular with stars and celebrities, shoes are all priced above £176. A pair of thigh-length black suede boots are priced at £385.

RAYNE
15 Old Bond St., W1 (tel. 493-9077)
Underground Station: *Green Park or Piccadilly Circus*
Hours: *Monday through Saturday from 9:30 a.m. to 6 p.m.*
Credit Cards: *AE, DC, MC, V*

Probably the only thing the Queen, Marlene Dietrich, Margaret Thatcher, and Barbara Cartland have had in common is that they've worn shoes made by Rayne. The shop was started in the 1880s by Henry and Mary Rayne and today is managed by their grandsons. With royal warrants to the Queen and the Queen Mother, Rayne has a very elegant interior and will give any woman the royal treatment. Styles range from work pumps to special-occasion heels. Prices for ready-made shoes start at £98.50, with white-and-beige kid sling-backs going for £126. You can also order custom-made shoes from any model in the shop, choosing your own color. Rayne also imports shoes from Italy which carry the Rayne inscription. Concessions are in Selfridges, Dickens & Jones, Harrods, and Harvey Nichols, and an additional shop is located at 57 Brompton Rd. (tel. 589-5560).

TRICKERS
67 Jermyn St., SW1 (tel. 930-6395)
Underground Station: *Green Park*
Hours: *Monday through Friday from 9 a.m. to 5 p.m., on Saturday to*
4:30 p.m.
Credit Cards: *AE, DC, MC, V*

In operation since 1829, this pleasant old shop still has wooden cabinets lining the walls, filled with its own ready-made men's shoes which start at £99. Bespoke (custom-made) shoes start at £330, while custom-made riding boots start at £385. Made-to-measure shoes and boots for women are also undertaken. Wooden lasts are kept for five years after the first order and for ten years after the second order.

SILVER

Because Britain was the foremost manufacturer of silver in the 18th century, it follows that British antique silver ranks as one of the most coveted for collectors around the world. The most famous silversmith of the times was Paul De Lamerie, who came to England from Holland as an infant and who dominated the silver market in the first half of the 18th century. As testimony to his skills, a silver dinner service he made for the seventh Earl of Thanet between 1742 and 1746 fetched £825,000 when it was sold at Sotheby's in 1984.

Few of us can afford such prices, but there are Victorian pieces that are not so precious, as well as items that are Sheffield plated. Sheffield plate consists of a copper plate sandwiched between two sheets of silver foil, a process discovered in 1743 by Thomas Bolsover of Sheffield. By 1765 Sheffield plate was being used extensively for wares previously made of silver.

For the amateur, it is often difficult to distinguish between objects that are sterling silver and the much cheaper items that are silver plated. Even before the advent of silver plate, there were forgeries of silver with too much alloying metal added to the precious metal. Toward the end of the 13th century in western Europe, it was considered a problem of such magnitude that stamps of approval, issued by an assay office, were required to protect the public.

These stamps are known as hallmarks and assure that the silver has been tested to see that it contains only the permitted amount of alloy. Today these hallmarks are used for determining where the silver was made and to some extent indicate the date. The London assay office, for example, stamped approved objects with a figure of a walking lion. From 1363 a mark denoting the maker was also added.

The best places to pick up inexpensive pieces of sterling silver or Sheffield plate are at one of London's antique flea markets, especially **Portobello, New Caledonian**, and **Camden Passage**. It's a buyer-beware situation at these markets, but I found most stallholders to be very honest.

At the other end of the silver market are the reputable, established dealers in silver, several of which have also been described in the "Jewelry" section. Both **Garrard** and **Mappin & Webb** deal in antique and contemporary silver, while **Tessiers** and **S. J. Phillips** sell the finest of antique silver. Tessiers' earliest piece, for example, dates from 1574 and is a London wine cup selling for more than £10,000. Refer to the "Jewelry" section for more information regarding these prestigious stores. More treasure houses in silver are listed below.

BOND STREET SILVER GALLERIES

111–112 New Bond St., W1 (tel. 493-6180)
Underground Station: *Bond Street*

Hours: *Monday through Friday from 9 a.m. to 5 p.m.*
Credit Cards: *Depends on individual dealers, but few accept them*

About a dozen dealers in antique, secondhand, and contemporary silver are housed on the first and second floors of this Bond Street building. Mainly large pieces are sold, including tea sets, pitchers, table flatware, candelabra, trays, bowls, and goblets.

LONDON SILVER VAULTS
53–64 Chancery Lane, WC2 (tel. 242-3844)
Underground Station: Chancery Lane
**Hours: Monday through Friday from 9 a.m. to 5:30 p.m., on Saturday to
12:30 p.m.**
Credit Cards: Most individual dealers accept major credit cards

Approximately 100 years ago a string of vaults was built underneath the ground in central London to house the valuables of the rich. Today these very same vaults have been turned into approximately 40 separate shops for dealers of antique and contemporary silver. The London Silver Vaults, therefore, has the largest concentration of silver you'll find anywhere in London, with gleaming tea pot after tea pot and tray after tray. No serious lover of silver should pass it up, and the public is more than welcome.

There are items for sale in all price ranges, including sterling silver and Sheffield plate, old and new. There are candelabra, wine goblets, sugar bowls, tea sets, salt and pepper shakers, toast racks, picture frames, napkin rings, trays, and cutlery. Prices begin at about £2 for plated-silver decanter labels. Sheffield-plated toast racks (which also make good letter holders) sell for about £30, while Sheffield-plated cheese knives are about £7.50 each. Sterling-silver serving trays run about £3,000 to £6,500. During my visit I saw a sterling-silver tea pot dating from 1933 priced at £985 and sterling-silver salt and pepper shakers made in London in 1790 priced at £209.

S. J. SHRUBSOLE
43 Museum St., WC1 (tel. 405-2712)
Underground Station: Holborn or Tottenham Court Road
Hours: Monday through Friday from 9 a.m. to 5:30 p.m.
Credit Cards: None

Located just a minute's walk from the British Museum, Shrubsole is a specialist in old Sheffield plate and sterling silver. Its silver collection dates from the late 17th to mid-19th centuries, with items ranging from about £60 to more than £10,000. Sheffield plate is much lower, with pieces ranging from £11 to £1,000. An 1810 Sheffield-plated Georgian chamber candlestick is priced at £180.

SHAPLAND
207 High Holborn, WC1 (tel. 405-3507)

Underground Station: *Holborn*
Hours: *Monday through Friday from 9 a.m. to 5 p.m.*
Credit Cards: *AE, DC, MC, V*

This quaint shop looks as though it has changed little since it first opened back in 1830. The old-fashioned interior dates from the early Victorian period, complete with a front door thick enough to contain its own built-in display case. The shop deals in silver and silver plate, as well as jewelry, clocks and pocket watches, cutlery, and decanters. A recent visit turned up a silver-plated serving dish from the turn of the century priced at £180 and a silver bookmark with a charming butterfly motif for £31.

SILVERWARE

Silverware is usually referred to as cutlery in England, and several shops covered elsewhere in this book also deal in silverware. In the "China" section, both **Chinacraft** and **Thomas Goode** carry sterling-silver and silver-plated sets of cutlery in various modern styles. Kitchenware stores are also good sources for cutlery. **David Mellor** is famous for his cutlery collections of stainless steel, stainless acetal, and silver plate. His cutlery has even ended up in the Victoria and Albert Museum and the museums of modern art in both New York and Philadelphia. **Divertimenti** also stocks cutlery of stainless steel. Other shops carrying some silverware can be found in the "Jewelry" and "Gift" sections of this book.

Antique silverware is abundant in London's flea markets, particularly along **Portobello Road.** I saw various sets of six fish knives dating from the Victorian period, for example, selling for less than £10. Knives and forks with handles of mother-of-pearl are also plentiful, though more expensive, and are often for sale as entire sets or as individual pieces. At the **London Silver Vaults** I picked up a long-handled relish fork with a mother-of-pearl handle dating from the 1800s for less than £15.

SOAPS AND TOILETRIES

In addition to the stores listed below, all the shops listed under "Perfume" carry their own range of soaps and other products to complement their scents. The **Body Shop,** described in the "Cosmetics" section, also stocks a large range of soaps, skin lotions, shampoos, and creams, all made from organic materials.

CRABTREE & EVELYN
6 Kensington Church St., W8 (tel. 937-9335)
Underground Station: *High Street Kensington*
Hours: *Monday through Saturday from 9:30 a.m. to 6 p.m. (on Thursday to 7 p.m.)*

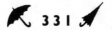
Credit Cards: MC, V

With a second shop opened at 134 King's Rd. at the beginning of 1987, Crabtree & Evelyn is well known for its beautifully packaged soaps, bath oils, shampoos, powders, and toiletries. Its products make inexpensive gifts, even for children. Soaps in the form of Peter Rabbit or Alice in Wonderland, for example, start at £1.80. For adults there's a wide range, from satinwood oval hairbrushes for £20.60 to Lily of the Valley gift boxes consisting of bath gel, soaps, bath cubes, a pocket aomizer, and toilet water, selling for £13.20.

CULPEPER
21 Bruton St., W1 (tel. 499-2406)
Underground Station: Green Park or Bond Street
**Hours: Monday through Friday from 9:30 a.m. to 6 p.m., on Saturday to
    5 p.m.**
Credit Cards: AE, DC, MC, V

In addition to its herbs, spices, mustards, and chutneys, Culpeper carries a range of soaps and toiletries made with natural ingredients. Soap scents range from Black Forest pine to lavender and jasmine and start at £1. You can buy boxed soaps with romantic messages such as "From One Who Loves You," scented in sandalwood. There are also bath salts, toilet waters, oils, herb-scented sachets, powders, shampoos, creams, and lotions. Another shop is located at 8 The Market in Covent Garden (tel. 379-6698).

SPORTING GOODS

In addition to London's largest sporting-goods store described below, department stores also stock sports equipment and clothing. For saddlery and riding accessories, refer to the "Riding Gear" section; hunting items can be found in stores listed under "Guns."

LILLYWHITES
Piccadilly Circus, W1 (tel. 930-3181)
Underground Station: Piccadilly Circus
**Hours: Monday through Saturday from 9:30 a.m. to 6 p.m. (on Thursday
    to 7 p.m.)**
Credit Cards: AE, DC, MC, V

Opened by cricket player James Lillywhite in 1863, Lillywhites boasts more than 30 sports departments. Covered are the areas of fishing, track, cricket, rugby, roller and ice skating, golf, skiing, tennis, badminton, squash, darts, snooker and billiards, shooting, and riding. The skiing and tennis departments are especially good, and Lillywhites carries the proper clothing and footwear in each of its sporting departments.

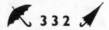
STAMPS

Be sure to check with auction houses, since **Christie's, Sotheby's**, and **Phillips** all have occasional philatelic sales. In addition, the **Trafalgar Square Post Office**, located at 24 William IV St. (tel. 930-9580), has a window where you can purchase all the current British stamps.

CECIL COURT STAMP CO.
6 Cecil Court, WC2 (tel. 836-6989)
Underground Station: *Leicester Square*
Hours: *Monday through Saturday from 10:30 a.m. to 5:30 p.m.*
Credit Cards: *None*

A surprising find in this narrow passageway lined mainly with antiquarian bookstores, this shop claims to have "the largest selection of modern stamps from around the world, especially topicals." Topicals, by the way, refer to stamps of a certain theme such as flowers or birds. Prices range from 30 pence for a stamp to £35 for a set of stamps.

LONDON INTERNATIONAL STAMP CENTRE
27 King St., WC2 (tel. 836-5871)
Underground Station: *Covent Garden or Leicester Square*
Hours: *Monday through Friday from 10 a.m. to 5:30 p.m., on Saturday to 3:30 p.m.*
Credit Cards: *Depends on stallholders, but most accept MC and V*

At last count, eight dealers were still located in this quaint-looking building. The stallholders I talked to vowed to remain, but in the past few years several dealers have relocated to the Strand to be closer to the large stamp houses. At any rate, it would be prudent to telephone before making a special trip. Dealers here specialize in various aspects of stamps, from new ones to old ones, from stamps issued in Great Britain in the 1800s to stamps from around the world. One dealer carries transatlantic mail with postage marks intact.

STANLEY GIBBONS
399 The Strand, WC2 (tel. 836-8444)
Underground Station: *Charing Cross, Leicester Square, or Covent Garden*
Hours: *Monday from 10 a.m. to 5:30 p.m., Tuesday through Friday from 9 a.m. to 5:30 p.m., on Saturday from 10 a.m. to 1 p.m.*
Credit Cards: *AE, DC, MC, V*

With a royal warrant as philatelists to the Queen, Stanley Gibbons was established in 1856 and proclaims itself quite simply as the largest stamp shop in the world. Located in a modern building in the heart of stamp land, it's like a

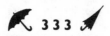
stamp department store, complete with all the necessary accessories such as stamp albums and magnifying glasses. It has the world's largest selection of British Commonwealth stamps, but also stocks stamps from other countries and both new and old stamps dating from about 1840. It also deals in old postcards, offers free evaluations on stamps that are brought into the shop, and holds regular stamp auctions. The *Stanley Gibbons British Commonwealth Catalogue*, available for £19.75, is considered the Bible for British and Commonwealth stamps and their current market prices.

STATIONERY

In writing this book I went through spiral notebook after notebook, and just when I needed a new one there seemed to be a **Ryman** or **W. H. Smith** right around the corner. These chain stores can supply your everyday needs in paper, pens, and office accessories, and are found everywhere in London. Consult the telephone directory for a shop near you.

For more esoteric desires, however, try some of the stationers listed below. Smythson must rank as one of the classiest stationers in the world, while the Italian Paper Shop has lovely marbled papers. If you're looking specifically for writing pens or nibs, refer to the "Pens and Pencils" section, though some of the shops below carry writing accessories as well.

FALKINER FINE PAPERS
117 Long Acre, Covent Garden, WC2 (tel. 240-2339)
Underground Station: Covent Garden
Hours: Monday through Saturday from 9:30 a.m. to 5:30 p.m.
Credit Cards: AE, MC, V

This shop specializes in artists' papers, including papers for calligraphy, book-binding, watercolor, painting, printmaking, and box making. Many papers are handmade, starting at £1.10 per sheet, and there are also colored and decorative Japanese papers and marbled papers. Supplies include bookbinding leathers, some pens, inks, nibs, bookbinding tools, and books on bookbinding, paper-making, and calligraphy. Uncut turkey quills cost 60 pence.

THE ITALIAN PAPER SHOP
11 Brompton Arcade, SW3 (tel. 589-1668), off Brompton Road
Underground Station: Knightsbridge
Hours: Monday through Friday from 10 a.m. to 6 p.m.
Credit Cards: AE, DC, MC, V

Using a method invented in the 17th century by the royal bookbinder of Louis XIII of France, a workshop in Florence produces the marbled paper sold in this shop. The iridescent colors used in the papers swirl like the delicate patterns of butterfly wings. Most of the products sold here are decorated with this colorful paper, from bookends to earrings and lampshades. Pencil holders cost £5.60, pocket-size address books are £3.30, and tiny chests of drawers useful for holding jewelry or paper clips start at £14.45. There are also diaries, notebooks, picture frames, albums, letter racks, and blotters. A sheet of hand-marbled Italian paper costs £8.25.

PAPERCHASE
213 Tottenham Court Rd., WI (tel. 580-8496)
Underground Station: Goodge Street
Hours: Monday through Saturday from 9 a.m. to 6 p.m. (on Thursday from 9:30 a.m. to 7 p.m.)
Credit Cards: MC, V

In addition to its stationery, greeting cards, postcards, pens and pencils, and party favors, Paperchase has a good supply of papers, including Japanese papers, metallic papers, and papers inlaid with maple leaves. It also sells Filofax, those wonderful notebooks with dividers and rings for refillable paper. A pigskin Filofax with two pockets costs £35. Another Paperchase is located at 167 Fulham Rd. (tel. 589-7839).

SMYTHSON OF BOND STREET
54 New Bond St., WI (tel. 629-8558)
Underground Station: Bond Street
Hours: Monday through Friday from 9:15 a.m. to 5:30 p.m., on Saturday to 12:30 p.m.
Credit Cards: AE, DC, MC, V

As the royal stationers to the Queen, Smythson is plush, dignified, quiet, very upmarket, and a leading authority on stationery etiquette. Did you know that a woman's visiting card is supposed to be bigger than a man's? Writing papers are Smythson's specialty, and a separate room downstairs in the basement is devoted to the cause. Here you can choose your stationery, invitations, name cards, and envelopes. The papers are in a variety of colors and may be hand-bordered, die-stamped, monogrammed, or printed in the style you choose. Twenty sheets and envelopes made by hand especially for Smythson cost £17.

On the ground floor is a large selection of diaries, address books, pens, leather-bound desk accessories, wallets, and attaché cases. Fishermen might enjoy the *Fishing Book*, where they can make notes of the fish they caught, which river they caught it in, the date, the weight, and other remarks. In the *Wine Cellar* book, which costs £38, connoisseurs can keep track of their vintages by noting the quantity, the date purchased, where it's stored, and the amount of stock remaining.

THE WALTON STREET STATIONERY CO.
97 Walton St., SW3 (tel. 589-0777)

Underground Station: *South Kensington*
Hours: *Monday through Friday from 9:30 a.m. to 5:30 p.m., on Saturday*
   from 10 a.m. to 5 p.m.
Credit Cards: AE, DC, MC, V

This shop specializes in engraved stationery and invitations in untraditional styles. The staff is happy to advise customers and work can be undertaken from a photograph or sketch. Also sold are the shop's own writing inks, starting at £3.55 in several colors, greeting cards, and unusual desk items gleaned from suppliers in other countries. "We're choosy about the products we buy for our store," an employee told me. Another specialty of the store are the Lefax personal organizers.

TAILORING

If you've never before inquired about the prices of made-to-measure suits for men, your first reaction to $750 to $1,500 suits might be that they are wildly overpriced. However, a well-made suit should last at least 20 years, and more important, it will flow with your body and should fit you like no store-bought suit ever could.

The differences between ready-made and bespoke (custom-made) suits are readily apparent in the interfacing, the color, the buttonholes and pockets, and the finishing touches. In a well-crafted bespoke suit the collar will have some life in it, curving slightly instead of lying flat. The

Royal stationers, Smythson of Bond Street

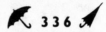
shoulders will be crisp rather than drooping pathetically from your body, and there will be no puckering where the sleeves meet the armholes. In short, your $1,000 suit will make you feel like a million dollars.

With one exception, all the men's shops listed below are located on the most famous tailoring street in the world, Savile Row. Savile Row is conveniently located in the West End not far from Regent Street. You'll need at least two fittings for a suit, perhaps even a third. Some of the shops will custom-make clothing for women as well, but more information on women's couturiers is given at the end of this section. If you want bespoke shirts to complement your new suit, refer to the "Clothing" section for shops specializing in this service.

MEN'S

ANDERSON & SHEPPARD
30 Savile Row, W1 (tel. 734-1960)
Underground Station: *Piccadilly Circus*
Hours: *Monday through Friday from 8:30 a.m. to 5 p.m.*
Credit Cards: *None*

Established in 1906, this men's tailoring shop is somewhat staid and reserved, dealing mainly with customers who come by recommendation. Decorated with wooden floors and wood paneling and filled with bolts of wools and tweeds, it charges upward of £785 for two-piece bespoke suits.

ANTHONY J. HEWITT
9 Savile Row, W1 (tel. 734-1505)
Underground Station: *Piccadilly Circus*
Hours: *Monday through Friday from 9 a.m. to 5:30 p.m., on Saturday to 12:30 p.m.*
Credit Cards: *AE, DC, MC, V*

Established about 20 years ago, this shop is very accommodating and offers some of the lowest prices on the street. Depending on the time of the year, it may be able to complete a two-piece suit within three days, charging £500 excluding the VAT. If you are unable to come directly to the shop, they may oblige by sending a tailor to your hotel for a fitting. Bespoke shirts cost upward of £60.

BERNARD WEATHERILL LTD.
KILGOUR, FRENCH & STANBURY LTD.
8 Savile Row, W1 (tel. 734-6905)
Underground Station: *Piccadilly Circus*
Hours: *Monday through Friday from 9 a.m. to 5:30 p.m.*
Credit Cards: *None*

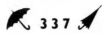

TAILORING

Both men's and women's tailoring is undertaken here. Bernard Weatherill specializes in hunting clothes and Kilgour, French & Stanbury produces suits and blazers. In addition to its bespoke riding and hunting breeches, overcoats, and topcoats, ready-made hunting clothes and riding accessories are also sold. The management declines to give specific prices because of the variance dependent on each customer's wishes, but since they are livery tailors to the Queen, the Duke of Edinburgh, and the Queen Mother, you can expect both high prices and excellent quality.

GIEVES & HAWKES
1 Savile Row, W1 (tel. 434-2001)
Underground Station: *Piccadilly Circus*
Hours: *Monday through Friday from 9 a.m. to 5:30 p.m., on Saturday to 1 p.m.*
Credit Cards: *AE, DC, MC, V*

Occupying a handsome town house built in 1732 for Lord Fairfax, Gieves & Hawkes possesses a large and prestigious-looking interior, complete with chandeliers, atrium, and ceiling fans. It's also so popular that you may have to wait for assistance, but there are plenty of ready-made clothing you can look at while you wait, including off-the-peg suits ranging from £220 to £600, ties, shirts, sweaters, socks, vests, and cashmere sweaters. Two-piece bespoke suits start at £800 and take up to two months to complete. Founded more than 200 years ago, Gieves & Hawkes possesses three royal warrants and early customers included Nelson and the infamous Captain Bligh of the H.M.S. *Bounty.*

HELMAN
10 Savile Row, W1 (tel. 629-2949)
Underground Station: *Piccadilly Circus*
Hours: *Monday through Friday from 9 a.m. to 5:30 p.m., on Saturday by appointment*
Credit Cards: *None*

Established in 1907, Helman charges upward of £935 excluding VAT for two-piece suits. Although it can complete orders within five days if pressured, the shop prefers to take more time and then mail the suit to customers if necessary.

HENRY POOLE
15 Savile Row, W1 (tel. 734-5985)
Underground Station: *Piccadilly Circus*
Hours: *Monday through Friday from 9 a.m. to 5:30 p.m.*
Credit Cards: *AE, DC, MC, V*

Since its founding in the early 1800s Poole has remained one of Savile Row's most distinguished tailors and has served such imposing customers as Charles

Dickens, explorer David Livingston, Winston Churchill, Charles de Gaulle, and J. P. Morgan. The staff is very friendly and personable. Excluding VAT, £675 is charged for a two-piece suit. Topcoats, capes, and riding clothes can also be custom-made, and accessories sold in the shop include ties and Brigg umbrellas.

HUNTSMAN
11 Savile Row, W1 (tel. 734-7441)
Underground Station: Piccadilly Circus
Hours: Monday through Friday from 9 a.m. to 1 p.m. and 2 to 5:45 p.m.
Credit Cards: AE, DC, MC, V

This classic men's tailoring shop makes bespoke suits and shirts, charging upward of £1,070 for two-piece suits and £58 for shirts, exclusive of VAT. Orders for hunting and riding coats are also accepted. Off-the-peg suits are also available for about £500, as well as ties, socks, and hunting shirts.

J. DEDGE & SONS
16 Clifford St., W1 (tel. 734-2248)
Underground Station: Green Park or Piccadilly Circus
Hours: Monday through Friday from 9:15 a.m. to 5:15 p.m., on Saturday
**   from 9:30 a.m. to noon**
Credit Cards: AE, MC, V

Men's and women's sports clothing are the specialty of this tailor's shop, including hunting, fishing, and riding clothes. It possesses a royal warrant as tailors to the Queen and charges an average of £715 for a two-piece suit and £770 for a topcoat. Suits take approximately two months to complete.

TOMMY NUTTER
19 Savile Row, W1 (tel. 734-0831)
Underground Station: Piccadilly Circus
Hours: Monday through Saturday from 9 a.m. to 6 p.m.
Credit Cards: AE, DC, MC, V

Having opened his shop in 1982, Tommy Nutter is more contemporary than his counterparts on Savile Row and his customers tend to be in show business. Since the start of his career in the late 1960s, Tommy Nutter has dressed Elton John, Mick Jagger, Eric Clapton, and members of the Beatles (three of whom wore his suits on the *Abbey Road* album cover). Everything from shirts, overcoats, and three-piece dinner suits are undertaken, and two-piece suits start at £770. Off-the-peg clothing is also available, with two-piece suits ranging from £313 to £410. Women also patronize the shop for tailored suits based on men's styles featuring padded shoulders and tapered trousers.

WOMEN'S

Bernard Weatherill, J. Dedge, and **Tommy Nutter** are happy to take orders for women's bespoke clothing. Other couturiers that will make made-to-measure clothing based on their own designs include **Catherine Buckley, David Fielden, Hardy Amies** (the only women's shop located on Savile Row), **Norman Hartnell, Ritva Westenius, Spaghetti**, and **Tatters**, all listed in the "Clothing" section.

ATISSU
29 Floral St., WC2 (tel. 836-9800)
Underground Station: Covent Garden or Leicester Square
Hours: Monday through Saturday from 10 a.m. to 6:30 p.m.
Credit Cards: V

Atissu is a unique shop, closing the gap between high-fashion couturiers and home dressmaking. Opened in 1986 by two ambitious young women, Atissu specializes in its own patterns and *Vogue* patterns cut from designer printed fabrics. Seamstresses will also take orders based on your own design. "The whole idea is to do whatever people like," one of the owners told me. It takes about four weeks to complete an outfit and usually a couple of fittings are required. Prices are based on an hourly rate of £8; dresses usually start at £165 and a lined, wool woman's suit averages about £192. Men's casual clothing can also be made, though the staff stresses that this is not a tailoring shop.

TARTANS

Tartans are twilled wool fabrics with plaid patterns, each forming a distinctive design worn by members of a Scottish clan. It stands to reason, therefore, that the **Scotch House** at 2 Brompton Rd. is the best place in London for tartans. It has devoted an entire room to tartans, with a large book listing over 300 tartans and family names. Tartans here begin at £16.50 per meter. Another store carrying tartans is **Westaway & Westaway**. Refer to the "Clothing" section for more information on both these shops.

THEATER TICKETS

If you know in advance what you want to see during your stay in London, you can order tickets prior to departure from the United States. **Keith Prowse and Co.** is located at 234 W. 44th St., New York, NY 10036 (tel. 212/398-1430, or toll free 800/223-4446), and **Edwards and Edwards** is at

1 Times Square Plaza, New York, NY 10036 (tel. 212/994-0290, or toll free 800/223-6108).

In London itself you can purchase tickets directly at the **theater box offices**, most of which are open from 10 a.m. to 8 p.m. The **tourist information centers** at Victoria Station and 4 Lower Regent St. also sell theater tickets, as do many of the upper-class **hotels**. Some of these include Browns (tel. 493-6020), Claridges (tel. 493-0130), Cumberland (tel. 262-1234), Grosvenor House (tel. 493-0364), Inn on the Park (tel. 499-1842), Inter-Continental (tel. 491-2884), Mayfair (tel. 493-9979), Mount Royal (tel. 493-0497), Park Lane (tel. 493-0823), Regent Palace (tel. 437-2625), Savoy (tel. 240-0285), Strand Palace (tel. 240-3181), and Westbury (tel. 493-1341). **Department stores** selling theater tickets include Harrods, which has a theater ticket counter on its fourth floor, and Selfridges, which has a counter on its ground floor.

Of course, there are many **ticket agencies** in London as well. A leading agency is Keith Prowse, which accepts AE, DC, MC, and V credit cards. You can order theater tickets by phone by calling 01/741-9999, sport tickets by calling 01/741-8999, and concert tickets by calling 01/741-8989.

If you're looking for bargain prices, the best place in town is the **Half Price Ticket Booth**, located in the southwest corner of Leicester Square. There is no telephone, which means you must pick up the ticket in person. Tickets are for same-day performances only and are usually half the normal price. Only cash is accepted. Hours are Monday through Saturday from noon to 2 p.m. for matinees and 2:30 to 6:30 p.m. for evening performances. Get there early and be prepared to take whatever they have to offer.

TOBACCONISTS

In addition to the shops listed below, other stores selling tobacco and smoking accessories include **Davidoff** and **Robert Lewis**, listed in the "Cigars" section, and **Astleys**, under "Pipes."

ALFRED DUNHILL

30 Duke St., SW1 (tel. 499-9566), on the corner of Duke and Jermyn Streets
Underground Station: Green Park or Piccadilly Circus
Hours: Monday through Friday from 9:30 a.m. to 5:30 p.m., on Saturday to 4:30 p.m.
Credit Cards: AE, DC, MC, V

Dunhill is an internationally famous company selling tobacco, pipes, cigars, lighters, humidors, and all the requisite smoking paraphernalia. Prices for single

cigars range from £4.40 for a Corona to £13.40 for a Dunhill Havana Club. The Havana Club comes in its own wooden box, making it a good give - away item for such special occasions as the birth of a baby. Walnut-veneer humidors start at £269 for a capacity of 25 cigars. Cigarette lighters include gold-plated ones for £154, silver-plated ones from £110, and 18-karat deluxe models for £4,600.

Dunhill also sells a wide range of men's clothing and gift items, including writing pens, wallets, luggage, watches, sunglasses, and fragrances. A Dunhill silk tie costs £38 and a polo shirt is £50. Dunhill products are also sold at Harrods, Harvey Nichols, and Selfridges, and at an additional shop in the Burlington Arcade.

G. SMITH & SONS
74 Charing Cross Rd., WC2 (tel. 836-7422)
Underground Station: Leicester Square
Hours: Monday through Friday from 8:30 a.m. to 6 p.m., on Saturday
from 9 a.m. to 6 p.m.
Credit Cards: AE, DC, MC, V

Established in 1869, this tiny shop specializes in snuff, producing more than 50 of its own kinds. Varieties range from Wild Strawberry, flavored with the natural oil of strawberries, to the Special M, pungent with almond flavor. Snuff starts at 30 pence, and cigarettes, tobacco, and pipes are also available.

SULLIVAN POWELL
34 Burlington Arcade, W1 (tel. 629-0433)
Underground Station: Green Park or Piccadilly Circus
Hours: Monday through Friday from 9 a.m. to 5:30 p.m., on Saturday to
4:30 p.m.
Credit Cards: AE, MC, V

Belonging to Benson and Hedges, this tobacconist shop is conveniently located in the Burlington Arcade and sells tobacco and sundries, including pipes, lighters, cigars, and cigarette cases. Sullivan Powell's Private Stock is priced at £1.75 for a box of 20 cigarettes.

TOYS

In addition to the shops listed here, other stores that carry children's toys are **Mothercare,** discussed in the "Clothing" section; **Dragons**, listed in the "Furniture" section; and **Games Centre**, covered under "Games." Bookstores that have good children's selections include **Heywood Hill, Hatchards, John Sandoe,** and **Peter Stockham at Images**, all described in the "Books" section.

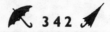

EARLY LEARNING CENTRE
225 Kensington High St., W8 (tel. 937-0419)
Underground Station: High Street Kensington
Hours: Monday through Saturday from 9 a.m. to 6 p.m.
Credit Cards: MC, V

This one-room shop specializes in toys for children under 8 years old. Toys are chosen that are both fun and educational, including those by Fisher Price, Duplo, Lego, and others. There are games, science kits, puzzles, crayons and paint, unbreakable music instruments, books, and games that help in learning how to read and write. A clock face to help kids learn how to tell time is £1.10, while a simple microscope is priced at £3.85. Half the items in the shop cost less than £3. What's more, there's a playing area where children can test out the toys in the shop while parents look around—the only drawback being that children enjoy it so much, some of them have to be dragged screaming and kicking from the shop when it's time to leave.

ERIC SNOOK
32 The Market, Covent Garden, WC2 (tel. 379-7681)
Underground Station: Covent Garden
Hours: Monday from noon to 6 p.m., on Tuesday and Thursday from 10 a.m. to 6 p.m., on Wednesday, Friday, and Saturday from 10 a.m. to 8 p.m., and on Sunday from 11 a.m. to 6 p.m.
Credit Cards: AE, MC, V

Although mainly a teenage and adult gift shop, Eric Snook also tucks toys in among the wares, including spinning tops for £9.35, teddy bears from £17, puppets, and games. The shop's specialty is tin toys from Germany, which are too fragile for younger children. A small tin chicken is £2.20, while a dump truck is £37.95.

HAMLEYS
188–196 Regent St., W1 (tel. 734-3161)
Underground Station: Oxford Circus or Piccadilly Circus
Hours: Monday through Saturday from 9 a.m. to 5:30 p.m. (on Thursday to 8 p.m.)
Credit Cards: AE, DC, MC, V

Six floors packed with toys has given this shop a place in the *Guinness Book of World Records* as the largest toy shop in the world. It's the Disneyland of toys, and the choice is so huge it's bewildering—even for grownups. As you walk through the store, model trains are whizzing on their tracks, toy parrots are squawking, plastic birds are flying, and demonstrations are being held showing the latest of the latest. This shop is worth a stop even if you don't have any children.

Departments include board games, electronic and video games, puzzles, dolls, dollhouses, building blocks, nursery toys, toy soldiers, model kits,

TOYS

mechanical toys, soft toys, building blocks, puppets, and magic kits. There are lots of teddy bears, and Galt educational toys. In the souvenir section, a six-inch Buckingham Palace guard is £1.90, while a London taxi with "Hamleys" written on it is £3.85.

POLLOCK'S TOY MUSEUM
1 Scala St., W1 (tel. 636-3452)
Underground Station: Goodge Street
Hours: *Monday through Saturday from 10 a.m. to 5 p.m.*
Credit Cards: AE, MC, V

This delightful museum filled with toys of yesteryear also has a gift shop where you can buy unusual toys rarely found anywhere else. Its specialty is cardboard cut-out theaters, which used to be sold for one or two pence during Victorian times and which almost disappeared after the turn of the century. This museum has done much to revive these cut-out theaters, which range from £2.20 to £45.

Also for sale are many old-fashioned toys (that is, made of wood instead of plastic and powered by hand rather than battery). There are inexpensive pocket toys from 5 pence that schoolchildren like to purchase out of their own pocket money, as well as collector's items for adults. The adult toys include rare teddy bears, German flats (stand-up figures from Germany), tin toys, and pre-1914 Dutch dolls that girls used to play with during the Victorian period. A smaller Pollocks shop is located at 44 The Market in Covent Garden (tel. 379-7866).

Hamleys bears en masse

TIGER TIGER
219 King's Rd., SW3 (tel. 352-8080)
Underground Station: Sloane Square
Hours: Monday through Saturday from 10 a.m. to 6 p.m.
Credit Cards: AE, DC, MC, V

The staff here is knowledgeable about children and toys, and it shows in their great selection of dolls, puppets, scooters, crib toys, building blocks, books, stuffed animals, and party favors. Pocket toys include marbles for 5 pence and whistles for 11 pence. Handcrafted British toys are a strong selling point for the shop, with a wide variety of soft, cuddly toys and wooden toys rather than plastic ones. String-puppet marionettes range from £9 to £55 and represent such personalities as Charlie Chaplin, royalty, witches, sailors, and fairytale figures.

YOUNG WORLD
229 Kensington High St., W8 (tel. 937-6314)
Underground Station: High Street Kensington
Hours: Monday through Saturday from 9:30 a.m. to 6 p.m., on Sunday
   from noon to 6 p.m.
Credit Cards: MC, V

This general toy store stocks board games, Lego, Galt educational toys, and lots of other usual items, and it has a large, excellent selection of children's books in the basement. Included are children's encyclopedias, books in science, geography, and history, and children's poetry, myths, and legends. *Tell Me Why*, put out by Hamlyn and costing £4.40, answers such questions as "Why don't we feel the earth rotate?"

UMBRELLAS

Given the number of wet and rainy days in London, umbrellas are a necessity of life in the capital city, and they come in all shapes and sizes. Originally made with cane or whalebone ribs, today they're made with fluted channels, and the discerning buyer will choose one that can double as a walking stick. The appropriate size is measured by holding the umbrella by your side and letting the tip touch the ground. Your elbow should be slightly bent, which will allow you to walk in an easy gait and swing it along your side. There are umbrellas for all occasions—for horse races, city life, and the countryside.

JAMES SMITH & SONS
53 New Oxford St., WCI (tel. 836-4731)
Underground Station: Tottenham Court Road
Hours: Monday through Friday from 9:30 a.m. to 5:25 p.m.
Credit Cards: None

This charming shop has changed little since it first opened more than 150 years ago, still selling umbrellas and walking sticks in all different price ranges and for all sorts of purposes. Umbrellas range from £9 to £192. The shop's own handmade umbrellas start at £44. I bought a combination umbrella-shooting stick (that is, a combination umbrella and walking stick with a handle that unfolds to form a seat) for £60. It's popularly used at horse races, though why anyone would want to sit down when it was raining was beyond either my or the store clerk's comprehension. But they do make great and unusual gifts. The shop also sells a wide range of walking sticks ranging in price from £6 to £450.

SWAINE, ADENEY, BRIGG & SONS LTD.
185 Piccadilly, W1 (tel. 734-4277)
Underground Station: Piccadilly Circus or Green Park
Hours: Monday through Friday from 9 a.m. to 5:30 p.m., on Saturday
   from 9:30 a.m. to 5 p.m.
Credit Cards: AE, DC, MC, V

Established in 1750, this famous shop caters to the country gentleman, supplying him with everything he needs for horse riding, hunting, and taking dignified country walks. Its stock of Brigg umbrellas is the largest in the world and is made in the shop's own workshops. Brigg gets its name from Thomas Brigg, a company founded in 1836 which amalgamated with Swaine Adeney after World War II.

The Brigg umbrella is produced in two basic forms: the Traditional, which has a handle and shaft made from a single piece of wood; and the Classic, with handles of cane, wood, and leathers that are mounted on a wooden shaft.

Swaine, Adeney, Brigg & Sons, home of the famous indestructible Brigg umbrella as well as of antique and contemporary walking sticks

Covers are available in either English silk or quality nylon. A Traditional nylon umbrella with a maple handle is priced at £71, while a silk classic with an ivory handle is £850. The shop also sells a wide range of walking sticks, from antique ones to contemporary and shooting sticks.

VIDEO

Unfortunately, videos sold in London will work almost anywhere in the world—except the United States. The systems for video are different, and you would need either a multisystem television range or an expensive adaptor in order to play the English version on your VCR back home. Since videos are widely available in the United States, you're much better off buying there. On the slight chance that you own a multisystem television or simply want to purchase, say, a British video unavailable elsewhere, try the store listed below.

VIDEO WORLD
260 Tottenham Court Rd., WI (tel. 631-1576)
Underground Station: Tottenham Court Road
Hours: Monday through Saturday from 9 a.m. to 6 p.m.
Credit Cards: AE, DC, MC, V

In the heart of audio-electronic land on Tottenham Court Road, this shop has what may be the largest stock of videos in town, with more than 2,000 VHS and Betamax tapes, starting at £22.

WALKING STICKS

Walking sticks are wonderful companions and are used as much for style and class as they are for support. You should choose a walking stick with as much care as you choose a piece of clothing—that is, it should "fit" both you and the occasion. The correct size is measured by holding the stick by your side with the tip touching the ground, and your elbow should be slightly bent. This allows both for support and ease of swing when you walk. A dress stick is often made of an exotic hardwood and is polished just like a fine piece of furniture. Rosewood and ebony are sturdy but heavy, while hickory and maple are lighter and beautifully grained. There are walking sticks called shooting sticks that unfold into seats (often called seatsticks by Americans) and walking sticks with tiny whisky flasks and even fishing rods concealed in the shafts.

Both **James Smith & Sons** and **Swaine, Adeney, Brigg & Sons Ltd.**, described in the previous "Umbrellas" section, carry a wide range of walking sticks. James Smith sells sticks ranging in price from £6 to £440,

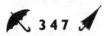
the price dependent mainly on the handle. There are hardwood, ivory, silver, and horn handles, some of which are one-of-a-kind. Shooting sticks here start at £33.

At Swaine, Adeney, Brigg & Sons, there are antique sticks, shooting sticks, and shotgun sticks. Shotgun sticks start at £1,100 and can be specially made to have anything put inside, though if a weapon is added the buyer must secure a license. An antique rhinocerous-horn walking stick from the Victorian age is priced at £1,925, while shooting sticks start at £88.

Another good shop for antique walking sticks is **Michael C. German**, described in detail under "Arms and Armor." Approximately 500 sticks are usually in stock, dating from 1680 to 1910 and starting at £50.

More shooting sticks can be found at **Purdey & Sons** and **Holland & Holland**, described in the section titled "Guns and Rifles," while **Saville-Edells**, listed in the "Gifts" section, has a range of unusual walking sticks such as those that contain flasks for whisky or fishing rods.

WATCHES

Many of London's first-rate jewelry stores sell top-name watches as well, among them **Collingwood, Cartier, Mappin & Webb, Garrard**, and **Kutchinsky**, all described in the "Jewelry" section of this book. In addition, **Asprey**, listed in the "Gifts" section, carries its own brand of watches in addition to Patek Philippe, Piaget, and others. The two shops listed below deal almost exclusively in wristwatches.

THE WATCH GALLERY
129 Fulham Rd., SW3 (tel. 581-3239)
Underground Station: *South Kensington*
Hours: *Monday through Friday from 10:30 a.m. to 7 p.m., on Saturday from 11 a.m. to 6 p.m.*
Credit Cards: *AE, DC, MC, V*

This upmarket shop displays and treats its watches like jewels. Prices range from £44 all the way up to £22,000, and the stock includes stylish watches of the 1920s and '30s (Cartier, Rolex, Patek Philippe, Vacheron Constantin) and elegant watches of today (Ebel, Baume et Mercier, Jaeger-LeCoultre, Hublot). There are also fun watches from Fortis and Heuer. A 14-karat-gold lady's Hublot watch with a black face, quartz movement, and rubber strap is priced at £3,000, while an Emerich Meerson lady's watch with a pigskin strap is £196. A man's antique Perry's Rolex Oyster dating from 1929 with a blue lizard strap is £1,095.

WATCHES OF SWITZERLAND
16 New Bond St., W1 (tel. 493-5916)

Underground Station: Green Park
Hours: Monday through Saturday from 9 a.m. to 5:30 p.m.
Credit Cards: AE, DC, MC, V

Watches galore are available here, including Baume et Mercier, Blancpain, Bueche Girod, Ebel, Hublot, Jean Renet, Longines, Omega, Patek Philippe, Rolex, Rotary, Seafarer, Tissot, and Vacheron Constantin. Watches start at £55, with a woman's 18-karat-gold dress watch from Rolex priced at £14,220.

WINES

It is an unfortunate fact of life that U.S. Customs will allow returning Americans to bring only one liter (33.8 ounces) of alcohol back with them duty free. Any amount more than this will be charged duty. If you're a true lover of wine, it may be worth it to pay the extra in order to bring back a few more bottles of really fine wines. Be sure to check whether **Christie's** or **Sotheby's** is having one of their frequent wine auctions. Some are collector's items, but many more are everyday wines sold in five- or ten-case lots or per dozen. Unless you have some friends with which to split the lots or plan to do a lot of drinking while still in London, you might have to forgo such purchases, but it's still worth attending these auctions if only to see what's on the market. Christie's claims to be the oldest established and largest wine auctioneers in the world, holding its first auction devoted solely to wine in 1769.

In addition to the two famous wine merchants listed below, the **Soho Wine Market,** listed under "Scotch," and the food halls of **Harrods** and **Fortnum & Mason** have good selections of wine.

BERRY BROS. & RUDD LTD.
3 St. James's St., SW1 (tel. 839-9033)
Underground Station: Green Park
Hours: Monday through Friday from 9:30 a.m. to 5 p.m.
Credit Cards: DC, MC, V

This is one of London's most charming wine-merchant shops, with a quaint exterior that has changed little since the building first went up in 1734. A family business since the beginning, the company itself dates back to 1699 when it first opened as a grocer's. By 1890 it had transformed into a shop selling only wines, and today it has a royal warrant as merchants of wine and spirits to the Queen. No wines are on display—rather, they are kept in the wine cellars that extend underneath St. James's Street. Wines range from the Berry Bros. own house wines costing £2.88 per bottle to French, German, Hungarian, Italian, Spanish, Portuguese, Australian, and sparkling wines. The owners of Cutty Sark, the company also sells port, sherry, madeira, brandy, and other spirits and apéritifs.

JOHN HARVEY & SONS LTD.
27 Pall Mall, SW1 (tel. 839-4695)
Underground Station: Piccadilly Circus or Green Park
Hours: Monday through Friday from 9:30 a.m. to 7 p.m.
Credit Cards: AE, DC, MC, V

Wine merchants since 1796, John Harvey supplies Buckingham Palace with wines. It's famous for its Bristol Cream sherry, which sells for £5.16 for 70 centiliters. Harvey's No. 1 claret is priced at £3.58, while Harvey's muscadet costs £3. It also sells wines from around the world, including English, European, Californian, and Australian wines, as well as ports, sherry, champagne, spirits, and even communion wines.

Berry Bros. & Rudd Ltd. supply wine and spirits to the Queen

Wedgwood

25·50

18·95

10·95

17·50

INDEX

FORTNUM & MASON

GENERAL INFORMATION

INDEX

ESTABLISHMENTS

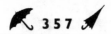

INDEX

INDEX

INDEX

INDEX

PRODUCTS AND SERVICES

INDEX

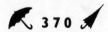

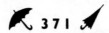

DESIGNERS AND OTHER PROMINENT NAMES*

*Designers with name boutiques in London may be found in the "Establishments" index

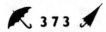

INDEX

THE
$35-A-DAY
TRAVEL
CLUB

DIEU ET MON DROIT

BY APPOINTMENT
TO HER MAJESTY THE QUEEN
COFFEE MERCHANTS
H.R. HIGGINS (COFFEE-MAN) LTD.

JAMAICA
BLUE
MOUNTAIN

Medium roasted

*This is reputedly the world's most
famous and most exclusive coffee.
Our consignment comes from the
famous Wallenford Estate which
gives its name to only the very best
Blue Mountain coffee. The flavour
is delicate, the coffee has full body
and light acidity in subtle harmony*

£12.80

The $35-A-Day Travel Club—How to Save Money on All Your Travels

In this book we'll be looking at how to shop in London, but there is a "device" for saving money and determining value on *all* your trips. It's the popular, international $35-A-Day Travel Club, now in its 26th successful year of operation. The Club was formed at the urging of numerous readers of the $$$-A-Day and Dollarwise Guides, who felt that such an organization could provide continuing travel information and a sense of community to value-minded travelers in all parts of the world. And so it does!

In keeping with the budget concept, the annual membership fee is low and is immediately exceeded by the value of your benefits. Upon receipt of $18 (U.S. residents), or $20 U.S. by check drawn on a U.S. bank or via international postal money order in U.S. funds (Canadian, Mexican, and other foreign residents) to cover one year's membership, we will send all new members the following items.

(1) *Any two* **of the following books**
Please designate in your letter which two you wish to receive:

Frommer's $-A-Day Guides
    Europe on $30 a Day
    Australia on $25 a Day
    Eastern Europe on $25 a Day
    England on $40 a Day
    Greece including Istanbul and Turkey's Aegean Coast on $30 a Day
    Hawaii on $50 a Day
    India on $15 & $25 a Day
    Ireland on $30 a Day
    Israel on $30 & $35 a Day
    Mexico on $20 a Day (plus Belize and Guatemala)
    New York on $50 a Day
    New Zealand on $40 a Day
    Scandinavia on $50 a Day
    Scotland and Wales on $40 a Day
    South America on $30 a Day
    Spain and Morocco (plus the Canary Is.) on $40 a Day
    Turkey on $25 a Day
    Washington, D.C., on $40 a Day

Frommer's Dollarwise Guides
    Dollarwise Guide to Austria and Hungary
    Dollarwise Guide to Belgium, Holland & Luxembourg
    Dollarwise Guide to Bermuda and The Bahamas
    Dollarwise Guide to Canada
    Dollarwise Guide to the Caribbean
    Dollarwise Guide to Egypt
    Dollarwise Guide to England and Scotland
    Dollarwise Guide to France
    Dollarwise Guide to Germany
    Dollarwise Guide to Italy
    Dollarwise Guide to Japan and Hong Kong
    Dollarwise Guide to Portugal, Madeira, and the Azores
    Dollarwise Guide to the South Pacific
    Dollarwise Guide to Switzerland and Liechtenstein
    Dollarwise Guide to Alaska
    Dollarwise Guide to California and Las Vegas
    Dollarwise Guide to Florida
    Dollarwise Guide to the Mid-Atlantic States
    Dollarwise Guide to New England
    Dollarwise Guide to New York State
    Dollarwise Guide to the Northwest
    Dollarwise Guide to Skiing USA—East
    Dollarwise Guide to Skiing USA—West
    Dollarwise Guide to the Southeast and New Orleans
    Dollarwise Guide to the Southwest
    Dollarwise Guide to Texas
    (Dollarwise Guides discuss accommodation and facilities in all
    price ranges, with emphasis on the medium-priced.)

Frommer's Touring Guides
    Egypt
    Florence
    London
    Paris
    Venice
    (These new, color illustrated guides include walking tours, cultural
    and historic sites, and other vital travel information.)

A Shopper's Guide to Best Buys in England, Scotland, and Wales
(Describes in detail hundreds of places to shop—department stores, factory
outlets, street markets, and craft centers—for great quality British bargains.)

A Shopper's Guide to the Caribbean
(Two experienced Caribbean hands guide you through this shopper's paradise, offering witty insights and helpful tips on the wares and emporia of more than 25 islands.)

Bed & Breakfast—North America
(This guide contains a directory of over 150 organizations that offer bed & breakfast referrals and reservations throughtout North America. The scenic attractions, and major schools and universities near the homes of each are also listed.)

Dollarwise Guide to Cruises
(This complete guide covers all the basics of cruising—ports of call, costs, fly-cruise package bargains, cabin selection booking, embarkation and debarkation, and describes in detail over 60 or so ships cruising the waters of Alaska, the Caribbean, Mexico, Hawaii, Panama, Canada, and the United States.)

Dollarwise Guide to Skiing Europe
(Describes top ski resorts in Austria, France, Italy, and Switzerland. Illustrated with maps of each resort area plus full-color trail maps.)

Fast 'n' Easy Phrase Book
(French, German, Spanish, and Italian—all in one convenient, easy-to-use phrase guide.)

Guide to Honeymoon Destinations
(A special guide for that most romantic trip of your life, with full details on planning and choosing the destination that will be just right in the U.S. [California, New England, Hawaii, Florida, New York, South Carolina, etc.], Canada, Mexico, and the Caribbean.)

How to Beat the High Cost of Travel
(This practical guide details how to save money on absolutely all travel items—accommodations, transportation, dining, sightseeing, shopping, taxes, and more. Includes special budget information for seniors, students, singles, and families.)

Marilyn Wood's Wonderful Weekends
(This very selective guide covers the best mini-vacation destinations within a 175-mile radius of New York City. It describes special country inns and other accommodations, restaurants, picnic spots, sights, and activities—all the information needed for a two- or three-day stay.)

Motorist's Phrase Book
(A practical phrase book in French, German, and Spanish designed specifically for the English-speaking motorist touring abroad.)

Swap and Go—Home Exchanging Made Easy
(Two veteran home exchangers explain in detail all the money-saving benefits of a home exchange, and then describe precisely how to do it. Also includes information on home rentals and many tips on low-cost travel.)

The Candy Apple: New York for Kids
(A spirited guide to the wonders of the Big Apple by a savvy New York grandmother with a kid's eye view to fun. Indispensable for visitors and residents alike.)

Travel Diary and Record Book
(A 96-page diary for personal travel notes plus a section for such vital data as passport and traveler's check numbers, itinerary, postcard list, special people and places to visit, and a reference section with temperature and conversion charts, and world maps with distance zones.)

Where to Stay USA
(By the Council on International Educational Exchange, this extraordinary guide is the first to list accommodations in all 50 states that cost anywhere from $3 to $30 per night.)

(2) A one-year subscription to *The Wonderful World of Budget Travel*
This quarterly eight-page tabloid newspaper keeps you up to date on fast-breaking developments in low-cost travel in all parts of the world, bringing you the latest money-saving information—the kind of information you'd have to pay $25 a year to obtain elsewhere. This consumer-conscious publication also features columns of special interest to readers: **Hospitality Exchange** (members all over the world who are willing to provide hospitality to other members as they pass through their home cities); **Share-a-Trip** (offers and requests from members for travel companions who can share costs and help avoid the burdensome single supplement); and **Readers Ask... Readers Reply** (travel questions from members to which other members reply with authentic firsthand information).

(3) A copy of *Arthur Frommer's Guide to New York*
This is a pocket-size guide to hotels, restaurants, nightspots, and sightseeing attractions in all price ranges throughout the New York area.

(4) Your personal membership card
Membership entitles you to purchase through the Club all Arthur From-

mer publications for a third to half off their regular retail prices during the term of your membership.

So why not join this hardy band of international budgeteers and participate in its exchange of travel information and hospitality? Simply send your name and address, together with your annual membership fee of $18 (U.S. residents) or $20 U.S. (Canadian, Mexican, and other foreign residents), by check drawn on a U.S. bank or via international postal money order in U.S. funds to: $25-A-Day Travel Club, Inc., Frommer Books, Gulf + Western Building, One Gulf + Western Plaza, New York, NY 10023. And please remember to specify which *two* of the books in section (1) above you wish to receive in your initial package of members' benefits. Or, if you prefer, use the last page of this book, simply checking off the two books you select and enclosing $18 or $20 in U.S. currency.

Once you are a member, there is no obligation to buy additional books. No books will be mailed to you without your specific order.

PURCHASES IN LONDON

DATE OF PURCHASE	STORE & PRODUCT	GIFT FOR	COST	DATE & PLACE MAILED	AIR OR SURFACE

PURCHASES IN LONDON

DATE OF PURCHASE	STORE & PRODUCT	GIFT FOR	COST	DATE & PLACE MAILED	AIR OR SURFACE

PURCHASES IN LONDON

DATE OF PURCHASE	STORE & PRODUCT	GIFT FOR	COST	DATE & PLACE MAILED	AIR OR SURFACE

PURCHASES IN LONDON

DATE OF PURCHASE	STORE & PRODUCT	GIFT FOR	COST	DATE & PLACE MAILED	AIR OR SURFACE

NOW, SAVE MONEY ON ALL YOUR TRAVELS!
Join Arthur Frommer's $35-A-Day Travel Club™

Saving money while traveling is never a simple matter, which is why, over 26 years ago, the **$35-A-Day Travel Club** was formed. Actually, the idea came from readers of the Arthur Frommer Publications who felt that such an organization could bring financial benefits, continuing travel information, and a sense of community to economy-minded travelers all over the world.

In keeping with the money-saving concept, the annual membership fee is low—$18 (U.S. residents) or $20 U.S. (Canadian, Mexican, and foreign residents)—and is immediately exceeded by the value of your benefits which include:

(1) The latest edition of any TWO of the books listed on the following pages.

(2) An annual subscription to an 8-page quarterly newspaper *The Wonderful World of Budget Travel* which keeps you up-to-date on fastbreaking developments in low-cost travel in all parts of the world—bringing you the kind of information you'd have to pay over $35 a year to obtain elsewhere. This consumer-conscious publication also includes the following columns:

Hospitality Exchange—members all over the world who are willing to provide hospitality to other members as they pass through their home cities.

Share-a-Trip—requests from members for travel companions who can share costs and help avoid the burdensome single supplement.

Readers Ask . . . Readers Reply—travel questions from members to which other members reply with authentic firsthand information.

(3) A copy of *Arthur Frommer's Guide to New York.*

(4) Your personal membership card which entitles you to purchase through the Club all Arthur Frommer Publications for a third to a half off their regular retail prices during the term of your membership.

So why not join this hardy band of international budgeteers NOW and participate in its exchange of information and hospitality? Simply send $18 (U.S. residents) or $20 U.S. (Canadian, Mexican, and other foreign residents) along with your name and address to: $35-A-Day Travel Club, Inc., Gulf + Western Building, One Gulf + Western Plaza, New York, NY 10023. Remember to specify which *two* of the books in section (1) above you wish to receive in your initial package of member's benefits. Or tear out the next page, check off any two of the books listed on either side, and send it to us with your membership fee.

THE ARTHUR FROMMER GUIDES™

(Pocket-size guides to sightseeing and tourist accommodations and facilities in all price ranges.)

☐ Amsterdam/Holland	$5.95	☐ Mexico City/Acapulco	$5.95
☐ Athens	$5.95	☐ Minneapolis/St. Paul	$5.95
☐ Atlantic City/Cape May	$5.95	☐ Montreal/Quebec City	$5.95
☐ Boston	$5.95	☐ New Orleans	$5.95
☐ Cancún/Cozumel/Yucatán	$5.95	☐ New York	$5.95
☐ Dublin/Ireland	$5.95	☐ Orlando/Disney World/EPCOT	$5.95
☐ Hawaii	$5.95	☐ Paris	$5.95
☐ Las Vegas	$5.95	☐ Philadelphia	$5.95
☐ Lisbon/Madrid/Costa del Sol	$5.95	☐ Rome	$5.95
☐ London	$5.95	☐ San Francisco	$5.95
☐ Los Angeles	$5.95	☐ Washington, D.C.	$5.95

FROMMER'S TOURING GUIDES™

(Color illustrated guides that include walking tours, cultural & historic sites, and other vital travel information.)

☐ Egypt	$8.95	☐ Paris	$8.95
☐ Florence	$8.95	☐ Venice	$8.95
☐ London	$8.95		

SPECIAL EDITIONS

☐ A Shopper's Guide to the Best Buys in England, Scotland, & Wales........ $10.95

☐ A Shopper's Guide to the Caribbean... $12.95

☐ Bed & Breakfast—N. America $8.95

☐ Fast 'n' Easy Phrase Book (Fr/Ger/Ital/Sp in *one* vol.) $6.95

☐ Guide to Honeymoons (US, Canada, Mexico, & Carib)................ $12.95

☐ How to Beat the High Cost of Travel ... $4.95

☐ Marilyn Wood's Wonderful Weekends (NY, Conn, Mass, RI, Vt, NH, NJ, Del, Pa) $11.95

☐ Motorist's Phrase Book (Fr/Ger/Sp) ... $4.95

☐ Swap and Go (Home Exchanging) $10.95

☐ The Candy Apple (NY for Kids)....... $11.95

☐ Travel Diary and Record Book........ $5.95

☐ Where to Stay USA (Lodging from $3 to $30 a night) $9.95

ORDER NOW!

In U.S. include $1.50 shipping UPS for 1st book; 50¢ ea. add'l book. Outside U.S. $2 and 50¢, respectively.

Enclosed is my check or money order for $_____

NAME _____

ADDRESS _____

CITY _____ STATE _____ ZIP _____

Date_____

FROMMER BOOKS
PRENTICE HALL PRESS
ONE GULF + WESTERN PLAZA
NEW YORK, NY 10023

Friends:

Please send me the books checked below:

FROMMER'S $-A-DAY GUIDES™

(In-depth guides to sightseeing and low-cost tourist accommodations and facilities.)

☐ Europe on $30 a Day	$13.95	☐ New Zealand on $40 a Day	$10.95
☐ Australia on $25 a Day	$10.95	☐ New York on $50 a Day	$10.95
☐ Eastern Europe on $25 a Day	$10.95	☐ Scandinavia on $50 a Day	$10.95
☐ England on $40 a Day	$11.95	☐ Scotland and Wales on $40 a Day	$11.95
☐ Greece on $30 a Day	$11.95	☐ South America on $30 a Day	$10.95
☐ Hawaii on $50 a Day	$11.95	☐ Spain and Morocco (plus the Canary Is.) on $40 a Day	$10.95
☐ India on $15 & $25 a Day	$10.95		
☐ Ireland on $30 a Day	$10.95	☐ Turkey on $25 a Day	$10.95
☐ Israel on $30 & $35 a Day	$11.95	☐ Washington, D.C., & Historic Va. on $40 a Day	$11.95
☐ Mexico on $20 a Day	$10.95		

FROMMER'S DOLLARWISE GUIDES™

(Guides to sightseeing and tourist accommodations and facilities from budget to deluxe, with emphasis on the medium-priced.)

☐ Alaska	$12.95	☐ Cruises (incl. Alaska, Carib, Mex, Hawaii, Panama, Canada, & US)	$12.95
☐ Austria & Hungary	$11.95		
☐ Belgium, Holland, Luxembourg	$11.95	☐ California & Las Vegas	$11.95
☐ Egypt	$11.95	☐ Florida	$11.95
☐ England & Scotland	$11.95	☐ Mid-Atlantic States	$12.95
☐ France	$11.95	☐ New England	$12.95
☐ Germany	$12.95	☐ New York State	$12.95
☐ Italy	$11.95	☐ Northwest	$11.95
☐ Japan & Hong Kong	$12.95	☐ Skiing in Europe	$12.95
☐ Portugal (incl. Madeira & the Azores)	$12.95	☐ Skiing USA—East	$11.95
☐ South Pacific	$12.95	☐ Skiing USA—West	$11.95
☐ Switzerland & Liechtenstein	$12.95	☐ Southeast & New Orleans	$11.95
☐ Bermuda & The Bahamas	$11.95	☐ Southwest	$11.95
☐ Canada	$12.95	☐ Texas	$11.95
☐ Caribbean	$13.95		

TURN PAGE FOR ADDITIONAL BOOKS AND ORDER FORM.